Once a
Legend

Once a Legend

"Red Mike"
Edson of the
Marine Raiders

Jon T. Hoffman

PRESIDIO

This edition printed 2000

Copyright © 1994 by Jon T. Hoffman

Published by Presidio Press, Inc.
505 B San Marin Drive, Suite 160
Novato, CA 94945-1340

Library of Congress Cataloging-in-Publication Data

Hoffman, Jon T., 1955–
    Once a legend : "Red Mike" Edson of the Marine Raiders /
    by Jon T. Hoffman.
           p.   cm.
    Includes bibliographical references and index.
    ISBN 0-89141-493-2 (hardcover)
    ISBN 0-89141-732-X (paperback)
    1. Edson, Merritt. 2. United States. Marine Corps—Biography.
    3. Generals—United States—Biography. I. Title.
    VE25.E37H64 1994
    359.9'6'092—dc20
    [B]   93-41682
                                          CIP

Printed in the United States of America

MARINES' HYMN

From the Halls of Montezuma,
  To the shores of Tripoli;
We fight our country's battles
  In the air, on land, and sea;
First to fight for right and freedom
  And to keep our honor clean;
We are proud to bear the title of
  UNITED STATES MARINE.

Our flag's unfurled to every breeze
  From dawn to setting sun;
We have fought in every clime and place
  Where we could take a gun;
In the snow of far off northern lands
  And in sunny tropic scenes;
You will find us always on the job—
  THE UNITED STATES MARINES.

Here's health to you and to our Corps
  Which we are proud to serve;
In many a strife we've fought for life
  And never lost our nerve;
If the Army and the Navy
  Ever look on heaven's scenes;
They will find the streets are guarded by
  UNITED STATES MARINES.

Contents

Acknowledgments

I could not have completed this book without the help of many people. Two important figures were Dr. Allan R. Millett and Dr. Williamson Murray, the professors at Ohio State University who enriched my initial studies in military history. Dr. Millett also played a major role by serving as my advisor and by pointing me toward the Coco River patrol and the Edson papers as a potential thesis topic. He then provided invaluable advice once I started down the road of writing a biography, and subsequently critiqued a number of chapters. Two other key individuals were Merritt Austin Edson, Jr., and Herbert R. Edson, the general's sons. Their recollections of their father were valuable, and they opened the door to numerous important sources that otherwise would have been closed to me.

The staffs of a number of state and federal archives assisted me in accessing a wide range of documentation on the general's life and times. Two archivists went above and beyond the call. Dr. Timothy K. Nenninger of the National Archives unearthed a key box of documents on the Raiders. Gregory Sanford, the State Archivist of Vermont, made available the relevant collections on Edson's time in state government and critiqued my chapter on the subject. The staff of the Manuscript Division of the Library of Congress helped me through Edson's mountainous collection of papers. Carol Johnson of the Photographic Division of the Library of Congress kindly provided access to the general's equally large, uncatalogued collection of photographs. All sections of the Marine Corps Historical Center answered questions and made available important resources. Brigadier General Edwin H. Simmons, USMC(Ret), director of the History and Museums Division, provided his own recollections of General Edson and the Service Command, as well as a valuable critique of several draft chapters. Benis M. Frank, the Chief Historian, helped me through the oral history collections and gave me his thoughtful analysis of several aspects of Edson's career.

I received valuable research assistance as well from Robert Sherrod; John Aldrich of the Vermont Militia Museum; Prentice Hammond and Ken Barrett of the town of Chester; Kenneth D. Fryer of the Medal of Honor Historical Society; Vern McLean of the Banana Fleet Marines; Dr. Stephen R. Wise of the Parris Island Museum; Elaine Wilson and Brother Paul Corceron of Australia; Ernest L. Carr of the 1st Marine Division Association; Tammy Sowers of Alpha Tau Omega national headquarters; and Francis Hepburn of the Marine Raider Association. Irv Reynolds and James Childs of Edson's Raiders Association deserve special thanks for providing records of the 1st Raider Battalion, assisting me in contacting many others who served with Red Mike, and critiquing the chapters on the Raiders.

I did the initial work on this book while I was on the faculty of the U.S. Naval Academy. The Naval Academy Research Council provided support for some of the basic research. Chairman Craig Symonds of the History Department kept the more onerous administrative tasks off my desk and provided valuable advice on the project. Professors Jack Sweetman, Bill Roberts, Bob Love, Mike Isenberg, and Brian Vandemark either read one of the initial chapters or gave me fresh perspectives on American military history. My other colleagues helped me develop as a historian, researcher, and writer. Connie Grigor and Alice Davis provided valuable administrative support.

The following people read parts of the manuscript and contributed vital critiques on style and content: Col. Joseph Alexander, USMC(Ret); Patricia and Hubbard Ballou; Martin Clemens; Brig. Gen. Gordon Gayle, USMC(Ret); Capt. Frank Guidone, USMC(Ret); Norman Harrison; Rev. Fred Henley, SJ; Capt. Judy Hession, USMCR; Brig. Gen. James Hittle, USMC(Ret); Maj. Gen. Carl Hoffman, USMC(Ret); Maj. Frank Hoffman, USMCR; Lt. Gen. William Jones, USMC(Ret); Col. Gordon Keyser, USMC(Ret); Col. Victor Kleber, USMC(Ret); Col. J. Angus MacDonald, USMC(Ret); Rev. Daniel O'Connell, SJ; Col. Mitchell Paige, USMC(Ret); Maj. Gen. Jonas M. Platt, USMC(Ret); Dr. Mark Reardon, MD; 1st Lt. Paul Starita, USMCR; Col. Houston Stiff, USMC(Ret); and Col. John Sweeney, USMC(Ret). Colonel John Greenwood, USMC(Ret), also read parts of the manuscript and provided valuable advice from his perspective as editor of the *Marine Corps Gazette*.

Many others contributed their valuable time to write me letters or give me interviews describing their personal knowledge of Red Mike. They are too numerous to mention in this all too brief acknowledgment, but most of their names appear in the list of sources at the end of the book. Without their assistance, this biography would not be as complete or as intimate.

Dale Wilson of Presidio Press deserves recognition for giving the manuscript a chance to become a book, and Joan Griffin rates special thanks for her insightful editing and for putting up with a long-winded author.

Last, but certainly not least, I dedicate this book to my family, especially my wife, Mary Craddock Hoffman. They put up with several years of long hours and helped me stay the course. Mary did double duty by creating the maps that illustrate this volume.

Foreword

He didn't fit the Hollywood image of a Marine. But few of the great men of the Corps that I've observed in war or peace have either. Short and wiry, of strong Vermont stock, he weighed only 140 pounds when in fighting trim; however, Merritt Edson had the heart of a giant. From his courage on the battlefield, highlighted by the incredible defense of "Edson's Ridge" on Guadalcanal (for which he was awarded the Medal of Honor), to his courage in dealing with the unsavory politics of the Pentagon and Capitol Hill, Edson became a legend in the Corps.

Edson intuitively know how to fight—a rare trait among many so-called warriors. He also knew that it took more to win than individual Marine valor and spirit, something a small, insular pre-World War II Marine Corps had difficulty understanding when catapulted into the Pacific campaign against the Japanese. For example, he argued, often successfully, for improved combat tactics and weapons. He also recognized that the outdated logistical system of the Corps was not adequate for the modern battlefield. Edson challenged the archaic supply system that was adversely affecting the way Marines were supported in combat. Perhaps the well-functioning logistical apparatus we enjoyed in Desert Storm can be traced to General Edson's haranguing of the supply department to introduce more modern and efficient means of providing Marines what they needed on the grim killing fields of the Pacific atolls.

More important to the nation and the Corps than the physical courage General Edson displayed in combat was the moral courage that enabled him to speak out against the demise of the Marine Corps in the post-war unification drives led by the U.S. Army and its supporters. Hell-bent to relegate the Marine Corps to a nonentity, they almost succeeded—not surprising since the movement's leaders were men of such status and ability as Truman and Marshall. Edson deeply wanted to be promoted to major general, but he willingly incurred the wrath of the defense hierarchy, including timid Marine Corps leaders. By speaking out publicly and in the Congress against the unification plan, he probably doomed his chance for promotion, but Edson and others such as Krulak, Twining, Thomas, and Hittle preserved for the nation a Marine Corps which almost immediately distinguished itself in battle again in Korea.

Despite a "blood and guts" reputation, Merritt Edson was courteous and polite, always concerned about his beloved Marines. His strength seemed to come from a quiet inner source. Like many, he was less than perfect in his personal life, though never embarrassing his Corps or his country. If anything, his human frailty allows us to better appreciate him as a person, not a mythological hero.

It is ironic that Edson is so much more appreciated by the Marine Corps after his death than he was during his active service. He probably went against the grain too often in an organization that can be jealous of its members who achieve unusual success or who advocate change too vociferously. Those things, combined with a promotion system that placed seniority over talent and his willingness to sacrifice his career for the good of the Corps, ensured that Marines would never benefit from Merritt Edson at its helm as their commandant.

Combat hero, leader, teacher, visionary; the Corps could use more Merritt Edsons today.

Gen. Walter E. Boomer
Assistant Commandant, U.S. Marine Corps

Prologue

The ridge was not imposing. At its highest point it rose just 123 feet above sea level. It stood out from its surroundings because it was a coral outcrop so meagerly covered with soil that it could support only *kunai* grass. At the base of its gentle slopes the jungle took over and nearly enclosed it in a sea of thick, towering vegetation. As a result, it provided no commanding view in any direction. The mile-long rise undulated along a generally north-south axis, though spurs thrust out at various points. Its southern end pointed inland, toward a spiny range of mountains rising beyond the jungle. At its northern terminus it overlooked a relatively open coastal plain, and therein lay its importance. In the center of that plain, less than a mile from the ridge, was an airfield.

In September 1942, planes of the U.S. Marine Corps, Navy, and Army operated from that strip, known as Henderson Field. The Japanese had begun constructing the field on the island of Guadalcanal a few months earlier in order to cut Australia's lines of communication to the outside world. The United States had reacted swiftly to the threat. On 7 August the 1st Marine Division had made the first Allied amphibious assault of the war. The nineteen thousand men of that organization now held a few square miles of ground around the field and several small nearby islands. The Japanese operated freely on the remainder of Guadalcanal, a land mass roughly ninety miles long and twenty-five miles wide. During the day, planes from Henderson Field controlled the surrounding waters, and the U.S. Navy was able to bring in supplies and reinforcements. At night, enemy warships prowled the seas and strengthened their own forces ashore. If Japanese soldiers wrested back control of the airfield, the 1st Marine Division would be cut off and destroyed.

On 12 September an unimposing Marine officer stood at the southern end of the unremarkable ridge. At five feet seven inches he was of less than average height. The close-cropped red hair, which had already begun an unrelenting retreat from his forehead, gave some indication of his forty-five years. Despite the arrival of middle age he was still athletic, with the slim frame of a baseball player and hiker. His spare build had been further pared by six weeks of reduced rations and a rigorous tropical climate. Since his helmet was too big and seemed to swallow up his head, troops sometimes referred to him among themselves as "the Mole." One of his men wrote of him: "He looks anything but a fighting man, small and sort of shrivelled up."

Neither was his outward personality what one would expect of a red-headed combat commander. Those who met him only briefly found him quiet, reserved, soft-spoken, mild-mannered. But his eyes revealed a strength of character at odds with the otherwise apparently gentle exterior. Their pale blue color resonated the steely determination and remorseless dedication to excellence that lay just beneath the surface. They invariably focused, unblinking, on an interlocutor and seemed to bore right through to the soul. Their stare could wither the toughest Marine. One combat correspondent thought the officer's eyes "as purposeful as a killer's and as unemotional as a shark's." No one who saw them in a tense situation could ever doubt the fighting heart of their owner, Col. Merritt Austin Edson.

At that moment a Japanese brigade of three thousand men was cutting its way through the jungle; its aim—to attack down the open ridge pointed like a spear at Henderson Field. Edson's mission was to stop them with his 1st Raider Battalion and the attached 1st Parachute Battalion. These troops had been handpicked from a service that already prided itself on being an elite. They had undergone intensive training designed to prepare them for combat both physically and mentally. They were also worn down by hard battles and tropic diseases. The two units numbered less than eight hundred men altogether, and many of these should have been in the hospital due to wounds or illness. All were weakened by poor diet and prolonged lack of sleep.

As they dug in across the nose of the ridge, their commander could take little comfort in the supposed superiority of the defense. The division's perimeter along this inland sector existed largely in name only, so his flanks hung almost unprotected in the jungles on either side. The hard coral lying just beneath the surface soil of the ridge made it impossible to dig proper fighting holes, nor were time or materials available to build shelters above ground. Barbed wire was in short supply, though the men worked busily to string what little they had across their front.

The elite nature of the units also presented problems. Because they had been designed to make lightning strikes in the enemy's rear, they were lightly armed and equipped. Their lack of heavy mortars and heavy machine guns left them far short of the firepower that a regular battalion could bring to bear for such a conventional mission. To top it off, the division commander's headquarters had just been relocated to a hollow at the opposite end of the ridge, and the airfield was not much farther back. The division's nerve system and aerial muscle had to be protected at all costs; there could be no thought of an elastic defense trading space for time and blood.

Given these handicaps and the tremendous challenge that lay ahead, the Marine Corps could not have found a better officer to command the defense of the ridge. Edson's wartime service stretched back more than a quarter century to the 1916 campaign against Pancho Villa on the Mexican border. Shortly afterward he was caught up in World War I and, though he saw no action, he trained very hard and very long for the desperate trench warfare of the western front. In the 1920s he spent more than a year fighting Augusto Sandino and his wily guerrillas in Nicaraguan jungles, and won a Navy Cross in the process. A decade later he stood eyeball to eyeball with the Japanese across Soochow Creek during their assault on Shanghai. And, in recent weeks, he and his men had wrested Tulagi from determined Japanese defenders (a second Navy Cross ensued) and savaged another enemy unit in the Tasimboko raid.

Edson's value went far beyond fighting experience. He was an able tactician who could outthink a foe as well as outfight him. His innovative Nicaraguan exploits won him a key billet as a tactics instructor in the Marine Corps Schools in the early 1930s, and he went on to rewrite the manual for counterguerrilla operations at the end of the decade. Later put in charge of the effort to create a commando-like force in the Marine Corps, he shepherded the Raiders from concept to reality.

A wide range of other experience gave him an unmatched perspective on the art of war. He trained as an artilleryman in World War I and earned his aviator wings soon thereafter, so he understood the capabilities and limitations of supporting arms better than most of his infantry peers. As a distinguished marksman, the preeminent leader in Marine team shooting, and a former head of the Corps's target practice program, he was an acknowledged expert on infantry weapons and firepower. His grasp of Japanese tactics was equally unsurpassed. During the Shanghai crisis, he had been able to observe their offensive operations at close range. On Tulagi he and his men had borne the brunt of the first Japanese defensive effort of the war and had emerged with the first American offensive victory over Imperial ground forces.

Chapter 1

"From the Halls of Montezuma"

The high-ceilinged room known as Wiley Hall was normally airy and pleasant. On this June day in 1911, however, the weather had turned unseasonably hot, and parents, students, and teachers crowded the large space located on the second floor of the L. A. Carpenter store. They gathered there for the graduation exercises of the Chester Grammar School. The traditional ceremony required each student to recite from memory a literary piece of his or her own choosing. Most wisely picked something short and simple. Merritt Edson had selected Mathew Arnold's *Sohrab and Rustum,* an epic poem of several thousand words. Although Edson edited out portions of it, the remainder still took twenty minutes to deliver, a time achieved after three weeks of daily memorization and practice.

When his turn arrived, the fourteen year old took his position in front of the assembly and began:

> Rustum strode to his tent door, and called
> His followers in, and bade them bring his arms
> And clad himself in steel . . .

The poem portrayed Rustum, an ancient Persian hero, as an older man proud of a lifetime of greatness:

> I have stood on many a field
> Of blood, and I have fought with many a foe—
> Never was that field lost, or that foe saved.

That day Rustum unwittingly engaged in single combat with his long lost son, who was equally unaware that he was fighting the father he had never known. The older warrior prevailed, and it was only as the younger man lay dying that the two learned of their kinship. In his grief, the old man vowed to kill himself. The son dissuaded him with a challenge: "Do thou the deeds I die too young to do." Rustum reluctantly agreed: "Till then, if fate so wills, let me endure."

There is no record of the crowd's reaction to the long-winded orator, but certainly no one present realized that the tale of martial glory and tragedy was so apt a metaphor for the future of the speaker. Eventually Edson would carve out his own legend as a warrior, and his last major victory would be the most bitter moment in his life.

There was no hint of military greatness in the bloodlines of the Edson family, traced back thirteen generations to Richard Edson, a prosperous yeoman farmer in England. In 1639, his great-grandson Samuel joined the wave of emigrants to the New World, where he settled in Massachusetts and became a successful farmer and businessman. At the age of sixty-two, he was appointed by the colony to a Council of War for one of the frequent Indian conflicts of that period. His three sons—Samuel, Josiah, and Joseph—fought in one engagement in 1676 and helped their company of volunteers destroy a marauding Indian band. These were the last and only direct ancestors of the young Merritt to demonstrate any military prowess.

The elder Samuel was better known for his religious activities. He served as a deacon and choir leader in the Congregational church. The younger Samuel was equally upright, but even more successful in the economic sphere. His only son, the third Samuel Edson, was both prosperous and religious. His ideas in the latter arena accorded more with those of his English forebears, however, and he helped create a new parish of the Episcopal church (the established Church of England). A grandson of the third Samuel sought his fortune in Vermont in the late 1700s, in the environs of the small village of Chester. The family later branched out across the state.

The Vermont Edsons were a close-knit group. Each August, in the lull between haying and harvesting, family members gathered in Chester for a day of eating, singing, playing, and talking. As many as a hundred relatives attended these reunions, all of them arrayed around a single line of tables placed end to end. The men were mostly small farmers and the women worked hard raising families and doing their share on the land.

Erwin Edson was typical of the clan. He was born in 1866 on a forty-four-acre farm several miles from Chester, in a region then called Poplar

Dungeon. At the age of twenty-one he married Lelia Moneta Davis, born just a year earlier than he on the neighboring farm. Erwin was of medium height, with a strong but spare build. Lelia was a "small, lively woman, with brown hair, grey eyes and a smile." They lived for a time in the bigger town of Rutland in central Vermont, where Erwin worked as a foreman in a creamery. There, on 25 April 1897, they had their third and last child, Merritt Austin. The other children were a brother, Myrton, and a sister, Mary. A year after Merritt's birth, the family of five moved back to the Poplar Dungeon farm, and two years later to a house and land that Erwin purchased on the edge of Chester at 5 Pleasant Street.

Erwin followed in the footsteps of his immediate forebears; he worked his farm and did other odd jobs, such as marketing dairy equipment. He had a hired hand to help him with the heavy labor, and a girl to assist his wife around the house. They took in occasional boarders, often young students from outlying areas attending the town high school. During the busy harvest season the number around the dinner table swelled to a dozen or more. Erwin was a strong supporter of the Grange movement, and founded the Chester chapter in his home in 1904. The Grangers were dedicated to promoting the interests of farmers through such means as enhancing agricultural education and fighting high railroad freight charges. Although the movement had been in existence for nearly four decades, it drew new strength from the Populist and Progressive campaigns around the turn of the century. Merritt would join the Grange when he was old enough, and take pride in a father who "look[ed] forward with plenty of zeal and hope for the future."

Despite the relative economic security of the Edson family, Merritt's horizon was fairly limited in his youth. He almost never traveled beyond the boundaries of his home state until he was a teenager, and then only rarely to nearby regions to visit friends and relatives. His primary window on the outside world was his classmate and best friend, Paul Ballou, son of Chester's Congregational minister. Paul spent his vacations in places such as Washington, D.C., New York City, and the Far West, and regularly sent postcards of these exotic locations to his chum.

As Merritt grew up, he had the same responsibilities for chores typical of all farm kids, but he found plenty of time for other activities besides school and work. He took music lessons for a while, but he seemed to enjoy the outdoors most. Although never very large for his age, he loved sports. He ran track and enjoyed skating, skiing, hockey, and tennis, but his favorite was always baseball. He hunted, trapped, fished, and swam, and took special delight in camping trips to nearby Lowell Lake. Some of his proudest moments were when he first swam all the way across the

William River, and when he shot his first deer. He played the role of big game hunter with zest, and had a picture taken of himself, his rifle, and the kill.

Merritt was an active participant in the many youth groups present in the area. His favorite was the Knights of King Arthur, a church organization for boys, which imparted a sense of idealism and adventure to its members. Later he joined the Boy Scouts. In high school he became involved in statewide organizations such as the Older Boys Conference, which sponsored motivational programs built around inspirational quotes ("Help me to stand for the hard right against the easy wrong"). In his senior year he attended a camp sponsored by the University of Vermont. It was designed to teach young men some of the business aspects of farming, but Merritt was most impressed by the man who administered the camp accommodations. He was Ira L. Reeves, then a captain in the Army and the professor of military science at the university. Merritt made his own impression, as well. He served as a tent leader and was elected president of a club formed by some of the students.

Another significant influence on Merritt's development was religion. His parents followed the Episcopalian line begun by the third Samuel Edson, but there were few of that faith in Chester and the parish had no active program for young people. Since the contemporaries of the Edson children were all Congregationalists, Merritt and his sister, Mary, voluntarily joined that church when he was twelve. With the zeal of a convert, he took wholeheartedly to every aspect of parish life. He sang in the choir, tolled the church bell, was elected president of his Sunday school class, and belonged to the Junior Christian Endeavor Society. Many thought he would become a minister someday. Both his parents and his church raised him to be a man of rectitude and integrity.

Merritt started classes in 1902 at the schoolhouse located in the center of town. An avid reader, he did extremely well in his early years and always finished near the top of his class, which numbered less than a dozen students. For the first two years of high school he continued his strong academic performance, but thereafter he took less interest in school, perhaps in part because of the retirement of his favorite teacher. Merritt disliked rote memorization and longed for more educators who could "awaken or keep awake the desire and ambition of the pupil to do something." Despite the decline in his grades, he graduated as the top male student in his class and third overall.

Another reason for Merritt's academic slide might have been his increasing interest in girls. In the ninth grade he and Paul Ballou graduated from building forts to attending dances. Although Merritt was a quiet youngster, he appears to have been quite outgoing with the female members of his school. They, in turn, liked his innate charm, blue eyes, and wavy blondish red hair. Considering the time period and the small-town atmosphere, the students had a great deal of leeway in courting. Even at the age of thirteen he was staying out past midnight after the summer dances at the lake.

Merritt's graduation as the top male student in his class earned him a hundred-dollar scholarship to the University of Vermont, generally known as UVM, for the initials of its Latin name. He had set his sights on college and had taken the Latin curriculum at Chester High, the equivalent of today's college preparatory course. The decision to seek more education was not preordained, for he would be the first in his immediate family to do so. The choice was complicated by a decline in the Edson family's economic situation, which may have been connected to the recession of 1913–14 and a drop in commodity prices. (By January 1916 Erwin would have to sell the farm and would be looking for a job.) Although the scholarship would pay for more than two-thirds of the first year's tuition and fees, there was the matter of room and board in Burlington, and the loss of Merritt's services around the farm. Despite the money problems, the Edsons scraped together enough to send Merritt to school in the fall of 1915. He intended to study agriculture.

The young Merritt heading off to college was cast very much in the mold of Deacon Samuel and subsequent generations of Edsons. He was a farmer, like most of his forefathers, though the most recent ones were not quite so successful at it as the earliest of the clan in America. He believed in God and had a strong moral upbringing. He believed in his community and nation, and stood ready to meet his "individual responsibilities in a democratic form of government." Insofar as he had political views, he was a staunch Republican in the progressive, big-stick wing of the party led by Teddy Roosevelt, who had dominated the national stage throughout Merritt's youth. Deacon Samuel would have been proud of this particular Edson.

The University of Vermont opened the school year of 1915–16 with a convocation for new students. They sang songs, listened to scripture passages, and heard an address from the president on "The Inspiration of Ideals." He challenged the 188 freshmen to follow their greatest ambitions. "The stirring power of infinite human possibilities should move you to high resolve in this supreme hour. Out of the obscuring mists of futurity comes the still small voice calling you to thoughts and deeds that, answered properly, will guarantee your immortality. . . . Your loftiest ideals may become realities.

You can be what you want to be." The students promptly turned to the most important task at hand, surviving UVM's traditional rite of passage in which sophomores cruised the town looking for freshmen to throw into Lake Champlain.

Merritt did not find his first year courses especially difficult, but let himself get distracted by campus social life on occasion. He still enjoyed dancing and staying out late at night from time to time, with the usual consequences for a college student. "Didn't wake up until about 1000 and I couldn't get my English theme done in time for class. . . . Foolish thing to do alright." During the fall semester he joined UVM's chapter of Alpha Tau Omega. Military cadets at VMI had founded that national organization after the Civil War and dedicated it to enhancing leadership, though Merritt and his twenty-nine fraternity brothers had their share of fun, too. Church activities kept him busy as well, and in spring he made the second team of the track squad.

Merritt was as much a hit with the girls of Burlington as he had been with members of the opposite sex in Chester. He always had a full dance card, and usually a different girl for each selection of music. That began to change early in his spring semester, however, as he developed a close friendship with Ethel Winifred Robbins. George Robbins, her father, was a successful representative of Dun & Bradstreet, and in January 1916 he hired Merritt's sister, Mary, as a clerk.

The two Edsons spent a lot of time visiting at the Robbins household, and Merritt was soon squiring seventeen-year-old Ethel to church, dances, and the movies. She shared his passion for those activities, and for reading. She was petite and pretty, with short auburn hair, brown eyes, and freckles. Like him, she was quiet, though not as outgoing. Merritt still dated others, but Ethel was the fixed star in a constellation of female admirers.

The final important interest of the freshman from Chester was the Army. The university boasted a military science department, and male students were required to take the subject for their first two years. The men were formed into a battalion of four companies, with Capt. Ira Reeves serving as the commandant, and upper class students filling other leadership billets. They wore regulation Army uniforms, which they had to buy themselves at a cost of fifteen dollars, and spent three periods per week in training (two of drill and one of lecture).

This forerunner of Reserve Officers' Training Corps (ROTC) was funded by Congress and staffed by the War Department. Company C had special status since it was also a part of the 1st Infantry Regiment of the Vermont National Guard. Participation in that unit was limited to those willing to take on that additional obligation. The battalion was fully equipped with an armory, sand tables, maps, and a military library of more than twelve hundred volumes. The battalion trained with older Krag rifles, except for Company C, which had the more modern Springfield Model 1903.

Most students were glad to reach their junior year and the end of the compulsory military course. In November 1915 Edson volunteered for Company C and the extra work that entailed. He may well have been inspired to it by Captain Reeves, who had gained his respect at the 1914 agricultural camp. The periodic day of pay for Guard training also would have been an inducement to the cash-strapped youngster. He took his duties seriously, sometimes skipping class to get his weapon ready for inspection. With war raging in Europe, Reeves directed training toward practical skills. There were the usual parades, but the battalion devoted considerable time to bayonet work and fencing, hikes and bivouacs, first aid and map reading, and even rifle marksmanship at nearby Camp Ethan Allen. Following an inspection in May 1916, the War Department placed UVM's detachment in the Distinguished Class for the second year in a row. Edson did well, too, and the company commander recommended him for promotion to student corporal.

Former President William Howard Taft spoke to the university in the middle of April 1916 on the theme of national defense. He stressed preparedness for war and the requirement for a large Navy. For a young college student keeping up with world events, danger seemed to be at every hand. The sinkings of the *Lusitania* and *Arabic* in 1915 and revelations of German espionage activities in the United States had strained relations between the two countries. The French were reeling under Germany's offensive against Verdun, launched in February 1916, and the Allied landing against Turkey at Gallipoli had stalled after heavy losses.

Nor were the threats limited to the European war. American Marines had intervened in the Caribbean nation of Haiti in 1915 and were still engaged in pacifying that troubled land. Political turmoil in Mexico directly threatened the U.S. homeland. Pancho Villa, part bandit and part rebel, led his followers on several raids against American territory. In an attack on Columbus, New Mexico, in March 1916 he and his men killed seventeen Americans. President Woodrow Wilson dispatched Brig. Gen. John J. Pershing and Army troops to track Villa into Mexico, but the expedition nearly became the flashpoint of war between the two countries. With tensions at a peak in mid-June, Wilson called up the National Guard.

The news fell like a thunderbolt on the University of Vermont, which had 10 percent of its student body in Company C. Most students found out about the call to active duty in the morning newspapers on Monday,

19 June. Mobilization was an easy task for the regiment, which had just completed a drill the previous month using automobiles to concentrate the entire force in eighteen hours. Captain Reeves, in his capacity as commander of the Guard regiment, assumed the rank of colonel. On 21 June UVM's company marched to the state reservation adjacent to Fort Ethan Allen, where it joined up with the rest of the regiment. In a hectic few days the men took the oath of federal service, received their physical examinations, and conducted hurried training to integrate new enlistees into their ranks. The War Department had slated the Vermonters for quick deployment to Eagle Pass, Texas.

Edson and his fellow students greeted the call to arms with high emotion. In addition to the excitement over the possibility of war, the mobilization order had come in the middle of final exams, and the president of the university had granted a reprieve from remaining tests. Cloudy skies, cool weather, and confusion over conflicting orders may have dampened their martial ardor somewhat over succeeding days, but if so, their send-off probably rekindled it. Monday, 26 June, was warm and sunny, and special trains brought fifteen thousand relatives, friends, and onlookers to Fort Ethan Allen. The crowd was so great that the regiment had too little space to complete all the maneuvers of its final parade. Tents and equipment were already packed and stacked by the rail siding, so the troops then gathered around impromptu fires, singing songs and saying farewells. When the trains did not arrive as scheduled, the men received their first experience of real military life; they spent the night on the ground.

They finally departed the next afternoon, in the midst of a rainstorm, for a trip of "five never to be forgotten days and nights." Due to a shortage of sleeper cars, the Vermonters made the long journey in regular passenger cars. The steady diet of corned-beef sandwiches grew monotonous, cinders from the locomotive kept everyone grimy, and the close-packed bodies turned ripe in the absence of washing facilities. The only relief was an occasional crowd of well-wishers, some of whom provided welcome treats of fresh food. The unit's arrival in Texas did not improve things at first. The woolen-clad troops had to pitch tents in temperatures exceeding 100 degrees. When chow call came in the evening for the first hot meal in days, a sandstorm promptly blew in to coat men and food with gritty dust.

Eagle Pass, the temporary home of the Vermonters, was a town of six thousand on the banks of the Rio Grande. Its most important feature was the bridge that crossed over to Piedras Negras on the Mexican side. The countryside was a virtual desert and generally flat, with the exception of steep banks along the river basin. Although temperatures reached up to 120 degrees during the summer, humidity was low and the troops soon became acclimated. Sandstorms proved to be less troublesome once the rainy season arrived, but then torrential downpours flooded tents and turned the bivouac area into a mudhole. The troops passed around the story that General Sherman had once said that if he owned hell and Texas, he would sell the latter and live in the former. Four more Guard regiments arrived and Eagle Pass took on the look of a major garrison.

Edson's transition to the life of a real soldier did not go smoothly, especially on 6 July, which was "one hang of a day!!" As Edson washed his face in front of his tent that morning, he failed to notice the approach of Colonel Reeves and "got beautifully bawled out." While standing watch that evening he let a man pass on his own authority and got into trouble again. The end result was an extra shift on guard. The rest of the time he was busy with kitchen police duty and work details incident to building the new camp. He found the demands on a private to be quite heavy: "I used to think I worked at home, once in a while, but I know now I was fooling myself."

Creature comforts were few and far between, and the only entertainment consisted of company sing-alongs in the evening. Inevitably, however, things began to improve. Shower facilities and electric lights appeared, the quartermaster finally issued cots, and before long movies were available in camp. The government had not yet paid the men, however, and Edson had to write home for some money. He wanted to purchase a few items from town to supplement the bland diet, which relied heavily on meat, potatoes, bread, and coffee.

The greatest disappointment to the eager Guardsmen did not involve physical hardship, but the complete absence of the war everyone expected. Each day Mexicans crossed the bridge to Eagle Pass to work or transact business; they did not act like the enemy. The nearest thing to a hostile force was the brief appearance of Mexican cavalry in Piedras Negras, but they made no threatening moves. The Vermonters had hardly arrived in Texas when the newspapers declared an imminent end to the crisis. Negotiations got under way even before the American show of force reached its zenith. The secretary of war announced that he would send no more units to Texas, and orders went out authorizing the release of any Guardsmen with dependent families. The conflict in Europe quickly reassumed its place on the front pages of American newspapers and the Mexican border issue all but disappeared.

That did not mean the Guardsmen were about to go home. In fact, the Vermonters received their first real mission in mid-July. While they had been building and improving their camp, the regulars had been outposting the Rio Grande and guarding the big ranches along the border. The 1st

Battalion drew the initial assignment to relieve the regulars. The men packed up their gear and boarded Packard trucks for their trip into the countryside. Half of Company C went to the Indio Ranch, a spread of 260,000 acres stretching along forty-five miles of the river.

The troops occupied the ranch's unused schoolhouse, an improvement over their oft-flooded tents, and had no work details other than guard duty, which accounted for only one day in three. There were occasional patrols and hikes, but these were more in the nature of sight-seeing excursions than military maneuvers. Their objectives were places such as the swimming hole and the fossil field. On the other hand, they no longer had access to the ice cream and sodas of Eagle Pass. Food continued to be Edson's biggest concern, and he poignantly wrote his family that other men were receiving packages of goodies from home. "Mary, if you love your brother at all, you and Ethel and Mollie [Ethel's mother, Mary Francis Robbins, went by the nickname Mollie] might make up a box of stuff and send it. Make enough to treat twenty-six other men beside myself . . . but for the love of Mike, *be sure and send it*!!!!!"

With plenty of time on his hands to think, Edson worried about things at home. Erwin had put the farm up for sale and was hoping to find work in Burlington, the state's biggest city. At the end of July, when the War Department announced that any units composed of students would be withdrawn from the border in time to start fall classes, Edson wondered how he would be able to pay for college. The family had been in severe financial straits during his first year, and it only looked worse for the near future. He wrote his sister that he was thinking about remaining with the regiment, which would keep him in money for the time being and put off tuition bills. At the end of the crisis he hoped to get a job and save up what he would need to finish school.

The folks back home launched an instant campaign to change his mind. Mary wrote a long letter that alternately pleaded with him to come back and chided him for not considering the feelings of his parents. His mother wrote to apologize for the bleak tone of her earlier letters and assured him that things were actually much better than she had indicated. A farmer near Burlington had hired Erwin, and she intended to rent a large tenement in town and sublet rooms to others. In addition, Mary was going to live at home and contribute a share.

The "most pleasant month of the entire summer" ended in mid-August when Company C trucked back to Eagle Pass and rejoined the regiment. They had to work even harder now, because the process of turning the temporary camp into a semipermanent base was in full swing. The men dug trenches, shoveled gravel, and put up wooden buildings. Training became much more demanding. In addition to daily periods of drill, the units now engaged in at least one tactical problem each day. By the end of August, Colonel Reeves had all the companies working together in a regimental maneuver. Once a week the regiment also hiked up to twenty miles with full individual equipment—a load of about forty-five pounds. Those who were observant learned a little about leadership in the process. Men who quit before the end received time in the guardhouse and additional work details. Unit pride soon had an even greater effect, as companies and regiments vied to see who was the toughest. If anyone dropped out or fell back, he and his fellows received jeers from competing units.

The students of Company C "came to know the army as no amount of college instruction could ever picture it." Many men did not care for the experience, and learned mainly that military life was a hardship. Edson saw things differently. "I am meeting every kind of nature here, rubbing elbows with every kind of man. It gives me a glimpse of human nature which every man must get to be successful. . . . I like this kind of life. I like the work. You know my liking for the military. Well this little session hasn't spoiled it one bit." He was proud of his promotion to private first class, and of his ability to shoot a rifle. He even exalted in the regiment's evening parade. "That is one of the most beautiful sights I know of, a thousand men passing in review, good men most of them, who are ready to serve their country and their country's flag." Whereas others welcomed demobilization, Edson did not: "I will be giving up something I like very much."

Orders came for Company C and it departed Eagle Pass on 15 September. The return trip to Fort Ethan Allen took five days, but the men enjoyed this train ride much more than their last one. On the way down they had been confined to their railcars. Lieutenant Burrage, a soon-to-be senior at UVM, was in command now, and they stopped to see the Alamo, Washington, D.C., and New York City.

The company arrived at Fort Ethan Allen on 20 September and mustered out of active service two days later. As it turned out, Edson's anguish over whether to remain with the regiment or return home was unnecessary. The 1st Vermont received its own orders soon after Company C departed, and the entire outfit was back home before the end of September.

Edson left Fort Ethan Allen with three months of military experience, a final pay of $36.77, and a discharge from the National Guard. He and his companions in Company C were now part of the brand new Reserve Officers' Training Corps, created by Congress in June 1916. The War

Department selected the sixteen campuses in the Distinguished Class of its old college training program to participate in the new setup. Students in ROTC schools would receive their uniforms free, and up to ten honor graduates from each unit would be eligible for commissions in the regular Army. In addition to those slots, graduates of each institution would be qualified to compete for four appointments to the Marine Corps.

As a sophomore, Edson was still not inclined to study, even though he was living with his family now. His strongest course continued to be Military Science, where he posted "A" grades, as usual, and he rose to the rank of student sergeant. He seemed to have little enthusiasm for school but considerable interest in the military. His priorities appeared to be in order by the middle of spring semester.

After a year-long hiatus, Germany launched a new program of unrestricted submarine warfare in February 1917 and resumed sinking American vessels on the high seas. Wilson broke diplomatic relations with Germany and authorized the arming of U.S. merchant ships. After further provocations, the president called Congress into special session and asked for a declaration of war on 2 April. The Senate and House passed the resolution by overwhelming margins. This time the nation was at war for real.

Edson faced a difficult choice. The government mobilized the 1st Vermont Infantry on 2 April. Although Edson was no longer a part of the unit, he had strong ties to the organization and would undoubtedly have found a ready home there as a noncommissioned officer. Another alternative was to enlist in the regular branch of one of the armed forces, as so many young men were doing in early April. Edson would have to start again at the bottom as a private, but he might expect to advance rapidly based on his prior service. The final option was to seek a commission as an officer. By mid-April the Army announced a plan to open officers' training courses around the country. It was looking for more than forty thousand young men, and Edson's background in the guard and ROTC made him a top candidate.

The former soldier's choice was an unexpected one. On 12 May he submitted an application for an appointment as a second lieutenant in the Marine Corps. His reasons remain a mystery. The Corps was waging an aggressive advertising campaign that saturated newspapers across the country with the slogan "First to Fight." That certainly would have appealed to him, and may have prompted his unexpected decision. In any case, he did not wait idly for a response to his application. The university suspended classes in early May to free students for the war effort, and Edson started work on a farm just a few miles south of Burlington. With an expanding economy and the sudden absorption of manpower into the military, workers were in short supply, and a large number of Edson's classmates went off to the countryside to do their patriotic share. Just to be on the safe side, Merritt also took the exam for enlistment in the Marine Corps on 24 May.

Near the end of the month Edson received word on his application. Brigadier General John A. Lejeune of Headquarters Marine Corps (HQMC) informed him that he was designated to take the examination for appointment in July. The general suggested that in the meantime Edson enlist in the Marine Corps Reserve. Those electing that option would be ordered to active duty immediately after the exam for a nine-week course of intensive training, by which time headquarters would know the result of the examination. Those who passed the test and the training program would receive promotions to second lieutenant in the reserve pending confirmation of their regular commissions. The Corps was expanding rapidly and needed to obtain officers fast. There had been only 341 Marine officers in June 1916. In June 1917 there would be 874, and the Marines wanted an additional 300 by October. For a service as tiny as the Corps, it was a virtual avalanche.

Edson went to the Marine recruiting station in Boston and signed his enlistment papers on 26 June. He then went back to Burlington and prepared for the five-day test, which began on 10 July. Thereafter he collected his things from the farm and waited at home for the promised orders. Determined to enjoy his last bit of freedom, he spent a day on the lake with his family, went to the movies every evening, and visited Ethel.

Time passed but no word came. In mid-August, after attending the Edson reunion in Chester, he returned to the farm and resumed work. He thought that the war was passing him by, especially when he received letters from Paul Ballou and another Chester classmate, both of them near the front lines in France with the American Ambulance Field Service. They regaled him with tales of submarine scares and artillery bombardments while he tended crops and cattle on the wrong side of the ocean. Whenever he visited friends in the Vermont Guard regiment at Fort Ethan Allen, it made him "homesick to get going."

Edson had passed the test (ranked fifty-fourth of the eighty-six successful candidates), but the Corps simply forgot to tell the candidate of his good fortune or even to follow through with the appropriate orders to active duty. That was not surprising given the unprecedented demands placed on the small peacetime staff. The Marine Barracks in Parris Island, South Carolina, the site of the training program, eventually took note

Chapter 2

"United States Marine"

There was a surprise for Edson when he arrived at Parris Island. He had missed the opportunity to train with his fellow officer candidates, so the officer in charge considered assigning him to the standard twelve-week boot camp for enlisted men (Edson was still technically a private in the reserve). While the appropriate leaders pondered his fate, they put him to work on a detail cleaning the mess halls. Edson was not pleased at being treated "like any bloomin' private," but a major came to his rescue the next day. The officer interviewed him, decided that he should receive seven weeks' credit for prior military service, and shifted him to a recruit company just beginning its eighth week of training. Edson skipped over the three weeks of "quarantine camp" devoted to the basics of marching, the two weeks of "maneuvers camp" dedicated to camp construction and physical hardening, and the first three weeks of "training camp" that taught advanced drill, the manual of arms, and basic tactical formations. He and 32d Company had before them just three weeks on the rifle range and two weeks of final polishing before graduation.

Edson looked forward to the marksmanship training, though he disliked the first week of "snapping-in" work. That consisted of practicing the various standardized shooting positions, none of them comfortable. He soon had raw elbows and sore muscles. The second and third weeks would involve actual practice firing of 350 rounds of ammunition. Marines took their shooting seriously, since success meant money, up to an additional five dollars per month depending on whether one qualified as an expert, sharpshooter, or marksman. Now that he was doing some real training, Edson was happy, though he still complained about the food and could not wait for the "*real* grub in the officers' mess."

After waiting so long to become an officer, things moved very suddenly in early October. On the fourth, Franklin D. Roosevelt, the acting secretary of the Navy, endorsed a list of men for appointment as second lieutenants. Merritt Edson was among those designated. Headquarters acted expeditiously for once and issued orders sending him to Quantico for the Officers Training School. He took his new oath of office as a lieutenant on 10 October and departed the next day, his sum total of boot camp being a week of snapping-in.

When Edson showed up in Quantico he found a camp under hurried construction on what had been raw land just a few months earlier. The new Marine base surrounded the village of Quantico, which was nestled between the Potomac River and the parallel railroad line from Washington, D.C., to Richmond, Virginia. Workers threw up more than 120 wooden buildings, each a long, single-story affair on low stilts, with a tar paper roof and small, screened windows. Tents held the overflow, as men poured in from the equally new recruit depots at Parris Island and San Diego, California. On these fifty-three hundred acres in northern Virginia the Marine Corps organized and trained units for deployment to Europe.

The original clerical error at headquarters continued to dog Edson's young career. The Marine Corps had launched a class for some four hundred of its newest officers in late summer, and that course was on the verge of graduating in early November. Instead of awaiting orders overseas with them, Edson was biding his time for the second class to start on 20 November. In the meantime, he went to the rifle range and picked up where he had left off at Parris Island. He found the going tougher here as freezing temperatures and snow made conditions miserable. The firing line became a muddy pit as successive relays of warm bodies defrosted the hard ground. Sitting or lying down to shoot meant a wet uniform and bone-chilling shakes as the cold seeped in to the skin.

Edson shrugged off the discomfort and fired a 263 on qualification day, ten points more than he needed to make expert, and the fifth highest score of anyone on the range that day. The group then fired the Navy marksmanship course on succeeding days, and he became one of only three men to pick up a second expert rating. Success gave him a cocky attitude, which he expressed in a letter written the night before additional shooting from eight hundred and a thousand yards. "Think you could hit the bull's-eye, three feet in diameter, at a thousand yards, Dad? Just watch me do it, for unless I am very much off, I will punch a few holes in it." The day prior he had hit a much smaller bull's-eye (the very center of the target) nineteen straight times from five hundred yards. He now rated an expert badge—two crossed rifles superimposed over a wreath—his first award for military distinction.

Shooting did not occupy all his time. He and a fellow junior officer spent some of their free hours preparing themselves for the challenges to come. On weekends they hiked through the woods and inspected the camp's complex of trenches and bunkers, built by troops training for the western front. Marines had cut down trees for construction materials, cleared brush for fields of fire, strung miles of barbed wire, and dug a warren of fortifications. The denuded, rough terrain looked as though it had been swept clean by artillery fire. The all-too-realistic site served as a chilling reminder of what lay ahead.

The apparent dedication of the two lieutenants was motivated in part by lack of money. Edson's pay account had not caught up with his rapid moves, and he had already borrowed $150 from his strapped family to pay for uniforms, so he had little alternative but to remain on post. He did take in the occasional free entertainment at the base YMCA, but he could not afford to dance at the officers' club. When payday finally came in mid-November, he sent his parents a first installment on the loan, and celebrated with a weekend in Washington.

The training course was only mentally demanding at first. The lieutenants concentrated on a host of manuals dealing with everything from uniform regulations to Navy signal systems, with primary emphasis on drill and guard. Anyone who scored unsatisfactorily on the weekly lessons lost the privilege of weekend liberty. Temperatures that fell below zero delayed the shift to outdoor work for a time, and then the class received ten days off for the Christmas holiday. Edson was glad to spend a day in January digging trenches: "I liked the exercise, for we get none too much here." He and three friends took walks in the woods on their own to keep in shape and to shout practice commands. The four musketeers also enjoyed playing cards by candlelight after the designated time for lights out, and meeting females on weekend liberty in nearby Fredericksburg. Edson found southern girls beguiling and "became smitten . . . according to my usual habit." Ethel, now a freshman at UVM, was far away and, apparently, not much in his thoughts for the moment.

As the war-shortened training course drew toward its mid-February ending date, the thing uppermost in Edson's mind was his next assignment. Of the 124 men in his class, only 40 would be going to France as replacements; the rest would fill out the Advanced Base Force, detachments on naval ships and yards, and training slots at the recruit depots, or go on to more training in aviation or artillery. A lucky few might get to Haiti, the next closest thing to a war involving the United States, and one soul would report to the legation guard in Peking. Edson listed his preferences as France, Haiti, and sea duty. He really hoped "to get 'over there' and start in on my bit," though he wondered if he would be up to the task. In one letter home he noted another Chester man who had already won a medal: "If I go over, will they be able to say the same thing about me?"

He also worried that any miscue in school would ruin his chances. During one stint as the officer of the day (OOD), a position that made him the commander's representative for twenty-four hours, he wrote in his logbook that the hash in the mess hall was unsatisfactory. He regretted his fixation with military chow when the school director, Maj. Presley M. Rixey, Jr., grilled him about the entry the next day. "I made something of an idiot of myself, being at a loss for words once or twice, and thereby helping kill my chances for overseas service." The incident probably had no impact on his assignment, but he was correct in his assessment that he would not be going to France.

On the last day of the course he received orders to the 11th Regiment, a month-old organization located at Quantico. The 11th was a light artillery unit designated to support the Advanced Base Force, which had the mission of seizing and defending bases in support of a naval campaign. The concept had arisen in 1900 in the aftermath of the Spanish-American War, but had not advanced much beyond the planning stage due to the Corps's chronic shortages of manpower and frequent distractions over Latin American interventions. Although the Navy had no use for the force in Europe, the Marine commandant, Maj. Gen. George Barnett, was turning it into reality under the loose purse strings of the wartime buildup. He was looking ahead to the next conflict while fighting the current one.

Edson did not appreciate the commandant's priorities, since he knew that the Advanced Base Force would not be participating in the war. "I was somewhat surprised and disappointed, for I really wanted but *one* assignment, and I never knew *how* much I wanted it until it was turned down." He was particularly upset because of the twenty-one lieutenants sent to artillery he was the only one who had not asked for it. "They tried to smooth it over by saying that they were sending picked men . . . and choosing the infantry officers afterwards. . . . If I had known what was coming I might not have done so well in topography, math, etc." The prospect of missing the fighting riled Edson. "I expect to tell my grandchildren that during the great war I was busily engaged in firing salvos of three-inch shells at a bunch of mosquitos along the Potomac, while someone else beat up the Germans."

The completion of Officers Training School did not make Edson an expert Marine. He had much to learn about the duties of a junior leader, as well as the intricacies of his new specialty. He reported to 130th Company of the 11th Regiment, unhappy over the turn of fate but ready to do his best. His unit consisted of four officers, 135 men, and four guns. Their daily routine began with an inspection of personnel followed by crew drills with the artillery pieces, classes on subjects such as signals and the computation of firing data, and then drills involving all four guns as a unit. Occasionally they did something new to break the monotony or to round out their skills. They spent several days constructing a model artillery emplacement near the trench complex. They fortified the gun positions with logs and sandbags and tunneled ten feet underground for troop shelters. In the process, Edson learned something practical about the difficulties of trench warfare: During a rainstorm the deep bombproofs filled up with water.

One day the company worked on infantry skills and physical fitness by making a tactical march. The Vermont lieutenant commanded the advance guard, but his excellent conditioning proved a handicap in that role. He kept his detachment moving so fast that he unwittingly outdistanced the main body following behind and lost contact with them. He did not join up with the company until he returned to camp, where he received an angry lecture from the commander.

In June the company put considerable effort into preparing a demonstration exercise for a group of admirals and congressmen. The Corps wanted increased appropriations for more tractors to draw artillery pieces, and 130th Company had to prove the efficacy of the new equipment in a simulated combat displacement over the rough ground of the trench complex. Edson thought that horses were better suited to the job.

Since there was little prospect of combat, the 11th Regiment performed a host of missions that did nothing to improve their fighting skills. They marched in several parades, stood their share of guard duty for the base, and for more than a month during the summer did nothing but clear sections of forest for an expansion of the camp. As the weeks dragged on, the inaction grew more grating. The outfit had never been near full strength, and each time a replacement draft sailed for France the 11th gave up a slice of its personnel. The well-publicized success of the 4th Brigade of Marines at Belleau Wood in early June only made matters worse. Edson's contemporaries, including classmates from the officers' school, were fighting and dying while he played lumberjack.

If the war seemed to be passing him by, Edson at least used the opportunity to improve his leadership. His stint as an enlisted man in the

Guard gave him one advantage, since he had an appreciation for the perspective of those at the lowest rungs of the military hierarchy. Perhaps it was that background, coupled with his inherently quiet nature, that accounted for his unusual style of command. He had been on the receiving end of tirades from superiors, but he was not quick to use that technique himself. As he explained to his mother: "You asked me if I was a very stern officer. I am afraid not, not nearly as stern and commanding as I should be to succeed A#1 in this work. Why, I have been here a week, and I haven't even bawled a fellow out once, yet."

He believed, too, that a leader had to be an expert at his trade, so he insisted on going to bayonet school, against the wishes of his company commander. "He tried to tell me that I wouldn't learn much more and that I could bluff it through anyway. But I didn't like the idea of trying to teach the stuff unless I knew it myself." And when it came time to do the dirty work, he was ready to pitch in with his men. In preparation for one inspection he donned coveralls and spent two days helping to disassemble and clean the company's artillery pieces. He soon discovered that the troops appreciated his efforts. At one point the mess sergeant asked him if he could accompany him if the lieutenant ever got his own command. "Things like that sure do make a chap feel good."

Life was fairly comfortable for the young lieutenant. Once he joined the 11th Regiment, he moved into his own sizable room in the barracks. With pay arriving on a regular basis now, he was able to hire an orderly for five dollars per month to make his bunk, shine his shoes, and perform other chores that saved a great deal of time for a "budding shavetail lieutenant." Some of that time went to professional improvements, such as practicing his French. A fair portion went to more personal pursuits, such as canoing on the Potomac, horseback riding, and more than one late night out on the town. Sometimes he landed in his bunk at 0500, only to awake an hour later at reveille for a full day of work. His career was on the verge of a substantial boost, too, as Congress passed a bill doubling the size of the Corps to seventy-five thousand men. Edson expected rapid promotion to first lieutenant followed by another quick jump to captain, which would net him the lofty salary of $200 per month.

The highest aspiration of Edson and most of the men of the 11th Regiment was about to be realized. Germany's spring offensive of 1918 had so dented the Allied lines that the War Department relented in its opposition to a second Marine brigade in France. On 2 May Acting Secretary of the Navy Roosevelt ordered Major General Barnett to form the additional brigade. Rumors swept the 11th Marines that it would convert to infantry and go to France. Edson, then attending an artillery school, found it difficult to concentrate on the work with the future so uncertain.

An announcement of the switch to infantry came in mid-August, but the new status did not protect the regiment from further personnel ravages. Headquarters transferred a number of trained gunners to remaining artillery units, and hacked off another large slice for a replacement battalion departing for the front. The fruits of unprecedented recruiting in July (a record 8,500 men) began to show up in early September. By 1 September Edson's company had 230 men and was near war strength; 1,800 Marines had joined the regiment in the past week, and 1,700 more were due in the following week.

The formal reorganization of the regiment into an infantry outfit came on 6 September, and for the first time the Marine Corps adopted the Army method of alphabetizing companies: the 130th became Company B. Edson had a new commander, Capt. Charles Grimm, a veteran of fifteen years in the Corps, much of it enlisted service. Many of the newer lieutenants were also former noncommissioned officers, since the Corps turned almost exclusively to that source in 1918. New recruits filled out the ranks and turned the military's old social order on its head. The Company B clerk, for instance, was a former college professor.

Training reached a feverish pace in September as the regiment sought to meld the quickly assembled and reorganized outfit into a functioning infantry formation. Many of the officers went through a one-week crash course at the Overseas Depot, the Quantico school for replacements. In addition to classes on machine guns, automatic rifles, mortars, field engineering, gas defense, scouting, and sniping, Edson and others got hands-on practice in grenade throwing, bayonet fighting, night firing, and terrain appreciation. Edson was still keeping late hours and rising early, but now his efforts were devoted entirely to studying for this "new kind of warfare."

The newly created 5th Brigade of Marines, composed of the 11th and 13th Regiments and the 5th Machine Gun Battalion, conducted one brigade-level exercise before the 13th embarked for France in mid-September. Since officers were still in short supply, Edson filled in as the adjutant of the 2nd Battalion of the 11th Regiment for the maneuvers, and got to know its commander, Maj. Charles F. B. Price. That was the beginning of a long and fruitful association between the two men. In early September Edson received his first promotion as a Marine, to the rank of first lieutenant. After a year of waiting he told his sister that he was eager to actually go off to war: "Here's hoping you feel as happy as I for this big chance." And he was especially glad to be going as an infantryman. "Artillery is all right, but I think I still prefer the real fighters, the infantry, the men who win the battles, the men who deserve all the credit."

The men of the 11th Regiment had defeated manpower shortages, War Department opposition, the Quantico landscape, and a host of other adversaries in their effort to join in the war, but there was one more enemy to conquer before they met their real opponents on the battlefields of France. In 1918 a flu epidemic began in Kansas and quickly spread to Europe, where it mutated into a virulent strain that made its way back to the States in the fall of the year. Unseasonably cold weather and the tremendous influx of new men contributed to a severe outbreak in Quantico that September. Late in the month 84 of the 238 men in Company B were ill, and the doctors were registering about five deaths out of every one hundred cases. The epidemic further disrupted training during the period when it seemed most critical.

Departure for Europe came suddenly. The orders arrived on 28 September, and the regimental headquarters and the 1st Battalion (including Company B) boarded a train the next morning. They made it to Philadelphia the same day and embarked on the transport *De Kalb*. The ship sailed on 1 October as part of a large convoy and arrived at Brest, France, without incident twelve days later. The day of debarkation for the 1st Battalion was sunny and beautiful, and the men broke into song as they set foot on foreign soil. They were happy to be there and had reason to take great pride in their Corps. The 4th Brigade of Marines had added to the glory it had won already at Belleau Wood: In mid-September the 4th Brigade helped reduce the St. Mihiel salient; in early October it seized Blanc Mont Ridge; and on 31 October it stood poised to kick off a new phase of the Meuse-Argonne offensive.

Edson and the 5th Brigade seemed to have arrived in time to join the action, but the brilliant performance of the 4th Brigade had not weakened General Pershing's resolve to limit Marine participation in the war. The commander of the American Expeditionary Force (AEF) assigned the 13th Regiment to stevedore and guard duty in Brest, and posted the 11th Regiment to Service of Supply work around the important logistics center of Tours. The situation also had changed drastically from the desperate days of spring that had given birth to the 5th Brigade. Allied hammer blows, fueled by American manpower and reinvigorated by fresh American spirit, now had the Germans reeling all across the western front. Germany launched peace feelers in October, and the Allies were on the verge of responding to them in early November. The most recent Marine arrivals had little hope of seeing action.

The Marines of the 11th Regiment received no grand welcome upon their arrival in France. Like hundreds of thousands of Americans before them they marched the few miles uphill to the receiving station at Camp Pontanezen on the outskirts of Brest. The ancient French base had permanent quarters for less than two thousand men. Since the site served as transient quarters for many times that number, nearly all slept on the ground under canvas. Sanitation and mess facilities were woefully inadequate, and frequent rains kept the area deep in mud. The flu epidemic made things worse, if that was possible. One transport that docked around the same time as the *De Kalb* brought ten thousand soldiers, 40 percent of them sick. The camp's condition, coupled with the orders to the Service of Supply, must have been a crushing blow to morale in the 11th Regiment.

Company B remained at Pontanezen for two weeks. Edson had been there only a few days when he became ill, but with a severe case of mumps instead of influenza. Several days later the doctors diagnosed an additional malady, orchitis, an inflammation in one of his testicles. By the time Edson caught up with the regimental headquarters in Tours in early November, it was clear that the war would be over in a matter of days. He tried to be philosophical about it in a letter to his sister. "I can't say that I am really pleased with my big efforts in this war, for it doesn't seem to me that it has amounted to very much. But why worry about that— 'c'est la guerre,' as the Frenchman explains everything."

Caught up in the excitement of the armistice celebration on 11 November, Edson brightened. "There is certainly something about this Corps of ours, the Marines, which *makes* a man soldier and take pride in it." But as he settled into a routine of "occasional work, much censoring of mail, and plenty of wasted time," his euphoria drained away. He looked ahead to 1919, "the year I had hoped to finish college and begin something worthwhile," and started thinking about his future. "I cannot make up my mind whether or not I want to get out. It will certainly do little or no good to put in a resignation over on this side."

The end of the war did not affect directly the 11th Regiment, which had been broken up and scattered about the environs of Tours to perform guard duty. Edson joined Company B near Issoudun, a small town to the east, where they guarded the 3d Aviation Instruction Center, one of the largest and busiest airfields in the world. He loved to watch the "birds" soaring above the wheat fields and soon prevailed upon the pilots to give him rides. "It gives one a most exhilarating feeling, this going through the air at a hundred miles an hour." A month later the company moved on to a new assignment, but flying had captured Edson's imagination during this brief exposure. The next stop for Company B was La Pallice, the harbor town for La Rochelle. The unit continued to do guard duty, though Edson had additional responsibility as the assistant provost marshal for the area. One of his primary tasks in that capacity was passing sentence on servicemen arrested in the town by the military police. His busiest day came after a race riot between white and black soldiers resulted in one death and a number of injuries.

The day after Christmas Edson received a most unwelcome gift. The area commander appointed him a judge advocate (prosecutor) for special courts-martial. Soon thereafter the area headquarters made him the assistant judge advocate for general courts-martial. In this capacity he had to work with a lawyer prosecuting the most serious crimes. He soon found himself overwhelmed. The general court sat in session afternoons and evenings, and the special court operated in the mornings. Somewhere along the line he had to learn the law and prepare cases for trial. The dockets filled up quickly in the aftermath of war; he prosecuted six special court cases in one day and eight general courts in two weeks. He neither wanted the job nor felt qualified for it, and experience confirmed that "there is mighty little [pleasure] in trying men day in and day out for mistakes they make."

He made his own miscue in March 1919. Three men of the 13th Machine Gun Battalion failed to return on time from their Paris leave. The paperwork that Edson received did not fully support the charges against them, but he rushed the case to trial before the main witness departed the area. He reasoned that he had no time to go looking for the missing documents anyway. The court acquitted the men. The area commander, an Army colonel, was irate and intimated that the lieutenant had gone easy on the men because they were Marines. The colonel filed a formal letter of reprimand in Edson's personnel record, an action designed to harm his career. The words were particularly harsh, accusing the Marine officer of "neglect of duty." In addition to the written reprimand, the Army commander canceled Edson's leave request and lectured him for an hour. There was one positive result to the affair—orders revoking his service as a judge advocate.

The world war had brought about a great deal of joint effort by the Army and Marine Corps. The 4th Brigade had served side by side with the Army's 3d Brigade in the 2d Division throughout all the fighting. An Army general had commanded the Marine brigade for a time and Lejeune had led the 2d Division for many months. That cooperation did not extend behind the front lines, though, and joint success in combat actually created additional friction. Through no fault of their own, the Marines had garnered an inordinate share of the publicity for the heroics of the 2d Division, and many Army officers would harbor a grudge against the Corps as a consequence. That feeling had contributed to Pershing's efforts to frustrate Marine hopes for more action in the war.

After his own brush with the Army as a judge advocate, Edson expressed the feelings common to many Marines:

Dad, if you only knew how much they don't like us!! Both men and officers! We all *think* that our men are better men, that we do our duty better and are more efficient—in fact, we not only think it, we know it—so the Army, unwilling to own up to the truth, takes every possible chance to run us down. It is interesting, but sometimes unpleasant, to have someone trying to get something on us, or make things unpleasant for us. For instance, lumber here is none too plentiful, so when we acquired some legitimately the other day, someone thinking that perhaps we didn't come by it honestly, immediately ordered an official investigation.

In June 1919 Company B made another move, this time back to Camp Pontanezen in preparation for the regiment's return to the States. Not everyone would be going home, however, since the Marine Corps needed to contribute its share to the occupation of German territory. Major Price received orders to cull regulars and volunteers from departing units and form the 15th Separate Battalion for occupation duty. He selected Edson, recently promoted to captain, to command Company D. The Vermonter was elated at achieving "the height of all captains' ambitions," and at the prospect of seeing Germany, but that did little to alter the present dull routine of guard duty.

The battalion ended up performing several ceremonial duties, which gave Edson an opportunity to see people such as General Pershing, President Wilson, and French leaders Clemenceau, Poincaré, and Foch, but the expected orders to Schleswig-Holstein never materialized. Edson did use his extended stay in Europe to play tourist, with trips to Paris, England, Scotland, and Ireland, but that benefit was offset by two bouts of malaria. Since his company was preoccupied with guard and ceremonies, professional rewards were few. He did develop closer relationships with seniors such as Price and Maj. Ross Rowell, and received some tutoring in tactics through the battalion commander's program of assigning battle studies to his subordinates.

Edson and the men were impressed by the changes wrought in their absence at Pontanezen: There were floors, and bunks with bedsprings, in all the tents; wooden walkways spanned the muddy paths; and the mess halls dished out extra helpings of hot food. Upon their arrival they went through a delousing station and received fresh uniforms and new equipment. The base had grown from a pest trap into a model of efficiency that housed up to a hundred thousand men on its thousand acres. The turnabout was due to Brig. Gen. Smedley Butler, who had taken command of the camp just before the end of the war. The legendary Marine had worked hard to boost morale and break through red tape. Shortly after the armistice, he personally had led a raid on the Brest warehouses to liberate an enormous quantity of duckboards. Those wooden slats, once destined to line the trenches at the front, became the floors and walkways of the transient center. The brigadier's exuberant personality radiated throughout the command and drew the best performance from men in trying conditions.

Edson had a different leadership style, but it was no less effective within the much smaller sphere of his own unit. He fully recognized that his positive, quiet methods of handling men were out of step with those of the majority of his colleagues and commanders: "Somehow, most all officers get that habit, all criticism and no praise." But his troops seemed to need little prodding to maintain their motivation. Just prior to the unit's departure from La Pallice, the men organized their own smoker, a traditional evening of boxing matches and amateur entertainment. They expressed their appreciation for Edson's work and closed the event with an impromptu, moving rendition of the Marines' Hymn. "It was a great night. . . . If you only knew just how it makes one feel to know that your men *like* you." Decades later, the Marines who served under him in France would still remember with fondness the young officer from Vermont. Lelia Edson, untutored in the ways of the military but a good judge of character, understood the secret of his success: "You always see some good in everyone, and so everyone sees good in you."

Feelings of success did not alter Edson's predilection to leave the service as soon as he could. He and his fellow officers called on Butler when they arrived at Pontanezen, and Edson found him eager to run the camp right up until the last soldier headed home. "He cannot conceive of any outfit of Marines not just as enthusiastic for peace time service as he is himself." The young captain felt especially bitter after a visit to the battlefields of Belleau Wood and Chateau Thierry, as he reflected on the men who died while he was "back in the States doing nothing." His letters home dwelt at length on the decision he faced. "About my staying in the service! I doubt it very much, for there is nothing in it. Although the pay is as large as I could hope to draw for several years in any civil occupation, the outgo is as large or larger, so one could never be ahead of the game. . . . I don't know what to do after I get out. College is out of the question, for I don't want to be a burden on you people any more."

There was also a question whether the choice would be up to Edson. The Marine Corps was undergoing an inevitable reduction in size following the end of hostilities, and that meant demotions and forced resignations. Most of the new officers brought on board during the conflict had received temporary or probationary commissions with just that eventuality in mind. Edson had already lost his captain's insignia after just a few months and was again a first lieutenant. For those wartime officers who wished to remain on active duty, HQMC raised two hurdles. The first was a four-day written exam covering eleven different subjects, from tactics to naval gunnery. That took place at all Marine units around the world in October 1919. Once the results reached headquarters, the commandant created a board of senior officers to review the scores in conjunction with fitness reports. They would determine which junior leaders the Corps would retain.

The process was delayed when Lejeune ascended to the commandancy in June 1920. He was unhappy with the results of the board appointed by Barnett, which had not given any preference to officers with combat experience in France. The former commander of the 4th Brigade and 2d Division convened a new group to reconsider each case. The extended period of uncertainty hurt the morale of those subjected to it. Edson took the tests and applied to stay in the Corps, though he was still leaning toward leaving the service. His objective was to avoid the "disgrace" of being "bounced out." He did not feel well prepared for the exam, because he had few manuals available and had spent little time studying. However, Major Price wrote the president of the board on behalf of his protégé and asked for special consideration given the handicaps.

Just after Thanksgiving the battalion received orders to board the transport *Henderson* (AP-1). In early December it weighed anchor and sailed for the States. It arrived at the Philadelphia Navy Yard just in time for Christmas Eve 1919. Major Price granted a few days of liberty to men who had families nearby, and most took their friends along with them for the first home-cooked meal in more than a year. Edson drew the assignment as officer of the day and spent the holiday on the nearly deserted ship. The Marine Corps was far away from announcing what his status would be in the postwar order, but he was finally in a position to submit his resignation if he so desired. In low spirits, he contemplated his future. He had joined the Corps

Chapter 3

"In the Air, on Land, and Sea"

I n the first few days after Christmas the 15th Separate Battalion remained on the *Henderson* and mustered out of the service the "duration of the war" men who had volunteered to remain behind with the unit in France. When the purge was over, Edson had two lieutenants and fifty-one men left in his Company D, and it was the largest of the four in the battalion. The skeleton of the 15th Separate boarded a train for Quantico and arrived there on the next to last day of 1919. The battalion reorganized itself into two companies, with Edson taking command of Company A. His contemplation over the holidays had provided no answers for the future, and after a month of leave and discussions with his family he was still no closer to a decision. In the meantime a number of his fellow officers had resigned. "If I only knew how to do something, I believe I would quit too—but I hate to stop earning anything." His family continued to face financial difficulties, which further limited his options.

It appears that Edson never did make a formal decision to stay in the Corps; things just happened. In early March HQMC disbanded the remnant of the 15th Separate Battalion and transferred Edson to the base's Guard Company. There he stood a three-day rotation, with twenty-four hours as the OOD, the next twenty-four as the fire marshal, and the final day off. His commander was Capt. Robert Blake, an officer with whom he became close friends. Edson also discovered through a connection at HQMC that he had scored well on the retention exam taken in France. Things looked a little brighter with that revelation and with an outstanding fitness report from Major Price: "This young officer has been placed in a hard and trying position as a company commander in this organization and has handled the situation exceedingly well for one of his age and experience. His retention in the service and grade is strongly recommended."

Price went from the battalion to staff duty with the base's Vocational School, an innovation of the camp commander, Major General Lejeune. He created the program as a means to improve efficiency, morale, and recruiting in the aftermath of the war. It utilized materials from a civilian correspondence school to teach classes during working hours. Enlisted men could take courses on a wide range of practical subjects, from reading and writing to various trade skills. Under Price's auspices, Edson volunteered to teach math during his days off. Since Lejeune was pushing the school and it had great appeal to the men, enrollment grew rapidly. Proponents of the Vocational School hoped to boost participation from the current 370 students to several thousand. Before long, the head of the program, Col. William C. Harlee, arranged for Edson to work full time at the school, though no formal transfer from Guard Company occurred. Edson took charge of the Instructional and Examining Force, and enthusiastically buried himself in the challenge of administering the expanding project. His day began at 0730 and stretched toward midnight, but the long hours did not bother him. "I like it. It is really the first thing worthwhile I have struck in the service."

Edson's responsibilities multiplied as the program expanded. In addition to teaching and grading, his section wrote congratulatory letters to the families of the enlisted men and contacted potential employers to arrange jobs for Marines about to leave active duty. The offer of vocational education and a future career was a powerful enlistment incentive at a time when the Corps was having difficulty filling its postwar ranks. Edson's efforts expanded with the increased duties. Harlee found the young officer invaluable, and the lieutenant worked more closely with the colonel as time passed. That proved especially demanding, since Harlee did much of his work at night. Edson soon gave up his rented room in Fredericksburg and simply slept in his office. He was so wrapped up in the cause that he turned down a six-month assignment to France that would have brought extra pay.

Although Edson was an enthusiastic supporter of the Vocational School, his motives were not entirely pure. "I am also working with men who can give a great deal in regard to promotion, good stations, etc." He soon discovered that he had hitched himself to the right stars. A few weeks later, Barnett unexpectedly resigned his post as commandant of the Marine Corps two years before the expiration of his term. The president appointed Lejeune to fill the slot, and Harlee went up to HQMC with him to take the Vocational School concept Corps-wide. Renamed the Marine Corps

Institute (MCI), the program continued its exponential growth. It had more than tripled in the three months of Edson's tenure, and was adding three hundred or more students per month. With Harlee's departure, Edson became the secretary of the Quantico branch of MCI, a position equivalent to being assistant director.

Although Edson realized that his seniors were the key to his future career, he was quite willing to speak his mind. He and Harlee had carried on a running debate over the choice of record-keeping systems for the infant program. Just before his transfer to HQMC, the colonel gave in and let the lieutenant have his way. He also gave his subordinate a glowing fitness report. "He combines a quick perception with remarkable talent for translating ideas and instructions into action. . . . I consider this officer one of the brightest and most efficient young officers in the Marine Corps." For the next few months Edson ran the MCI office in Quantico, since his nominal boss was on extended leave and running for Congress from New York. That created clashes with the captains on the staff, who did not relish taking direction from a lieutenant.

With Lejeune and Harlee now at HQMC, Edson also discovered "a great deal of opposition to this progressive idea." His determined proselytizing on behalf of the program apparently angered senior officers who were less enthusiastic about it. In November 1920 he found himself "thrown out" and transferred to the 17th Company of the 5th Regiment. The vocational school concept died soon after and MCI evolved into a correspondence program dedicated wholly to military subjects. Still, Edson had the satisfaction of knowing that he had helped give the infant idea a start.

The MCI crusade was not the only thing that kept the Vermonter in the Corps in 1920. A more important factor was his increasing family responsibility. His father had continuing difficulties in finding steady jobs, and his mother required hospitalization for an extended illness, so he sent money home each payday to help them. He also started a family of his own. He had apparently been thinking about it for some time, since he had spent one-fourth of his savings in France on a diamond. He married Ethel Robbins in the First Church in Burlington on 16 August 1920. The newspaper account of the wedding gave a lengthy description of one of the gifts, a tea set sent from Japan by a cousin of the bride. The ship that carried it sank, and the only thing recovered at the scene was a single floating box with the tea set inside. The newlyweds spent their honeymoon on a two-week canoe trip along Lake Champlain, followed by a brief stay in New York City. Ethel, with just one more year to go at UVM, dropped out of college and moved to Quantico.

The couple's early days together were somewhat difficult, mainly due to an acute shortage of housing around the still-new base. They lived for a time in the quarters of another officer on leave, then rented rooms in a home in Fredericksburg, and ended up in the Quantico Hotel, a "wretched" building, but convenient to Edson's work. Just when the single, cramped room threatened to grow too oppressive, they finally obtained a small house on base. Ethel fell in love with the close-knit military life-style of bridge parties, dances, and "calls" at the homes of other officers. She and Merritt indulged their love of the outdoors with frequent picnics, long walks, and horseback rides. In their letters home, each waxed poetic about these early days of marriage. She described one lazy day spent on the banks of Quantico Creek, with her husband sleeping on one side and their German shepherd, Rex, contentedly chewing a stick on the other. He wrote at length on the wonder of a sunrise and a stroll along the water. "All in all it was a glorious morning, one of the best I have had in a long, long while."

With his parents and wife depending on him, Edson no longer had the freedom to resign his commission and make a fresh start. During that first year home he also realized that there were important tasks to perform in the peacetime military. And it became clear that there was plenty of room for him in the Corps. So many officers had resigned by 1920 that those remaining had no worries about being able to convert their temporary or probationary commissions to permanent ones. The only question that remained was where one would stand on the list in terms of rank and seniority, a matter to be determined by the Neville Board, which Commandant Lejeune had convened in June 1920.

Headquarters announced the results of the Neville Board in March 1921. Some officers, particularly those with distinguished combat records, jumped dramatically in standing on the lineal list. Edson landed in the upper half of the first lieutenants, about where he would have been based solely on his prior seniority. One problem persisted, and it could not have been prevented by any reasonable action by the Marine Corps or Congress. The rapid wartime expansion of the Corps had created the "Hump," a block of hundreds of officers, all commissioned within the space of about one year, and all of roughly the same age and same amount of time in service. One group of 140 officers, for instance, had received their original commissions between 10 August and 15 September 1917. In the small Corps after the World War there would be very little room for advancement; consequently one's placement on the lineal list could make a significant impact on promotion and pay. As an example, Robert Blake, commissioned on 10 August 1917, received a permanent appointment in 1921 in the upper third of the captains list. Edson, commissioned just thirty-six days later, would hold his rank of first lieutenant for the next *six years*!

*   *   *

The 5th Regiment, Edson's new home after the divorce from MCI, was an important element in Lejeune's rejuvenation of the postwar Corps. The old Advanced Base Force was gone, replaced by the East Coast Expeditionary Force, a more flexible organization that could perform a wider range of missions. The new force consisted of the 5th and 6th Regiments of infantry, the 10th Regiment of artillery, a small aviation group, and supporting units. There was some training, including a reenactment in 1921 of the Civil War's Wilderness campaign, but often as not the troops were engaged in endless peacetime tasks such as guard duty. Those distractions were multiplied by Smedley Butler's penchant for base building, which included construction of a twenty-five-thousand-seat stadium carved out of a Quantico hillside. The labor came exclusively from Marines, with most of the task accomplished by pick and shovel.

Edson, who had wanted to be an infantryman so badly in 1918 because they were "the real fighters," chafed at the lack of action. During his first six months in the States, headquarters turned down his requests for duty overseas (twice) and for a transfer to the aviation field. The only thing Edson had to look forward to was shooting. His company went to the rifle range for annual qualification in April 1921 and he set himself the goal of making the top score in the unit. He finished second, but his score of 267 out of 300 was outstanding, and he set his sights on a new and higher objective, competitive marksmanship.

Rifle matches were still a comparatively new thing in 1921. The Army had instituted standardized shooting competitions as early as 1882, but President Teddy Roosevelt, a strong nationalist and avid big game hunter, provided an important boost in 1901. He established the National Board for the Promotion of Rifle Practice (NBPRP) to encourage marksmanship, as a means to enhance America's international prestige and improve readiness for war. Two years later the board instituted a national-level shooting competition for civilians and service personnel. The National Rifle Association (NRA) soon joined in sponsoring the National Matches, which eventually found a home at Camp Perry, Ohio. Army shooters initially dominated the National Matches because of that service's established program. The Marine Corps soon initiated the practice of bonus payments for shooting qualifications and adopted the Army's distinguished marksmanship award program two years later. In 1909, HQMC created the Marine Corps Matches as a means to select its team for the National Matches. With increased attention and training, the Marines were soon holding their own against their rivals.

In spring 1921 Edson hoped to earn a coveted slot on the Marine team, a high honor in a service that was building up rifle marksmanship to the level of a religious cult. To achieve that goal he needed to qualify for the base team, finish near the top in a regional competition that served as a qualifying round for the Marine Corps Matches, and then do well enough at that level to gain the attention of the team captain and coach. Of the more than twenty thousand Marines around the world, barely thirty would make the cut.

Just days after recovering from a severe case of boils and carbuncles on his face and neck, Edson went to Annapolis with the Quantico team to face off against the Naval Academy's best. They defeated the midshipmen, and soon thereafter the lieutenant shot his way through the Eastern Division and the Marine Corps Matches. The captain and the coach did not rely solely on scores to pick the best. They wanted men who could perform under pressure, work well in a team atmosphere, and absorb the knowledge they would provide. Edson, three other officers, four warrant officers, and twenty-four enlisted men made the team.

They began training at Quantico, then moved to the Navy range at Wakefield, Massachusetts, in June to take advantage of weather conditions there, which more closely resembled those of Camp Perry. The training program consisted of several hours of firing each day, supplemented by coaching on the necessary techniques. The latter included the extremely difficult skill of "reading the wind," the process of judging its direction and speed so the shooter could adjust his sights to compensate. Even a small breeze could affect trajectory and throw a bullet off by inches; at long range a strong wind could move the point of impact several feet. In addition to a steady hand and good eyes, shooters needed physical stamina. Each man wore a heavy woolen undershirt under his padded shooting jacket and spent hours in the summer sun each day. Those who could not stand the heat did not last long in the sport.

Edson did very well in his first week at Wakefield, posting the highest scores among the first-time team members. Thereafter he went into a tailspin, but he eventually broke his slump. By the time the Marine contingent arrived at Camp Perry at the beginning of September, he had earned a spot among the top ten shooters. That was significant, because the premier event of the upcoming competition was the National Trophy Rifle Team Match, which pitted ten-man teams in a contest based on the combined total scores of all ten. The title brought with it bragging rights for the coming year; the service that won could lay claim to having the preeminent marksmanship program in the nation.

The match was composed of five stages with a total value of thirty-five hundred points (three hundred fifty per shooter). The first stage consisted of ten shots in ten minutes from the difficult standing position at a range of two hundred yards. Edson did poorly here with just thirty-eight points out of a possible fifty. He recovered marvelously at the next stage, ten rounds fired in one minute from the sitting position on the two-hundred-yard line. All ten of his shots went into the five ring for a "possible" of fifty points. The teams then moved out to three hundred yards for another rapid-fire string, this one from the prone position. Edson did almost as well, with a forty-nine. Next it was the six-hundred-yard line and twenty shots in twenty minutes from the prone. The shooters then repeated that sequence at the thousand-yard line, a range so great that the blackened circle of the target, though several feet in diameter, appeared to be about the size of a pinhead above the front sight post of the rifle. The lieutenant did reasonably well, with a ninety-three and an eighty-eight, respectively, at each of the final two stages. His score of three hundred eighteen placed him eighth on the team, just ten points shy of the best Marine shooter. Most important, the Marine Corps defeated the Army and carried home the title.

Any member of a national championship rifle team was a hero to fellow Marines. He was also certain to catch the attention of senior officers; the commandant traditionally congratulated each man with a personal letter. In addition to pride and renown, Edson got to know a number of other officers and men in the Marine shooting elite. Some were already legends, such as Capt. Joe Jackson, the perennial team leader; Maj. Littleton W. T. Waller, Jr.; and Gunners Otho Wiggs and Calvin Lloyd. Others were Capt. William W. Ashurst and Lt. William J. Whaling, who would climb to the top ranks of marksmanship in their own right. For an officer who loved shooting, it was an enjoyable summer of hard work, tough competition, and good fellowship, all crowned by success. Edson returned to Quantico in the fall of 1921 with the shooting bug firmly implanted.

The Marine reputation for straight shooting had utility beyond war and recruiting. Following an epidemic of robberies against the U.S. mail system, in November 1921 the president directed that the Marine Corps provide guards on railroad mail cars. Merritt and Ethel returned to Quantico from leave in Vermont and found the base in an uproar as it rushed to organize detachments for the mission. Edson received orders to New Orleans, where he would serve as the executive officer of a seventy-six-man group working parts of Louisiana, Texas, Arkansas, Alabama, Tennessee, and Kentucky. The duty quickly settled down to dull routine, since no bandits chose to test the well-known mettle and marksmanship of the Marines. On 5 December Edson received another surprise, as HQMC issued orders for him to report by the end of the month to the Naval Air Station in Pensacola, Florida, "for aviation duty at that post." There is no indication that he had renewed his previous application, so headquarters may have simply drawn it out of their files for action.

Marine aviation was still in its infancy. At the time of America's entry into the war four years earlier, the entire force had consisted of just seven pilots. During the war it grew to 282 officers supported by 2,180 enlisted men, but peace brought the same rapid decline that withered all branches of the armed forces. In 1921 HQMC set aviation strength at 6 field officers (majors and above), 16 captains, and 79 lieutenants. Since there were only 35 qualified flyers on hand, it promulgated a request for applications, especially from junior officers. The announced criteria were brief: Candidates were to be physically qualified, no older than twenty-eight years, and preferably unmarried. The latter element gave a hint of the extreme danger involved, even in peacetime. In 1922 the Corps would acquire 17 new pilots, giving it a total of 52. During that same period it lost 9 of that number to fatal crashes. Although Edson was married, he had volunteered when few officers were doing so; headquarters accepted.

The Vermont lieutenant entered aviation at a time of tremendous excitement, which tended to override concerns for the hazards involved. A few months earlier Army Brig. Gen. William ("Billy") Mitchell had stunned the Navy's hierarchy by sinking the former German battleship *Ostfriesland*. Mitchell, Britain's Gen. Sir Hugh Trenchard, and Italy's Gen. Guilio Douhet were advocating air power as the arbiter of future conflict. The Navy was about to commission its first aircraft carrier, and the Washington Naval Treaty authorized the United States to turn two battle cruiser hulls into flattops four times the size of that experimental ship. Aviation had already demonstrated its utility in the World War, and the Marine Corps was vigorously incorporating planes in combat in Haiti and in its Civil War battlefield maneuvers. Flying promised equal parts adventure, danger, and career opportunity (if one lived long enough). It was just what Edson wanted—a chance to make his own mark instead of living in the shadow of the World War heroes.

Edson's reception at Pensacola included a reminder of the risks of his new line of work. As the current class of candidates finished up its training, the top student of that group and the school's senior instructor died in a crash. Edson might have easily changed his mind at that point, since he failed the physical examination for being underweight, but he asked for a waiver and headquarters granted it. His choice was courageous if not wise. Of the eight Marine officers in his class, four would die in aviation accidents, and only one would spend his entire career as a flyer. Edson was fatalistic and nonchalant about the prospect of death. "I do not know as it makes so much difference whether one be young or old. In either case, one's life is run and someone else carries on their work." There is no indication of Ethel's thoughts on the matter, though she was three months pregnant and must have been concerned. In the spirit of "living fast," which permeated the ranks of aviation pioneers, Edson bought his first automobile, a considerable expense given his salary.

The Pensacola program began with about four weeks of ground school, followed by a month or so of flying under instruction, with a qualified pilot in the plane at all times. The aircraft was an N-9 Jenny, a two-seat biplane built specifically by Curtiss as a trainer. The student took about three flights per week, none of them more than an hour in duration, some as short as five minutes. On 16 March Edson went up five times, with a different instructor along on each of the first four hops. With their approval, his fifth flight was a solo. It lasted twenty minutes.

For the next month he continued solo flights. After every five hours of time in the air, an instructor went up for a check ride with the student pilot. It took a month to accumulate twenty-five hours of solo time, a period capped by test flights for formation and stunt flying. The next two weeks consisted of long-distance flying under instruction in a Curtiss HS-2, with flights up to three hours in duration. The remaining six weeks were filled with training in advanced skills such as navigation, communication, spotting, gunnery and bombing, and flying at night and with instruments.

Edson did reasonably well in the demanding program. His best marks were in the ground school, and the next best in gunnery. He had taken "more than the usual time to solo," but he performed acceptably in the air, and his overall score placed him twenty-first of the forty-seven Marine and Navy officers in the group. On 12 June Edson received an appointment as a naval aviator. The only shortcoming of the Pensacola course was its total focus on seaplanes. Marines did most of their flying from land bases, and that required further instruction at the main airfield of the Corps in Quantico. Edson asked for a delay in his transfer there, since Ethel was close to giving birth. Headquarters granted it, so he joined the Marine Barracks at Pensacola and honed his flying skills with more practice.

It was an idyllic few months for the young couple. Despite the pregnancy and the demands of flight school, their honeymoon spirit had not waned. While walking the dog one morning, Edson decided it was such a great day that he loaded Ethel, Rex, blankets, and food in the car, and drove to a secluded beach for breakfast. On the way back, they became stuck in the sand. He gave his wife a quick lesson in operating the gearshift and then he began to push. The car broke free and went careening down the road, with Ethel unable to control it. Luckily the engine died and the car coasted to a stop against a tree. After that adventure, Edson stopped along the way to pick some flowers for her. The Edsons' first child arrived on 2 July, a tad over six pounds and flailing so vigorously that the nurses nicknamed him Wiggles. The parents christened him Merritt Austin Edson, Jr. To top off the first half of 1922, Congress passed legislation granting a 50 percent boost in pay for aviators, just in time to take care of the expansion of the Edson household.

At the end of August Edson joined the 1st Aviation Group in Quantico. It possessed two of the Corps's five squadrons and served as the air component of the East Coast Expeditionary Force. The nominal organization of a squadron was three divisions of six planes each, plus three spare planes in each division for replacements (an indication of early maintenance problems). Due to budget constraints, squadrons actually had just one or two divisions, with the others on paper for activation in wartime only. In addition to the Quantico squadrons, there was one each in the Dominican Republic, Haiti, and Guam. The Marine Corps of 1922 had a total of about forty active aircraft.

Edson took his training in landing on an airfield in outmoded Curtiss JN Jennies and Vought VE-7s. Instruction was cursory at best. He made two flights of fifteen minutes each before soloing in the Jenny, and a single flight of twenty-five minutes prior to going it alone in the Vought. Thereafter he logged a considerable amount of time in the air, and brought his solo flight time to 131 hours. With that final practice complete, headquarters granted Edson's wish to go overseas, but it was not quite what he wanted. Of the three aviation detachments on foreign duty, only one was in a peaceful location and he was headed there. He would join Marine Scouting Squadron 1 (VS-1M) in Guam. The trip via the Panama Canal, San Francisco, and Honolulu took nine weeks.

The United States had taken possession of Guam during the Spanish-American War. The island's primary value was its location astride the sea route from Hawaii to the Philippines. It figured prominently in war plans that envisioned a U.S. fleet rushing across the Pacific to protect the latter archipelago. The problem after World War I was that Guam lay in the middle of a Japanese pincer. It was the southernmost major island in the Marianas chain, an island group owned primarily by Japan. To the south were the Carolines, also dominated by the Japanese. Guam was the potential stopper in the bottle against reinforcement of the Philippines. Under the recent Washington Naval Treaty, the United States gave up the right to fortify the island in return for Japanese acceptance of naval inferiority. That clause only enshrined reality, since Congress had no intention of spending money on overseas bases.

There was a minimal military presence on the island, which served as a refueling point for ships and a way station for the Trans-Pacific Cable. Most activity centered around the harbor of Apra on the west coast of the island. The term *harbor* was a misnomer, because reefs prevented most ships from using the small, enclosed bay, but the Navy installed coal bunkers on Cabras Island at the entrance to Apra, and set up a small naval station across the way at Piti. Orote Peninsula, on the opposite side of the harbor, held the cable station, the barracks of the Marine garrison force, and the base for the small detachment of seaplanes of Scouting Squadron 1. The naval headquarters was located at Agana farther up the coast.

The Edsons received a royal welcome. The squadron speedboat, a twenty-four footer, came out of the harbor to meet the ship and take them in ahead of the rest of the passengers. Crystal clear water showcased multicolored corals along the reef, and the crumbling walls of an ancient Spanish fort rose from a tiny island in the harbor. The blue-green sea gave way to the vivid greens of the island, which rose into high hills in the interior, a landscape of natural beauty. A car waited at the landing to take them to their quarters, a fairly large bungalow of several rooms, to include a bathroom with a shower (though no hot running water). The quarters came complete with two servants.

Scouting Squadron 1 was a small force of half a dozen officers and less than a hundred men. Its planes reflected the mixed bag of hand-me-downs that characterized most of the Marine air corps. There were three HS-2Ls (a Curtiss pusher biplane, meaning that the propellers were behind the wings), two N-9 trainers, and an F-5-L (a five-seater patrol bomber and the largest Marine aircraft type to date). All were seaplanes. The squadron had arrived on Guam in 1921, and had occupied the collection of buildings that formerly housed the Marine garrison. The latter unit had moved to its new barracks in 1919 when the old buildings had grown too expensive to maintain, an indication of the present condition of the seaplane base. The officer bungalows were relatively new, but that hardly counted in their favor. The aviators had built them from aircraft packing crates and other scrap material. The only structure in good shape was the hangar, a steel frame building put up specifically for the squadron.

As the squadron's name indicated, its purpose was not to fight, but to provide long-range eyes for the island commander. That task was not easy given the capabilities of the equipment. Fuel and speed constraints limited search patterns to less than a hundred miles, and that only in good weather. The planes were so prone to breakdown that most long flights ended up in a forced landing at sea. Each aircraft carried two mechanics in addition to the pilot, and though they were adept at repairs away from base, the planes were not sufficiently seaworthy to stay afloat in rough conditions. The squadron commander recommended against operating beyond the distance from which a plane could glide back to the island. A greater handicap was the lack of radios. Communications relied on carrier pigeons, which transported information at the stately rate of about fifteen miles per hour, if they made it home at all.

As the newest lieutenant, Edson received the additional assignment of squadron engineering officer. That gave him a wide range of responsibility for everything from aircraft maintenance to upkeep of the base. He felt overwhelmed initially, since he knew little about the work, but he came to enjoy it, particularly when he requisitioned an entire year's worth of supplies valued at one million dollars. The other benefit of the position was the requirement to test-fly all planes after any repair work. That provided him with considerable stick time. Long stints in an open cockpit were hard on the fair-skinned redhead, though, and he suffered from severe sunburns.

There were some drawbacks to life in the tropical outpost. Food was expensive. That worsened the money crunch that Edson already faced despite the extra flight pay. In addition to helping his parents, he had incurred debts making the long move to Guam. He determined to earn a little extra any way he could, and soon set to work on a chicken coop and a garden. The latter was a major project, since the ground was mainly rock and he had to haul soil from another part of the island. The poultry never quite seemed to work out; disease wiped out his profit margin more than once. To put off the expense of another transfer, he requested an extension of his two-year tour, which HQMC granted. He drew the economy line at the servants, though, and insisted that Ethel keep them on.

The officers and their families formed an especially close community here, as they were far from any other semblance of American society. There were dances at the club, frequent bridge tournaments, and a regular round of parties. The Edsons took the opportunity provided by the seclusion to spend even more time reading, and they signed up for the New Century Library, which provided a steady stream of classics through the mail. By the time they left Guam, books would account for one-fourth of their entire shipment of household goods. Edson kept in shape with swimming, tennis, golf, and other sports. His crowning moment came when he started up a squadron baseball team. He played first base and also coached the new organization to the island championship during its first season in 1924–25. That turned out to be the most dangerous thing he did on the island. A baseball struck him hard on the chest and after ten days of increasing pain he finally had the doctor take a look at it. He had been playing with a fractured rib.

With an unusual amount of time on his hands, Edson tried to get Ethel interested in some of his activities. He taught her chess and golf, and got her up in the air for a plane ride. Early on they still had time for romantic interludes: a canoe trip out to the Spanish fort in the harbor, and a moonlight swim in a deserted cove. In the last year of their stay on Guam, however, they both seemed too busy to spend much time together. Ethel took a month-long trip with several other wives to Shanghai, China, and Miki, Japan. Edson made his own voyage to Miki and the Philippines several months later. He played baseball every Saturday and Sunday, the days they used to reserve for themselves, and when he came home every evening he was so tired that he went to sleep right after dinner.

The last year of duty with the squadron was not always pleasant for Edson. The commander, a captain, was a hard man to work for and not much of a leader. His priorities could change overnight. One month he cut out all flight operations so the Marines could practice drill in preparation for a general's visit. The very next month he cut back dangerously on maintenance to set a record for the number of hours flown. His conduct did little to set a positive example for his subordinates, since he frequently showed up late for formations and otherwise performed his job poorly. He seemed more interested in his own perquisites than anything else, including basic manners. One evening he and his wife came to the squadron movie just before it started and found no seats left. Edson got up and offered his chair to the captain's wife, and the CO had the temerity to suggest that Ethel stand up as well so he also could sit down. That incident came just after Edson's extension went through, and it made him regret having arranged to remain longer in the squadron.

The slow pace of Edson's career also was frustrating. With the exception of his short stint as a captain, he had been a first lieutenant since 1918, and there was not much hope for a promotion anytime soon. Advancement to higher rank in the Corps was at that time based entirely on seniority, as long as one passed the requisite qualification exams, which was not too difficult. That comforting certainty of eventual elevation to the next rank was offset by an accompanying lack of openings. There was no method to force less competent officers out of the service, and little reason for any of them to leave until they had completed a full career of thirty years or more. With few senior officers retiring and the size of the Corps remaining stable, advancement was painfully slow. During the course of 1924 only eleven lieutenants made captain.

The transport *Chaumont* (AP-5) delivered several new officers to VO-1M in mid-June 1925, one of them a replacement for Edson. He made his last flight on 1 July and boarded the *Chaumont* the next day. He and his wife were both glad to be heading home. If they needed evidence that they had been in the tropics too long, Ethel discovered it when they attended the dedication of the new enlisted mess hall a few weeks prior to their departure. She took Austin into the walk-in refrigerator, and he cried because he had never felt cold before. The trip to the States was another long one, with the ship taking six weeks to get to San Francisco. They made it to Vermont by late August and took a month of leave to get reacquainted with their families.

The Edsons arrived in Quantico in late September 1925 and Merritt joined VO-4M. The assignment could not have pleased him very much, since the commander of his flight division was none other than his old CO from Guam. That marked the beginning of a run of bad luck that would dog him for some time. A week later he and the captain flew a plane up to Long Island as part of a detachment participating in the Pulitzer Races. While there, high winds damaged the plane and delayed their return. When they finally departed, the division commander had the controls, with Edson as copilot. Bad weather set in over Maryland, with the cloud ceiling dropping to four hundred feet and visibility to just two hundred yards. The captain decided to set down on what appeared to be a smooth field, but it turned out to be rough and soft. The strut supporting the right wheel gave way and the DeHavilland DH-4B, a World War I–vintage observation plane, came to rest with one wing in the dirt. A crew had to disassemble the plane and truck it back to the base, but both men walked away unscathed.

Two weeks later Edson received orders making him the commander of Service Squadron 1 (SS-1M). A mixed blessing, it got him out from under the thumb of a man he disliked and gave him his first command since Company A of the 15th Separate Battalion. On the other hand, the squadron was a catchall unit of drivers, mechanics, and assorted other ground personnel, not a fighting outfit of planes and pilots. His duties involved the supervision of these 160 men, as well as responsibility for all the accompanying paperwork.

The reassignment did not take Edson completely away from flying, though he soon had cause to wish that was the case. In January 1926 he flew to Philadelphia to pick up parts from the Naval Aircraft Factory there. On the return flight he became lost and ran low on fuel. He decided to set down for gas and directions, but in the short time at Quantico he had not yet had the opportunity to perfect the land-plane skills he had learned so briefly so long ago. He broke a wheel on the VE-7, though not so badly that it could not be repaired. The replacement parts arrived the next day, but overnight the water pump had frozen and burst (the temperature was hovering around zero).

Three days later he was finally ready to go again. His navigation was no better this time and he had to ditch on low fuel again. He came in too fast, the wheels stuck in soft ground, the plane nosed over hard; he and the copilot ended up hanging upside down from the fuselage, only their safety belts holding them in the cockpit. The propeller and radiator were ruined, so they had to disassemble the aircraft and truck it to a rail station for shipment. In fairness to Edson's flying ability, the extreme temperature, worsened by the windchill of high speed in an open cockpit at altitude, probably made it difficult to navigate or control the plane. His face was so frozen that it swelled up, and layers of skin peeled off over the next few days.

In March 1926 HQMC ordered Edson to attend the Army's Advanced Flying School at Kelly Field, Texas. After six weeks of training the Army determined that he was not physically qualified to fly because of defective depth perception. This was not a new discovery; the Navy had noted the same problem during tests in January. Upon Edson's return to Quantico the doctors gave him a series of fresh exams. Although he improved somewhat in the last two checks, the flight surgeons recommended that he be grounded for a period of two months and undergo weekly vision tests. They told him that the disability "was probably permanent." In the meantime, headquarters decided to send the lieutenant to the Company Officers Course, which would keep him occupied at Quantico pending the final determination of his physical status. Although no one made a formal connection to his earlier string of crashes, the defect may have contributed to his propensity to hit the ground too hard.

The Company Officers Course was part of another Lejeune innovation, Quantico's Marine Corps Schools, which also included the Field Grade Officers Course. Both training programs were an attempt to match the Army's emphasis on advanced professional education. The ten-month company course was supposed to prepare students to be company commanders and staff officers for battalions and regiments, but its focus tended heavily toward small-unit tactics and weapons proficiency, subjects more germane to commanders of platoons rather than companies. Many of the attendees were in fact lieutenants, oftentimes men with combat experience from the World War. They had little interest in rehashing the use of the bayonet, techniques of patrolling, or the functioning of the rifle. Their instructors were not inclined to press them too strongly, either. The students had liberty from noon Friday till Monday morning, and the commandant of the schools stated plainly that "too much study without proper time for relaxation and exercise is not good."

The lax program left time for Edson to keep up his interest in aviation. He flew regularly throughout the fall as a passenger and took the weekly eye exams. A Navy flight surgeon examined him on 22 October and watched him make landings. The doctor noted that the vision tests were mixed, but he felt that they were good enough to recommend that Edson resume flying, with continued monitoring of his eyes. Edson made a handful of solo flights in December but did not get up in a plane again until nearly a month later, on 22 January 1927. He drew out an O2B-1 and took it on a cross-country hop to Hampton Roads, Virginia. On the return leg, the engine began to miss and lose power, so Edson had to land in a farmer's field near Ark, Virginia. As he came in, he realized at the last moment that he was going too fast and thus might overshoot the landing area. In a flash he decided not to circle round for another attempt and instead put the plane down very quickly and very hard. He and the lone crewman walked away unhurt, but the aircraft was heavily damaged. The reaction to this latest crash was swift and negative. The same flight surgeon who had recommended Edson's reinstatement now came to the exact opposite conclusion after the crash. He thought that the lieutenant showed "bad judgment" and "inaptitude for flying." Unwilling to let the matter rest on a simple evaluation of skills, the doctor attacked Edson's mental state. A 1924 physical had found him "quiet, shy, studious." The exam done two days after the crash turned this into the possibility of "an inferiority complex," and averred that the pilot "had lost his head" during the landing. The surgeon's final conclusion was more justifiable: "To allow this pilot to continue to fly would only result in a further destruction of government property and ultimately disaster to himself."

Considering that the annual averages at this time for the entire Marine Corps were twenty-five crashes, five fatalities, and five serious injuries, Edson had already done more than his share of damage and used up more than his share of luck. The official accident board took a more lenient view than the doctor and recommended that Edson receive remedial training and another opportunity to prove himself. The base commander was less forgiving. He claimed that he had restricted Edson to local flights and forbade him to pilot the O2B-1s. Headquarters revoked the lieutenant's flight status.

Edson never explained why he did not follow the rules imposed by his superior, though he later intimated that his commander had contrived them after the fact. That interpretation seems possible in view of the absence of any sort of disciplinary action, which surely would have followed the disobedience of a lawful order that had such drastic consequences. Even the loss of flight status was less of a sanction than might be supposed at first glance. Under the rules then in force, Marine pilots could serve in aviation billets for only five years before switching back to line duty for at least three years. Edson was due for a job on the ground at the end of his current schooling no matter what. He did not feel prejudiced by the revocation, and headquarters later allowed him to petition to regain his flight status without dredging up his accident record. He never lost his love for flying, and for the rest of his life he would indulge in it whenever he had an opportunity. And the golden wings of an aviator remained a permanent fixture on his uniform. The experience also provided him with an invaluable background that most of his ground contemporaries did not possess. They could talk about aviation, but he had 530 hours of firsthand knowledge in a cockpit.

Edson completed the Company Officers Course in mid-April. The school may not have been challenging, but it did exempt him from most of the exam for promotion to captain. He was finally reaching the appropriate level of seniority for advancement, and headquarters had him take the remaining portions of the test, which he passed. It was now only a matter of months until he regained the "railroad tracks" he had lost eight years earlier. His orders took him to the Marine Barracks at the Philadelphia Navy Yard, where he took command of one of the guard units. He barely had time to get settled when headquarters directed him to report back to Quantico for temporary duty there. Due to the heavy overseas commitments of the Corps that year (a brigade each in China and Nicaragua), it was impossible to hold the normal qualifying competitions for the Marine Corps Matches. The Target Practice Section at HQMC solved that problem by sending seventy-three of the best marksmen in the Corps to Quantico to compete with Marines stationed there. Edson had failed to make the team in 1926, but his consistently high annual scores, his 1921 experience, and his ready availability in the States made him an ideal candidate in 1927.

After the Marine Corps Matches, the final team selections included nine lieutenants, one of them Edson. The thirteen officers and twenty-six enlisted men of the team spent most of July and August at Wakefield, with a break to compete in the United Services of New England matches. Based on his prior experience as a shooter, Edson served as the assistant statistical officer for those matches. He also worked on the board named by headquarters to test the Cutts Compensator. Fitted on the muzzle of an automatic rifle or a submachine gun, the device was designed to direct the flow of gases coming out of the muzzle so as to counteract the natural tendency of the weapon to rise during automatic firing. Thus more bullets would strike closer to the original point of aim. Edson had been a simple trigger puller up to this point in his marksmanship career; now he was moving up to a higher level as an official and as a weapons expert.

During the course of the summer he performed well behind his rifle. He won his third competitive shooting medal, which qualified him for the prestigious Distinguished Marksman classification. Only twelve other shooters reached that plateau in 1927. In the long-range Wimbledon Cup competition he demonstrated the skill that had made him so cocksure as a second lieutenant many years before. He placed all twenty shots in the bull's-eye, and eleven of those within the smaller V-ring inside the bull's-eye. That was good for eighth place; the winner had fourteen V's.

A few months of shooting proved to be a good tonic for Edson, but he was not eager to return to Philadelphia at the end of the summer. The vast majority of his fellow Marines were overseas and he wanted to join them. In August, while still at Camp Perry, he made a request for transfer to the Gendarmerie d'Haiti. Haiti was no more active than Nicaragua or China at that time, but a Marine officer with the *gendarmerie* filled a billet at the next higher rank in that organization, and that meant more pay. Edson had no more success with this request than he had with similar ones in 1921.

Headquarters, however, took a step that was both surprising and fortuitous. In early November, orders appeared transferring Edson from the barracks to command of the Marine Detachment of the USS *Denver*. This was highly unusual, since Edson had been in Philadelphia for only a few months, and he was going to a first lieutenant's billet even though he was approaching promotion. He received word of the orders while on leave in Vermont and rushed to carry them out. He arranged to put his household effects in storage in Philadelphia, left Ethel and Austin with her parents in Burlington, and headed for the *Denver*'s home port of Boston. It was not Haiti, but a tour at sea was certain to be better than the dull routine of guarding a Navy yard.

Chapter 4

"To the Shores of Tripoli"

S ea duty, a tour with a Marine detachment on board a Navy ship, was the traditional backbone of the Corps. The Continental Congress had created two battalions of Marines in 1775 for precisely that purpose. In that era Marines at sea served as sharpshooters or alongside the ship's complement as gun crews and boarding parties, and they formed the heart of any naval force landing on a hostile shore. This unique role as half soldier, half sailor had allowed the Corps to weather a number of attempts by both the Army and the Navy to abolish it.

But sea duty was rapidly becoming an anachronism. After the World War, Commandant Lejeune redirected the focus of his service toward a new and more important mission, the amphibious assault. Seagoing Marines still performed one important task: They were the strong arm of American diplomacy, ready to go ashore at a moment's notice to intervene in minor trouble spots around the world. The locus of their efforts in the 1920s was China and Central America. The latter area was so busy that in 1920 the Navy Department created a new unit, the Special Service Squadron, for the specific purpose of keeping order in that turbulent region.

The handful of ships in this squadron were hardly first-line. The flagship, USS *Rochester* (CA-2), commissioned in 1893, was the oldest American warship in active service. The light cruisers *Denver* (CL-16), *Galveston* (CL-19), and *Cleveland* (C-19) were of a similar vintage. *Denver,* commissioned in 1902, wore her obsolescence for all to see; most of her ten five-inch guns were mounted in the sides of the hull instead of in turrets on the deck. At 3,200 tons, she was dwarfed by the 10,000-ton "treaty" cruisers that came off the building ways following completion of the 1922

Washington accord. *Denver* had a complement of just over three hundred men and a top speed of twelve knots. The only modern ship was *Tulsa* (PG-22), a gunboat built especially for shallow-water missions. Each ship had a nominal home port in the States but reached it only every other year or so for a yard overhaul. Their real base was the anchorage off Balboa, on the Pacific end of the Panama Canal Zone.

In the summer of 1927 Capt. John W. Thomason, Jr., the literary light of the Corps, wrote an article in the *Gazette* on the squadron and Panama. If Edson noticed it during his busy days at Camp Perry, he must have read only the first page, which described a tour there in glowing terms. "Why, it's just like shore duty. Got any family? Sure—take 'em down on an Army transport. Fine place. Sleep ashore every night. Golf. Tennis. Swimming." The *Denver*'s new lieutenant intended to do just that, and arranged for shipment of his household goods and automobile to the Zone, where he expected Ethel and Austin to join him. He apparently missed Thomason's accurate observation buried in the body of the article: "You regret, when your two years in the Squadron are finished, that you didn't get to see something of [Balboa]."

The *Denver* pulled away from its berth on 10 December 1927 and pointed its bow south for the long run to Panama. It was a beautiful winter morning, but the 0900 muster spoiled Edson's mood. Privates Barton and Hoffman had failed to return from their final night of liberty. That left him with his first sergeant, eight NCOs, and fifty men. By midday he was more concerned with a personal matter. The Atlantic gave the old cruiser a rough reception, and Edson was one of many who could not eat a thing. He gained his sea legs within a few days, though, and got a daily routine under way. After breakfast he inspected the Marine compartment and the men. The detachment spent the balance of the morning in physical training, drill, and instruction on professional subjects. Afternoons were devoted to ship's work, largely the never-ending task of chipping and painting, or to cleaning weapons, equipment, and clothing. Edson tried to get in an occasional class for the NCOs on leadership or tactics.

Conditions were none too pleasant for the troops. The living spaces below decks were hot and crowded; many slept on deck at night to stretch out in the cool air, though rain often drove them back to their muggy hole. Personal hygiene consisted of a saltwater bath with a sponge and bucket on the main deck. The old ship had outmoded coal-fired boilers, which necessitated a backbreaking transfer of fuel by hand. At the end of hours of labor, both men and ship were coated with the black dust, and that meant hours more of cleaning. Training could grow tiresome given the limitations of the environment. Much of the training was concentrated on drill with the ship's five-inch guns, several of which had Marine crews.

The *Denver* arrived off Colón, the Caribbean terminus of the Panama Canal, on 19 December. Befitting the treatment that the Navy typically gave Marines, Edson drew the assignment as the ship's senior shore patrol officer, which meant that he would have that duty the first night of every port visit. Since the ship often stopped for only a day or two, it was not a good deal. It did not take him long to decide that the skipper "dislikes Marines most cordially." Once in Balboa Edson got his men ashore for drill and baseball. The detachment celebrated Christmas day with a turkey dinner and a victory over the *Rochester*'s Marines. Edson opened his gifts, all books, but it did not seem like much of a holiday and he confided to his diary that he missed his family.

As Captain Thomason had predicted in the *Gazette,* finding quarters was "something else again," and the newest lieutenant on station had to break the bad news to Ethel. "Do not think I am trying to paint the picture any worse than it is, for you must know that I only wish you and Austin were down here." Thomason soon proved right about the lack of time in port, too. The day after Christmas the *Denver* received instructions to sail immediately for Cabo Gracias à Dios (Cape Gracias), a small town on the Caribbean coast of northern Nicaragua. There was a report of bandits menacing American citizens there.

It took a day to pass through the Canal and another to reach the objective. Edson spent that time instructing his men on landing force duties and weapons. Upon arrival, the ship's captain, Edson, and a small group took a local boat into the town, a ride that included a hair-raising passage through heavy surf over a sandbar. Once ashore, they discovered that they were on a "fool's errand." The cry for help had come from an American whom local authorities had arrested and fined for rum smuggling. The landing party let matters lie and the ship headed south the next day.

The *Denver* returned to Panama in mid-January to take on coal. The ship soon made another run to Nicaragua, to transport Maj. Harold H. Utley to Bluefields and to pick up a diplomat for return to the Canal Zone. After that delivery it was back to Nicaragua again at the very end of the month. The ship took Utley on board for a tour of the Nicaraguan towns along the Caribbean coast. The major had no authority over the ship's Marine detachment, but he gave it a "quite thorough inspection" anyway. Edson then accompanied him ashore on inspections of the various Marine outposts, all garrisoned by parts of the 51st Company, which did fall

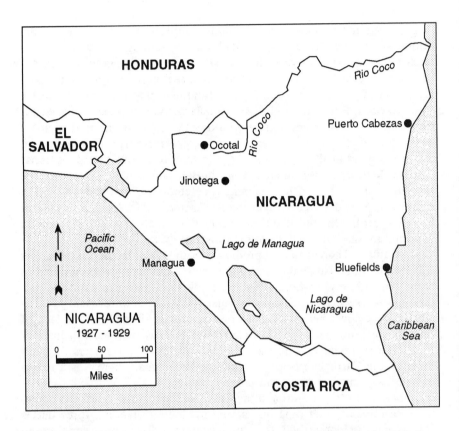

HONDURAS

Rio Coco

EL SALVADOR

Rio Coco

Puerto Cabezas ●

● Ocotal

Jinotega ●

NICARAGUA

Pacific Ocean

N

Lago de Managua

Managua ●

Bluefields ●

Lago de Nicaragua

Caribbean Sea

NICARAGUA
1927 - 1929

0   50   100

Miles

COSTA RICA

under Utley's command. By mid-February the *Denver* had been in Central America for eight weeks, six of which it had spent in the vicinity of Nicaragua. The highlight of the latest trip was Edson's receipt of the long-awaited promotion to captain, which came on 11 February 1928. Except for a brief period as a captain during the war, he had been a first lieutenant for nearly ten years.

The *Denver*'s quick response to the report of bandits, and Major Utley's arrival on the scene, were symptomatic of larger events in Nicaragua. The United States had been intervening militarily in that unstable Central American country from time to time since 1853, but various incursions had not alleviated the underlying hostility between the dominant political movements, styled as the liberals and the conservatives. In the mid-1920s the liberals launched yet another revolt, this one backed by Mexican arms and money. The Marine

Corps's 5th Regiment, supported by a squadron of planes, arrived on the scene and forced a peace treaty on the parties in May 1927. In accordance with this agreement, most revolutionaries turned in their arms and awaited the elections scheduled for the coming year. The United States then began to withdraw its force.

One recently established Liberal leader, Augusto César Sandino, refused to endorse the treaty. He took his small group of armed men into the difficult countryside of Nueva Segovia, pillaged a mine and a town, and gathered recruits with patriotic harangues and promises of loot. The Marines of the time referred to Sandino and his men as bandits, mere outlaws seeking personal gain. That accurately described some of the marauding bands that professed allegiance to the rebel cause, since they were opportunists taking advantage of the general disorder. Sandino's background and politics were obscure, but he portrayed himself as a strong nationalist who rejected American intervention in the affairs of his country. His focus on politics raised him to a level seldom seen by Marines in the early twentieth century. Whatever his actual motives, he acted like a true revolutionary seeking to overthrow the established government for reasons beyond immediate personal greed. Those Marines who missed that distinction would have a difficult time trying to deal with an enemy they badly misunderstood.

In July 1927 Sandino led a force of several hundred men against an outpost of Marines and Nicaraguan constabulary at Ocotal. The defenders and their aerial reinforcements inflicted numerous casualties on the massed attackers and drove Sandino out of town. Thereafter, the rebel leader decided to avoid conventional confrontations with his better-armed opponents. Years later Edson would discuss the difference between a rebel who had the support of a majority of the populace, and one who represented only a minority faction. The former would be in a position to launch a full-scale civil war; the latter had to follow a different path if he hoped to have any chance of victory. In the classic style of a weak revolutionary, Sandino adopted Edson's alternative course: the strategy of guerrilla warfare against a stronger foe.

After the attack on Ocotal, the flow of Marines out of the country reversed, and reinforcements poured in, mainly the 11th Regiment. That organization and the 5th Regiment became the 2d Brigade. These strong forces pushed into Nueva Segovia and drove the rebel band out of its stronghold. Rumors and intelligence assessments then indicated that Sandino would move into eastern Nicaragua. This sparsely populated region stretching from the central highlands to the Caribbean coast made up two-thirds of the nation. It contained the bulk of foreign investment in the country, mainly lumbering, mining, and plantation operations. Nine rivers and one small railroad carried products to the handful of coastal towns that served as commercial centers. Roads did not exist; overland traffic moved by foot or mule on rough jungle trails. Much of the population consisted of Miskita Indians and other tribes. The few Nicaraguans of Spanish and mestizo descent were strongly liberal and had supported earlier rebellions against conservative rule. Here, Sandino hoped to garner support, strike at lucrative economic targets, and avoid his enemy's main forces.

It was this suspected rebel movement to the east that kept the *Denver* so busy in early 1928. When Sandino's plans became apparent, brigade headquarters reacted by reinforcing the single company that garrisoned the coastal towns. Major Utley assumed command of the newly formed Eastern Area when he arrived in Bluefields on 22 January. He had no maps, few troops, and an area of responsibility loosely defined as "the east coast of Nicaragua and such territory inland as can be controlled by troops supplied from the east coast of Nicaragua." He established his headquarters, which consisted of himself and a bugler, at Puerto Cabezas on 24 February. Since brigade had its hands full occupying the more populous western portion of the country, the commander of the Special Service Squadron (COMSPERON) contributed his ships' detachments to the reinforcement of the Eastern Area. The first unit to land was the *Denver*'s; Edson and fifty-six men went ashore at Puerto Cabezas on 19 February.

The brand-new captain had already spent time poring over intelligence reports and a map of Nicaragua. The Coco River drew his attention. It was one of the country's major transportation arteries; with headwaters in the central highlands, it flowed hundreds of miles to the east into the Caribbean. It was a potential supply channel running into the rebel-dominated interior (one already used by Sandino in 1927), as well as an escape route if government forces from the west coast pursued the guerrilla bands into their lair. Edson had taken advantage of Utley's presence on the *Denver* in early February to discuss possible plans centered on the Coco. He recommended three separate actions: reconnoitering the river, garrisoning it to deny its use to the rebels, and sending a combat patrol upriver into the heart of Sandino's territory. Meanwhile, he hoped that rumors of a pending attack by Sandino proved true: "If so, may I do more, or at least all, of my share in stopping him." He would have nothing to worry about on that score.

The major soon implemented the first two courses of action recommended by his subordinate. Utley ordered Edson to begin reconnaissance patrols in late February. He then formulated a plan "to guard the line of the [Coco] as far up as Bocay." Edson dispatched a five-man team up to Sacklin on the Coco and another four-man group toward the Pis Pis mining district in the interior. On 7 March the captain and five of his Marines sailed north to Cape Gracias, where they hired a boat, a guide, and three native crewmen for a trip up the Coco River. Benny Müller, an American contractor who lived along the river, volunteered to join the effort. The patrol hoped to gather information on the terrain, the enemy, and the local Indian population. Edson belittled the hazards of the upcoming operation in a letter to his wife: "Outside of the discomfort of living in the bush there will be no more to it than any other camping trip."

Preparations for the river patrol foreshadowed the logistic problems that would plague all future operations in this remote region. Edson had to use his own money to cover expenses. The patrol's motor launch was a small, open craft powered by a converted Ford Model-T engine. Its top speed of ten miles per hour was often less than the river's current, and that presented considerable problems heading upstream. The boat had barely enough room for the Marines and the crew, but it was the largest one the patrol could hire. They had to lash another boat alongside to carry their fuel and provisions. Nearly all craft on the river were dugouts made from mahogany or cedar logs. The standard version, called a *pitpan*, could usually

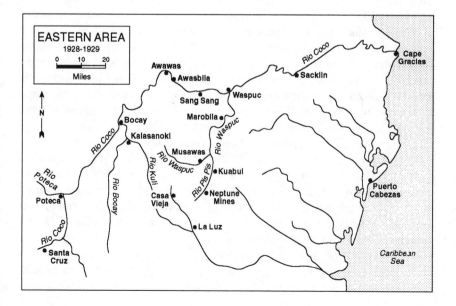

carry an eight-man squad in addition to its crew of four Indians. Occasionally the locals used wooden ribs and boards to build up the sides of a larger dugout and increase its carrying capacity. These bateaux had a crew of up to a dozen Indians, and might be up to forty feet in length and five feet at the beam, yet they drew just two feet of water when fully loaded.

The patrol departed Cape Gracias the morning of 8 March. It moved well in the navigable lower river and made sixty miles before the motor burned out a bearing. The Marines had to wait three days for one of the crewmen to travel back to the cape for parts. With the engine finally repaired, the patrol then moved another fifty miles up the river to Sacklin. At that village Edson met up with the overland patrol commanded by Sgt. Melvin Mosier. The NCO reported that his arrival had come as a surprise to the natives, whereas news of the boat unit had preceded its landing. The Indians closely watched the river, the route of most traffic into the region—a lesson Edson would put to use later on. The local government representative, the *commandante,* informed the patrol that Sandino had 40 men in Sang Sang and more than 150 soldiers farther up the river at Bocay. Edson discounted that report and determined to push his reconnaissance to the latter location.

The patrol arrived at Waspuc around midday on 14 March after portaging a number of large rapids. In addition to these delays, the men frequently had to wade next to the boats and pull them through shallows created by the dry season. The continued soaking took its toll on shoes and feet alike.

Waspuc, the largest settlement in that area, consisted of seven frame houses and a store. The patrol halted there for a day while the Indians overhauled the motor again. The Marines did not rest but took a *pitpan* ten miles up the Waspuc River, which branched south toward the Pis Pis mining district. With the engine work complete, movement up the Coco resumed. On 18 March Edson reached Awasbila. Directly ahead lay the Kiplapine Rapids, a half mile of whitewater dropping down a forty-degree gradient. That marked the head of navigation for motorboats. Only native dugouts could negotiate the difficult stretches of water upriver.

Edson hired local Indians and a dugout to take himself and the two men farther up the river, but on 23 March the patrol met a resident of Bocay coming downriver. The Nicaraguan acknowledged that rebels frequented his village but claimed that there were presently no forces in that location. Edson, who had traveled just a few miles beyond Awawas, now decided to go no farther. "The story seemed straight enough and my opinion of it was confirmed by a Cuban living nearby whom I knew to be distinctly unfriendly with the bandit element." Müller must have influenced that judgment, since Edson could hardly have assessed with any surety the trustworthiness of the local inhabitants. Another factor in the decision to go back was the dwindling supply of rations. The patrol covered the distance from Awawas to Cape Gracias in just three days—a demonstration of the effect of the current on waterborne traffic.

The captain considered his operation a success. He and his men had penetrated 260 miles into the interior, to a place where no Marines and few Nicaraguans had ever been before. They had gathered a wealth of information on the waterway, the surrounding terrain, the transportation assets available, the state of rebel activity, and the "attitude of natives towards [the] Marine occupation." Edson counted this last element as the most important outcome of the venture: "It is my belief that, if we were to succeed in our mission of eradicating the bandit element in Nicaragua, we should make every effort to gain the friendliness and cooperation of the peaceful citizenry." In particular, he hoped to use the Indians as a tool against the guerrillas. "They were inculcated from the time of their birth with a hatred of the Nicaraguans whom they called 'Spaniards' and so were potential allies if properly approached and handled." Edson decided to woo the Indians "by learning enough native words to make my wants known to them; by showing an interest in them and their mode of living; and by always treating them fairly."

His initial activities in Puerto Cabezas revealed the energy that must have sustained him during the three-week patrol. The first night back he stayed up till 0400 briefing the major and reading mail, then got only ninety minutes' sleep. At 2300 that second night he was still awake and working on a letter to Ethel. He told her all about the long trip and proudly described the rare acquisition, for a Marine, of facial hair. In his eagerness to explore, he had decided not to waste any daylight hours on shaving. "Being the 'Old Man'—I overheard some of the men calling me that among themselves the other day—it was of course absolutely necessary that I surpass them all in the raising of . . . a full beard." He also passed on the exciting news that he had received orders to relieve Capt. Franklin Hart as commander of the *Rochester*'s Marine guard. This was a distinct elevation, since the flagship normally rated a senior captain. At 2 officers and 103 men, it was also the largest ships' detachment in the Navy. Edson considered it "something of a compliment to be picked for the place."

Despite his apparently inexhaustible supply of energy, the rigors of the expedition had taken their toll, and two days later Edson was confined to his bed with chills and a high temperature. The medical people thought it was a relapse of malaria, but the blood test came back negative. They gave him quinine anyway and a few days later he was on the way to recovery. The patrol had not encountered Sandino and his men, but it had met the toughest enemy the Marines would face in the coming campaign—the hardships dished out by the forbidding Eastern Area.

The first patrol up the Coco had uncovered little about the rebels except rumors that they were coming. In early April the enemy finally turned those expectations into reality. The former Liberal *commandante* of Cape Gracias moved down the river and took control of Sang Sang. Another Sandinista lieutenant attacked the Pis Pis area, seizing the La Luz and Los Angeles mines on 12 April, and the Bonanza works shortly thereafter. The rebels destroyed the facilities, carried off gold and supplies, and kidnapped an American manager. The Sandinista actions galvanized the Eastern Area command, which had thus far been content to make small reconnaissance patrols while it gathered strength from the arriving detachments of the Special Service Squadron. Report of the Sang Sang raid came to the headquarters at Puerto Cabezas on 6 April. Within a few hours Edson rose from his sickbed, gathered a force composed of 2d Lt. Jesse Cook, thirty-seven Marines, and a Navy corpsman, and embarked on a ship for movement to Cape Gracias.

The captain organized his patrol into a headquarters group and two sections of two squads each. A squad contained seven riflemen and one man armed with a Browning automatic rifle (BAR). The detachment carried along two Lewis machine guns but had no grenades. Each man carried a poncho, shelter half, mosquito net, an extra uniform, and four spare pairs of socks. Logistics had improved only slightly since the earlier patrol. The unit brought along a new American outboard motor, but Edson again had to rely on his own funds to finance the expedition. The communications situation was unchanged; it depended solely on messages carried by runners and boatmen. At least the Marines had plenty of ammunition and thirty days of rations on hand.

The unit debarked at Cape Gracias on 7 April and received a lukewarm welcome from citizens fearing imminent occupation by Sandinista forces. Reports indicated that more than two hundred men intended to raid as far as the cape. The residents had no confidence in the puny American group and most refused to aid the Marines. They expected the rebels to win and dreaded the prospect of future reprisals. The patrol commandeered a motley collection of vessels and proceeded upriver without the benefit of Indian crewmen. Mechanical breakdowns slowed the first day's advance. Edson made up for the lost time by traveling all the next night and stopping only briefly for breakfast in the morning, but lower water levels resulted in damaged outboard propellers and longer portages. On 10 April the Marines finally reached Sacklin, where five men remained behind as a message relay station.

Four days later the patrol made it to Waspuc, where Edson learned that Aguerro had retreated up the Coco River to Bocay with his loot. The Marine captain established his main body at Waspuc, then moved on and set up an outpost at Sang Sang on 17 April. That same day he took seven men and proceeded farther west, with the intention of placing an ambush at the rapids near Awasbila. The advance patrol had hardly gotten beyond Sang Sang when its boat overturned in rough water. The mishap cost two rifles, a BAR, and four days of rations. Edson reorganized and reequipped the squad and moved out overland the next day. After a two-day march they reached the Kiplapine Rapids; they scouted the area but found no sign of the enemy. A runner from the main body brought news of a large Sandinista force in the Pis Pis mining region, so Edson returned by himself to the camp at Waspuc on 23 April and contemplated his next move.

Clearly, the maintenance of outposts and patrols would take more men than the tiny outfit could muster. With detachments at Sacklin, Sang Sang, and Kiplapine, and a half-dozen men on patrol up the Waspuc River, the main body boasted just six souls. The situation was complicated with the enemy on two fronts: Aguerro's force up the Coco, and the band raiding the mining district up the Waspuc. Reports on the latter described a group of seventy-five well-armed men on horseback and another fifty on foot with shotguns and machetes. Concerned about the weakness of his far-flung detachments, Edson shuttled back and forth between his posts and never spent more than two consecutive nights in the same location. He asked Major Utley to reinforce him with the remainder of the *Denver* Marines. The Coco Patrol did receive one important attachment at this time. Arthur Kittle, a nineteen-year-old resident of the area, half American and half Miskita, joined the group as a guide and interpreter. His knowledge of languages and the backwoods would serve the Marines well in the next several months.

The patrol received its first support from the outside world on 28 April. Two Marine biplanes landed on a sandbar in the river. The captain's flight experience came in handy on this occasion; both pilots entrusted him with the decision of whether or not they should land. They passed on the results of aerial reconnaissance in the region and a most welcome box of chocolate-covered almonds from Ethel. These aircraft came from the distant Northern Area facility at Ocotal, which significantly limited their operational capability in the eastern reaches of the country. The shortcomings of the old planes in speed and range were partially offset by their versatility in being able to land and take off in the most primitive settings. The Eastern Area was about to get its own air force in the next week, in the form of two Marine amphibian planes. They would be immensely valuable along the rivers in the trackless interior of Nicaragua.

The main purpose of this particular air mission had been to see if Edson was still alive. Major Utley had received word from four different sources that the captain and nine of his men had been killed in battle. Utley sent the planes to investigate and rushed reinforcements up the river. It turned out that a single Indian heading down the river had generated the multiple false reports. The incident illustrated the problems Utley faced in communications and intelligence, but for once those things worked to Edson's benefit. The reinforcements consisted of Lt. Milo R. Carroll, twenty Marines, and a Navy corpsman. They arrived at Waspuc in early May and brought with them a "portable" radio, built on the *Denver* out of spare parts and a wooden field desk. It weighed 125 pounds. The Coco Patrol now had a strength of three officers, fifty-seven Marines, and two sailors.

At about the same time, the Eastern Area received its first substantial reinforcements—two companies from Edson's old 11th Regiment. With a significant force now in hand, Utley began to plan an operation against Sandino. He outlined his intentions in a 24 April message to brigade. The Coco Patrol would block the northern exit to the mining area by holding Waspuc, while three other units moved westward from the coast by separate routes. Utley requested that the Northern Area occupy the trails and rivers to the west of the mining district and thereby close the trap on the guerrilla army.

While brigade mulled over this proposal, they questioned the wisdom of Utley's dispositions: "Experience here shows it is not repeat not desirable to divide small isolated detachments into widely separated groups." Then on the last day of the month, brigade responded to the Eastern Area request for support: "Much easier to block river and trails at Bocay at your area if you have sufficient men." The only troops that could reach that sector, of course, were the handful of men on the Coco tied to defending that sector, and headquarters had already told the Eastern Area not to stretch them so thin.

Faced with a shortage of assets and no prospect of outside aid, the major decided to alter his plan. On 2 May he sent a coded radio message to Edson instructing him to move up the Waspuc and Pis Pis rivers and close off avenues of escape to the west. Both officers realized the need to act fast to spring the trapdoor before the rebels recrossed the rivers. Edson decided to obtain Indian boatmen for the move, because his troops were unfamiliar with the upper reaches of the Waspuc and not yet skilled in the use of poling boats (the only craft that could navigate this waterway). Edson had no more money and knew that the natives would be unwilling to join in a risky expedition, so he lured them into his camp with promises of good wages for local work. Only when the patrol was ready to depart did he inform them of the true situation. During the ensuing operation the Marines had to guard their boatmen as well as look out for the enemy. It was one of the rare occasions when Edson violated his own dictum to treat the Indians well.

The captain concentrated his forces to meet the twin missions of keeping the Coco basin secure and attacking up the Waspuc. He drew in his outposts, left a small group in the base camp at Waspuc, and formed a combat patrol of himself and thirty-one Marines. This force left Waspuc early on 4 May. One boat carried five men acting as the point element. The rest of the patrol followed at a distance, with an appropriate interval between craft so that not all would be caught in the crossfire of an ambush. Edson brought the makeshift radio and rations for eight days.

As the unit progressed upriver, the advance guard boat pulled farther and farther away from the main body. In the early evening that lead vessel approached the tiny village of Marobila. As the boat began to pull into shore, the point received fire from the huts. The native crewmen immediately dived over the side and the Marines soon followed, since they had no cover in the boat. They made it to the opposite bank and returned fire as their craft drifted out of sight downriver with their packs and supplies. In the melee one rifle disappeared in the river. Since the tiny unit estimated enemy strength at thirty to forty men, and had no means to cross the river in any case, the corporal in charge broke off contact and took his men into the bush. The next morning they headed downriver until they met up with the main body, which had made camp for the evening. The captain was not pleased with the reaction of the advance guard, though he also realized he had "blundered by letting it get too far ahead."

The main force reached Marobila that day. Edson landed one squad well before the village and had it circle around the objective, but the area was deserted. A thorough search turned up nothing but the remains of recently slaughtered cattle and the tracks of about eight men, who had apparently split up and departed in three directions. The patrol continued upstream to the junction of the Pis Pis River, where it detained a Nicaraguan and two Indian boatmen. They indicated that the Marines had run into a force of seventy or more poorly armed men, the same ones who had played a part in the raid on the Neptune Mine in April, and that those men were now "poling as fast as possible" up the Waspuc. The mounted force had allegedly left the area fifteen days earlier and was headed toward the interior.

Edson at first decided to execute his orders and continue up the Pis Pis to the designated blocking position at Kuabul. The enemy had smaller boats, which could travel farther up the shallow Waspuc than could Edson's craft. The detainees claimed that there were no trails out of the upper reaches of the Waspuc, so it appeared that the rebels eventually would have to return down the Waspuc or move overland to pick up the Pis Pis River. Edson left a squad to cover the river junction and moved out with the main body. Darkness caught the Marines in the middle of a rapids set in a deep canyon, and they spent the night huddled on a flat boulder projecting from the turbulent water.

Early the next day the patrol reached Kuabul and set an ambush on a nearby trail. After a fruitless morning, Edson marched the unit overland to the Waspuc River to search for signs of the rebels, but he found none and assumed that they had continued westward over some trail. He wrote off the incident as a lesson on the reliability of information from unverifiable sources. It further highlighted the intelligence problem in this type of combat. His advance guard had reported contact with dozens of the enemy, and the detainees enlarged upon that estimate, but the guide had found signs of just a fraction of that number. Such conflicting reports would bedevil all Marine operations in Nicaragua.

Edson learned another lesson that night. He led the patrol back down the trail to Kuabul in the evening, but they soon lost their way in the total blackness. He finally called a halt at about 0330. When the Marines awoke the next morning, they discovered that they were only a few hundred yards from their destination, but on a different path from the one they had taken to Waspuc. This experience, and several like it in the coming months, made a lasting impression on the captain. "I am thoroughly convinced that night movements in bush warfare should be confined to exceptional circumstances, where the objectives to be gained are clearly defined and can be gotten in no other way, and that such movements will be successful only by the greatest of luck in new and strange territory. . . . In my opinion the supposed advantages of night marches in bush warfare can not begin to equal their disadvantages."

Major Utley's shoestring counteroffensive had now reached an impasse. The enemy had escaped to the west and there was no hard information on their location. The lone rumor placed Sandino and his units at Casa Vieja, which was not much help since it was not on Marine maps. The Eastern Area commander was not about to give up, however, and he outlined fresh moves to Brig. Gen. Logan Feland, the brigade commander. "My general plan briefly is in conformity with my previous mission to deny territory to the bandits. . . . Then I propose to push into the area between the Waspuc and [Coco] as far as my means of supplying my patrols permit." Plans were one thing, execution quite another. In answer to Edson's earlier pleas for reinforcements, the major rushed the *Galveston*'s Marine detachment up the Coco River. Other than that he could do little. His other patrols continued to move slowly westward, into an area the guerrillas had already vacated.

The Coco Patrol did not wait idly for new instructions. Edson decided to shift his force to Musawas, where he could control key avenues into and out of the mining region and find better forage. The patrol had just one day of rations left, and the tiny village of Kuabul yielded little in the way of provisions. Edson ordered the majority of the patrol to travel by water, while he set out with five men by an overland route. Each man had a single can of beans.

The trek to Musawas revealed many of the difficulties of operating in the Nicaraguan interior. The terrain was "as mountainous as any in Vermont," and the trail ran cross-compartment, which meant that it did not follow a valley or ridgeline but instead cut across many of them. At each one the Marines had to climb a steep slope, make an equally tough descent, then wade a stream and start the process all over again. For men already weakened by illness and poor diet, it was an exhausting movement. Getting their shoes wet at the bottom of every valley did not help, either, and their feet were soon raw. The captain found it "as hard as any hiking I have ever done."

Edson ended up carrying the pack of one man who came down with a malarial fever. After awhile, the Marine refused to go any farther even with his lightened load. The others could hardly carry him in the rough terrain, nor could he remain there. When talk failed, Edson simply led the rest of the patrol away. "Realizing then that I was not bluffing, he decided that perhaps, he, too, could manage to go along. But the rate of march was slowed down." Then the trail ended and the Marines had to cut their way through the jungle growth. Eventually they reached the river and constructed a makeshift raft. Later they came upon two rotting native dugouts, which they patched with bark. The detachment pulled into Musawas at noon on the third day.

The town, the most substantial in the region, consisted of a missionary compound surrounded by squalid native huts. The Moravians were hospitable, but the Indians were much less so at first. They were of the Suma tribe, which feared and hated the Miskitas. Most abandoned the area at word of the patrol's approach, and they did not return until Edson paid off his Miskita boatmen and sent them back down the Waspuc. The intertribal dispute was only part of the problem. During his brief foray into the area, Sandino had "instilled in the minds of the natives that the Marines if they came would rape, murder, and steal." The missionaries helped to overcome that propaganda, and Edson took steps to prevent worse things from happening. Concerned about increasing aerial activity, he counseled caution in the use of planes: "Do not bomb towns Waspuc River, only source information, guides, boatmen. Indians here neutral."

The patrol spent its time in Musawas recovering from a month of life in the bush. The men feasted on the local fare of beans, bananas, beef cattle, and an occasional monkey. Edson sent three sick Marines to the rear, and awarded three days on bread and water to another for shirking his duty. (There is no record what he actually ate, since bread would have been a luxury in the bush.) After a few days of rest the captain wanted to push on in pursuit of the rebels, and Major Utley obliged on 15 May with new orders. The *Galveston* detachment would relieve those *Denver* Marines still on the Coco, and the latter would then reinforce the unit at Musawas and bring along fresh rations. Some of the patrols coming from the east would garrison the mining district. Edson and one other officer would lead their respective contingents to the west. Their objective was Bocay, the suspected location of Sandino's new headquarters.

Since the Coco Patrol possessed the only radio in the field, it had to send out runners to inform the other units of their fresh assignments. To conserve the precious supply of batteries, the patrol employed the radio only for short periods at fixed intervals each day. Airplanes supplemented electronic assets, but they were almost as scarce and equally cumbersome. When not deterred by weather, they could drop messages to a patrol, if they could find it. The infantry communicated with the pilots through a system of panels (frequently undershirts) laid on the ground. If that shorthand code was insufficient to convey a long message, the planes made a "pickup." Two Marines stood on either side of an open area, each holding aloft a pole. The message was tied to a string running between the poles. As the pilot swooped low his observer dangled a lead-weighted rope from the plane in hopes of hooking the string. If successful, he pulled rope, string, and message up into the plane.

Captain Wesley Walker brought a platoon into Musawas on 20 May. His orders were to turn over his thirty-six mules to the *Denver* detachment to support their westward movement, while he and his men took boats back down the river. Thereafter Walker called Edson's men "the horse thieves," and he joked that the *Denver* officer must have been "the major's fair-haired boy" to get the prime assignment. Edson echoed that thought in a letter to Ethel. "The major must think I like this kind of stuff for he keeps giving me the hardest and best details in the field." He was not so pleased with brigade's conduct of affairs, since it had reacted too slowly to the threat to the east coast. Prospects were not much brighter now that brigade had belatedly created and reinforced Utley's command. "I do not see how we can finish [Sandino] this year. The rains have already begun and I am of the opinion I shall wake up some morning and find my outfit rained in up here in the interior and no chance to get out until Christmas."

The eager captain's reinforcements from Waspuc were slow in arriving. They meant not only additional manpower, but a resupply of canned rations, shoes, and uniforms—items badly needed for the upcoming operation. Logistics were fast becoming a primary occupation for Edson, and he recommended that Area Headquarters act immediately to send supplies up the Coco to meet him at Bocay. He foresaw problems with his mule train, too. A sergeant from Texas took charge of the animals obtained from Walker and reported that they were in poor condition—worn out from their long trek, underfed, and covered with sores due to improper handling. The Jamaican *muleros* hired on the coast had failed to use saddle blankets. The NCO tried to remedy the defects as best he could.

Meanwhile the rainy season came on with full force. The continual downpours turned the trails into deep quagmires. Each passing day increased the difficulties of the pending march. To add to his woes, Edson came down with another bout of malaria at Musawas. He refused the corpsman's recommendation that he should go to the rear, but started another quinine course. In a few days the fever, chills, and headaches disappeared. Illness, shortages, weather, and the seemingly endless pursuit of an unseen foe must have taken their toll on everyone in the patrol. Edson radioed Utley: "Motto for June necessary for morale of field troops."

The rest of the *Denver* men finally arrived on 24 May. That gave the

Coco Patrol a total strength of two officers, forty-four Marines, and one corpsman. The unit prepared to move out the next morning, but a message received that night indicated that the operation might be called off. Edson did not bother to turn on the radio at the next appointed hour, and proceeded with the original plans. "I later learned that my guess was correct and that if I had not acted as I did, we would have received orders which would have kept us at Musawas indefinitely to 'block the rivers and trails in that vicinity.' Once under way we were not ordered back there, and I never saw the place again."

The movement to Bocay proved to be another battle against hardships rather than the enemy. Food remained a scarce commodity, a situation exacerbated by the difficulties of transport and weather. The constant rain ruined some of the rice and beans carried in cloth sacks. One mule fell and broke open its load, which saturated a bag of rice with kerosene. The men wolfed down the spoiled rations that night, because the alternative was no meal at all. To stretch out the small quantity of canned corned beef, salmon, and sardines, the patrol subsisted on just two meals a day, and those were always cold or at best lukewarm because the firewood was wet.

The mules went hungry, too, because there was little grazing available in the dense woods. The animals soon were as exhausted as their masters; in addition they seemed to have a maddening propensity for snagging their pack loads in the brush along the trail. Private Raymon Clark thought they did it purposely to get a rest. Both men and mules found it hard going in the sucking mud. One of the surefooted creatures ended belly up in a creek, temporarily knocking out the radio strapped on its back. By this point, the dampness had ruined every watch in the patrol, which added an unreal sense of timelessness to the misery.

Edson employed simple tactics on the move. Three of the squads rotated daily between the advance guard, main body, and rear security; half of the advance guard unit served as the point element. The fourth squad took permanent charge of the pack train, which traveled with the main body. The men advanced in single file and maintained dispersion throughout the length of the column. When the trail closed up or vanished, as it frequently did in this sparsely inhabited area, Suma Indians preceded the point and cut a fresh path.

On 28 May the Coco Patrol made Casa Vieja, where it caught up with Capt. Henry D. Linscott's unit. That officer had faced a somewhat tougher situation than Edson's, since his unit consisted largely of young Marines straight from boot camp. Linscott, the senior officer, took charge of the combined patrol, and it departed for Bocay on 30 May. The first day out they moved well and covered twenty-one miles, which got them to the Kuli River. The second day of fourteen miles proved tougher. The trail crossed that waterway numerous times as it switched from one bank to the other; often the men were neck deep in the rainy season floods. The third day was an even rougher ten miles, but it got them to the Suma Indian village of Kalasanoki, not far from the Bocay River. An old Indian told them that the rebels had passed through three weeks before and continued south. He also indicated that other guerrillas would supposedly be gathering in Bocay on 3 June.

The officers conferred over the alternatives. Their land-bound patrol could follow a cold trail south, or cut a time-consuming new path north to Bocay, in which case they would not arrive in time. They decided to leave the vast majority of their units in place and head for their original objective by water. The two captains and eight men commandeered the three available boats and set out on 2 June. Edson and a corporal were in the smallest craft by themselves, and they nearly drowned when it capsized in a rapids. Despite the delays, they reached their destination the same day. It turned out to be a rather large settlement of fifty thatched huts and a single building used as a store and house by the local English *patrón*. The two officers decided that one of them had to go back and lead the patrol to Bocay overland. They drew straws and Edson won; he chose to remain and set up an ambush with six men. The next day the Marines learned that their quarry had passed through the town on 1 June.

Edson planned a new operation and outlined it in a message to Area Headquarters. He expected the *Galveston* detachment to arrive in Bocay with a ration resupply on 4 June. He wanted to ferry the stores up the Bocay and Kuli rivers to his patrol at Kalasanoki, and then move overland to Poteca, where he expected to find the guerrilla main body. Two problems developed immediately. Walker arrived in Bocay later the same day with his waterborne patrol coming from Waspuc, but he had no spare supplies with him. Then Major Utley withheld approval of the scheme.

Later, the captain maintained that he could have dealt a severe blow to Sandino if Area Headquarters had implemented his plan. According to his account, the men "were full of ambition and keyed up to the highest morale." That contradicted his earlier message about flagging enthusiasm; two weeks of intervening hardships could hardly have improved the situation. Even if the patrol had been able to muster the necessary rations and will to go forward, there was little likelihood of a spectacular success. Edson more nearly captured reality in a subsequent comment: "It was so difficult to obtain decisive results from any single contact. An engagement was a signal for them to disperse the forces and to move on to new territory." A move against Poteca in early June would have driven the guerrillas from that place, but it would not have seriously altered the course of the conflict.

The improved morale was probably only Edson's. The malaria was gone and his attitude was entirely changed by the time he reached Bocay. Before, he had only wished to be out of the interior as soon as possible; now he wrote a buoyant letter to Ethel. He sarcastically compared his "grand life" on the trail with that of an officer doing garrison duty. "But I would not change places with him if I could, for this is a man's job if there ever was one. . . . In spite of it all, I like it."

He and the other officers of the three units now in Bocay also had some fun at Utley's expense. The major told them he was coming out by amphibian plane for a visit, so his subordinates sat around the campfire dreaming up the perfect bush welcome. They decided on meals of fermented rice and beans, beef without seasoning, muddy river water to drink, and no coffee, sugar, or salt. They would give him a ride on a boat and capsize it, then build a standard native bamboo bunk for him, except the split staves of the "mattress" would have the sharp edges facing up. A few pigs and chickens would keep him company for the night. And when he went to leave, a heavy rainstorm would ground the plane and keep him there. The officers found the chance to sit around with friends and unwind a welcome change from three weeks of tension on the trail. There was no malice against their leader despite the hard edge to the joking. Edson wrote Ethel that "he has certainly been good to me so I am all for him."

The major came out to Bocay on 8 June for a conference with his officers to determine "future movements," a phrase that left open the possibility of offensive operations against Poteca. By that time, however, brigade had already issued orders to stabilize the current line of outposts. One unit would garrison the Coco as far as Bocay, another the mining district, and a third the eastern coastal towns. The *Denver* detachment, with the most time in the interior, would withdraw to Puerto Cabezas for a refit period. Thereafter Area Headquarters would establish a rotation policy for frontline units. These arrangements recognized the logistics crisis that affected the far-flung Eastern Area. The operations report for 10–16 June noted that Marines in the field subsisted on just one-half to one-third of their authorized ration allowance. The rainy season made overland supply routes impracticable. The rising rivers were exceedingly dangerous;

a substantial quantity of the provisions and equipment sent by boat simply disappeared in the rapids. It would take time to build up sufficient stocks in the forward areas to support fresh moves to the west.

The same weekly report summed up the tactical situation. "Although we have had little contact with hostile forces, we have secured a large area for our forces, have denied a comparatively rich mining section to the enemy, and are in a position to advance rapidly into the area now controlled by the bandits." The Marine position was much better than it had been in mid-April; however, Sandino still occupied the central strip of the nation, beyond the reach of the geographic commands. As long as he held this sanctuary, he could build his forces and threaten the stability of Nicaragua.

The *Denver* detachment boated down the Coco to Waspuc, arriving on 15 June. An amphibian plane met the unit there with orders for Edson to fly back to Puerto Cabezas, where he would yield his command to 1st Lt. Ralph B. DeWitt (also from Chester) and await the arrival of the *Rochester*. The ship would eventually transport him to the Pacific coast of Nicaragua so that he could link up with his new detachment on garrison duty in that region. After "twiddling thumbs" for several days in Bocay, Edson was eager to do something useful, so he penned a special intelligence report. Although not particularly long, it was most unusual, for it made no mention of the enemy. Instead he focused on topics such as the "attitude of civil population towards Marines," "economic conditions," "friction between Marines and civilians," and the "political situation." He concluded that the population had a vital role to play in the conflict, and that the Marines had to win them over "by good treatment, an attempt to understand the people, and [the] actual example of our forces."

This was not a revolutionary theory, but it was one more often honored, if at all, in word rather than deed. Edson counseled against such a failure. "Any sign of oppression, poor faith in fulfilling obligations, etc., will result only in hindering our operations and may lead to active opposition. The more intelligent inhabitants will become pro-Marine if properly handled." A relative newcomer to guerrilla warfare, the captain had perceived the key to victory in such a contest. Many others with greater experience, from time immemorial until well after his day, would fail to grasp that salient fact.

Edson returned from this patrol with yet another beard. He explained the growth in practical terms. "It is too much trouble to shave after getting up at 3:30 a.m. and keeping on the move until late in the afternoon and the beard protects the face from rain, sun, mosquitos, and whatnot."

Chapter 5

"We Have Fought in Every Clime and Place"

T he Marines had successfully driven Sandino from the populous west coast and then from the valuable Eastern Area, but he and his followers were still at large in the interior. Reports indicated that four hundred Sandinistas were concentrated at the village of Poteca, at the confluence of the Coco and Poteca rivers. This was much closer to the Northern Area than to Utley's command, but a patrol led by Maj. Keller E. Rockey had decided that the terrain prohibited movement into that sector from the west. Although Sandino was not an immediate threat, brigade could not simply ignore him. The American government wanted to bring the conflict to a swift conclusion and thereby end the rising chorus of domestic and international opposition to the intervention. The timetable called for elections in November 1928, followed by a speedy withdrawal. If Sandino remained free in the central mountains after the American departure, his strident nationalism might undermine a new Nicaraguan government created out of the intervention.

The *Rochester* arrived in Puerto Cabezas on 28 June, with General Feland and RAdm. David F. Sellers (COMSPERON) on board. Edson's messmates at Eastern Area Headquarters joked that the two senior officers had come to escort him to his new command in the west. They were not far wrong. The general and admiral came ashore and asked to see Edson. As he approached them and saluted, Feland asked him if it was possible to get a patrol to Poteca from the east coast. Red Mike replied in the affirmative. Without hesitation, the brigadier answered: "Well, I am going to give you the chance to do it." The brigade commander had decided that the aggressive Marine captain was just the man to track Sandino into his lair. Red Mike soon would be making his third foray up the Coco River, and he predicted to Ethel that it would be "the hardest thing I have ever had yet."

Utley drew up the new plan. Northern Area units would operate along the Jicaro River, while Edson seized Poteca and chased Sandino into the trap. As he moved westward, the captain was supposed to establish outposts along the Coco from Bocay to Santa Cruz, a distance of more than one hundred miles. Area Headquarters assigned DeWitt's *Denver* Marines and Cook's *Galveston* detachment to the third Coco Patrol. This gave Edson a force of two officers, eighty-seven men, and two corpsmen. Half of DeWitt's troops were already on their way to Waspuc to relieve Cook's force at that outpost. Under the new orders, part of the coastal garrison force would assume that mission and the two lieutenants were to move forward to Bocay, where Edson and the remainder of the *Denver* detachment would join them as soon as possible. Red Mike hoped to have the patrol assembled at Bocay and ready to move out by 23 July.

The rainy season dictated the method of movement. Continuous downpours made overland routes impassable, so the troops and supplies could move only on the waterways, though the latter were much more dangerous. Edson noted the changed character of the river as he moved up the Coco in the middle of July. Motorized bateaux could operate along much greater stretches due to increased depth. Poling boats, on the other hand, were limited to shallow water. Since the river had overflowed its banks, the *pitpans* had to make their way through a tangle of trees and jungle growth. Each time a boat crossed the river to avoid obstacles or deep water, the current swept it downstream, since paddling could do little against the strong flow.

Reliance on the rivers presented another problem. The Eastern Area could gather barely enough craft on the Coco to transport all of Edson's patrol at once. Obviously, these same boats were the only ones available for making supply runs to the rear. The patrol leader had to choose between tactical lift and logistics; the more troops he carried, the faster his supply situation would deteriorate. Edson planned to supplement his stores with airdrops and local provisions, but neither constituted a reliable source of supply. The rainy season limited aerial capabilities, and the sparsely inhabited region produced very little food. The shortage of water transportation placed a restriction on the movement of reinforcements, too.

Other facets of the logistic situation had not improved appreciably. A few new outboard motors had arrived, but the lack of space for fuel and spare parts made their employment impractical. The Eastern Area still had only one radio in the field, the one built by the *Denver*. Edson decided to leave it in Bocay, since the bulky set and its batteries took up too much precious boat space. The patrol left behind shelter halves, mosquito nets, and machine guns, too. Many of the Marines, fed up with government shoes that were "not worth a damn," bought the rugged civilian footwear preferred by the lumbermen. Although the Corps possessed considerable experience in bush warfare at this point, it could not meet basic needs such as boots and boats.

Edson arrived at Bocay on 24 July, one day after the scheduled start of the operation. Transportation problems also had delayed the movement of Lieutenant Cook and his twenty-five men (still at Waspuc) and the buildup of supplies in the assembly area. Captain Walker's garrison at Bocay possessed only a week's worth of rations for themselves and none for the Coco Patrol. And Area Headquarters had recalled Lieutenant DeWitt for duty elsewhere. Edson reluctantly dispatched his largest boat downriver to Cape Gracias to pick up supplies and evacuate two sick men, but he was determined to kick off his offensive on 26 July with whatever assets were available.

The local *patrón* balked at permitting the use of his Indians for offensive action, since he feared eventual reprisals. Edson brushed aside that objection and had his men appropriate the handful of native boats and crewmen in the area. These draconian tactics netted him enough transport for the sixty-five members of the patrol present in Bocay. He anticipated "nothing serious" but placed a guard on the boats and boatmen, and positioned an outpost upriver to prevent the passage of any villager with information on the patrol. As much as he wanted to build up trust with the inhabitants, shortages forced the patrol leader to do "absolutely necessary" things that undermined his other, more positive actions.

On the night of 25 July it rained more heavily than usual. In spite of Edson's precautions, the rising current carried off two of the boats, and twelve Indians slipped away into the jungle. When morning came, the Marines had to delay their departure while they reorganized to fit the available transportation. The third Coco Patrol finally got underway later in the day with just one officer, forty-six enlisted men, one corpsman, and seven boats. Half its strength remained at Bocay or was still on the way there from Waspuc. Except for a single morning of sunshine, it rained steadily for the next five days.

A boat capsized on 28 July. The occupants survived and recovered their craft, but they lost two BARs, a rifle, and over a hundred pounds of rations. That night the patrol moved its bivouac site three times to escape the rising water. By morning they were clinging to a steep slope, thoroughly sodden and exhausted. The river had risen more than twenty feet in twelve hours, to the highest flood stage in the recent memory of the locals. The conditions rendered travel impossible. In addition a tree fell onto a boat; the men managed to salvage the *pitpan,* but they had lost yet another load of precious rations. The "depressing, demoralizing, unceasing" rain was taking its toll.

The main patrol resumed its advance on 31 July. Farther up the river the Marines discovered an abandoned guerrilla camp and indications that a small party had used it within the past few days. Edson was certain that the rebels knew of his approach, and he became concerned that they might attempt an ambush in Callejon Canyon. The Indians were worried, too; seven of them left the campsite on the pretext of looking for firewood and never returned. The next morning Edson advanced two squads overland to the head of the canyon to secure the passage of his small fleet through the rapids. The obstacle spelled trouble, but not of the guerrilla variety. Two boats capsized in the turbulent waters, including the largest one. The patrol lost the majority of its food, cooking utensils, and medical supplies, as well as another BAR and a case of ammunition.

The lost rations must have particularly galled the men, who had subsisted on just two small meals a day to stretch their meager stocks. All they had left now was coffee, rolled oats, flour, lard, and a little bacon—no condiments. Edson described the monotonous diet to Ethel a few days later. "We mix the flour with water, fry it in lard, eat rolled oats and coffee with it, and call it any meal we feel like."

The next day another boat capsized, though without any significant loss. Red Mike suspected that the Indians were purposely engineering the mishaps to sabotage the patrol. They were not willing participants and had little to gain from an encounter with the rebels. He let it be known, probably through Arthur Kittle, that he was aware of the game and might take some drastic action if it happened again. Thereafter the boats were steadier. The accidents revealed yet another problem. Due to the frequent loss of supplies, Edson decided to break open the cases of reserve ammunition and issue the bandoliers to the men. The ammunition was of World War vintage, so it had been picked over prior to shipment to Nicaragua to cull out those rounds that had deteriorated with age. These crates were marked as hand selected, but the contents turned out to be the rejects that should have gone to disposal. Nearly all were unusable.

On 3 August Edson sent one boat and its Indian crew back to Bocay. They carried his report of events, a request for resupply, and one Marine too sick to continue. The patrol was down to its last day of rations; with absolutely no forage available along this uninhabited stretch of the river, things looked rather bleak. The entrails of a freshly slaughtered steer came by on the current, however, indicating that someone was not far upstream. With one less boat available and the enemy possibly nearby, Edson altered his standard tactics for movement on the river. Instead of relying on an advance guard boat, he now placed a squad on each bank. They would precede the main body and provide security to the front and flanks. If they came upon an impassable area, a *pitpan* could ferry them beyond it, but at least one of the squads had to remain on shore at all times.

The patrol pulled into shore below Mastawas on the afternoon of 4 August. A squad went overland to the village and surprised two men on the edge of the settlement. The Marines fired and missed, and the guerrillas escaped. The Americans did not come up entirely empty-handed; they seized a rifle, pistol, two shotguns, explosives, and various papers. The latter had no intelligence value, but they made interesting curios. Red Mike sent Ethel one letter signed by Sandino. The rebel leader's seal showed a Nicaraguan using a machete to decapitate a prostrate Marine. The weapons were much more valuable; they replaced those lost in the river. Failure to capture the lookouts, however, removed any remaining chance of surprising the enemy.

Against his "better judgment," Edson decided to lay over in Mastawas on 5 August, one of the first dry days since the beginning of July. He would have liked to press onward before the rebels had time to react to news of his approach, but the men badly needed a day of rest, mainly for their feet. Most had worn out all their socks, and the constant friction of wet leather on flesh had taken its toll. In a message to headquarters the captain requested an emergency resupply of 150 pairs of socks "to combat sore feet epidemic." He did not consider it a minor matter. "Those feet are going to be their best friends from now on and will spell success or defeat of my plans here."

He also asked for mosquito netting. Sand fleas and mosquitoes were making it nearly impossible to sleep at night, which was having an adverse effect on physical strength and morale. Eating was another order of the day, and the Marines made short work of a hapless steer, the first they had seen since leaving Bocay. Edson thought the need for rest was only partly due to the tough conditions. "I am sorry that I and my men ever went back to Puerto Cabezas. It softened everyone, got them out of the habit of woods living, and it has been a long drag trying to get them back into shape again."

The patrol moved out again on 6 August and encountered increasing signs of recent enemy activity in the area. That confirmed the results of aerial reconnaissance missions. Since 21 July, planes had traded fire with rebels on several occasions. Edson advanced to Yamales and Ililiquas the morning of 7 August. His men uncovered another arms cache in the first village and some of the items plundered from the mining region in the

Within a half mile of the settlement, the terrain grew steeper and began to form a gorge. When they reached that area, both flank units requested boat transportation around obstacles: heavy brush and bamboo on the east bank, and a cliff topped by another bamboo thicket on the western side. Porter and his men had just gotten into a *pitpan* when a guerrilla ran from his concealed position on the west bank. Marines in the lead boat fired at him and Edson ordered his force to deploy on that side of the river. His *pitpan* was the first to reach shore and he literally stumbled onto a rebel position. In his first contact with a real enemy, Red Mike's pistol misfired. The guerrilla got off his own shot from a range of just a few feet, but it missed as the captain fell to the ground, his foot caught in a vine. Private First Class Anthony Yelanich, his runner, killed the rebel.

Two other boatloads, to include Porter's, landed nearby. The captain formed them into a line and yelled for Mosier to cut his way through the brush and join them. By this time everyone was shooting. Two enemy machine guns opened up, and rifle fire seemed to come from all points of the hillside on the western bank. The remaining men of the patrol, still in their boats, took to the water to avoid the fusillade. They clung to the sides and drifted downstream out of the action.

The firing died down after about forty-five minutes. Edson had stabilized a line of three squads running uphill from the riverbank, and the Marines in the boats had gathered under Schoneberger at Ililiquas. The captain sent Mosier to the rear with orders. The men at the settlement would drive upriver and clear the eastern shore while the squads under Edson performed the same mission on their side. Flankers along the water would maintain visual contact between the two units. Mosier would bring up the boats but keep to a safe distance in the rear.

The Marine attack began at 1500, about an hour after Edson issued the order. The patrol met little resistance initially, but eventually it encountered rifle and machine-gun fire. The guerrillas soon retreated when Marines on both banks returned the fire. Red Mike's section continued to advance until 1630. By then he had lost sight of his unit to the east, so he decided to return to Ililiquas and regroup his forces there.

Red Mike found the remainder of the patrol at the settlement. Mosier had been wounded when his boat came under fire as it moved upriver in support of the attack. Mosier's Indian boat captain aided the sergeant in driving off the rebel force, and then shepherded him to safety. The other wounded were Sergeant Schoneberger and Drummer Thomas Paine. Private Meyer Stengel was killed as he moved along the east bank, maintaining contact with the rest of the Marine force. Edson later recommended Stengel, Mosier, Schoneberger, Yelanich, and seven others for the Navy Cross.

The Marines counted ten guerrilla bodies and believed they had wounded at least three others. They captured twelve rifles and a small quantity of ammunition. More important, the patrol gained considerable knowledge about their enemy. Documents indicated that Sandino had concentrated his entire force in the vicinity. Rebel actions also confirmed that they were more than mere bandits. They wore a uniform of blue denim, with red and black armbands and hatbands. For the most part the guerrillas fought with courage and did not hesitate to engage the Marines at close quarters. Their positions consisted of individual holes and slit trenches, all well placed to enfilade the river and provide mutual support. The rebels had carefully chosen and thoroughly camouflaged the ambush site. Sandino and his men were rapidly learning the guerrilla art.

The Coco Patrol spent the first part of that night recovering from the fight. The corpsman treated the wounded with makeshift dressings, since he still had not received medical supplies to replace those lost in the rapids. Edson sent the casualties downriver to Bocay, along with one private unfit for duty due to sore feet. The patrol now had just forty-one enlisted Marines and five boats. They also were short of ammunition. In addition to the rounds fired, the men had lost a considerable amount from the bandoliers they had slung from their shoulders. Bullets seemed to be a hard commodity to hold onto no matter where the patrol carried them.

Edson was none too comfortable with his position. He planned to move forward the next day, and expected to meet the enemy in even greater strength, possibly the several hundred men that intelligence ascribed to Sandino's force in the area. His report to Utley, taken downriver with the wounded, contained an alternate plan for the patrol to fall back if necessary, destroying everything in its wake that might be of use to the rebels. A similar message to Cook, still making his way upriver, cautioned the lieutenant to keep one eye on his Indians and the other on watch for a rebel attack. In that mood, Edson drifted off to sleep after his first exposure to combat.

A couple of hours before dawn a Marine outpost detected movement on the trails leading downriver to the patrol's rear. Edson, roused from sleep by the news, made a quick decision. He and his men would withdraw to Mastawas to avoid any prospect of being surrounded and to speed the linkup with Cook's detachment. They were in boats and on the way within the hour. On 9 August the lieutenant and twenty-one men finally joined up with their parent unit. Red Mike later considered the withdrawal a mistake, but at the time it must have seemed the prudent thing to do given the potential odds. The unrelenting pressure of the tough situation also may have taken the edge off his normally aggressive attitude. A letter to Ethel revealed some of his concern: "Thinking Sandino all day long, looking for him just around every corner, or for some of his men, seeing signs of him all along the way, rather gets on one's nerves after awhile. And some sixty-two-odd men to look after besides!"

Another letter to Utley poured out the captain's frustrations: too few Marines, too many of those he had debilitated with bad feet or malaria, not enough boats or crewmen, and no resupply of desperately needed items such as shoes and socks. Edson then turned to the tactical situation:

> I have a territory some 200 miles long by 50 miles wide to cover with a force of sixty men. There are no supporting troops within 100 miles in any direction. The territory to be covered is that in which it is certain Sandino has concentrated his entire force. I would like a definition of my mission. At present my mission, as assigned, is to proceed to Santa Cruz, establishing outposts at contact points. With the force at my disposal, I cannot reach Santa Cruz and adequately garrison my lines of supplies. . . . If, however, my primary mission is to destroy the bandits, it seems to me best to keep my entire force intact, at least to Poteca, and depend upon mobility, rather than outposts. . . . If you can supply me with food and clothing by air, I believe that my command can make it decidedly uncomfortable for the outlaws. There will be several casualties, probably, but we hope the results will justify them. If this is approved, I shall cut loose from boats, and using captured animals, move by trail.

Utley made no immediate response, but he seemed prepared to support whatever decision Edson reached on tactics. He radioed brigade headquarters and asked them to airdrop rope and other pack train equipment to the Coco Patrol as soon as possible. He also requested maximum air support from brigade, since their airfield was now much closer to the scene of action.

Things looked up for the patrol after a little rest, another aerial resupply, and the arrival of the reinforcements. Edson sent a squad upriver on the afternoon of 9 August; it uncovered a cache of thirty-four rifles. With improved weather, planes began making daily forays into the area. They accomplished nothing spectacular, but they raised Marine morale and undoubtedly undercut that of the enemy. Results were nil because the guerrillas were becoming "plane wise." They avoided movement during the midday hours when aircraft commonly appeared, and they made good use of camouflage and concealment. The air corps found it increasingly difficult to spot targets, as Maj. Ross Rowell reported to his superiors. "Pilots fly around houses at altitudes that permit the observers to look into windows and doors. Bursts of gun fire and occasionally bombs are employed . . . to attempt to draw hostile fire." Anyone who ran or hid assumed the status of an enemy.

On 10 August the patrol resumed its advance upriver. On the thirteenth the unit made it to Espanolita, just a few miles beyond Ililiquas. There Edson discovered nine campfires less than a day old, which indicated a force of sixty to ninety men. There were several fresh graves, as well as evidence of aerial bombing. Red Mike remained here the next day and sent out small patrols. A squad heading upriver made contact with some rebels, but there were no casualties on either side. Another patrol went downriver. It encountered a rebel boat bringing supplies from the Bocay River. Although the guerrillas had successfully slipped past the Marine outpost at Bocay, they were not as lucky this time. The Americans killed four of them, and the remaining five surrendered. One of those captured was Abram Rivera, a Sandinista chieftain. The supplies consisted primarily of clothing and boots taken earlier in the summer from the mining region. Since most of the Marines were in tatters and nearly shoeless, Edson turned the booty over to his men. The straw hats and overalls served the purpose, but as Red Mike later noted, they were hardly the height of military fashion. "Add to that the fact that no one had shaved in over a month and one can imagine what a fine looking outfit we were."

The entire patrol moved forward again on 15 August. The next day the Americans came upon two men. In the ensuing firefight the patrol killed one man and captured the other, an Indian boatman who claimed to have been pressed into Sandino's service. The tiny action netted a shotgun, some dynamite, and the information that the rebel force had split up and scattered. Aerial reconnaissance seemed to confirm this, because planes made numerous contacts with small bands during this period. The aircraft attacked observed or suspected targets every day between 11 and 18 August.

The Coco Patrol pulled into Poteca early on 17 August. The Marines were surprised by the size of their long-sought objective. Despite its prominence on the map, the settlement consisted of just one house, albeit a substantial one of mahogany walls and a tile roof. The building had taken a direct hit from a thirty-pound bomb, but that had done little more than create a skylight. The aviators may have been accurate with their dive-bombing, but ordnance had not kept pace with tactics.

The payload of the typical two-seater plane was also lacking when it came to supply; the infantrymen had nothing more than a few sacks of beans over the last several days. But the airmen made up for that on 17 August. Shortly after the patrol arrived at Poteca, two Fokker cargo planes made an unprecedented drop of twenty-two hundred pounds of rations.

Edson's original orders had envisioned an advance beyond Poteca and a linkup with Marine units from the west. A flurry of messages modified that goal several times during the final drive up the river. Utley initiated the process with his frequent messages to brigade headquarters seeking news of the Northern Area patrols that were supposed to assist Edson in drawing a net around Sandino. There were none in action, but in response to the major's constant pleas, Northern Area finally decided to launch its own expedition down the Coco. Since that command possessed no boats of its own, the brigade operations officer, Maj. Oliver Floyd, ordered Red Mike to take his flotilla upriver to Santa Cruz. There he was to turn it over to a Northern Area unit that would then go downriver toward Poteca. That message left brigade on 7 August.

The resulting switch in places was hardly the combined operation that Utley and Edson had envisioned back in June. When Red Mike received the order, he added his thoughts and sent it on to area headquarters. He noted the obvious stupidity of the plan and summed up his feelings on the matter: "You may answer Brig.—I haven't the nerve to do it." The major simply filed the message, but first appended his own opinion: "What the Hell's the use answering them?" On 8 August Major Floyd forwarded some helpful advice to the patrol in the wake of its encounter at Ililiquas: "Press operations up Coco River with all due caution." Edson sent it on to Utley with annotations echoing the theme of his earlier long letter to his superior. "Why not press *down* the Coco River a bit? I have a force of sixty men to cover an area 200x50 miles, with no supporting troops of any kind within a week's travel. No kick to make but this is rubbing it in."

Shortly thereafter brigade asked the Eastern Area to salvage a plane that had crashed on the Coco. Utley refused to do so. "Until additional planes arrive here for duty the supply of Edson's patrol depends solely on the very few boats now available. Ration situation above Waspuc found unsatisfactory and believe that every available resource should be devoted to supplying arms and provisions to outposts and patrols." The major's response brought an immediate reply from brigade. On 12 August planes dropped a copy of that message to the detachment on the Coco. "The

Commanding General does not require that the patrol under Captain Edson now advancing up the Coco River advance up that stream beyond the vicinity of Poteca for the present time. This is because of the difficulty of the supply problem." This exchange culminated in the diversion of the Fokkers to the Coco operation and the massive drop of 17 August.

The Eastern Area commander wrote a personal letter to Edson on 14 August. He clearly hoped to cheer up his hard-pressed subordinate. "I am glad to note that you have not yet lost your sense of humor, for I must admit that the communications which you annotated had already driven me to extreme and unpunctuated profanity." The letter then lauded the captain and his men with the observation that they were his "shock troops" and were "making history." Finally, he recounted his efforts to increase support for the Coco Patrol and summed up the meager results: "Lord knows, there seems to be little we *can* do."

Many senior officers believed that Marine efforts had broken the back of the revolutionary movement. During that summer more than sixteen hundred "self-confessed bandits" had taken advantage of a generous amnesty program. Air missions to the Poteca region now dropped leaflets to induce the "demoralized" rebel remnants to surrender. Utley even passed to Edson an Associated Press (AP) story in which Admiral Sellers reported that the Nicaraguan campaign was "virtually ended." The admiral stated that Sandino had fled to Honduras and that his followers were abandoning him due to the Marine blockade of their last stronghold. The news surprised Red Mike, who queried his boss about the press release. "How about this? Is any part of it correct?"

In the rear areas the conflict did seem to be almost over, and attention turned to parceling out rewards for the victory. General Feland heaped praise on Red Mike in a letter to Utley. "As you undoubtedly know we are all pleased with what has been accomplished on the Coco River. Edson's persistent advance and successes gained make up one of the striking stories of the campaign. Please do not be sparing in your recommendations for awards or commendations." To Edson himself, Feland wrote: "Nothing finer has been accomplished in Nicaragua." With the general's admonition in mind, the major passed Edson's earlier Navy Cross nominations up the chain of command. Along with them, he sent a Navy Cross citation for the patrol leader. The secretary of the Navy would approve it later that year.

Thousands of miles to the north, the newspapers and radio waves carried daily bulletins on the latest actions of the Marines in Nicaragua; one name seemed to crop up on a routine basis. The *Burlington Daily News,* proud of its hometown boy, editorialized that Edson "seems to be conducting about the only war that is being staged in the world today." Despite the opinions expressed by Admiral Sellers in the AP bulletin, that conflict was far from over yet; there remained an extraordinary tale of heroism and hardship.

Edson wasted no time in strengthening his hold on Poteca, which he considered a "strategical position." The site, high ground overlooking the confluence of the Coco and Poteca rivers, controlled the best transportation routes in the area and served as an outpost in the heart of Sandino's once impenetrable stronghold. On his first full day there Red Mike instituted a vigorous program of patrolling in all directions, sent two of his boats down to Bocay to bring up supplies, and scribbled messages on a host of topics. Despite the many difficulties, he believed the morale of his force was "excellent," though soon after, he would admit that the men were "anxious to go back at any time." The indomitable captain told them to have their Christmas presents mailed to Poteca.

With its proposed voyage down the Coco canceled, Northern Area finally pushed an overland patrol into Poteca on 21 August. The commander was 1st Lt. Stan Ridderhof, a flyer who had served with Edson on Guam, where the two pilots had become friends. After comparing notes, Red Mike thought his counterparts in the west lax in pursuing the bandits, since "patrols are sent out for a few days only and if no contact is made it is taken for granted no bandits are in the area."

Edson's forecast of the need for a long stay soon proved correct. On the morning of 30 August one of his patrols discovered a fresh rebel camp just a few miles downriver near Wamblan. A good system of outposts apparently saved the guerrillas; the Marines made no contact but found breakfast cooking on the fires. The camp had sheltered about thirty men; the squad came away with thirteen rifles and some explosives. Three days later, another patrol went upriver to Yacalwas to investigate a reported rebel outpost of five men. The squad walked into an early morning ambush of about twenty guerrillas. The Americans killed one man but suffered a much greater loss themselves—Arthur Kittle, the invaluable Nicaraguan guide. The small patrol broke contact and returned to base. Lieutenant Ridderhof led out a much larger group the next day. This time the Marines surprised two men near the site of the ambush. They killed one rebel and captured three weapons.

The Coco Patrol submitted its first weekly patrol report on 8 September. The last of the force's scattered detachments had finally joined the main body on 22 August, which brought unit strength to two officers, seventy-six men, and one corpsman. Edson stressed several themes that would recur throughout subsequent reports. One of the major ones was health problems. Eight of his troops were on the sick list, and the number had been as high as fourteen. Skin ulcers and infections were prevalent, and more than half the unit was undergoing quinine treatment. (Ridderhof had commanded the patrol sent to avenge Kittle's death because Red Mike was down with malaria again.) In the following two weeks, three men required evacuation.

Illness not only reduced manpower, it often had an even more direct effect on operations. "Stamina of men considerably affected by malaria and—to some extent—unsatisfactory rations. Several men unfit for patrols being retained for garrison duty only. Men cannot stand up under arduous patrol duty as they did last May—every long patrol being handicapped before its completion by some one or two men succumbing to fever or intestinal trouble." The resulting slow rate of march made it even more difficult to make contact with guerrilla forces.

Logistics continued to occupy a prominent place in Red Mike's thoughts. Rations, which had gotten low again in early September, were only part of the problem. After months in the jungle, much equipment and clothing required replacement. In addition, the patrol needed an endless number of items in order to turn Poteca into a permanent base camp. Edson's supply requests included a trench mortar, heavy machine guns, hand grenades, signal rockets, shovels, slings, ammo belts, cartridge belts, targets, toilet paper, tents, and barbed wire (forty-two hundred yards of the latter).

The availability of aircraft, their minimal cargo capacity, weather, and the method of delivery all limited the usefulness of aerial resupply. The last factor proved most conspicuous, since the amphibians could not land near Poteca. Other types of aircraft delivered cargo by dropping it, without parachutes; the ensuing impact damaged many items, particularly canned rations. Boats were only slightly more effective. The long trip upriver took more than a week, and a significant portion of the goods never reached their destination due to accidents. Useful river craft, primitive and inexpensive, mysteriously remained almost as scarce as planes. Overland movement of supplies was out of the question given the slowness of mules and the problem of feeding them. When Edson asked whether he should look to brigade or to Area Headquarters for supplies, Utley replied, "The answer is God."

Despite the problems, higher headquarters met most of Edson's requests, to include sending him Lt. Floyd A. Stephenson, one of the few available officers fluent in Spanish. Red Mike quickly turned Poteca into a fortified camp. During September the Marines cleared fields of fire, constructed a single apron barbed-wire fence, and dug kneeling trenches around the entire perimeter. As other assets trickled in, they added three Browning heavy machine guns, a mortar, and further wire entanglements. They test-fired the heavy weapons and developed range cards. The unit regularly practiced defensive drills, so that squads could man the defenses on a moment's notice. Although this gave the appearance of a fortress mentality, Red Mike's purpose was exactly the opposite. He mainly hoped to deter any guerrilla assault and thus free up men for offensive patrols. He often left just two squads to guard the camp.

Morale was another constant concern for Edson. He stressed the positive impact of supply deliveries on his unit's attitude, and noted that the hum of a motor was "one of the most musical and best beloved noises ever heard by all the men here." After one airdrop, he acknowledged that Utley's description of the source of supply was not far off the mark. "God is great. Supplies from heaven yesterday to feed the starving and clothe the naked. Visit from our planes raised morale 500%."

Edson's concern was based on experience. He had already conducted several disciplinary hearings and imposed punishment for infractions such as malingering and disobeying the orders of an NCO. In late September four privates deserted their outpost at Wamblan, stole a boat, and headed downriver. They surrendered the next day at Bocay after their craft overturned in the rapids, but their action revealed the level of desperation among some of the men. The harsh conditions on occasion overwhelmed even the iron Marine discipline of that period. Red Mike ascribed the actions of the deserters to "lack of adequate rations," which did not deter him from recommending a court-martial.

Edson's own spirits were high after his recent successes, however, and he found it easy to ignore the hardships. Although a few men were ready to desert, he could look around and enjoy the scenery, which he described in a letter to Ethel:

Last night was one of beauty—one of those which is always connected with the name of the tropics—a large, round, bright full moon shining over the rim of the mountains around us, the clouds of white puff drifting by so that the silver lining turned to gold— the Coco River running at the foot of the hill on which the camp is built and the moon lighting up its waters—our fleet of native *pitpans* tied along the sandy beach—and the smell of wet, green earth all around! You remember those nights in Guam—so many of which were like that.

The hardships of the advance up the Coco had not kept Edson from remembering their anniversary. He wrote a letter in late July in hopes that it would get to Vermont by 16 August. As a backup, he sent a message to Major Utley on the fourteenth via plane pickup and asked him to pass on the sentiment in a telegram to Ethel. "You may know that I am loving you more—if possible—than I did eight years ago, that my thoughts are always with you, and that I am missing you and Austin more than you can guess." That he had been so thoughtful in the midst of his battles really touched her: "If you never do another thing in this life for me, I shall always cherish that message as my dearest possession."

Adoption of a stable base did allow Edson to improve his communications with the outside world. A radioman and a set arrived at the camp on 19 September. Prior to that, the patrol had sent its messages by boat to Bocay or had them picked up by plane. Often the aircraft came from Managua, in which case information passed directly to brigade and then eventually down the chain of command to area headquarters. The advent of radio communications did not cut the general's command post out of the loop, since it could still listen in on message traffic. That may have influenced the habit that Edson developed of writing frequent, lengthy personal letters to Utley, many of them honest appraisals of his own situation or critical of policies originated outside the Eastern domain.

Since Sandino was still around in September—two months after Admiral Sellers had declared the conflict all but over—the Marines had to decide how to finish him off. As the month opened, brigade policy remained unchanged: Edson was to stay at Poteca and conduct short patrols in the surrounding area. The operations officer tried to spell out an objective for the Coco Patrol, but his letter on the subject was confusing and unfocused. Red Mike asked Utley for clarification or more specific directions, but the major replied that he was in the dark, too. "I think the General is . . . your immediate C.O."

Edson, the leading proponent of offensive roving patrols, faced the task of implementing a static, defensive policy, but he never abandoned the idea of a bigger operation against the rebels. The captain summarized his view in a formal "Estimate of Situation" submitted to Utley on 3 October. He guessed that Sandino had about two hundred men in the area northeast of Murra. Many of these were probably "forced recruits," and all suffered from shortages of food and ammunition, but their position did give them some strength. Due to the limited avenues of approach in that rough terrain, they could readily detect any moves in the vicinity and slip away if hard-pressed.

Red Mike briefly stated the operational choices available to him: "(1) To sit still and await bandit actions, (2) To attempt to keep bandits moving and unable [to] formulate or carry out definite plans." Edson, of course, favored the latter approach. Despite his meager assets, he proposed an immediate operation against the guerrilla stronghold. He would take most of his force up the Poteca River. He hoped that Northern Area patrols would move east in support, in line with a recent brigade message that had called for coordinated patrolling between the geographic commands.

The aggressive captain did not wait for his superiors to develop an alternative. On 4 October Edson and forty-six men moved out for Gulke's Camp on the Poteca. Two days later they made contact with the enemy at the mouth of Arenal Creek, just a short distance from their initial objective. The patrol captured food and a small quantity of ammunition, but the four-man rebel outpost escaped unharmed. Before the pursuit could move very far, higher headquarters intervened. Brigade had adopted Red Mike's idea for joint action, but the staff redesigned the scheme of maneuver. On 7 October a plane dropped a message to the detachment that halted its operation and placed it under the tactical control of the Northern Area.

Edson notified Major Utley of the change and expressed his dismay. "Success [of] my operations depended largely on rapidity of movement and surprise by following unexpected route. Both these elements now lost." The Coco Patrol's temporary superior issued an order the next day that directed the detachment to remain in place until 12 October and then proceed southwest to the headwaters of the Tamis River near Murra "for the purpose of clearing that area of reported bandit forces." Red Mike chafed at the delay, not only for tactical reasons, but also due to the adverse effect on health and morale.

The Coco Marines finally moved out again on 12 October. The new orders required them to cut ties to their boats and proceed overland, for which they were ill-equipped. They had no pack animals, so the men had to carry everything on their backs. A series of particularly difficult trails complicated the task; in one day they crossed the Congojas River seventy-two times. Two men became sick and further slowed the rate of march. On 14 October the patrol discovered an abandoned rebel camp but seized only a few papers and a typewriter. (The latter perked the interest of one staff wag at area headquarters. A subsequent intelligence report commented: "Note for tacticians and strategists: not even bandits in the bush can fight a war without typewriters!")

On 15 October the detachment reached the deserted mining town of Murra and linked up with Capt. Maurice Holmes of the Northern Area.

Red Mike described the reception to Utley. "Both Stephenson and I got the impression that we were not particularly desired over there in the NA playground. . . . They all seem glad to extend us a fine welcome at home— but not to run around in their backyard stirring up or digging out something they have thus far failed to find. Do I make myself clear?"

A squad out looking for pack animals did stumble onto a guerrilla band. The Marines killed a single rebel and retrieved a rifle and twelve rounds from the body. The Northern Area patrol donated three of its mules and two days of rations to Edson's force, which moved out the next day, headed in the general direction of the Poteca River. This time Red Mike followed even worse trails in hopes of increasing the probability of contact. The tactic turned up only another abandoned camp. At one point the path narrowed into a ledge on a canyon wall, with the river 250 feet below. One mule fell over the precipice and took with it a fourth of the rations and some of the confidence of the Marines.

Conditions on this patrol were the worst of any of Edson's operations. Moreover, the Marines had been out in the bush for nearly four months, and the strain was beginning to tell on them. One night two sentries complained out loud about being lost in the middle of nowhere. Edson got up and quietly reprimanded them. The next morning he called the patrol together and tried to boost their sagging spirits. He also told them he was tired of the "bellyaching," and if anyone wanted to find their own way back to base, they were welcome to do so. No one accepted the offer, but the incident highlighted the challenge of leading men under extremely trying conditions.

The patrol reached the river on 22 October and boated down to Poteca that day. In a letter to Utley, Edson repeatedly registered his "disappointment" over the results, but he thought the patrol had accomplished something just by demonstrating the ability to penetrate any guerrilla lair, no matter how inhospitable the terrain. He also noted that the rebels had abandoned two good ambush sites and now appeared to be motivated by one goal—to avoid combat with his Marines.

Based on this last operation, Red Mike guessed that the rebels had vacated the area for a less dangerous location, and that "the period of active and long patrols for this organization is about over." He would continue small forays from the base camp but did not expect to encounter the enemy. With that in mind, he described a new policy to Utley. "We are now in the process of transition from field to garrison duty with patrols of one-two-four days duration, in line with the opinions expressed above." The switch in emphasis may have been driven partially by the low morale of some of his men, which continued to result in frequent disciplinary problems. There were cases of men feigning illness to avoid patrols, and one Marine simply refused to obey an officer's order. Within hours of that offense Red Mike sentenced the man to five days on bread and water.

The amenities of the camp had come a long way since August. The airmen had dropped tents, and everyone now had a bamboo bunk and a mattress made of rice sacks stuffed with straw. Edson decided to go well beyond those basics. He requested a long list of recreational items for the men, erected a volleyball court, built an oven, and made plans for a complete Thanksgiving dinner, including turkeys and eight kegs of beer. At the same time, Red Mike tightened up the military routine. He reintroduced shaves and daily inspections, and typed up eighteen pages of regulations governing camp life and guard responsibilities. When not on patrol, squads participated in classroom and field training. The troops dug model trenches and constructed samples of different kinds of wire obstacles. They also competed for various awards, such as scarce cigarettes and first place in the chow line.

Lieutenant Edwin A. Pollock and his detachment of *Tulsa* Marines soon joined the patrol, which now numbered four officers and ninety men. The Coco Marines made one joint patrol with a Northern Area unit in November. The combined outfit searched the Santa Cruz area without result. The experience only confirmed Edson's doubts about his compatriots to the west. They did not share his predilection for predawn departures to avoid native observation, and they kept mainly to the *paso reals,* wide, well-traveled trails that the rebels avoided.

The irrepressible captain could not endure for long the quiet garrison life. Shortly after his return from Santa Cruz he wrote Utley: "My feet are getting nervous again and I desire to see more of Nicaragua à la cavalry mounted on mules." He hoped to outfit his patrol with the horses and mules he had observed in the upper Coco valley. Those animals would provide overland mobility during the upcoming dry season. He soon coupled this idea with an expanded version of his earlier tactical scheme:

Somewhere in my letter I mentioned a pair of itching feet. . . . My idea is the organization of a patrol of about 40–50 men, with no fixed limits of patrolling, free to move in this territory as outlined, following such clues as it can pick up and reporting in at the nearest post in any one of the three areas for rations about once every fifteen days. . . . The idea would be an outfit as near like bandits as possible—using the side trails they use—becoming bush men like them—and living like them. . . . This would be damned strenuous work—it would require an outfit of 100 men, for this kind of patrolling would wear out half the command a month, and it might not bring any better results than we have had already. But I would certainly like to give it a try. Even tho it by itself gets no contact with the outlaws, I believe that a roving band of this kind would be quite likely to chase them into the hands of some other patrol with equally as good results.

Red Mike also renewed an earlier invitation for the major to visit his remote outpost. "The main idea is that I crave to see and talk with you personally. There are numerous questions of policy which should be considered and decided in the very near future. . . . I believe these things can be talked over and decisions reached much better in person than by letter."

Over the course of the next few months the Coco Marines maintained an active patrolling program throughout their area. It was Edson's policy that every patrol scour at least one new location, both to improve knowledge of the countryside and to ensure that no routine developed that would give the enemy a respite. Lieutenant Pollock made the only contact during this period. On 17 December his unit came upon a rebel group that surrendered without a fight. The band—a Sandinista colonel, four other men, eight women, and eighteen children—was armed with a sword, two shotguns, and a small quantity of explosives. A late December intelligence summary noted that there had been no enemy activity east of the Poteca-Garrobo outpost line since its establishment in the fall. Edson seemed fully justified in concluding that he had "badly . . . hurt the bandit morale and organization."

Further evidence of success came from the local inhabitants. Reports from September onward painted an increasingly positive picture of relations between the Marines and the Indians. Several factors probably contributed to this process. Aerial propaganda leaflets and American actions dispelled some of the fear instilled by Sandinista agitators. Edson and Utley also enlisted the help of the influential Moravian missionaries in this task. Employing the natives as boatmen, guides, and informers provided a source of income to replace that lost with the disruption of the logging and mining industries. Lastly, the extended Marine presence promised an indefinite reprieve from rebel exactions and disruptions. In January 1929 twenty families requested and received permission to settle near the base at Poteca. Edson was certain that many of them had served with the Sandinistas, but he preferred to ignore their past: "Every house within fifty miles of our camp has some ex-bandit in it, but so long as they behave themselves, it is all right with me." His policy of concern for the Indians had begun to generate results.

Red Mike sometimes found it harder to deal with his own men. His attempts to improve camp life continued, and brigade came through with most of what he needed for his Thanksgiving celebration. The troops had a genuine holiday meal of roast hams, fresh potatoes, and even apple pie, but rain dampened spirits, and the feast hardly made up for months of hardship. Just prior to the airdrop of the fresh supplies, the patrol had been living for days on slim rations of beans and rice for breakfast, lunch, and dinner. They had also gone four weeks without cigarettes and soap.

Disciplinary problems continued, though they were largely confined to a handful of men. The problem, of course, was figuring out how to deal with the few malcontents. The simple answer was to send them back to Puerto Cabezas for a court-martial, but a warm bunk in a dry cell and three full meals a day would have been a reward. Red Mike preferred to keep them in the bush and invent some way to punish them in a situation where everyone already was deprived of just about every semblance of civilization. A sentence of bread and water came to mean being last in the chow line, where one would get the burned food scraped from the bottom of the pot. Even that measure was sometimes not enough. After one meal a private complained loudly about the chow doled out to him at the end of the line. Edson tried to talk quietly to him, but the Marine paid no heed. In an unusual display of frustration and anger, the captain punched the much bigger man in the jaw, and a fight ensued. The momentary slip in composure cost Red Mike a cracked rib.

The captain put together a holiday of sorts for Christmas, too—another good meal, a supply of cigars, and a Santa Claus handing out Red Cross packages. Even so, it was not much of a holiday for the men. The brigade newspaper carried an account of the Coco Patrol's celebration: "Weather: 57 varieties, Visibility: poor, Spirits: depressed." The entertainment program led off with the "Marines' Hymn," but ended with the troops singing "Show Me the Way to Go Home."

Despite the occasional problems, Edson's outlook remained positive, and with good reason. Praise poured in from all quarters for his performance. Captain Jacob Lienhard told the commander of the Northern Area that Edson was "the best General in Nicaragua." Upon Stephenson's return to Managua, the brigade commander invited him to dinner and pumped him for details on the Coco Patrol. The lieutenant later described to Edson the impression he received from the general and his senior officers: "From a momentary hero you have become a symbol of aggressiveness, level-headedness and good tactics—in effect an institution—something that Brigade can turn to on almost any phase of the situation up there, assuming that you will deliver the goods or give them the right dope." He told his former patrol commander that "you have made history for the Marine Corps and carved a place for yourself in its annals, and future."

Ethel told her husband that the wives of an admiral and some Army colonels had invited her to a party in Vermont. "Everyone knows who you are now. You're famous. I bask in the glow shed from your aura." Red Mike did not let the flattery go to his head. "If I believed all that I hear, I should need several large-sized hats to replace the one now being worn." His explanation for success was luck, and the freedom of operation that brigade had given him from time to time. For the latter reason he wanted very much to remain at Poteca, where he felt he was nearly on a par with the area commanders. He was quite displeased by rumors of a pending transfer and radioed brigade to make certain it was not true. He was in no hurry to get away from the hardships of the bush as long as there was the possibility of more action. "But I would like to be lucky enough to bag old Sandino himself—that would be something to write home about."

Operations reached a hectic pace during the winter months. Edson led a patrol of forty-one men into the upper Coco valley on 14 January and spent three weeks conducting a thorough search of the region, while another detachment of sixteen men scoured a nearby area. The Marines followed tracks and discovered several abandoned camps, but they were always one step behind the guerrillas. Red Mike spent just one night at Poteca and launched a new patrol on 5 February into the district northwest of Cua. The rapid turnaround resulted from the offer of an Indian to guide them to Sandino's hideout.

This time the Marines made contact, though bad luck allowed the enemy to achieve surprise. The patrol heard voices on a trail and fell in behind a small group of men. After awhile another group came up on the rear guard of the patrol, which opened fire too soon and let those rebels escape unharmed. Thus alerted, the guerrillas ahead of the Marines took off running, with the patrol in hot pursuit. When the Americans reached the top of a ridge, they ran into an ambush. The guerrillas kept up the fight for fifteen minutes with automatic weapons and dynamite bombs, then melted away when one of Edson's squads threatened to out-flank them.

The Marines pursued briefly and overran a brand-new camp, but they could not regain contact. They returned to the site to take care of their only casualty, an Indian wounded in the leg. They inflicted no losses on the guerrillas. A close inspection of the site revealed a carefully crafted, V-shaped position, with the trail leading into the mouth of the V. That allowed the rebels to fire on the Marines from two directions without putting themselves in their own line of fire. Edson estimated that twenty-five men had conducted the ambush. After evacuating the wounded man by boat, the patrol made its way overland to Poteca through terrain that rivaled that encountered on the Murra patrol.

A letter from the new brigade operations officer was waiting for Edson when he returned to base. Major Harry Schmidt was searching for fresh methods to deal with the rebels, and he suggested offering a thousand-dollar reward for information leading to the demise of Pedron Altamirano, then the most active of the guerrilla chiefs. Red Mike held out no hope of success for that option. In a memorandum to Schmidt he described the Nicaraguan's tactics, which relied heavily on night movements and the maintenance of outposts around his camp. This security system made it unlikely that even good intelligence would allow the Marines to achieve surprise. Edson then resurrected his earlier proposal for a roving patrol, one that would relentlessly pursue the enemy band. With support from standard combat patrols working planned routes, one might expect to eventually flush the guerrilla group into open battle. "If the infected area is kept constantly filled with patrols moving, Pedron fleeing from one may easily run into another."

Red Mike had not been waiting idly for a chance to express his opinion. Utley had visited Poteca in January, and the two officers had spent four hours discussing tactical possibilities, particularly the roving patrol described by Edson in his earlier letters to his commander. Not content to rely on straightforward arguments, the captain had brought to bear a more subtle means of persuasion. The troops had serenaded the major, and one of the verses of their homemade song had predicted, "There's going to be some mounted patrols." Before departing, Utley had told his subordinate that he would try to arrange a trip to Managua, where the two of them could have "a final show-down" with General Feland.

The latest letter from brigade seemed to be the opening that Edson sought. He radioed Utley and asked for the promised conference on tactics. The major agreed. Red Mike made a hasty journey by boat to Bocay, then by amphibian plane to Puerto Cabezas. After a two-day visit there, he flew on to Managua on 22 February. Edson visited briefly with the general that evening and met with the staff the next day. There was no need to argue his point. They gave him a copy of Brigade Special Order #11 and supplemented it with verbal instructions. The captain paraphrased his mission statement in a letter to Utley. "Go where you please, do what you please and return when you feel like it. If then you feel like going into the wilds again, it is alright with us, for the rest of the time here you will be foot loose and fancy free." Edson finally had his roving patrol.

One restriction promised to limit his effectiveness; he was to return to Poteca prior to 1 April to execute orders to join his ship in the States. The *Rochester* and its detachment had left Nicaragua more than a month earlier, and there were rumors of more troop withdrawals. The successful November elections in Nicaragua had fueled political opposition at home to the continuing intervention. Red Mike gathered intelligence for his commander in after-hours conversations with the staff officers. They indicated that troop cuts loomed for the Eastern Area. Utley's command was already the smallest in Nicaragua, with just six hundred men of the brigade total of five thousand Marines. When Edson questioned how a smaller force would cover the immense territory, the staff officers had no reply. The Poteca commander summarized his findings for the major: "It is the same old stuff of no definite policy to look to or work on."

The order specified an immediate start for Edson's patrol, but malaria hit him hard and delayed his departure from Managua. He got up in a plane on 3 March for a reconnaissance of the projected area of operations, then flew to Quilali the morning of the fifth. From there it was a mule ride to Santa Cruz, where one of his *pitpans* picked him up for the last leg to Poteca. In the meantime, the personnel ax had fallen. On 2 March brigade informed Area Headquarters that COMSPERON wanted his Marines back on ship by 3 April. Those men made up the whole of the garrison at Poteca, but a supplementary message kept the roving patrol alive. Edson and his men would move through the rebel zone and end their operation in the Northern Area, then receive air transportation to the east coast.

The last patrol began on 9 March. Edson and twenty-six men departed Poteca by boat and met up with their pack train at Guiguili the next day. They then proceeded overland to the southeast, their eventual objective the headwaters of the Cua River. On 14 March the detachment came across a freshly cut trail showing signs of heavy traffic. At successive villages along the path they received reports that Altamirano and forty men had passed through the area about three days ahead of the patrol. At each stop the rebel leader had enlisted new men into his ranks, sometimes against their will.

Around noon on 17 March the point man spotted a guerrilla on the trail and killed him. The patrol recovered a Springfield rifle and four rounds from the body. Twenty minutes later the detachment walked into a well-concealed ambush. About fifteen rebels opened fire with rifles at point-blank range and then fled five minutes later when the Marines gained fire superiority. Edson led most of the patrol in pursuit, but he could not regain contact on the difficult trail. Signs along the path indicated that the ambush had covered the retreat of a larger force of more than forty men. Red Mike broke off the chase after two hours and returned to the site to care for his casualties.

The initial fusillade had wounded two Marines, one of them the point man, Private Savulich, who had been hit three times. He died that afternoon. The men found one rebel body in the brush. The patrol buried Savulich according to Marine custom in Nicaragua—in the center of a hut, which they burned down to conceal the grave. Edson turned the detachment west and arrived at Jinotega on 20 March. Both he and the wounded man flew to Managua. The patrol leader made a personal report of the operation to the brigade staff and flew back to Jinotega the next day. Four cargo planes transferred the entire group to Puerto Cabezas that morning. The last Coco Patrol had come to an end.

The failure of this operation did not shake Red Mike's confidence in the roving patrol. His afteraction report focused on the modified rebel tactics he had faced in his last two engagements. Their ambush was no longer the opening move of a battle, as it had been at Ililiquas. Now it was nothing more than a means to inflict a few casualties, slow the advance of Marine patrols, and thus protect the rebel main body. He did not think his own ideas would have to change drastically. The patrol would have to be prepared to split into two elements at the end of an ambush. One would pursue the guerrillas while the other looked after the pack train and any casualties. There would be a cost in lives, but he still thought that a roving patrol would eventually run any rebel band into the ground.

Edson spent one week in Puerto Cabezas waiting for a commercial steamer to take him to New Orleans. A thorough physical found him in good health, the best since his baseball days on Guam. The only effect of a year in the backwoods of Nicaragua seemed to be a ravenous appetite for sweets; he bought four pounds of chocolates and polished them off in two days. Utley gave him a perfect fitness report and appended recommendations for two more medals.

Red Mike was much more concerned about his homecoming after such a long absence. He planned a week in New York with Ethel, followed by thirty days of leave in Vermont. Oddly enough, he wanted to go trout fishing "out in the hills" for part of it. Less surprisingly, he hoped that Ethel would leave Austin at home when she came to New York to meet him. "Lord knows I want to see him bad enough, but he would not really enjoy the week in the city and we can have such an excellent time during that week."

It had taken ten years, but this time he could return from overseas a hero.

Chapter 6

"Where We Could Take a Gun"

Red Mike's homecoming went smoothly enough, but his plans for a well-deserved vacation went awry. A Standard Fruit Company steamship got him to New Orleans, where he picked up a train for the two-day ride to New York City. Ethel met him at Pennsylvania Station and they spent a week at the Embassy Hotel while he checked in with the *Rochester*. The couple barely made it home to Burlington when Ethel became seriously ill. She was confined to bed for the remainder of his leave, which he extended until the day before the ship sailed for Central America. He spent those several weeks close by her side; Ethel's mother remarked that she "never dreamed any man could be so kind to anyone." During the last four days before his departure she was finally recovered enough to sit up. He made arrangements for her to come down to Panama when she was well again.

The *Rochester* sailed from New York on 27 May 1929. This time Edson had all his men on board, and he was quite pleased with the detachment. Of the ninety-nine enlisted, sixty-four were fresh from sea school, where Sergeant Schoneberger had taken care of his old *Denver* commander by handpicking the replacements from the latest class. Red Mike saw to the promotion of Mosier and Yelanich and their transfer to the *Rochester*. Things were much the same as they had been on the *Denver,* though the bigger *Rochester* rode the waves a bit easier. The only thing different this time was Edson's appetite. The first shipboard meal was baked beans, something he hoped never to see again after his time in Nicaragua.

The *Rochester*'s senior Marine had a special day on 15 June. All hands turned out on deck that Saturday morning to honor two heroes of the

Coco Patrol. As the ship's captain read the citations, the admiral pinned Navy Crosses on Edson and Yelanich. Then the band played the "Star Spangled Banner."

Major Utley was not receiving quite the same treatment for his part in the battle against Sandino. He had not been getting along well with the manager of the lumber concern in Puerto Cabezas, and the latter used his considerable influence to instigate an official investigation of the major's stewardship of the Eastern Area. Based only on a cursory review of rumors regarding drunkenness and womanizing in the organization, the new brigade commander called Utley to Managua and relieved him. Threats of a court-martial subsided when Utley brought the facts to light; then General Feland intervened from his new position at HQMC to put the matter completely to rest.

The Eastern Area itself was already just a shadow. The Marines had deserted Poteca, and a force of just one company garrisoned the coastal towns and the mining district. Eventually even those men would be withdrawn. Although the Nicaraguan Guardia Nacional took up some of the slack, Sandino's forces revived. By 1931 they were able to establish a base at Bocay and raid all the way down the Coco River to Cape Gracias. The situation was as bad as it had been in early 1927. Only the deceit of Anastasio Somoza, a Guardia commander, would bring the rebellion to an end. Under the guise of a truce in 1934, he brought Sandino and some of his officers into Managua for a meeting and assassinated them.

At this crossroads in his career, Edson was thinking about his own future, which was not that bright, even with his new status as a hero. The hump of World War officers continued to clog up the promotion system. Edson finally had made captain after ten years in the service, but the rank of major was a distant dream. He described the problem to Ethel with a simple example. He, Bob Blake, and Frank Cowie each had eleven years in the Corps. Blake was now near the top of the captains list, Edson was near the bottom, and Cowie had just made first lieutenant. If officers continued to retire at the mandatory age, in eighteen years (1946) Blake would be a lieutenant colonel and Edson would just be making major. Lejeune had submitted a bill to Congress that would create a system of promotion by merit, thus allowing the Corps to remove the deadwood and speed up promotions for the most capable officers. For Edson, there was the chance of moving up eighty places on the list, which would result in promotion in 1933, assuming that he was not one of those forced out. He was willing to take that risk. The House passed the bill in December 1927, but the Senate refused to act and the legislation died.

❧ Despite those dashed hopes, Edson gave no thought to getting out of the Corps. That still left him with a choice between aviation and ground duty. He missed being a pilot; many of his Coco Patrol messages sent via plane had carried that sentiment to the squadron. "Good luck to the gang. Would sure as hell like to be with you." During his February 1929 visit to Managua, one of the aviation commanders had broached the subject of his return and implied that all he had to do was ask for it. Edson was in no hurry to decide, but he wanted the choice, once made, to be for the remainder of his career. On the *Rochester* in 1929 the appeal of more adventure in the air outweighed the dull routine of shipboard life, even after one of his friends died in a plane crash on the Coco River. His reaction to the event was revealing about his attitude toward death. "It is too bad, for I liked Howard a great deal and I hate to see him finish. But that is all in the game, I guess."

The remainder of Red Mike's tour of sea duty was uneventful, except for two more bouts of malaria. Ethel made it down to Panama for a few weeks, but her husband was at sea most of the time. The admiral took the *Rochester* on a grand tour of Central America, with visits to Guatemala, El Salvador, Honduras, and Costa Rica. Orders came through in early August for Edson to report to the Navy Yard in Philadelphia, and the couple boarded a commercial steamer for the States near the end of the month.

Red Mike reported to Philadelphia for duty as one of seven instructors of the Basic School. This course for new Marine lieutenants had been in existence in one form or another for many years; Edson had gone through it in 1917 under the rubric Officers Training School. Starting with the class entering in the fall of 1929, the program doubled in length to nine months. As its name implied, it focused on teaching basic skills to brand new officers. About half of the lieutenants were graduates of the Naval Academy; the rest entered the Corps via ROTC or received their commissions from the ranks. With the exception of the latter, these young men had no practical experience in the Marine Corps. The Basic School aimed to fix that and turn out officers with sufficient competence and confidence to lead Marines.

The new program of instruction consisted of 1,200 hours of classroom training, capped by five weeks of range firing and field exercises. Nearly half the hours were devoted to weapons, a similar amount to general subjects such as first aid and guard, and the remainder (130 hours) to tactics. Edson specialized in the latter. Given his experience in trying to outsmart Sandino, he was a perfect match for the position. There was no prepared syllabus, so he spent much of his first year studying and developing his lectures. It was hard work, but tactics were the "most interesting" part of the curriculum, so he did not mind.

Red Mike did not put much stock in principles when teaching his specialty. "Unlike most subjects there are practically no hard and fast rules to be learned and rigidly adhered to. Each problem, like a game of chess, has any number of correct solutions, which takes all monotony out of teaching the subject." Edson certainly communicated that spirit to his pupils. Four of the fifty-three students of the class of 1929–30 went on to be generals, and each remembered Edson as the man they most admired at the Basic School. Brigadier General Frank Schwable made Red Mike his role model: "He was so direct, he knew his business, he knew how to put it across, he was stimulating." Another of those future generals, Samuel B. Griffith II, would get to know Edson a lot better in the years to come.

Some of the lieutenants were able to translate their studies into practical application in short order. Lieutenant Joe Tavern joined Nicaragua's Guardia after graduation and soon found himself in a firefight with Sandinistas. He reported back to Edson that the time spent on weapons and tactics had proven valuable. However, his preparation was not what it might have been considering the Corps's long history of interventions. In fact, the first action to codify some of the lessons of guerrilla operations, then known as "small wars," was an unofficial effort completed by a student at the Field Officers Course in 1922. For a time the Corps used Maj. Samuel Harrington's "The Strategy and Tactics of Small Wars" to train other students, but it fell out of use by 1930. When Utley arrived at Quantico to teach the small-wars curriculum that year, he was reduced to "the time honored custom of 'bulling' on the subject."

Utley visited Edson in Philadelphia in March 1930. The two discussed the need for more information on small wars, since they had muddled through with little to guide them during their own stint in Nicaragua. They soon opened a correspondence on tactics. Red Mike bemoaned the shortcomings of the current instruction at the Basic School, which consisted of just four hours on "Bush Warfare." He thought it was a "worse situation" than Utley had inherited, but the major replied, "TAINT POSSIBLE." The Quantico instructor could find little in the files at headquarters, so he began sending letters throughout the Corps to officers who had participated in previous campaigns.

His effort was hardly novel. In November 1928 the 2d Brigade staff had asked every officer in the command to furnish a summary of his experience in the field: "It is the intention of this office to compile a pamphlet covering the important problems, together with their solutions which have confronted this Brigade during its service in Nicaragua. This pamphlet will be intended as a guide for future, similar expeditions." Both the brigade and Utley received little response. Edson was one of the few to answer his former commander's plea.

Red Mike's long letter to Utley developed several points. He attacked the practice, common in Nicaragua, of arming the point man with an automatic weapon. In his view, the point man was most likely to become the first casualty, which would deprive the patrol of an important asset when the unit most needed it. Furthermore, the demands of point duty required men to rotate into that position at frequent intervals, which necessitated a confusing swap of weapons. Nor did he think that NCOs should be armed with automatic weapons, because that would cause them to focus on firing a weapon instead of controlling their squad. He also addressed the practice of reconnaissance by fire, in which units used mortars, rifle grenades, or automatic weapons on suspicious areas in their path. He thought that tactic had many drawbacks, not the least of which was the sacrifice of the possibility of surprise. (Utley agreed, saying that it was like a "small boy whistling as he passes the graveyard to keep his courage up.")

Senior officers were impressed with Edson's ability to develop and describe tactical doctrine. After he gave a lecture on the Coco Patrol to the staff and students of the Basic School, his commander contacted Col. R. C. Berkeley, head of the Marine Corps Schools in Quantico. Berkeley already was familiar with Edson's expertise, since he had been chief of staff of the 2d Brigade during the time of Red Mike's exploits. He arranged for the captain to make the same presentation in Quantico. Edson accompanied his ninety-minute talk with slides made from his original photographs. Even the Army had taken an interest in his exploits. Captain Mathew B. Ridgway's official report on Marine operations in Nicaragua described the Coco Patrol as "the best example of river patrol tactics which has occurred here."

The major continued to do research on small wars to build upon the earlier efforts of others. In addition to articles in the *Gazette* by Marines such as Harrington, there was C. E. Callwell's turn-of-the-century book *Small Wars*. Utley sent copies of his own work to Edson and asked for the captain's comment and criticism. Red Mike obliged with several letters outlining more of his ideas. The major refined his notes into a treatise and published excerpts from it in the *Gazette* from 1931 to 1933.

Although the Marine Corps Schools officially adopted the project, Utley and his successors never found the time to complete it. The demands of teaching and the drain of manpower and attention toward brushfire conflicts in places such as Nicaragua prevented much progress. Tired of the delay, the major general commandant suspended classes for the 1933–34 academic year and set both faculty and students to work developing doctrine on small wars and the amphibious assault. Two publications emerged from that process, the *Tentative Manual for Landing Operations* and *Small Wars Operations*. It is unclear how much of the latter manual was attributable to Utley, but certainly he and Edson had a hand in starting the process. The book's sample diagram for defense of a campsite was the fire plan sketch of Poteca, which Red Mike had sent to Utley in 1930. Many of its ideas, however, contradicted those that Edson had championed. It would take awhile, but the hero of the Coco would eventually get the chance to stamp his own imprint on Marine Corps doctrine in that field.

The Corps's first work on the theory of amphibious warfare initially proved more durable than its effort on guerrilla warfare. With the move away from interventions in the mid-1930s, Marine planners were shifting their focus toward the concerns of the next big war, which many believed would be a naval war with Japan. Edson was not on the cutting edge of this revolution in Marine thinking, at least not in 1930. He still had his mind fixed on the problems of fighting guerrillas and he saw little reason to change. "I may have the wrong idea, but it seems to me that here at the Basic School the young officers should be given plenty of instruction in 'Small Wars' and 'Overseas Operations,' with less emphasis placed upon instruction as part of larger forces. As a matter of fact, I think this criticism applies to our entire system of schools."

In the summer of 1930 the Corps had need of Red Mike's more specialized skills in another area—competitive shooting. He received orders to the Marine Corps rifle team on 30 May, while he was in the field with the Basic School class, but he still arrived in Quantico by 2 June. This last-minute call left him unprepared, which showed in the East Coast matches on 4 and 5 June. He finished fifty-second out of one hundred twenty competitors. That was the third highest score among officers, however, and it earned him a chance to fire in the Marine Corps Matches the following week. He did little better there, with a finish of fifty-fourth out of seventy.

The team captain, Maj. Harry L. Smith, was not interested in Edson's scores. He needed to develop officers for future leadership positions in the shooting community. The requisite rank, experience, and personality were hard to find; Red Mike was one of the few to fit the profile. He had competitive spirit, and he knew how to build a team. One of the shooters arriving at Quantico for the Marine Corps Matches that summer was Cpl. Raymon Clark, formerly of the *Denver* and the Coco Patrol. When Edson saw him on the practice range with jury-rigged equipment, he arranged to get him a real shooting jacket, then brought out his own scope and stool and spent time teaching the young Marine. Smith ended up making Red Mike the team's assistant coach.

The 1929 Marine team had not fared well in the National Matches. Things looked equally bleak in the early going at Camp Perry in 1930. Marine shooters were doing poorly in the individual competitions until Smith decided to take things into his own hands. The team captain traditionally shot in practice with the rest of the men to get a feel for daily conditions, though he never fired in competition. Upset at his team's poor showing, Smith drew his own weapon from the armory and entered the Scott Match, fifteen slow-fire shots at nine hundred yards. When the smoke cleared he had bested several hundred others to take first place. Thus inspired, the Marines went on to win several team competitions, to include the preeminent National Trophy Rifle Team Match.

Edson was back on the team in the summer of 1931. Despite a second year of economic depression, the Camp Perry competition had continued to grow. This year there were more than twenty-five hundred military and civilian shooters on hand. They were supported by an additional three thousand servicemen manning the targets, toting up scores, serving meals, and performing all manner of other chores. This large assemblage lived in a tent city located just a few hundred yards behind the firing lines. By tradition, the previous winner of the National Trophy Rifle Team Match pitched its tents under the single large tree that dominated the encampment. The Marines occupied that site in 1931 and eventually won the right to return to that spot in 1932. Edson was an assistant coach of the rifle team again, as well as coach of the pistol team.

Red Mike made a lasting impression on everyone at Camp Perry in 1931. In one of the individual matches he made what he thought was a poor shot. The target crew pulled it down and ran it back up in the air showing a score of five, a bull's-eye. Edson asked the officials to have his score posted again, something done only when one challenged it for being too low. The target went down and came back up with the five still showing. The captain then insisted that a pit officer verify the target. The inspection revealed a mistake and the target came up with a three this time. Edson was no longer one of the best shooters, but he was building a reputation as a coach and a sportsman.

With that expertise in mind, headquarters transferred Red Mike in the summer of 1931 to the Depot of Supplies in Philadelphia for duty as the ordnance officer. That position would serve the dual purpose of further grooming him to assume a position in the hierarchy of Marine competitive shooting, and placing him where he could support the team during off-season periods. The technical emphasis on weapons and ammunition suited Edson just fine at first, because he had an interest in the field. Just a few months earlier he had arranged to spend part of his Christmas in Quantico firing the Thompson submachine gun, because he wanted to find out for himself if it matched the manufacturer's claim of accuracy at ranges of several hundred yards. Lieutenant Colonel W. Dulty Smith, the commander of the Basic School, was sorry to see Edson go. He thought he'd done "some very excellent work" as an instructor and was "one of our best officers."

Edson spent the winter of 1931–32 immersed in his new duties, which included everything from planning and constructing rifle ranges to overseeing the design and testing of new weapons. One effort involved the Army competition for a new rifle to replace the venerable Springfield, which had been in service for nearly three decades. There were other tests at Quantico on various modifications to the BAR, and visits to several arsenals to learn about the production of munitions. The job lost a lot of its luster, however, when Congress deleted funds for the 1932 National Matches from the budget. The enforced economy of the Depression was putting a crimp in competitive marksmanship.

The tour at the depot was supposed to last for three years, but Red Mike began casting about for a substitute in the spring of 1932. His primary goal was aviation, which seemed especially attractive since the foreseeable future held no prospect of commanding troops or shooting. Edson took a flight physical in May and passed, though the surgeon provided a lukewarm endorsement. He passed another exam at Quantico at the end of May, but failed the final one done at headquarters on 10 June. Surprisingly it was not his vision that created the problem, but a finding that he had poor circulation and an abnormally fast heartbeat. Headquarters rejected his request for flight status. Occasionally Red Mike would think wistfully about what might have been, but thereafter he gave up any serious ambitions to fly. Nevertheless, the gold wings of a naval aviator would grace his chest for the rest of his career. For the time being Red Mike was stuck in Philadelphia.

The National Matches were suspended, but the shooting game was not entirely dead. The Marine Corps held its usual series of matches to pick a team, though the number of competitors was about half that of 1931. Edson served as the coach of the 1932 team, which spent the summer shooting in regional matches. Money was even tighter in 1933, so the Corps held separate matches on each coast. The result was two Marine Corps teams that year, each competing in its own area. Headquarters made Edson captain of the East Coast team, a distinct honor that elevated him to the highest ranks of the Marine shooting program.

The results proved the wisdom of the choice. In regional competition in Quantico his men won seven of ten individual matches and two of the four team matches from a field representing civilians and all the services. His own shooting was none too shabby either—his aggregate score for all competitions placed him eighth. The major general commandant recognized his performance with a personal letter of congratulations: "The results of your team give ample evidence of your excellent leadership."

In 1934 the Marine Corps had two official teams again. Edson was the East Coast team captain, but additional duties as chief range officer for several competitions kept him busier than usual. His reputation in the shooting world continued to grow. The head of the Massachusetts branch of the National Rifle Association commended Red Mike for his performance as an official in the Wakefield matches. "This year Captain Edson called coaches and team captains together, and gave one of the finest talks I ever heard on what the range officers expected of competitors."

Edson's career prospects brightened considerably during this period. In 1934 Congress finally passed a law authorizing the Corps to junk the old seniority system and selectively promote officers to major, lieutenant colonel, and colonel. Those who failed to make the next rank would have to retire once they reached a certain number of years of service, or sooner if the Corps so decided in individual cases. A captain commissioned in 1917 would thus have to leave the Corps no later than 1938 if he had not yet made major. In 1933 Congress also had granted the Corps an increase of seventy-three majors, a significant boost, since there had previously been barely a hundred officers of that rank. Those two actions vastly accelerated the timetable for Red Mike's advancement. A selection board meeting in February 1935 picked him for promotion.

The tour at the Depot of Supply marked a turning point in Edson's personal life. He had been a loving husband to Ethel for more than a decade, and the couple had a second son, Herbert Robbins Edson (the family called him Bobby), the day after Christmas in 1931. At some point, however, probably in 1934, Red Mike met and fell in love with Lillian MacLane, a married woman with a family of her own. It is impossible to say whether this event precipitated trouble in his marriage or came about as a consequence of it. In either case, he was profoundly unhappy for a time. It did not help that he would not turn to anyone for advice or consolation, a feeling he expressed in a doleful letter to his sister in February 1935. "If I could only discuss things freely. I would so like to do it—but I have never found it an easy thing to do. Perhaps someday I shall surprise you with all the things I wanted to talk over with you last fall, but which I could not bring myself to do. For after all, we each have our own problems and no one else in the world can solve them but our own selves."

The difficulty in his personal life did not carry over to his work. Congress authorized money for renewed National Matches in 1935, and headquarters named Edson captain of its first real team since 1931. He chose Captain Whaling to be his coach and Gunner Cal Lloyd to be the assistant coach. With funding for a full series of qualifying matches, Edson was able to handpick the best forty-eight team shooters from Marine units around the world. By this time he and his predecessors had perfected the selection process. Scores were not the only criteria. Red Mike favored big men because they could more easily absorb the recoil of the rifle, men with blue or gray eyes because they seemed to have better vision over a wider range of light conditions, and even-tempered men because they remained calm in competition. The latter characteristic was most important to Edson. "Rifle shooting has as many ups and downs as shooting golf and if a man cannot take it without losing his temper he has no business playing at it."

The shooters trained steadily from selection of the team in June until the end of the season in September, though Edson made sure that the effort did not become arduous or monotonous. The men never shot on weekends, except to make up for days missed due to bad weather. Red Mike had no strict rules for periods off the range, since he believed that enforced modifications of behavior would have a greater negative effect on scores than any supposed improvements from additional rest or abstinence from cigarettes or alcohol. The men had liberty from the end of the shooting day till 0700 the next day, and from Friday evening until Monday morning. If anyone abused the freedom to the point of hurting his scores, he soon found himself off the team for poor shooting. Edson employed the same low-key, positive leadership style that was his trademark. He thought it important to "give a word of encouragement instead of a growl to the man who, after working his heart out, leaves the line with a low score instead of his highest for the season."

The results were spectacular. The Marines swept into Camp Perry and picked up where they had left off in 1931. They won a majority of the matches, including three of the four premier competitions sponsored by the NBPRP. They took the National Trophy Rifle Team Match by a record sixty-two points against a field of 113 military and civilian teams. That made it three times in a row for the Corps, but the *Gazette* noted that "this performance is considered by the veteran Marine shooters as our 'Blue Ribbon' year."

Those achievements amply justified the faith that headquarters had placed in Edson that spring. After six years at Philadelphia he had been due for an overseas tour, and the Personnel Section had slated him for a transfer to the 4th Regiment in China. Orders from higher up canceled those plans and kept Edson on at the Depot of Supply so he could head the 1935 team. When fall arrived, he was getting too close to promotion to put him in a captain's billet, and there were no openings for majors overseas. Colonel Seth Williams, the depot commander, tried to hold onto him. In the end, headquarters decided to send him to Parris Island to take charge of marksmanship training at the recruit depot. It would be the first time he had set foot there since his brief stay in 1917.

Colonel Williams took the unusual step of writing directly to the commandant about the performance of his ordnance officer, whom he had been able to observe for more than four years. He complimented Red Mike for "valuable improvements" in the Ordnance Section and the School for Armorers and extolled his virtues. "Captain Edson is one of the very outstanding officers of the Corps. He has that sustained intelligent interest in all phases of his profession, which makes him more and more valuable to the Marine Corps each year of his service. I have never had an officer serving under my command who has given more satisfactory service." In view of the traditional discord between the staff and line, this was high praise indeed coming from a senior quartermaster officer.

The Edsons went to Vermont for an extended vacation in the fall of 1935. Home was not the happy place it once had been, for the Depression had wreaked its havoc on both families. George Robbins had lost his job with Dun & Bradstreet, so Ethel's parents had moved from Burlington to Maine, where they shared ten-acre Eagle Farm with another relative. It was a steep decline in fortunes. Wood provided the fuel for cooking and heating, and there was neither indoor plumbing nor electricity. The pastoral setting of an adjoining tidal cove and forest was a delight to young Austin, though, and he and Bobby would spend many youthful summers at this place.

The bad economy merely added to Erwin and Lelia's already hard times. He had been in poor health since the 1920s, and Red Mike had been sending home money to help with medical and living expenses. With a promotion and pay raise pending, he decided to purchase a small farm for them outside Chester. That would not only support them, but double as an investment for him. He borrowed $4,500 from the Chester Savings Bank and bought the fifteen-acre place.

Red Mike reported to Parris Island just prior to Thanksgiving 1935. His tour here would be only slightly longer than his last one, and not much more pleasant. There seemed to be some potential, since the base commander was General Berkeley, who thought highly of Edson. Red Mike's skills went to waste, however, as his superiors shuttled him back and forth between the duty of assistant range officer and assistant training officer, and never let him do either for any extended period. After training the finest shooters in the world, he was frustrated at trying to teach the fundamentals to recruits who seemed happy just to hit the target.

It did not help that he tried to serve several masters at once. In addition to the demands of his billets, which kept him busy six days a week, he had two other important assignments to complete. The commandant appointed him to head the 1936 team; that required extensive preparation, and it was hard to coordinate things now that he was no longer the ordnance officer at Philadelphia. He also was writing up the story of the Coco Patrol for the *Gazette*. Editors of that journal had been pestering him for an article on the subject since 1932, and he worked steadily on the project in his off hours through the fall and winter at Parris Island. The result was a large manuscript that the *Gazette* published in three installments.

The real source of his dissatisfaction probably had little to do with the nature of his job or the long hours, but with continuing problems in his personal life. The attempt to help his parents was going badly. The plumbing and heating systems failed in the house and it needed painting. He became mired in details such as ordering chickens and fruit trees and arranging for repairs. Then the bank announced that the property could support a mortgage of only $2,900, so he would have to come up with collateral for a personal loan to cover the remaining amount. He had no other property suitable for that purpose and ended up having to ask two other officers to cosign his personal note. Moreover, Erwin and Lelia were not particularly pleased with the farm. Edson displayed his exasperation in a letter to his sister that noted the efforts she had made in the past to help their parents. "I shall try to make up for that now by trying to furnish them with the means of making their own living. That is what I should have done sixteen years ago instead of foolishly getting married."

The last sentence of that letter went to the heart of his unhappiness. He was still in love with Lillian and she was far from Parris Island. His physical condition soon reflected the constant mental strain. His weight crept up and he went back to smoking after giving it up in preparation for his aborted return to aviation. His outlook on life was as bleak as that of any recruit in the first day of basic training.

The anticipated promotion to major finally materialized in March 1936. He had been a captain for eight years, but he had reason to be pleased at his progress, since he had expected at one time to remain in that rank until 1946. The advancement itself was less exciting to him than the event it set into motion. Within days, orders came in from headquarters for Edson to report there for duty. That was "just what the doctor ordered." In May he packed up the family and sent them to live in Chester, while he settled into his duties with the shooting team.

If marksmanship had reached the status of a religion within the Corps, it was certain that Red Mike was now one of its gods. He thus wielded considerable influence in 1936 as he pursued another national championship. When Edson arrived at Wakefield, he found the range detachment billeted in the prime barracks reserved for the team. The senior major in charge was uncooperative. Red Mike described the problems to a friend at headquarters in charge of shooting matters, Maj. William W. Ashurst. Orders soon arrived relieving the major and putting Edson in charge of the range detachment until a replacement reported aboard. Red Mike also led a campaign to overturn the ruling in the brand-new *Marine Corps Manual* that prohibited the use of recreation funds to support intramural shooting. It made no sense to him, since that was the one sport most closely allied to military service. "If I said all that I think about it, the paper would burn with the heat!" A month later the commandant signed a change to the manual. The team captain's clout extended well beyond the Corps. He tested ammunition from one manufacturer and found it less accurate than promised. Although he had no responsibility for procurement, he did not hesitate to threaten to refuse to accept all production until the firm corrected the problem.

Red Mike looked after his shooters on a personal level, too. During the off season, even before it was certain that he would captain the team, he wrote letters to those men he thought would be able to contribute in the coming year. The communications had the desired effect of maintaining motivation, as one of many responses noted. "Thank you for the little Christmas note and the genuine interest you take in me. I felt like beating my chest when you said you were counting on me for this year's team." The interest was indeed real, as evidenced by Edson's negotiations with the Personnel Section over the assignment of one officer. "As much as I would like to have him I do not want to interfere in any duty assignment which would help him toward any later selection and promotion."

There was no matter too small to escape his notice. At the last minute headquarters decided to downgrade the number of cooks going to Perry in support of the team, as well as the rank (and therefore experience) of those who would go. Edson sent a long letter to the colonel in charge of the matter to try to change his mind. He explained that a special diet was every bit as important for shooting as it was for any athletic team, and this was the most important one in the Corps. It made no sense to go to great expense to assemble these talented men and then scrimp on feeding them. Later he fought to ensure that the cooks received their promotions at the earliest opportunity.

Edson could be hard on his shooters when it was appropriate. Before the season started he explained to one captain known for his drinking bouts that "the time has passed when a member of the pistol team can shoot on it if he feels in need of fortifying himself before or during the match." If the officer wanted to try out, it would be on those terms or not at all. Just prior to the Perry matches Edson received word that two of his shooters were adding points to their practice scores. The three men assigned to check on them at the next practice confirmed it. Less than four hours later the pair had packed their seabags and were on the way to their duty stations. Someone in Washington took exception to Edson's authority to issue travel and transfer orders, but he explained that it "was a case of emergency." Headquarters submitted in this as in all other things.

As the big matches approached, Red Mike's greatest concern was the potential for overconfidence. He made sure that this team realized that the previous year's success would have no bearing on the results this time around. After that, his main problem was keeping the visiting generals away from the team so the men could concentrate on the job at hand. In the end, all his effort was handsomely rewarded. The Army Infantry team provided tough competition in the National Trophy Rifle Team Match, but his Marines beat their 1935 score by fourteen points and outdistanced the Infantry by forty-eight points. It was a fourth victory in a row for the Corps, an unprecedented achievement for any service. The pistol team, also under his charge, placed second in their most important match, and the Marines won a majority of all the other events. The success was every bit as complete as in 1935. Edson tried his hand in a few individual events and did quite well in that realm, too. He finished tenth in the Marine Corps Cup Match with the rifle and twenty-fifth in the National Trophy Pistol Match.

Red Mike would be intimately associated with competitive shooting for the rest of his life, but this was his last hurrah on the actual firing line. Others, such as Cal Lloyd, had established a greater reputation for their shooting ability, but Edson had carved out his own huge niche. From his first year as a firing member of the championship 1921 team, through his part as a team official in the unprecedented four straight rifle team national trophies, he had exhibited his thorough mastery of every facet of the game. He was not solely responsible for the dominance of the Corps in the field, but he had contributed mightily to the team effort that made it possible.

Prior to the start of the shooting season, headquarters had indicated that Edson finally would be going overseas when fall came. He wanted to go to the 4th Regiment in Shanghai, though he was also interested in attending the Senior Course at Quantico. When it came time to make the transfer, there were again no billets open in China, so he was on his way to school. He was "glad to get it," because he thought it was time he "went some place to be educated." The family came down from Vermont and moved into a new brick apartment complex in the hills overlooking the site of the old World War wooden barracks, most of which were now gone and replaced with equally new brick buildings for the troops. Edson had no time to rest, since the course already had been in session for six weeks while he was off shooting. He reported to the school just four days after winning the championship match.

Edson found that the Senior Course required no more studying than the Company Officers Course of 1926, although it was a much more challenging program. The course consisted of a series of problems revolving around the attack and defense of an advance base, with an additional exercise devoted to a small-war scenario. The fifteen students, along with the instructors, filled the roles of commanders and staffs charged with planning and executing the operations. At the end of the ten-month program, students were supposed to have learned a great deal about strategy and tactics, aviation, ordnance, and gunnery, along with a smattering of field fortifications, weapons, training programs, and military and international law.

Already working under the handicap of missing the introductory material, Edson made no heroic efforts in class, though he did take the program seriously. Instead, he focused on completing the story of the Coco Patrol for the *Gazette*. In the last few weeks of 1936 he churned out a further twenty-two thousand words on the subject to take his tale up through the seizure of Poteca. He hoped to describe the conclusion of the operation in another installment, but never completed the work.

As the school wound down in spring, Red Mike received the long-overdue orders to Shanghai. He was looking forward to the prospect, not least because the commanding officer of the 4th Regiment was Colonel Price. Over the years Edson had maintained close contact with his old battalion commander from France and was eager for the chance to serve under him again. His personal life had not improved, but he did not let that interfere with his work. He seemed to be following the advice he had given Austin several years before. "Keep the head and eyes up and look the old world in the face even tho at times it does seem rather hard to do."

Chapter 7

"They Will Find the Streets Are Guarded"

The trip to China was not a happy one for Red Mike. The Edsons left Quantico in late May on a cross-country drive to Seattle. Austin and Bobby enjoyed the new sights, but their father felt "cooped up" in the automobile packed with family and luggage. After seventeen days on the road, they boarded the SS *President Grant,* which took them to Shanghai via Yokohama, Japan. Red Mike slept in one stateroom with Austin; Ethel and Bobby shared another one. The extra space did not improve his mood. He explained in a letter to Mary that she could "imagine how pleasant it all is . . . two weeks on board ship with someone you despise—for whom there is no mutual respect."

The steamer arrived at its destination on 6 July. As the ship stood up the mouth of the Yangtze River and thence into its tributary, the Whangpoo, the passengers had their first look at Shanghai. In the 1930s that metropolis had the distinction of being one of the most cosmopolitan and unusual cities in the world. Great Britain had won extraterritorial rights to a large chunk of it following the 1842 Opium War. The resulting International Settlement now covered fifty-five hundred acres and was home to about a million people representing numerous nationalities. There were about seventy-five thousand foreigners in all, with the Japanese, Russians, British, and Americans predominating. The remaining residents were Chinese. The city within a city had its own municipal council run by the foreign settlers. The French had a separate concession adjacent to, and about half the size of, the International Settlement. Another million and a half Chinese lived in the rest of the city, which surrounded the foreign quarters.

Greater Shanghai was the leading port of China and the door to the important Yangtze River valley.

The 4th Regiment of Marines had come to the International Settlement in 1927 to join the other foreign units protecting the area against the turmoil of the Chinese civil war. Once the Nationalists were firmly in control of the Chinese portion of the city, tensions relaxed, but the Marines stayed on. Things heated up again briefly in 1932 when fighting flared between the Chinese and Japanese after the latter's forces occupied China's northern province of Manchuria. By 1937 the Marines had adapted to the comparative luxury of a garrison force in an economy with an endless supply of cheap labor and a wide variety of available vices. The most significant change had been the redesignations of the early 1930s: Companies were now alphabetized rather than numbered, and the organization was now the 4th Marines instead of the 4th Regiment.

The Edsons discovered very quickly that the life of a foreigner in China was not as inexpensive or as easy as they had pictured it. They finally settled on a four-room apartment on the fourth floor of a five-story building. It was one of the best bargains they could find, but it still cost $230 per month, almost as much as a half year of payments on the farm in Bartonsville. They had three servants, but Ethel was not satisfied with their performance. On laundry days the bathtub doubled as the washing machine, and wet clothes festooned lines stretching across the rooms of the apartment. Within a month Ethel was "ready to leave as soon as possible." Her husband adjusted to the life more easily. Edson had been in the city only a day when he purchased a polo pony (for the grand sum of one dollar) and applied to join one of the elite social clubs, Le Cercle Sportif Français.

In 1937 the 4th Marines was at a peacetime strength of just fifty-nine officers and slightly more than a thousand men. Of that meager number, a portion was dedicated to service and support functions normally performed by a base unit. It had two battalions instead of three, each consisting of only two rifle companies and a machine-gun company. The regimental commander, Colonel Price, had been in charge since the previous summer. His subordinate commanders were Lt. Col. William H. Rupertus, a recent arrival heading the 1st Battalion, and Lt. Col. Roswell Winans, in charge of the 2d Battalion. Although there were a number of majors who had been in Shanghai for some time, Price placed Edson in the plum job of regimental plans and training officer (R-3).

Edson had precious little time in which to assimilate his new assignment before the work turned serious. On 7 July, the day after he arrived in Shanghai, the Japanese precipitated war with China when units on

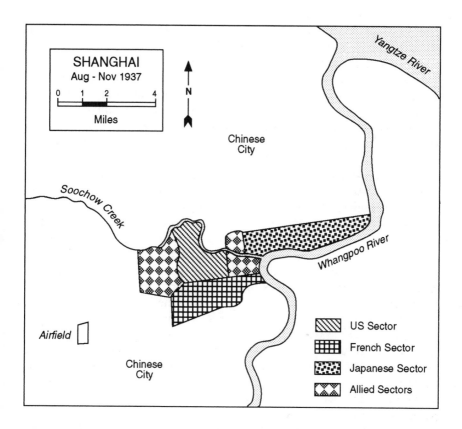

"maneuvers" clashed with Chinese troops at the Marco Polo Bridge near Peking. With that incident as a pretext, their army in Manchuria launched a full-scale invasion of north China. Within a month they captured Peking and Tientsin. The Imperial Japanese Navy rushed ships to Shanghai and sent Special Naval Landing Force units ashore to reinforce the garrison in the Japanese portion of the International Settlement. Both sides avoided hostilities in the area until 9 August, when a Japanese motorized patrol tried to enter the airport west of the city. In the ensuing firefight with Chinese militia guarding the field, two Japanese soldiers died.

On 11 August nine more Japanese ships arrived, which gave them a fleet of twenty-seven. That night a Chinese division moved into northern Shanghai to bolster the militia garrison surrounding the Japanese enclave. With the city on the verge of war, western forces began to take their prearranged positions on the boundaries of their portions of the settlement to prevent entry by either of the belligerents. The Municipal Council also mobilized the Shanghai Volunteer Corps, a force of fourteen hundred trained western militiamen. On the morning of 13 August, the Japanese and Chinese began fighting along their common boundary in the city. Both sides pledged to respect the remainder of the settlement as neutral territory—an iffy proposition given the close quarters.

The Marines were responsible for sector C, which required them to occupy a seventy-two-hundred-yard frontage formed by the south bank of Soochow Creek. Given the size of the regiment, that was no simple task. The 1st Battalion was on the left, the 2d on the right, with all companies in the line. The regiment's twenty-nine machine guns occupied sandbagged positions with overhead cover; each battalion held its platoon of 37mm guns in the rear. A provisional unit formed from the service and support detachments constituted the reserve. The creek at least provided a defensible line. In addition to the water itself, the vertical concrete banks and wide streets on either side made for a formidable obstacle easily covered by fire. Luckily there were only a few bridges in the American sector.

Reinforcements were not long in coming. The USS *Augusta* (CA-31), flagship of the Asiatic Fleet, landed its detachment of fifty Marines along with fifty-seven sailors. By 26 August two companies of Marines arrived from the Philippines to flesh out the understrength battalions of the 4th Marines. A brigade headquarters and the 6th Marines were on their way from the States. As an emergency measure, the regiment even enrolled fifty-six young men into an auxiliary force, issued them uniforms, and set about training them in weapons and drill. At the same time, the U.S. consul and the admiral ordered the evacuation of government dependents and encouraged the departure of all American civilians. Ethel and the boys left on the SS *President Hoover* on 20 August, headed for Manila.

With pluck and superior numbers, the Chinese repulsed the initial Japanese attacks and launched an offensive of their own, which kept their enemy pinned against the banks of the Whangpoo River, where the Japanese had ample support from the guns of their fleet. On 24 August fresh elements of the Japanese Army made an amphibious assault from the Yangtze River in an effort to outflank the city from the north. They advanced several miles inland and linked up with their comrades in the International Settlement, but the drive stalled. The Chinese skillfully turned the urban area into a fortified zone of basement bunkers and rooftop observation posts, with barbed-wire obstacles and antitank ditches closing off the streets. To prevent a flanking attack to the south, they barricaded the Whangpoo with sunken ships. The fighting settled down to a duel of aerial bombing and artillery.

The Marines could do little during this period except hunker down in their own defenses and watch the "greatest show on earth" unfold just a few hundred feet away. Price and his staff had no great challenges to meet once they manned the defensive line. They spent the days monitoring reports, updating training, and making periodic inspection visits to the front lines to keep up morale. One of Edson's primary jobs was maintaining liaison with the city police and with forces guarding the neighboring sectors. Price's greatest concern soon became the massive influx of refugees, perhaps as many as a million during the first few days of fighting. These added souls burdened resources, increased crime, and brought on a cholera outbreak. Despite the liberal use of firepower by both sides and the proximity of the Americans to the targets, the Marines on the perimeter suffered only three wounded in the course of the entire campaign. Civilians inside the settlement fared less well; a few errant bombs landing in the refugee-crowded city killed hundreds.

American reinforcements arrived on 19 September, and the 6th Marines took over the entire Soochow Creek line on the twenty-third to give the weary 4th Marines a rest. The 2d Brigade commander, Brig. Gen. John C. Beaumont, had been Price's predecessor as commander of the 4th Marines, so he was familiar with the situation. Despite the welcome addition of manpower and firepower, some of the officers of the 4th Marines were not entirely pleased with the new arrivals. Edson thought Beaumont was weak willed and he wished Price was still in command. The men of the 6th Marines, anxious to demonstrate their professional skill, tore down the sandbag bunkers built by the 4th Marines and reconstructed them according to their own tastes. They proudly told reporters that these were the type their predecessors had used at Belleau Wood. The "constant criticism" and "lack of friendly cooperation" irritated Red Mike.

As the inconclusive fighting dragged on north of Soochow Creek, things regained a semblance of normality in the western zones of the settlement. The theaters were open again by the end of September and the 4th Marines resumed their sports schedule of baseball games and polo matches. It was relaxed enough that Price and Edson went to the movies, yet Red Mike thought it was "like living on the edge of a volcano." The buildup of forces was continuing; with hundreds of thousands of troops in the area, something was bound to happen.

The 2d Brigade assumed a new posture on 3 October. The 4th Marines took over responsibility for the eastern half of the American zone, while the 6th Marines continued to hold the western portion. Each regiment put one battalion in the line, with the other in reserve and available for rotation to the front. The Japanese offensive finally came on 23 October. A powerful assault breached the Chinese lines north of the settlement, and the Nationalist forces began to withdraw from the city. A two-division landing by the Japanese south of Shanghai in early November threatened an envelopment and hastened the Chinese retreat. The two wings of the offensive linked up to the west of the city by 9 November: The area was entirely in Japanese hands, save for the western portions of the settlement.

The Chinese troops had set fire to the city as they withdrew, which only added to the devastation caused by weeks of shelling and bombing. The Marines now looked north from Soochow Creek over a smoking ruin. As the war receded into the distance, western forces in the settlement relaxed their guard a bit more. Each of the Marine regiments stationed just a company along the creek, and the Shanghai Volunteer Corps demobilized. Some foreign civilians began to return to the city, though the American government refused to allow its dependents to come back just yet.

The danger and the separation did not improve things between Ethel and Red Mike. If anything, both of them had additional reasons to be unhappy. She found the cost of living high and the quarters cramped at Camp John Hay in the mountains north of Manila. Rumors and arguments flared among the military wives, who had nothing better to do. Since Ethel received few letters from her husband, she depended on secondhand news from others. It varied from positive reports about Edson's work as the plans officer to frightening stories that he was ill and near death.

The rumors about his health had some basis in fact. In early October he developed a cough and cold, which turned severe enough that he went into the regimental hospital on the tenth. Nausea and vomiting followed each coughing fit. Edson went home after a few days, but burning pains in his stomach persisted. He had suffered a similar attack during his last summer at Camp Perry, and had experienced recurring indigestion since then. After a series of tests, the medical people decided that he had a duodenal ulcer. He went on a strict diet of soft, bland foods and took medication. In addition to orders to stay away from alcohol and cigarettes, the doctor advised him to avoid mental strain.

The latter task was not easy. Money was an increasing source of worry, since the war had driven up the cost of food to six times its normal level. There were also the dual expenses of maintaining households in Shanghai and the Philippines. And he was just as unhappy as before over his personal life. His few notes to Ethel were cold and unfeeling in contrast to his long, loving letters from Nicaragua. He skipped any semblance of sentiment and merely signed them with his name. For the first time a note of bitter fatalism crept into his writing. He closed one letter with the postscript: "Do not worry about me. . . . I am not worth worrying about anyway."

The Japanese presented another type of concern. Shanghai was now a major base for their drive up the Yangtze River. Surrounded by a fleet and two hundred thousand troops, the western forces guarding the remainder of the International Settlement were in a perilous position. They were too weak to serve as anything more than a tripwire; the only thing that kept the Japanese at bay was the possibility of war with the western powers. Edson thought there was little reason for the Marines to remain in the city for that purpose, especially since the U.S. government was reluctant to threaten the use of force to uphold its position. In late November he predicted that the Japanese would use some incident as a pretext to seize control of the settlement. "It is just like sitting on a keg of powder wondering when someone is going to throw a lighted match into it. But it is interesting, and I would not miss it for anything."

On 3 December the Japanese insisted on conducting a victory parade through every zone of the International Settlement. The American admiral ordered all his military personnel to remain away from the route of march, but Edson changed into civilian clothes, borrowed Price's camera, and stationed himself on the second floor of a building on the border between the French and American sectors. From that vantage point he photographed and counted the stream of six thousand Japanese soldiers. The city government had ordered all Chinese to stay indoors, but someone emerged to throw a grenade and wound three Japanese before the municipal police gunned him down. Red Mike was "sorry it did not do some real damage." He suspected that the man was a provocateur hired by the Japanese for the purpose. Japanese businesses and personnel were the targets of similar attacks in the weeks to come.

Nine days after the victory parade, Japanese planes bombed and sank the *Panay* (PR-5), a U.S. gunboat plying the Yangtze. Many of the Marines were furious. Edson thought it was time to declare war. Price took out his anger on the commander of the Japanese garrison when that officer came to the headquarters of the 4th Marines to express his regrets. The colonel leaned over his desk and shook his finger in the face of his visitor: "You sons-of-bitches will never get away with this." But they did, at least for the time being. The Japanese continued their game of testing American will and readiness for the next four years. Patrols and truck convoys periodically violated the western zones of the settlement. Each time the Marines and their European allies had to deal with the situation through tough talking and a show of force.

In this atmosphere of high-stakes poker, training for combat took on a new meaning in the 4th Marines. Once brigade headquarters and the 6th Marines departed in February 1938, the regiment was master of its own destiny again and instituted a number of new initiatives. One was the Special Training Platoon, which arose from the use of service and support troops as provisional infantry units during the 1937 crisis. Those men were not fully prepared to fill that role because the everyday demands of their regular duties made it difficult to carry on any useful training in weapons and tactics. Beginning in March 1938, each rear-echelon unit had to rotate a portion of its manpower through the Special Training Platoon, a two-week course on basic infantry subjects. During that time the men had no other duties or distractions. The program was demanding; participants found it "almost as rigorous as that of the recruit depots." More than two hundred Marines went through the course before the end of the year.

The regiment also elevated the standard of field training for the infantry companies. Prior to 1937 Chinese restrictions on foreign troops prevented any exercises in the countryside around Shanghai, so the only tactical training consisted of platoon-sized operations in one of the city parks. Starting in June 1938, the 4th Marines rotated one or two companies at a time up to Camp Holcomb, a small American enclave on the coast near Peking. Here the officers and men could stretch their legs in bigger tactical formations and undertake a full range of live-fire training with all their weapons. The exercises included night firing and the use of tear gas.

These innovations were "the fruits of Edson's energy and resourcefulness." He inspected Camp Holcomb for suitability prior to the start of Marine training there, and he was the officer reviewing the graduation of each Special Training Platoon. First Lieutenant Victor H. ("Brute") Krulak, then the assistant intelligence officer of the 4th Marines, described Red Mike's impact on the regiment. "Edson injected dynamism into his office—training programs, training inspections, exercises. He had a great deal of input into the training schedule—a real breath of fresh air." The major's success was evident in his longevity in the R-3 billet. When Colonel J. C. Fegan took over the 4th Marines in October 1938, he kept Edson on in the job.

The increased pace of training in 1938 did not turn the Shanghai garrison life into an endless grind of work. Edson started out his day at 0800 and was usually done by 1600. As the Japanese and the westerners settled into their uneasy standoff, the city's nightlife regained a veneer of its old gaiety. The return of military families in December 1937 contributed to the sense of normality. Before long the officers and their wives had reestablished the social practices of the prewar period. There was a constant round of parties, bridge games, and other entertainments. Hardly an evening passed without the Edsons going out or having someone over to the apartment. In the process, Red Mike developed friendships with a number of foreign officers, though he was most partial to the British.

The frequent lunches and dinners eventually had an undesired effect. By the end of 1938 Edson had regained the weight he had lost due to his ulcer diet and was up to an unprecedented 148 pounds. The stomach pains had disappeared for the most part, though, and his only medical problem was a recurring rash on his face from playing mah-jongg, a Chinese game using small wooden tiles. It turned out that the varnish was made from a vine related to the poison ivy family.

In January 1939 Edson learned that the commandant had slated him to relieve Ashurst in a few months as the inspector of Target Practice at HQMC. Red Mike had hoped to use some of his remaining time in China to see more of the country, but a lack of funds prohibited that. Instead, he made an "observation trip" up the Yangtze with a few other officers of the regiment. They boarded the Navy gunboat *Luzon* (PR-7) on 10 April and sailed to Nanking and then fifty miles beyond that to Wuhu. There was a vacation atmosphere, with visits to the Ming tombs and Sun Yat-sen's mausoleum, and some duck hunting off the bow of the ship. There also was surreptitious study of Japanese activity.

That experience added to Edson's store of knowledge of the Japanese, which was considerable after watching their combat operations at close range in the summer of 1937. Opinion varied on the capabilities of these potential opponents. Krulak thought they were "professional, disciplined, serious, and competent." An Army officer echoed the belief that the Japanese were "an efficient fighting machine." The 4th Marines newspaper had expressed a more contemptuous view in October 1937: "We cannot but wonder just how much of a war it would be if the contestants knew how to use the implements they have at their command."

Edson looked at the Japanese effort from a much wider perspective. "Each additional mile of coastline they take, each mile they advance inland, increases the difficulty of their supply problems—makes them more and more vulnerable and susceptible to defeat in detail. . . . Over a million and a half [Japanese] troops are over here now, and many more will be necessary, and the war has only begun." Red Mike's January 1938 prediction, that the continent would be like quicksand for the Japanese, was prophetic. Seven years later more than a million men still would be trying to subdue the Chinese even as American forces closed in on the Japanese homeland.

During his tour in Shanghai Edson got acquainted with more than potential enemies and allies. The 4th Marines was blessed with some of the finest young officers in the Corps. Several would be generals someday: Krulak, Capt. Robert E. Hogaboom, Capt. Wallace M. Greene, Jr., Capt. Robert H. Williams, and 1st Lt. Herman N. Nickerson. Greene, a native of Burlington and Edson's assistant in the plans and training shop, would end up as commandant of the Marine Corps. Lieutenant Colonel Clifton B. Cates, the new commander of the 2d Battalion and a hero from the World War, was a future commandant, too.

Red Mike continued to build his own reputation in the Corps. Just before his departure from China, the admiral sent letters of commendation to Fegan and Price for their handling of the Shanghai crisis. He asked that the colonels forward copies of the document to subordinates meriting recognition. Price singled out Edson for special praise in an endorsement sent to headquarters. "Due to his position and to devotion to duty, initiative, energy, intelligence, tact, and professional ability displayed by him, [he] was outstandingly the most valuable officer on my staff." When Red Mike checked out of the 4th Marines, his orders bore the standard formula: "Detached with regret." Before Fegan signed them, he penned in the word "much."

The trip home was much more pleasant for Edson than his voyage to China. At the end of this journey he wrote Mary a buoyant letter about smooth sailing and agreeable weather. His love for Lillian was undiminished, but the bitterness and cold indifference he had directed toward Ethel in the summer of 1937 were gone, never to reappear. The family arrived in San Francisco late in May. They purchased an Oldsmobile sedan and drove to Washington, D.C., where Edson reported to headquarters before taking leave and heading to Vermont. The week he spent there would be his last real vacation for years to come.

In 1939 Headquarters Marine Corps was located on Constitution Avenue at 18th Street, between the Lincoln Memorial and the Washington Monument. The large stone and glass structure, known as the Main Navy Building, looked more like a warehouse or a factory than an office complex. It was one of several buildings thrown up during the emergency expansion of the military for the World War. The staffs of the sea services had been there ever since.

Headquarters was not a large entity (at that time the entire Marine Corps numbered barely nineteen thousand officers and men), but it suffered from poor organization. It was a relic from an era when the Corps was a much smaller collection of ships' detachments and Navy Yard guards. Brigadier generals headed the three largest staff sections: Adjutant and Inspector (A & I), Paymaster, and Quartermaster. A colonel headed the Operations and Training Division, later renamed Plans and Policies. There was no chief of staff to coordinate their efforts, and competing sections jealously guarded prerogatives carved out in the past with no regard for logic. Reorganizations in the late 1930s had sometimes made things worse. Edson's billet, inspector of Target Practice, was one of those anomalies. His primary duties concerned marksmanship, clearly a training function, but his shop was in the A & I division. The byzantine nature of headquarters politics would cause him many headaches before his tour was through.

The target practice job was not an obscure one in the post–World War Corps. The current commandant, Maj. Gen. Thomas Holcomb, had held it from 1915 to 1917. He also had fired on the first Marine squad to win the National Trophy Rifle Team Match in 1911. His personal office in Main Navy now housed all the trophies won by Marine shooters over the years. His considerable interest in marksmanship was a fact of potential importance in bureaucratic battles, though there was no certainty it would help Red Mike. The commandant had to balance all the interests of the Corps, and he himself had shifted the Target Practice office from Plans and Policies to A & I in a recent reorganization of headquarters.

One of Edson's first tasks was to get the Marine Corps's competitive marksmanship program back on track. The 1937 team had won a fifth straight National Trophy Rifle Team Match while he was in Shanghai, but the 1938 team had lost for the first time since 1929. The 1939 shooting season was already well under way by the time the new inspector of Target Practice got his feet on the ground. He watched the team practice for two days at Wakefield, and then reported to Camp Perry, where the Army officer in charge assigned him at the last minute to be the assistant range officer. That was no small job. Perry's four side-by-side rifle ranges boasted 378 targets and a firing line that stretched for nearly a mile.

The Marines fielded a strong team and did well in many matches, including putting all 160 shots in the bull's-eye for a perfect team score in the thousand-yard Herrick competition. But they faltered again in the premier National Trophy match. That result "shocked" Ashurst, Edson's predecessor, but he absolved Red Mike of any blame. "If there was a way we could get all our teams in the stage of training and mental attitude you had your 1936 team we would win by fifty points or more every year. The 1936 team was the best team I ever saw in the eleven years I have been at Camp Perry. It was not luck either but excellent leadership and the proper technique in training."

There was drama of another sort that year. During the course of the matches, Germany invaded Poland and war broke out between the major European powers. Before the last shot went downrange at Perry, President Franklin D. Roosevelt declared neutrality and a limited national emergency. He also authorized an expansion of the Marine Corps to twenty-five thousand men, which had a significant personal impact on Edson. The 1938 promotion board had looked at twenty-two majors and selected four for elevation to lieutenant colonel. The board meeting in November 1939 picked thirty majors for advancement, one of them Red Mike. He took his promotion exams in January 1940 and passed them with ease. The doctors found no trace of his ulcer, and Colonel Price headed the board evaluating his professional qualifications. Edson pinned on the silver oak leaves of a lieutenant colonel in April 1940, just four years after his last promotion.

Duties in the Target Practice office were normally not too onerous, but senior officers were not content to let Red Mike rest. Headquarters regularly assigned him to teams inspecting Marine facilities around the country; each trip took several days. In addition, he sat on a number of enlisted promotion boards. He also became involved in the process of picking a replacement for the venerable Springfield rifle. Ashurst noted the increased responsibilities. "You have had a hard job so far in Target Practice and much more work and different than when I took over the job."

One other additional duty occupied a large share of Red Mike's time during his first year at headquarters. Even before Edson had reported aboard, the commandant had assigned him to a board to revise *Small Wars Operations.* The senior member was Rupertus, now a colonel commanding the Marine Barracks in Washington. The other members were Maj. Vernon M. Guymon, the aviation officer in the War Plans section, and Maj. Ernest E. Linsert, secretary of the Marine Corps Equipment Board. The four men were to complete their effort by the end of the calendar year.

In the past such a task would have fallen to the Marine Corps Schools in Quantico, the organization that had created the doctrine in the first place. Holcomb, however, was not inclined to follow the niceties of staff procedure; instead, he made regular use of ad hoc boards established for particular purposes. The officers he selected for the small-wars assignment had a wide range of experience in the field. Rupertus had served in Haiti from 1919 to 1922. As a major then, he had held senior billets as inspector of constabulary and as chief of police in the capital. Linsert spent time in Nicaragua in 1932 as the brigade intelligence officer just prior to the Marine withdrawal. Guymon was one of the pilots who flew in support of the Coco Patrol.

Several things conspired to make Edson the most important member of the board. Only he had any experience in combat on the ground in a small war. He also was best suited by inclination, since he had considerable interest in doctrine in the field and in writing. (He now had several articles in the *Gazette* to his credit and had been a member of that journal's editorial board for the past few years.) Moreover, Rupertus spent most of the winter of 1939–40 in the Caribbean as chief umpire for the annual Fleet Landing Exercise, and Linsert's role in the development of new landing craft kept him preoccupied throughout this period. The board members were so busy that they hardly accomplished anything before their deadline expired.

Red Mike went to work on the manual in January 1940. He hoped to complete his effort in a few weeks, but it stretched into late June with many postmidnight sessions in his office at Main Navy. The result was an entirely new book, the *Small Wars Manual,* which bore little resemblance to its predecessor in either organization or content. Evidence indicates that most of the 1940 version, if not all of it, was a product of Edson's personal efforts. His influence certainly was overwhelming in the tactical sections, which reflected his often-uncommon views. For instance, the new manual counseled against reconnaissance by fire and the use of automatic weapons by the point man of a patrol—heretical ideas that Red Mike had been espousing since 1929. The book took a number of passages verbatim from his previous writings, both published and private. He even wrote the chapter on aviation, as well as the introductory material on the work of the staff.

The manual was a tour de force for what amounted to a one-man board. Regrettably, it also was irrelevant even before it went to the printing press. The Marine Corps was gearing up for a major conventional war and would soon be shunting the *Small Wars Manual* out of its mount-out boxes and into museums. Red Mike's effort did not go completely to waste, however. It added to his already considerable reputation as a tactician and marked him as an authority in the field of unconventional doctrine.

Edson's stock in the shooting world continued to rise, too. Shortly after the 1939 National Matches, members of the NRA elected him to a seat on the board of directors. A few months later the Marine Corps assigned him to be its representative on the NBPRP. During the same period he worked to inject new dynamism into his service's competitive shooting program. One of his methods was to require each battalion in the Corps to field a team in the qualifying matches, with at least one novice shooter (known as a tyro) on each team. That change boosted interest and participation in the program, and developed some fresh faces for the Marine team. Ashurst thought it "the biggest improvement in the [Marine Corps] matches for years."

The 1940 rifle squad had all the makings of a winner, but there was concern after the two consecutive losses. Red Mike thought there was a tendency among the shooters "to blame everything except themselves for a poor score," and he made his opinion known to the team. Ashurst thought the pressure to succeed was making them work too hard; he urged Edson, the "past master in the art of applied psychology," to go to Perry and "help them out of it." The *Gazette* later reported that the ten men chosen for the National Trophy Match went out for a party prior to the competition to enhance their sense of being a team. That may have been the result of the "one or two suggestions" that Edson made to the team officials. In any case, the Marines finally recovered the prize trophy for rifle prowess. Red Mike had played his part again in restoring Marine Corps marksmanship to preeminence.

That success did not erase Edson's own doubts about the future of a more important aspect of shooting—the ability of the average Marine to hit his target. The continuing emergency was playing havoc with the marksmanship program. Part of it was the rapid increase in the size of the Corps. The earlier authorized expansion and the October 1940 activation of all Marine reserve ground units added ten thousand men to the rolls that year. While manpower exploded, ammunition grew scarce as production went into war reserves or overseas to aid various allies. During 1939 the Corps had dedicated four hundred fifty rounds of ammunition per man to recruit rifle training, three hundred for the annual requalification of every other Marine, and three hundred more for each man for field firing in combat problems. Faced with shortages in 1940, headquarters decreed a reduction in the allowance for recruits to one hundred rounds and for requalification to just sixty. Field firing remained at its previous level.

Edson vehemently opposed the change. He argued that the lack of initial training would never be rectified, especially with an even more limited requalification allowance. Although combat firing sounded like the right area to emphasize, it did nothing to teach a man how to hit a target, since no one received feedback from this type of shooting. Worse still, there was a movement afoot among some senior Marines "near the throne" to incorporate field-type firing within the qualification course itself, so that even fewer rounds would be dedicated to actual marksmanship training. Red Mike thought the real solution to the problem lay in diverting ammunition from automatic-weapons allowances to rifle firing, and from field firing to qualification courses. His efforts met with some success. He managed to maintain the normal shooting schedule for lieutenants at the Basic School and won a promise from the commandant to reestablish the old program for recruits the following year.

Red Mike was deeply involved in another major debate in 1940 that reverberated beyond the halls of headquarters. This one concerned the procurement of a new rifle. The Army had chosen the semiautomatic M1 Garand in 1936, but the Marine Corps was still wedded to the bolt-action Springfield. With the demands of the European war and American military expansion outstripping readily available production capacity, the government ordered an end to the manufacture of the outmoded M1903. The Corps now had to pick its successor. The Garand was the obvious choice because of the benefits of commonality with the Army. In fact, the Corps had already outfitted one unit, Ashurst's 1st Battalion, 6th Marines, with M1s in 1939 to test the new rifle.

The problem was that most Marine small-arms experts disliked the gas-operated Garand, which had significant problems that its manufacturer had so far not corrected. The other candidates were a gas-operated Winchester model and a recoil-operated weapon developed by Melvin Johnson, a Marine reservist from Boston. In addition to his natural ties to the Corps, Johnson possessed a considerable amount of clout in Massachusetts political circles. Moreover, his weapon's revolutionary design promised to be more accurate and more rugged than the Garand. The Army was disconcerted by the Marine interest in a different rifle. Production of a new weapon would divert manufacturing resources from the M1 and slow the Army's conversion to its chosen design. It might even call into question the wisdom of the Army's choice, with possibly even more dire consequences for that service's future procurement.

The issue drew high-level attention. In May 1940 the Senate held hearings on a bill to adopt the Johnson as the standard rifle for all services. The Corps sent Red Mike to testify before the Senate Committee on Military Affairs. He told the senators that it was Marine Corps policy to follow the Army lead in procurement, *if* the weapons were suitable for landing operations. He explained that the expected additional durability of the Johnson could make a difference in that respect, though there had been no field comparison tests yet: "And, after all, that is the final test of any piece." Seven Army witnesses all argued against any government purchases of the Johnson rifle. In private, Edson thought that the Johnson might be the better weapon, but he expected that it was "too late" to overcome the entrenched Garand.

The Senate bill languished in committee, but the Marine Corps took definitive action in late 1940. In accordance with his usual habit, the commandant bypassed the Equipment Board and formed a special task group to evaluate the three candidate rifles and compare them with the Springfield. Newly promoted Colonel Ashurst headed the effort, which consisted of extensive practical testing. Edson, one of two other experienced shooters assigned to assist Ashurst, designed the tests and went to San Diego for two months to conduct them. The program was a challenging one. The Marines fired the weapons under various extreme conditions: after dragging them through the surf and across a beach, after letting them sit under a sprinkler for fourteen hours, after submersing them in seawater for ten hours, and so on. At the end of four weeks of testing, each weapon had fired twelve thousand rounds, equivalent to several years of normal use.

The results indicated that the Springfield was more rugged than any of the three semiautomatics, but the Garand showed up best over its two similar competitors. The Winchester suffered because it was so new the manufacturer had yet to work out all the bugs. The problems with the Johnson centered on the number of breakdowns during the test. Edson thought that may have been due to factors other than poor design. All the other test weapons were factory fresh, whereas the two Johnson models already had fired more than ten thousand rounds in earlier demonstrations and were badly worn. The board's January 1941 report recommended procurement of the Garand, and the commandant accepted it in February.

That was not the end of the matter, since Winchester and Johnson both hoped to sell their weapons overseas, but the War Department moved to withhold their access to the necessary machine tools. The Army also selectively leaked portions of the report supporting the M1 and making its competitors appear to be "entirely unsuitable for military use." The Marine Corps preferred to remain silent, but Edson convinced his seniors to let him publish a more accurate summary of the tests in the NRA's magazine and in the *Gazette*. Once the commandant decided to purchase the M1, the Army allocated a large portion of its monthly production to the Corps. Edson thought it was an attempt to "saddle it on us before the thing proves unfit in the field, before we change our minds." This was Red Mike's introduction to the workings of Congress and the political savvy of the War Department; the experience would stand him in good stead in the future.

Edson's work on the West Coast in the winter of 1940–41 may have settled the rifle controversy, but opponents of marksmanship at headquarters took advantage of his prolonged absence to launch a new effort against the shooting program. The main thrust of their proposal was a change in the qualification course to just thirty shots, with twenty of those devoted to field-type firing. Red Mike's assistant acquiesced in stopping requalification firing altogether rather than changing the course of fire. At the same time, Plans and Policies deleted all ammunition for any form of marksmanship competition from unit supply requests. The commandant also decided that the Corps would hold no qualifying matches for the year. The Marines were not alone in this regard. The Army already had announced its intention to forgo participation in the National Matches, cease requalification firing, and end the special payments for rifle qualification.

Much of the opposition to marksmanship training came from Plans and Policies, particularly from one officer, Col. Thomas E. Watson. He was a small man, shorter than Red Mike, but he had a temper that was "fiery and monumental." He had served in the pre–World War Corps as a junior NCO and bore the nickname "Little Corporal." His acerbic personality was encompassed in his other monicker, "Terrible Tommy." Edson had been dueling with him for some time. In early 1940 Red Mike had submitted a recommendation for the reauthorized use of campaign covers, the wide-brimmed hats that provided excellent protection from the sun, an especially important feature for troops working on the shadeless rifle ranges. He sent the proposal up the chain of command without first getting the concurrence of Plans and Policies. Watson, then the acting head of that division, briefly squelched the attempt because he had not been consulted beforehand. Edson eventually got the campaign covers approved, but Watson remained a steadfast opponent of anything related to marksmanship.

Red Mike fought a running battle to preserve as much of the marksmanship program as he could, but he lost more and more often. He believed that a man's confidence as a fighter began with his ability to hit a target with his basic weapon, the rifle. If Marines lacked that capability and confidence in themselves as individuals, that was a step backward toward the massed formation tactics of an earlier era, when a single soldier was meaningless because he could not hit anything with his musket. Ashurst agreed that "hits per gun per minute is firepower, not the number of shots. . . . The troops here are learning to ride in boats, etc., but they know little about shooting." Edson thought the changes were "criminal." His inability to make an impact on policy left him with the feeling that "I might as well give up my job!"

The infighting at headquarters only added to Red Mike's other worries, which continued to center on Lillian and money. His pay barely covered the monthly expenses of his family and parents, and he had little in the way of investments to show for more than two decades of work. His assets outweighed his debts at the end of 1939, but most of what he had consisted of the cash value of life insurance policies. His savings account held just $91.26. When a senior official at the NRA retired in the spring of 1941, Edson thought wistfully of resigning his commission to take the job, since that income plus his retirement pay would be more than he could ever hope to earn in the Corps. That was not an option, of course, with the country confronting a possible war.

Lillian was by far the worse problem. She lived in Chicago now and he saw her only rarely. They managed to get together in New York for a visit to the 1939 World's Fair, and he took time out from the 1940 National Matches to meet her in Dearborn, Michigan. He also stopped in Chicago for a few days on his return trip from the West Coast in February 1941. In the long interludes he wrote her nearly every day.

Although he missed Lillian a great deal, he was most concerned with her unhappy marriage and what he should do about it. His options were limited. Under the divorce laws then common in the United States, one could not initiate proceedings to dissolve a marriage unless he or she could establish that the spouse had done something to destroy what the state had sanctioned. The acceptable grounds for divorce were all disreputable: adultery, drunkenness, mental cruelty, insanity, and so forth. Thus he could bring an action for divorce against Ethel only if he accused her of some heinous conduct and proved it in court. Even then, if she did not want to be divorced, she could stop the proceedings by making counterallegations. If she could prove them, the court would not grant a divorce, since the party asking for it had to be free of any blame for the failed marriage.

Edson had no desire to hurt Ethel in that way, but that left him unable to help Lillian. The dilemma caused him considerable mental anguish. "Am terribly worried about [Lillian] and know not what to do—knowing all the time what I want to do. But how?" He felt the pressure even more because she placed such high expectations on him, a fact he kept before him with a quote from one of her letters inscribed in the front of his diary. "Remember I love you and that you are the most important thing in life. Don't ever let me be disappointed." As time passed, he increasingly berated himself for his inability to solve the problem. "Two letters from Lillian today—the second one so blue and downcast— and so disappointed in me. Please, dear God, make me worthy of her and do not let me fail her." "She left Dearborn today for Chicago and hell-worry, while I, louse that I am, stay here, loving her and yet doing nothing about it." "What an existence! Living a coward's life because it is the easiest thing to do, while loving someone else who is actually dying because of me!!"

The constant worry, coupled with long hours devoted to various Marine projects, continued to affect his health. His weight ballooned to 160 pounds, he felt exhausted all the time, and his nerves were "absolutely on edge." A series of minor ailments plagued him: hives, stomachaches, headaches, and bad colds. He felt a complete lack of "ambition or pep." Despite his unhappiness and the physical symptoms, he made every effort to maintain a normal life at home and at work. He treated Ethel with respect. He spent time introducing Bobby to some of the more fascinating things in the capital (a dirigible ride one weekend, the top of the Washington Monument on another). He helped Austin reach his decision to enroll in Georgetown's School of Foreign Service. To his family and to most of the outside world he was a good husband and father.

The difficulties in his personal life and at HQMC continued to weigh heavily on Edson. By spring 1941 he seemed to be fighting "daily battles" with Watson. The latest blowup involved the new allowance for marksmanship practice with the .45-caliber pistol; Plans and Policies had set it at a paltry eight rounds without consulting the Target Practice section. After yet another struggle, Red Mike got it raised to twenty rounds, still far below what he considered adequate. He did not fare so well against a "concerted effort" by Plans and Policies to wipe out the last vestiges of the competitive marksmanship program. In an April 1941 letter to Ashurst, then heading to China duty, Edson closed with the lament, "Needless to say, I would much prefer to be out there with you than sitting here under the conditions which exist." He was much closer to getting his wish than he realized.

Chapter 8

"Our Flag's Unfurled to Every Breeze"

O n Tuesday, 27 May 1941, Edson had a welcome visitor in his office at Main Navy. Captain Krulak, now an aide to Maj. Gen. Holland Smith, commander of the 1st Marine Division, told Red Mike that Smith would like to get Edson down to Quantico, where "things were moving rapidly." At lunch the next day Krulak said that the general was hoping to get the major general commandant to approve his release from HQMC. Edson immediately started working the levers of the bureaucracy on his own behalf. He put the question of his transfer directly to the general in charge of personnel matters and suggested that Col. Littleton Waller, Jr., would make an excellent replacement. Waller, a former team shooter, was retired and presently employed by the NRA.

The morning of 2 June was a whirlwind. Smith himself called to tell Edson that he wanted him specifically for command of a rifle battalion. Waller dropped by to give his assent to recall to active duty. Before noontime the commandant approved Red Mike's transfer with a date of detachment just two days hence. The news invigorated Edson's flagging morale. Not only would he be escaping the dreaded halls of Main Navy (his "two most unsatisfactory years . . . spent in the Corps"), but the division commander had promised him 1st Battalion, 5th Marines. The 5th Marines had a long history of distinction reaching back to the legendary battle at Belleau Wood in World War I. Since then the 1st Battalion had been commanded by people such as Leroy P. Hunt, a hero of Belleau Wood; Archer Vandegrift, now the assistant commandant; and Harold Utley, Edson's mentor in Nicaragua. His regimental commander would be his old friend Robert Blake.

There was something else special about the unit; it was "a rubber boat outfit embarked on APDs." In recent months the 1st Marine Division had conducted some amphibious training with small units landing from inflatable craft. Although the initial tests were done with three companies, one from each battalion of the 7th Marines, the Corps now intended to consolidate and enlarge that experiment by turning it over to 1/5. That battalion would work exclusively with a special Navy detachment of destroyer transports (designated as APDs). These ships were World War I vintage flush-deck, four-stack destroyers that had been in mothballs since 1922. The Navy had just finished converting six of them by removing two boilers and their associated stacks, which left a small hold amidships for cargo and troops. The addition of davits for hoisting and storing four landing craft completed the job. The high speed and small size of these vessels made them ideal for conducting raid operations. The 1st Battalion, 5th Marines, would be no ordinary outfit, and it would need an extraordinary commander to mold it along fresh lines.

General Smith never revealed why he picked Edson for the job. He knew Red Mike from their common tour in Philadelphia, and they overlapped briefly at headquarters in 1939, but they had never been close associates. It is possible that the division commander gave Blake a free hand to choose his own people, and Edson would have fit the bill as a trusted friend of many years. However, Smith's personal intervention in the assignment process would indicate that he made the selection. Since Edson was not a friend, the general's choice must have been based on capability. Red Mike had demonstrated his courage and aggressiveness in Nicaragua. He was a noted tactical thinker, particularly in the field of small wars, which were often much like raids; he was one of the top weapons experts in the Corps; and he was a proven leader who could get the most out of men when the going was rough.

Edson reported to Quantico on Saturday, 7 June 1941, a little worse for wear from years of staff duty. He was overweight and did not have the physical conditioning that had allowed him to range at will across the rough hills of the Coco River basin. Though his body may have been a bit weak, Edson was definitely willing and ready to command again. As some of the troops got their first hands-on experience with an APD on Monday morning, Edson called all the officers to a conference. He introduced himself, talked with them for a while, and then reassigned several of them to new jobs. As if to emphasize his own dedication to the task, he moved into the duty officer's room in the barracks so he would not have to waste time commuting from Washington. The next day the battalion implemented a new organization that would allow it to fit companies aboard the confined spaces of the APDs. If it was not clear to the men before, they knew now that they had a new commander and that they were going to be different from any other battalion in the Corps.

The reorganization of 1/5 was largely tactical in nature. While in garrison, the battalion would maintain the standard setup of three rifle companies (A, B, and C), a machine-gun company (D), and a headquarters company (which included an 81mm mortar platoon). At the time of embarkation aboard ship, 1/5 would rearrange itself into six reinforced rifle units (RRUs), one for each of the available APDs. Each RRU consisted of half a rifle company (one and a half platoons), a section of two water-cooled heavy machine guns from Dog Company, a section of two 81mm mortars, and a share of headquarters.

Other than breaking up companies and platoons, the only significant change to the standard organization of a rifle battalion was the addition of eight 81mm mortars (for a total of twelve), forty men to man them, and sixteen communicators. The new grouping was not intended as a mere administrative convenience for purposes of shipboard life, however, since orders specified that RRUs be prepared to act independently in a landing from an APD, as a reinforced company if landed from two APDs, or as a rump battalion if landed from a division of three APDs. Action ashore as a complete battalion was just another option and by no means the standard one.

If the orders were precise in specifying how the new APD battalion should be organized, higher echelons were much less informative about its purpose. For weeks to come Edson operated on assumptions regarding his potential missions. He saw his unit performing reconnaissance, feints, raids, secondary landings, diversions, covering operations, or attacks on the enemy's rear area. The lack of direction from seniors may have been more the result of uncertainty rather than inattention. Just two weeks before Edson took on his new assignment, two junior officers at Parris Island received word that they would form "mobile landing units" for use from APDs. They set about drafting tables of organization from scratch, only to have the orders canceled at the end of May. The sudden switch in name to reinforced rifle units, the shift in locale from Parris Island to Quantico, and the absence of a doctrinal mission all point to a hasty, ill-defined decision. The rationale for altering 1/5 may have been based largely on the need to utilize the six available APDs at a time when the Navy had precious few transports for amphibious operations, though the creation of the RRUs indicates that there were tactical considerations at work as well.

Edson's battalion was not alone in adapting to change in mid-1941. The entire Marine Corps was undergoing a transformation. As manpower authorizations increased in preparation for war, reservists and recruits streamed into the service. In February 1941 Holland Smith had read out orders changing his 1st Marine Brigade into the largest unit the Corps had ever fielded, the 1st Marine Division. At that time it consisted of the veteran 5th Marines, the month-old 7th Marines, and the just-created 1st Marines. The latter remained largely a paper organization for many months to come; the division boasted only a few thousand men, well below its authorized strength of fifteen thousand. A similar metamorphosis occurred on the West Coast, with the 2d Marine Brigade becoming a division, too. Other new units began to spring up in response to various perceived or actual needs, everything from parachutists to barrage balloons to defense battalions. It was a time of tremendous ferment and experimentation, so the inception of the APD battalion drew little notice.

Change was afoot at even higher levels. In June the Army assented to creation of a joint corps, to consist of the 1st Marine Division and the Army's 1st Infantry Division. Extending interservice cooperation even further, the Army also consented to put the organization under command of Major General Smith. Its mission was primarily training, but as war drew nearer, it became more concerned with possible contingency operations in defense of the Western Hemisphere. After a series of redesignations, it became known as the Amphibious Force Atlantic Fleet (AFAF).

The understrength 1st Marine Division had spent the winter of 1940–41 in the Caribbean participating in landing exercises with the fleet and had just returned to Quantico in spring. During that time the Corps had scoured the Atlantic Coast for a more suitable base, one that was roomy enough for its growing formations and readily accessible from the sea for amphibious maneuvers. Officers found just such a location in North Carolina at the mouth of the New River and purchased 110,000 acres of land. The site lacked all the requirements of a base, from barracks to roads to rifle ranges, but the Marines determined to put it to immediate use. Smith scheduled his two divisions for amphibious exercises and shore maneuvers at New River, with the APD battalion to lead the way at the end of June.

Edson's first days with the battalion had been busy ones. He got acquainted with the APDs as they arrived one by one at Quantico. He participated in a regimental command post exercise, worked with his staff on plans for embarkation and operations, and inspected the units to ensure that their uniforms and equipment were ready to go. Many nights he was in his office till very late, though he made time to get up to Washington to see Austin's school play and graduation. The family also came down to stay with the Blakes for a few days so they could see a bit more of him. The last APD anchored off Quantico on 17 June and the battalion began embarkation. With that task complete on the nineteenth, Edson called his officers together on the dock and stressed their responsibilities and the importance of the upcoming training. For some reason, however, sailing was delayed for several days. He used the time to swim in the base pool to begin the process of getting into shape, and he took the battalion ashore for a twelve-mile hike, culminating in an advance guard problem and selection of defensive positions.

The flotilla of APDs finally got underway on 25 June and arrived at New River on the twenty-seventh. On alternate days the battalion landed in the morning, trained ashore for a while, and then went back to the ships in the evening. Heavy seas made it difficult to climb down the nets from the tossing destroyers to the landing boats. Once ashore, the troops found a troublesome terrain of thick woods heavily populated by mosquitoes and ticks. Most of the time it rained. After several days the APDs made a port visit in Charleston for fuel. Despite the risk, Edson arranged liberty and a special pay for his men, and ended up with an expected handful of absentees when the flotilla departed the next day.

Things were little better upon the return to New River. Heavy rain delayed H hour for a night landing, and then high winds forced one of the APDs to drag anchor once the landing craft were finally launched. When the distressed ship signaled the rest of the squadron, many of the boat crews interpreted the flashing lights as a recall. Edson made it ashore in the driving rain with just two platoons.

Sunny days seemed little better. A sixteen-mile hike from the coast inland to the emerging tent camp took more than six hours, an average time for men on foot, but in the process a large number of Marines failed to keep up with the formation. The battalion had to send seventeen men back to the ship with sunstroke or sore feet. At 0500 the next morning Edson had the troops up and on the way back. This time they took a shorter route and there were fewer stragglers, but the pace was much slower. To his chagrin he found "this outfit is certainly in very poor condition at the moment."

On 11 July "the armada" arrived: the ten large transports carrying the 7th Marines, the rest of the 5th Marines, and portions of the 1st Infantry Division. Up to this point 1/5 had been operating by itself and reporting directly to the 1st Marine Division headquarters. Now it reverted to the customary role of another element in a regiment. Blake, anxious to get a look at one of his units in action, decided to accompany 1/5 in a night landing scheduled for 0300 on the fifteenth. The weather was rough again and the battalion missed its assigned beach by almost a mile. Edson found the error more than a little disconcerting, since his men stormed ashore directly in front of Smith's quarters. In addition, a sailor died in a mishap on the beach.

The fouled-up operation highlighted some of the shortcomings of the Higgins boat, the relatively new landing craft that was the mainstay of the amphibious assault. Each of these wooden boats carried a platoon of infantry. Their flat bottoms made them good beaching craft; on the run into shore two ring-mounted machine guns in the bows were available for suppressive fire. The boats were not sturdy enough to operate in rough weather, however, and suffered significant damage every time they nestled against the bobbing APDs. A model with a bow ramp was only just coming into production, so most passengers had to debark by jumping over the side. Manhandling supplies out of them was even more difficult. In addition, their compasses were designed poorly and prone to malfunctions, and there was a severe shortage of experienced crewmen to operate the growing fleet. It was just about impossible to conduct an efficient landing under these conditions.

Red Mike's string of bad luck did not end there. On 16 July the regiment was to conduct a demonstration landing for the secretary of the Navy. The APD battalion braved yet another stormy passage ashore, only to find out upon reaching the beach that force headquarters had canceled the exercise. After two more days of rough weather and disrupted operations, the squadron put into Charleston Navy Yard for a much-needed rest. In an effort to get the troops off the crowded "tin cans," Edson disembarked the battalion and began to set up a tent camp. Even this went awry, as a heavy rainstorm soaked all the men's bedding and gear before they could complete their temporary homes.

More bad news followed when Smith's chief of staff, Col. Graves B. Erskine, arrived in Charleston. A member of the battalion had written his congressman and complained about the stark living conditions aboard the crowded destroyer transports; the result was a high-level investigation. Erskine spent a day interviewing troops and found their grievances justified. The Marine compartment on each ship housed more than a hundred men but had just four washbasins, which had running water for only brief periods in the morning and evening. There were saltwater showers on some vessels but none on the others. One ship limited each Marine to two baths per week, to be accomplished with no more than two buckets of fresh water.

The living space was nothing more than an empty compartment, with no bunks and insufficient floor space for all the men to lie down at once. Erskine discovered that the ventilation was inadequate when the compartment was empty and suspected that it had been insufferable when troops were crowded aboard. Men often slept on the deck in the rain just to escape the fetid air. No fresh bedding had been issued during the month-long stay on the ships, nor had there been an opportunity to wash it. For appearance's sake, Navy officers forbad the hanging of wet clothes anywhere, so men had been forced to put sweaty, rain-soaked field uniforms in their seabags. The small Marine living spaces were further crowded by mounds of bulk supplies that had overflowed from the equally cramped stowage holds.

Not surprisingly, Erskine thought morale was very low in the unit and recommended substantial changes. Some necessitated structural improvements to the ships; others required the Navy to rethink its responsibilities toward its Marine passengers. Simple creature comforts such as mess tables, cafeteria trays, and wash buckets quickly appeared on the Charleston docks. The battalion also transferred most of its supplies to other ships to free up space in the living compartments. The force headquarters canceled a scheduled training stint and sent the APDs and their embarked Marines south to Miami for two days of liberty. A few unlucky souls had not stuck around long enough to hear about that positive development; when the unit sailed from Charleston, Edson had to report a further twenty-eight absentees.

The small flotilla arrived off New River again on 3 August and rejoined the main task force. Edson participated in staff conferences with force headquarters on the battleship *Wyoming* (BB-32) and with division on the transport *Barnett* (APA-5), all in preparation for a major amphibious exercise to begin the next day. Red Mike and his men would not go ashore until D+2 (two days after the initial landing), since they were the corps reserve, but it was obvious that their role in the operation would be an important one. In confirmation of its unique status as the APD unit, the battalion was an addressee on the operations order, a privilege otherwise reserved for division-level commands (and the fledgling 1st Parachute Battalion). In effect, 1/5 was no longer fully subordinate to its parent regiment. Force headquarters even took to calling it the "light battalion" and separating it out from the other five infantry battalions of the 1st Marine Division when making various reports.

The two-division operation, probably the largest amphibious exercise conducted by the United States up to that time, demonstrated that the Navy's capabilities were still closer to the concept stage than to reality. During the course of the entire first day, the task force was able to put ashore just one battalion from each regiment. The second day was a repeat of the first, so that at the end of forty-eight hours the regiments still had just two-thirds of their fighting strength available on the beach. Red Mike spent D day developing his plan with the battalion staff and then called his company commanders together for a conference to issue the order. Their mission was in line with the special nature of the battalion. They would land at 0745 on D+2 at a point in the rear of enemy lines, advance overland, destroy the opposing reserve force, and take control of important lines of communication. To assist in the effort, the entire tank force of the 1st Marine Division (one company) and the 1st Parachute Battalion (itself still consisting of just one company) would be attached to 1/5. In order to enhance command and control, the RRUs would revert to the standard organization once ashore.

Edson's task force made it to the beach in good order for once and the mobile units achieved the desired surprise against their opponents. With support from the force's entire air contingent, they seized their objective and took fifty prisoners in the process. That night, as his men set up defensive positions in advance of friendly front lines, Red Mike could take comfort in something that finally went right. When the rest of the division caught up the next day, 1/5 reverted to regimental control and resumed the advance. For the next three days the force fended off attacks by scout cars, a parachute landing in its rear, and the ever-present mosquitoes. After a simulated fighting withdrawal, the Marines and soldiers began reembarkation. Red Mike, "thoroughly covered" with bug bites, finally made it back to his APD at 0300 on 10 August.

That marked the end of the exercise, and the various units began to make their way home. For some, that would no longer be the crowded base at Quantico. The 5th Regiment's 3d Battalion would temporarily stay at the Navy Yard in Norfolk pending a permanent return to New River, the ultimate destination for all units of the 1st Marine Division.

The hectic first ten weeks of command had taken Edson's mind off his personal troubles, but his return home brought them back to center stage. The APDs arrived in Quantico on 13 August and he dutifully went up to Washington to spend the night. He took time out to write Lillian, though, and to privately bemoan his unhappy state of affairs: "How I wish that it was she who had been waiting for me in Washington tonight—and every day and night!" If his heart was in Chicago, he nonetheless put his family first in more practical matters. During his time at sea he had taken the opportunity to make out a will in which he left some money to his parents and everything else to Ethel. The document was a normal precaution for a man on the verge of war, but it sent a chill through Austin when he received his copy.

The return to Quantico did not mark the start of a vacation. While his men settled into the brick barracks on the main part of the base, Edson took up residence in a tent located on the waterfront a few hundred yards away. Everyone kept busy cleaning gear and clothing, marching in battalion and regimental parades, and standing inspections. Red Mike spent much of the first week consulting with his officers and drafting a report on the recent exercises, which he expanded into an evaluation of the APD battalion concept. He catnapped for only a few hours in the course of a long weekend of writing and finished the rough draft near midnight on Sunday, 24 August. The unlucky duty clerk typed until dawn. The result was twenty-seven single-spaced pages of thoughts on what worked, what went wrong, and how it might be fixed.

The primary focus of Edson's epistle was the organization of the battalion. He began by noting the difficulties it posed aboard ship, since every unit was split between two or more vessels. Company commanders and first sergeants were not in a position to provide leadership to all of their men (a significant problem given the inexperience of many junior officers and NCOs in the rapidly expanding Corps), nor could they properly meet basic responsibilities, such as accounting for personnel and equipment. The machine-gun and headquarters companies had it worst, with elements of each spread among all six ships. This affected even Red Mike's staff, also dispersed throughout the squadron, and made it tough to plan an operation while at sea. Things were worse during the landing phase. The RRU was theoretically capable of independent operations, but if the battalion were to function as a whole, it could do so only when organized as a proper battalion. The mortars and machine guns needed to recombine to provide effective firepower, the staff needed to assemble into a command post (CP), and commanders needed to gain control of their split platoons and companies. This could be done only on the beach—a poor time to get organized if one were landing into the teeth of enemy opposition.

Red Mike next analyzed what the battalion was supposed to do. He assumed that its missions would involve reconnaissance, raids, and other special operations; in his mind his men were a waterborne version of the parachutists. As such they had to be lightly armed and extremely mobile. Furthermore, in fulfilling these duties they would undoubtedly be operating directly under force or division control. The current setup met none of these requirements. The APD battalion had even more weapons, equipment, and supplies than a regular battalion, so it was too heavy to be foot mobile.

At the same time, the nature of the APDs left the battalion with no organic motor transport, since none could be carried on the small ships. Thus it could move only by foot once ashore, an obvious contradiction. As an example, the mortar platoon had three times as many guns as normal, but only 50 percent more manpower. It could carry all its weapons but not a single round to shoot. Or it could carry ammunition, but only by leaving two-thirds of its guns behind. Furthermore, since the nature of the battalion's missions required it to operate independently, the regiment generally would be short one-third of its combat power, oftentimes during the initial assault when it would need that extra battalion the most. Edson concluded that "the idea of employing a standard infantry battalion as a permanent mobile landing group is unsound."

Based on his detailed critique, 1/5's commander recommended the creation of a unique battalion attached directly to force or division headquarters and specifically organized to operate from destroyer transports. He described three different proposals, but all were based on two considerations: first, that the units fit in the available space on board the APDs; second, that mobility supersede "heavy sustained firepower" as the primary ingredient of their combat power. In accordance with these guidelines, Red Mike's initial suggestion was a battalion consisting of a headquarters unit and five rifle companies. The latter were much like the recently adopted standard for regular rifle companies, except that the APD variant would give up one of its three rifle platoons and one Browning automatic rifle squad within each of the two remaining rifle platoons. On the plus side, it would have a beefed-up headquarters element with intelligence specialists, demolitions personnel, and a small shore party group to handle supplies.

Unlike the old rifle company organization presently used by 1/5, the new one also boasted a weapons platoon of two light machine guns and two 60mm mortars. The headquarters company was substantially pared down, to just eighty-six officers and men. Among the deletions was the entire 81mm mortar unit, so that the battalion's heaviest firepower now resided in the light machine guns and mortars of its rifle companies. Each of the six companies would occupy its own APD; Edson was willing to risk all of his command-and-control eggs in one basket in order to facilitate planning for operations. The resulting battalion would be light on its feet and ready to hit the shore fighting.

The remaining alternatives were variations on the same theme with increasing allowances of firepower. Organization number two traded off the fifth rifle company for a two-platoon machine-gun company with eight heavy guns. The third possibility maintained the additional machine guns and exchanged another rifle company for an 81mm mortar unit of four tubes. Both of the heavy-weapons organizations had a high ratio of men to guns so that they would have no trouble carrying adequate ammunition on foot. In either variation the new companies would each have their own APD and not be parceled out to the rifle companies while afloat. In Red Mike's eyes, the advantages of having concentrated firepower readily available to the battalion commander immediately upon landing outweighed the risks of losing a ship at sea. Edson noted that the options providing heavy-weapons units would increase the defensive firepower of the battalion. That his first choice was the all-rifle company organization indicates that he desired to emphasize offensive striking power, a conclusion in line with his assumption that the battalion would concentrate on raids and similar special operations. His provision for demolitions men further highlighted that point.

The battalion commander's concerns ranged far beyond mere reorganization. He noted the need for numerous improvements in equipment, especially the rubber boats, which would not stand up well under heavy use or enemy fire. Each boat could hold ten men sitting athwart the gunwales with their individual equipment piled in the center, but even something as small as a machine-gun cart was too bulky for the small craft. The outboard motors were notoriously unreliable, and even when they could be coaxed into running properly their top speed was just five knots. Their roar also carried for miles, which made stealth impossible. Paddling was quiet but even slower, and would quickly exhaust the men.

Among other things, Red Mike pressed for the provision of radios, which would allow the battalion to control close air support. At this point the planes operated from orders received before takeoff, or through a clumsy system of reading panels laid out on the ground by the infantry. He asked for the M1 rifle, since its higher rate of fire would compensate for the decreased number of men and weapons in his smaller companies. Not one to be parochial, he argued that the Marine Corps should adopt the Army's trucks and field kitchens, which were superior to their USMC counterparts. In a short but telling note, he recommended that the troops should be issued two canteens instead of one. (More than a year later, in the aftermath of Guadalcanal, he would still be pushing for this simple but important improvement.)

Another set of comments focused on tactics and training. Red Mike stressed the need for more frequent practice of night landings. "Any organization that can make a satisfactory night landing can land effectively under extremely adverse conditions during daylight hours." To do this, Navy boat crews needed to learn how to follow a compass heading. He also noted the unrealistic nature of some parts of the recent exercises.

Since the battalion lacked a shore party element, that duty had been performed by the cooks and messmen. Once they moved forward to fulfill their real mission, the simulated casualties that had been evacuated to the beach took over the job of unloading the landing craft. Last, he called for increasing emphasis on marching, an obvious requirement for a unit that would henceforth depend entirely on its feet for mobility.

As Edson's document worked its way up the chain of command, Smith was making his own report on the exercise to the commander in chief of the Atlantic Fleet. The general commented at length on 1/5's landing at Brown's Cove and referred to the APD battalion/tank/parachute/close air support combination as "a spearhead thrust around the hostile flank." This had been much more than a mere tactical response to a particular situation; the force commander had been testing what he saw as an innovation in amphibious doctrine. His experience indicated that the assault across the beach developed too slowly and was thus vulnerable to counterattack. To remedy this, he envisioned making future landings in three elements. The first wave would consist of a parachute regiment, an air infantry regiment, a light tank battalion, and "at least one APD battalion." These fast-moving forces could quickly seize the beachhead and secure it for the more ponderous units of the rest of the division, which would then do the yeoman's work of expanding the initial enclave. The third wave would consist of the reserve forces and service units. Edson's quest for a lighter, faster, independent organization thus dovetailed nicely with Smith's perceived requirements.

As these doctrinal issues swirled around the heads of concerned officers, most of the division focused on issues of more immediate practical concern. At a conference on 26 August Bob Blake announced plans for the move to the base at New River. The transfer would begin on 15 September, though it would take some time for all elements to concentrate at the wilderness site. In a sign that the APD Battalion was evolving beyond the experimental stage into a distinct entity, it would not be going to the new base at all, but would remain indefinitely at Quantico with force headquarters. In effect, the 5th Marines was becoming a two-battalion regiment. This split had its good and bad points. Since liberty spots and base amenities were nonexistent at New River, Edson saw it as "good news for the boys" of his battalion. From the point of view of the rest of the division, soon to be living in muddy tent camps, 1/5 was a pampered lot. Even senior leaders such as Lt. Col. Gerald Thomas, the division operations officer, felt that way; he derisively referred to the APD battalion as "the plaything of [force] headquarters."

While the rest of the division packed for its pending move, Red Mike turned his attention to training and leading his battalion, which was still a long way from meeting his rigid standards. A surprise visit at morning guard mount elicited the observation "Pretty lousy!" After inspecting one company's rifles he declared that one-third of them were unfit for firing. Most of his "wandering lads" had returned to the fold and he spoke to them for a few moments in the hope of preventing any recurrence of desertion. Many of them had turned themselves in at various posts (two enterprising men did so in California) and received government transportation to the base. Their commander, always looking for a tool to shape motivation, recommended that the Marine Corps deduct from their pay the cost of travel to Quantico. Two other Marines had gone home and then sent requests that they be discharged for family reasons. Edson wrote each in a firm tone and explained that they needed to return to duty before any action could be taken.

Red Mike concentrated most of his efforts on his junior leaders, both officers and NCOs. He instituted regular battalion-level schools for them. In addition to teaching them the basics of their jobs, he sought to prepare them for even greater responsibilities. Officers, for instance, learned all about the battalion operations section, even though that was a billet normally held by a major. Some got to temporarily move up and actually do the work. Even Maj. Edward F. Doyle, the executive officer, occasionally got to lead the battalion through its paces. In staff meetings the battalion commander sought to develop his subordinates by forcing them to do most of the talking. He opened each gathering by presenting the subject and then giving them the floor to discuss it and offer suggestions. When he had heard everything, he issued his decision, as often as not incorporating their ideas.

He was also willing to listen after he had made up his mind. During one field exercise an "enemy" patrol from one of the companies managed to capture and deflate all the rubber boats of the main force. Since reinflating the craft was difficult and time-consuming, Red Mike was angered by the resulting disruption of the training plan, and he ordered those responsible to perform the disagreeable task. Their company commander, Capt. Henry Cain, protested that Edson's punishment sent the wrong message to the troops, since the perpetrators had shown initiative and skill in accomplishing their mission. Edson relented and canceled the order; those who had failed to guard their boats suffered the consequences.

Red Mike practiced the same method in more informal settings, too. One Saturday two lieutenants clambered onto the train to Washington and were surprised to find their commander heading home by the same means.

He motioned for them to sit with him, then occupied the next fifty minutes eliciting their observations about the relative merits of light versus heavy mortars and the best personal weapon for those officers and enlisted men not armed with the rifle. Instead of giving them the "benefit" of his years of experience, he was genuinely interested in their ideas. The young officers found it a heady experience.

Invariably, every field exercise resulted in a detailed critique. The day after a battalion operation lasting a few hours, the officers and senior NCOs spent almost that much time appraising their performance exhaustively. Red Mike had an even more unusual method of evaluation. Due to his background in flying he had a keen appreciation of the role that air would play in battle, and he had the connections to make use of that knowledge. On occasion he arranged for planes to overfly the battalion during field exercises; the pilots were to try to spot the forces on the ground and take photographs to simulate enemy aerial reconnaissance. The results of the overflights were enlightening. One photo demonstrated just how difficult it could be to use camouflage in an effective manner. It revealed a neat row of dark green rectangles under the trees—pup tents outlined by their arrangement and the overuse of branches to conceal them. Red Mike continually stressed that units keep off the roads and trails and move instead through the woods. He developed in his own troops the wariness of aircraft that Sandino's men had exhibited along the Coco so many years before.

Edson made frequent trips to the Marine Corps Schools located on the base and borrowed their materials for classes and tactical problems. The latter sometimes involved force on force operations, with one part of the battalion simulating the enemy. Another common feature was land navigation. The officers and NCOs learned it individually at first, and then had to incorporate it into field exercises. As might be expected, the former team shooter emphasized marksmanship skills with all weapons, including crew-served ones. The troops spent a lot of time on the ranges firing at targets and getting feedback on their accuracy.

Hiking was the final training staple. These were no casual walks in the woods, but tough contests of endurance. The battalion could often be found snaking along the back roads of the Quantico area, each man suffering under the weight of a full pack and his weapon. Occasionally they broke into "double-time," a slow run at twice the speed of the normal walking cadence. Sometimes the backbreaking, day-long hikes were only the prelude to a night field exercise. As if to highlight the demanding nature of the marches, in the middle of one Captain Cain dropped dead from heart failure. Nevertheless, the incident resulted in no discernible slackening of the pace in subsequent training.

If Red Mike was a tough taskmaster, he at least made it clear to the troops that he expected as much from himself as he did from them. When they went out to the range, he shot right alongside them. Whether it was hot or cold, windy or wet in the field, he was there laboring under the same conditions. On hikes, Edson often turned and walked back the length of the battalion column to observe his men. He then trotted back to the head, a distance of several hundred yards. He earned the respect of his men not only for this display of stamina, but also because they realized he was checking on their well-being. Decades later this habit of his would be one of the first things his men recalled about him. That is not to say they loved him for it at the time: "When you are tired, hungry, and thirsty and keep plodding on and on, there is no one to blame or cuss other than the leader. I have heard the troops call Edson every name you could come up with."

Whenever possible Red Mike balanced his hard-nosed approach to training with morale-boosting events. One was a battalion dance, but he went a step further and arranged for a serviceman's welfare organization to provide 150 young ladies (most of them secretaries in the burgeoning Washington bureaucracy) to ensure that the occasion would be a success. Still not content, he asked the Virginia Highway Patrol to escort the buses from D.C. to make certain that the guests did not arrive late. After one particularly grueling, wet, cold exercise, the battalion arrived back at its barracks late at night to find the messmen doling out hot coffee laced with medicinal brandy— just the tonic they needed. For Thanksgiving the battalion commander did more than simply ensure the standard turkey dinner. He, Ethel, and the boys showed up to eat, as did all the other officers—a nice touch that made it seem more like a family occasion.

Although the battalion was growing closer together, its connection with its parent regiment was becoming increasingly tenuous. The men of 1/5 stood in ranks and rendered honors on 26 September as the Headquarters Company and 2d Battalion of the 5th Marines entrained for New River. Just days later Krulak informed Edson that his battalion was on the verge of being formally redesignated as a part of force headquarters. Smith was strongly in favor of the idea but was holding off until sufficient troops were available to make the 5th Marines whole again. Meanwhile Red Mike was continuing to ruminate on possible organizations and missions. In early October he requested orders to observe the annual Army maneuvers scheduled for Camden, South Carolina, where he hoped to get a good look at that service's air infantry units. "I believe their strength and armament as well as the type of operation assigned to them will closely parallel the functions of an APD Battalion." Smith was looking at a different, albeit similar model for his new unit; in November he suggested that Edson might go to England for a month to observe the commando units there.

Red Mike spent a week watching the Army maneuvers in mid-October. He initially attached himself to the 102d Mechanized Cavalry of I Corps, and later joined II Corps. His impression was that the Army had solid leadership at the top, but capability grew increasingly diluted as one progressed down the chain of command. At the company, battalion, and regimental level he found leadership and tactics "extremely poor," with formations generally roadbound and unaggressive. The Army, even more so than the Marine Corps, was suffering from rapid expansion.

In the latter part of October, 1/5 got the chance to demonstrate its own capability before a much larger audience. As part of the celebration of Navy Day, elements of the APD battalion conducted a simulated amphibious assault at Fairlawn Park, located along the Anacostia River in suburban Washington. The Navy, perhaps desiring not to appear to be too eager to participate in the ongoing European conflict, wrote a scenario reminiscent of the Banana War era. The Marines were invading the nation of Neutralia, its forces depicted by men in dungarees and straw hats. At the appointed time two companies of 1/5 made their appearance in rubber boats, but rain had forced the cancellation of their supporting elements—a bombing run by Marine air and a drop by parachutists. They nevertheless put on an enthralling show replete with blank fire from rifles and machine guns, puffs of smoke simulating artillery rounds, and a climactic bayonet charge that carried the enemy fortifications.

Shortly thereafter the 1st Marine Division ordered Edson down to New River, to lead 2/5 during a large-scale exercise. Whaling, the battalion's normal commander, was away on detached duty, as was 2/5's executive officer. In a switch from the usual emphasis on amphibious assaults, the scenario involved a lengthy approach march from the interior, with the division deploying to defend the coast from enemy attack (a mission with which it would become intimately familiar in 1942). Later in the month Red Mike went back to New River to assist in an exercise with 3/5.

Vandegrift, now the division commander, may have valued Edson for his aggressiveness in the training environment. Many senior officers had grown too cautious and were unable to adapt to the tougher requirements of wartime. Red Mike felt most at home in that environment. He regularly exercised his own men with live fire, and was fond of saying: "If no one gets hurt in a training cycle, the training is so artificial that it is probably of little value."

As fall turned into winter, Red Mike grew progressively more confident in the capabilities of his own battalion. In the middle of November his force made a two-day tactical movement covering thirty-one miles. Only one man dropped out, and several planes sent to look for the large formation could not find it. On 4 December the unit was out again on a classic Edson training exercise. The companies departed the barracks just after midnight, made a long approach march to an assembly area in a distant part of the base, arrived there at dawn, received the attack order, and then launched into the assault soon thereafter. Upon completion of the maneuver they hiked back to the barracks area, with the final miles at double time. After five months they were finally reaching the standards of performance Edson had set his sights on.

On Sunday, 7 December, Edson went shopping for a puppy for his youngest son's birthday. The news that day of the Japanese attack on Pearl Harbor shocked much of the country, but it seemed to make little impression on Red Mike. He briefly summarized the initial radio reports in his diary, then described his successful acquisition of a cocker spaniel and the performance of other mundane family chores. His words were devoid of foreboding or elation, either of which might have been expected from a soldier thrust into war. A British friend from Shanghai had written weeks earlier about the advent of war for the United States: "Like ourselves you will be trying to do in twenty months what should have been designed and developed properly over twenty years." Although that observation might have been accurate for the country as a whole, Red Mike and his men were ready for war. He approached it calmly as a professional ready to do the things he had spent a lifetime preparing himself to do.

Merritt Edson poses in 1912 with his first deer. (Library of Congress)

Second Lieutenant Edson in the Quantico trench complex, constructed in 1917–18 to simulate the battlefields of France. (Library of Congress)

Captain Edson stands on the duck boards of Brig. Gen. Smedley Butler's Camp Pontanezen in Brest, France, in 1919. (Library of Congress)

Ethel Robbins around the time of her marriage in 1920 to 1st Lt. Merritt A. Edson. (Library of Congress)

First Lieutenant Edson's official photograph for 1922. (USMC)

First Lieutenant Edson created a stir in Chester, Vermont, when he landed his Marine biplane there in the 1920s and visited with his parents. (Library of Congress)

This hard landing typified the difficulties that Edson and his fellow aviators experienced in the 1920s when making emergency landings during cross-country flights. (Library of Congress)

Four generations of the Edson family: grandfather Azro, father Erwin, Merritt, and son Merritt, Jr. (Austin). (Library of Congress)

Captain Edson displays the beard he grew on the first of his Coco Patrols. (Library of Congress)

A contrast in technology: modern planes and native dugouts both proved important in the hunt for Augusto Sandino. (Courtesy Raymon Clark)

Nicaraguan Indians pole boatloads of Marines up the river during one of the Coco Patrols. (Courtesy Raymon Clark)

The outmoded *Denver* and her sister ships comprised the special service squadron that patrolled Central American waters between the world wars. *Denver* contributed its detachment of Marines, commanded by Captain Edson, to the hunt for Augusto Sandino. (U.S. Naval Institute)

Captain Edson poses at Poteca with the officers of the Coco Patrol. *Left to right:* Unidentified navy dentist, 2d Lt. Jesse Cook, Edson, 1st Lt. Edwin Pollock, 1st Lt. Ralph DeWitt. (Courtesy Raymon Clark)

Captain Edson takes a break during a rifle match in the 1930s. (USMC)

Major Edson with his 1936 Marine Corps Rifle Team, winners of the National Trophy Rifle Team Match. Seated next to Edson are his two principal assistants: Maj. William Whaling (*left*) and Chief Marine Gunner Calvin Lloyd (*right*). (USMC)

The commander of the 4th Marines, Col. Charles F. B. Price (*second from the right*), inspects the lines in Shanghai during the 1937 Japanese assault on the city. He is flanked by his operations officer, Major Edson (*far right*), and Lt. Col. William Rupertus (*with hands on hips*). (Library of Congress)

Major Edson poses with a mounted Japanese officer in occupied Shanghai. (Library of Congress)

Colonel Edson joins senior Marine leaders for a tour of Guadalcanal not long after the battle of Edson's Ridge. General Thomas Holcomb, commandant of the Marine Corps, is in the front seat of the jeep. Major General A. A. Vandegrift is seated in the back with Edson. (USMC)

Colonel Edson issues an operation order to his staff officers and subordinate commanders in the 5th Marines during the campaign on Guadalcanal. (USMC)

Brigadier General William Rupertus congratulates Colonel Edson after pinning the Medal of Honor on him in February 1943. (USMC)

Colonel Edson participates in the interrogation of one of the rare Japanese soldiers captured on Tarawa. (USMC)

Colonel Edson rests on Bairiki Island, Tarawa Atoll, in the aftermath of the battle. (Julian Smith Papers, Marine Corps Historical Center)

Colonel Edson accompanies senior officers on a tour of the beaches of Betio soon after the Marines secured the island. Vice Admiral Raymond Spruance (*center*) commanded the Fifth Fleet, and Maj. Gen. Julian Smith (*right*) led the 2d Marine Division. (USMC)

Edson wears the Legion of Merit that he has just received for his part in the assault on Tarawa. (Library of Congress)

Brigadier General Edson, without a helmet as usual, surveys the scene from a forward observation post during the battle on Saipan. (USMC)

Brigadier General Edson checks on the progress of operations at the 6th Marines command post on Saipan. (USMC)

Edson discusses the Tinian operation on a command post telephone as his aide, Lt. Carl Mesmer, looks on. (USMC)

Edson delivers the principal address at the August 1946 veterans homecoming celebration in Chester, Vermont. Public speaking occupied much of his time during the 1946–47 debates over the unification of the armed forces. (Library of Congress)

As executive director of the National Rifle Association in the early 1950s, Edson kept a close watch on military shooting programs. Here he tries out a new rifle being tested by the Army and Marine Corps. (Library of Congress)

Chapter 9

"We Are Proud to Claim the Title"

I
f the war started suddenly and violently for Americans in places such as Pearl Harbor, the Philippines, and Wake Island, it still seemed far away to military men at home in the States. Some units stepped up training, but for those under command of men such as Red Mike, it was just more of the same. Nevertheless, it was still practice combat, while their comrades were fighting and dying thousands of miles away. The threat became more real when German submarines appeared off the Atlantic seaboard and began sinking merchantmen plying the coastal trade routes.

Reality and simulation clashed in late December 1941 as AFAF made final preparations for maneuvers that had been scheduled since October. Originally the 1st Infantry Division and 1/5 were supposed to land at New River while the 1st Marine Division defended its home base. General Smith evaluated the submarine threat and called off that risky endeavor. The new version called for landings at Fort Story, an Army base located on Cape Henry at the mouth of Chesapeake Bay. With the Navy's huge Norfolk base a few miles away and the guns of the coast defense artillery overlooking the beach, the chance of unwelcome enemy interference seemed much reduced. Now two regiments of the 1st Infantry Division and 1/5 would attack aggressors played by coast defense units and Marine artillerymen. Smith's earlier plan to employ Edson's battalion against the 1st Marine Division was a product of his continued search for refinements to amphibious doctrine. The general saw the exercise as another test of his three-echelon landing scheme, "the air-tank-paratroop team designed to strike the initial blow and gain the initiative during the debarkation of the main landing force."

The battalion left Quantico on its APDs on 7 January, with the thermometer registering a frosty twenty degrees. The transports sailed to New York, linked up with the remainder of the task force there, then headed south again for Chesapeake Bay. The scheme of maneuver called for Edson's men, reinforced by a company of Army tanks and a platoon of engineers, to land on a flanking beach one and a half hours before the main assault and secure the primary road junction leading into the area. Naval gunfire and an air strike would pave the way, with the tanks landing first and the infantry following close on their heels.

Things did not work out according to plan. The landing craft carrying the tanks moved faster than expected, which soon put them ahead of the designated time schedule. When they came upon sandbars near the beach, they unexpectedly slowed down because the coxswains were unsure if they could clear the obstructions. This caused the following waves of infantry to bunch up on the tanks, though the brief deceleration was not enough to make up for the time gained earlier. The tanks hit the beach five minutes ahead of schedule, and the infantry came ashore almost simultaneously. The planned air strike came in right on time and hit the forces that were supposed to be still offshore. The ships also kept prepping the beach according to schedule. The umpires promptly labeled all tanks and 50 percent of the infantry as destroyed due to the combination of friendly and enemy firepower. (The result would have been almost as bad even without mistakes, because Smith had already told the umpires to assess heavy casualties due to insufficient air and naval gunfire support. For the next few years the crusty general would be pushing the Navy to provide more preparation fires for the amphibious assault.)

Edson's effort looked good by comparison to the rest of the division. At least he had made it to the right beach in good order, a feat that no other unit was able to match. The Army battalions came ashore at the wrong places and in complete confusion; one was spread out over two miles of coastline. To add to the problems, the below-freezing temperatures posed a severe threat to the troops who had gotten soaked in the course of the assault. In order to give the men a chance to dry off and to let their commanders get organized, Smith declared a ninety-minute "armistice." After a break around old-fashioned campfires, the Marine battalion continued its attack and seized the assigned objective. Then it became the regimental reserve for the Army's 18th Infantry. The next morning Edson sent out patrols that discovered a Marine aggressor force on a nearby ridgeline. He got permission to attack and captured the enemy by lunchtime. That evening the division conducted an amphibious withdrawal covered by Edson's men.

Red Mike and his battalion came out of the exercise with an enhanced reputation. Although Smith declared the ship-to-shore movement "a complete failure," he did note that the Marines had at least made it to the right beach. Erskine asked Edson how he had managed to do it when all others had failed. Red Mike must have had a twinkle in his eye as he recounted the process. "I told my men to look at the beach, that's where you land, and you make that coxswain take you there. If you have any trouble with him, take your gun and stick it in his back. . . . They said they didn't have to do that more than once or twice." The real story was more matter-of-fact. Since the landing craft compasses were unreliable and their crews untrained in navigation, Edson asked for bearings from one of the APDs just before starting the run to the beach; the ship provided the proper heading and he merely went in that direction.

The umpire accompanying the battalion filed a glowing report on its operations ashore. He frequently referred to the use of cover and concealment, to constant patrolling, and to alert leadership. He especially praised the attack on the ridgeline on D+1, in which Edson used a small force to keep the aggressors' attention focused to their front while the rest of the battalion executed a surprise attack on their flank. The umpire's summary seconded the feeling of confidence that Red Mike himself now had in his unit. "This appeared to be a well trained, efficient battalion. In combat work, the men showed evidence of a thorough grounding in combat principles, and it was particularly noted that they always acted as though they were facing a real enemy. Their morale was of the highest, and they were at all times possessed of a strong initiative."

Edson's own report of the operation was typically detailed and insightful. He questioned the prevailing tactical wisdom of the time regarding the use of tanks in amphibious landings. In exercises the tanks went ashore first, probably due to the not illogical assumption that they had armor and could better withstand the initial fire of the defenders. Red Mike came to the opposite conclusion. He noted that the tank landing craft were bigger, slower targets than the Higgins boats carrying the infantry and were consequently much less likely to survive the run to the beach. He recommended that infantry units take the lead in the future, so they could gain an initial foothold on the shore and cover the landing of the tanks. As was his habit, he took the matter up with senior officers through informal channels. Although there is no evidence to indicate that his efforts caused the change, later amphibious assaults would reverse the landing order of infantry and tanks.

Tactics were not the only thing in flux as the Marine Corps adjusted to a real war. The APD battalion concept, born just seven months earlier, was undergoing a major transformation. Edson's long list of recommendations made after the August exercise had received no official response from higher headquarters, but he went ahead and implemented those changes that were within his power. When the battalion embarked for the Fort Story exercise, it did so in accordance with his ideas about proper organization. Each of the three rifle companies and the Headquarters Company went on board its own APD. Company D, composed of all the mortars and machine guns, took up the remaining two ships. Edson had quietly laid to rest the unwieldy RRU concept. Bigger changes were already in the works.

The previous October Smith had broached the subject of reorganization of AFAF to the commander in chief of the Atlantic Fleet. The general wanted to bring his force into line with his concept of a three-echelon amphibious assault. The APD battalion was both a cornerstone of that idea and an organizational anomaly, since it was still technically a part of the 5th Marines. In early January 1942 Smith took steps to address the problem. In a letter to the major general commandant he recounted the history of the APD battalion, described how he intended to employ it as an independent unit under AFAF control, and noted that the upcoming switch to new infantry tables of organization would make it too big to fit on destroyer transports. He then recommended that HQMC formally redesignate the unit, place it directly under force headquarters, and authorize creation of a new 1/5 at New River to replace it. Once the Fort Story maneuvers were complete, he hoped to forward suggestions for a reorganized APD unit. The commandant reacted quickly. While at sea on 7 January, Edson received word that he now headed the 1st Separate Battalion.

Smith and Edson were not the only ones pushing for a small, mobile force capable of quick strikes from the sea. At about this same time, similar ideas were percolating throughout the Marine Corps, the other services, and the Allies. The British were actually far ahead of the United States in this respect. In 1940 they had organized commando units—forces equipped and trained to raid enemy territory. They conducted their first significant operation against Norway in December 1940. The British were more than willing to share their knowledge and experience. The American military attaché in London began a series of reports on commando training and operations in July 1941. In November the Marine Corps sent two officers to England to observe the commandos in greater detail. Captains Wallace Greene and Samuel Griffith remained there for several months but sent home their initial observations in a January 1942 report.

Two other Marines were also interested in the commandos. One was Evans Carlson, a capable officer with experience in Nicaragua and as an observer with Mao Tse-tung's guerrilla army in China. He became enamored of Mao's style of warfare, and with the zealousness of a convert preached its value upon his return home in late 1938. The Communist origins of his military doctrine did not sit well with superiors, however, and Carlson soon resigned his commission in protest when they tried to muzzle his ideas. By summer 1941 he was able to return to active duty, albeit as a reservist. His faith in guerrilla tactics was as strong as ever, and he had managed to pick up one valuable adherent, Capt. James Roosevelt, a fellow reservist and the son of the president. (Holcomb had commissioned Roosevelt a few years earlier as a favor to the president. The young man's military experience prior to mobilization had consisted of service as his father's aide.) In January 1942, with the war going badly for the United States and the Japanese running wild in the Pacific, the time seemed ripe for Carlson's ideas. If the American military was too weak to fight it out toe to toe with its enemies, guerrilla warfare and raids might be viable alternatives. On 13 January the younger Roosevelt wrote to the commandant and recommended creation of "a unit for purposes similar to the British Commandos and the Chinese Guerrillas."

Yet another source pushing the idea was William J. Donovan, an Army hero in World War I and now a senior intelligence official. His plan also mentioned the commandos, but it was even more dedicated than Roosevelt's to the guerrilla concept. He hoped to mold a force that would support fifth columnists and local guerrillas in occupied territory, something more akin to the original mission of today's Special Forces than to the raiding concept of the commandos. He forwarded his formal recommendation to the president on 22 December 1941. His influence with Franklin Roosevelt was strong, and his ideas most likely filtered down to the major general commandant (MGC). Holcomb certainly was thinking a great deal about the subject in early January 1942. He received Smith's request for redesignation of the APD battalion on 6 January. The next day the MGC forwarded copies of the London attaché's reports on the commandos to the commanding generals of his divisions and corps training commands. On the seventh he created the 1st Separate Battalion.

The pressure from Donovan and the Roosevelts for a Marine counterpart to the commandos was growing very strong and soon would have an effect on Edson and his men. By now Holcomb's superiors had told him of a scheme to appoint Donovan a brigadier general in the Marine Corps with a portfolio to develop a commando force. On 14 January the commandant wrote to Smith and to General Price (now commanding general of the 2d Marine Division) and asked for their thoughts on the Donovan proposal. Both abhorred the idea and noted obvious objections: the current lack of trained manpower, the potential drain of the best men into a few elite units, the resentment at the appointment of an outsider to high rank in the Corps.

Holcomb had little difficulty in developing a counter to the commando-guerrilla concepts. He wrote Jimmy Roosevelt on 20 January that all Marines were essentially capable of such operations. In addition, "the APD Battalion . . . is organized, equipped, and trained for this duty, including in particular the use of rubber boats in night landings." The commandant expressed the hope that destroyer transports would be made available on the West Coast in the near future to support organization of a second such battalion there.

The Navy, perhaps under pressure from the president, got into the act a few days later. On 23 January Adm. Ernest J. King, commander in chief of the U.S. Fleet, directed the head of the Pacific Fleet to "develop organization and training of Marines and naval units of 'commando' type for use in connection with expeditions of raid character." Admiral Chester W. Nimitz complied the very next day by passing the task on to the 2d Joint Training Force (the West Coast version of Smith's AFAF, commanded by Maj. Gen. Clayton B. Vogel). Although King had mentioned submarines as possible transports, Nimitz spoke of APDs as being "the most suitable vessels." He envisioned four commando units, each one capable of being carried in an APD, and all falling under a single battalion-level headquarters. He also requested four destroyer transports from the Atlantic Fleet for this purpose. Nimitz's efforts seemed to play directly into Holcomb's hand. The Marine Corps might get an additional APD battalion, something it saw as desirable, rather than an autonomous organization of an indistinct nature.

The commandant took steps to encourage the development of the West Coast unit along the lines of Edson's battalion. On 4 February he arranged for a one-third slice of the 1st Separate Battalion to go to California and serve as the nucleus for the new outfit. (By design, perhaps, it was not until then that the 2d Joint Training Force finally acted on Nimitz's directive and created a separate battalion in the 2d Marine Division.) That same day a staff officer from HQMC called AFAF headquarters to inquire about the table of organization (T/O) of its 1st Separate Battalion. Holcomb intended to send to Vogel those tables of equipment and personnel as a guide. In addition, on 10 February he offered to transfer Edson himself out to the West Coast to command the new battalion.

The commandant's actions were little more than suggestions; he gave no firm orders to Vogel and Price. In that spirit, the commander of the 2d Marine Division disregarded most of the commandant's wishes and went his own way. Price may very well have been trying to curry favor with the president, an attitude evident in his response to Holcomb's earlier query on the Donovan proposal. He had sent an official letter that praised some aspects of the idea, and a private letter that strongly objected to the entire scheme. Price also named Major Carlson as commander of the new outfit and appointed Jimmy Roosevelt as his executive officer. Holcomb would soon have difficulty reining in the creative proclivities of these two officers.

In response to HQMC's 4 February request for tables of organization, Smith asked Edson for fresh input. Red Mike had obviously been putting much thought into the subject. By 8 February he produced a document even longer than the one he had submitted in August. He recommended that the rifle company have three smaller rifle platoons rather than two larger ones. Also, he believed that a battalion of one weapons company (with machine guns and mortars) and four rifle companies would produce the best possible mix of firepower and maneuverability.

Smith put an enthusiastic endorsement on the document, and the next day Edson hand carried it to HQMC, where it met with approval from the commandant. Holcomb passed it on unchanged to the 2d Marine Division, but the West Coast outfit had already developed its own ideas on the subject and sent them to HQMC. The competing proposals passed in the mail, an apt metaphor describing the two battalions, which always seemed to be heading in opposite directions on nearly everything.

The commandant did put his foot down on two issues. One was the name to be given to the new units. No one liked the title separate battalion. Edson referred to it as "nondescript." He thought that a distinctive designation that described the mission would be more in line with Marine custom (defense battalions, parachute battalions) and "a decided morale booster." One step ahead of the commandant, he suggested a new name in a 6 February memorandum. His genius for tactics and weapons did not carry over to titles, however; "1st Destroyer Battalion" never had a chance. Smith threw a more likely candidate into the ring three days later when he forwarded Edson's tables of organization to the commandant. His suggestion of "1st Shock Battalion" at least had an elite connotation. Price wanted to stay with the commonly accepted term "commando," but he offered "raiding battalions" as an alternative. By the time the commandant asked for input on 10 February, several ideas were already heading his way. He made his decision quickly. On 12 February he directed that the units be called Marine raider battalions; Edson's would be the 1st, Carlson's the 2d.

The other point of concern that Holcomb addressed was the mission of the new units. Donovan, Carlson, and Roosevelt had argued for an outfit that would fight like guerrillas. Smith thought of his former APD battalion as part of his three-echelon doctrine for use in the amphibious assault. Edson generally concurred with his immediate boss, though he had foreseen as far back as August 1941 that such a unit would be ideally suited to commando-like raids. Since then he had developed an organization designed to operate more like a conventional battalion than Carlson's notional guerrilla bands.

The commandant made it clear what he expected from both outfits. As far as he was concerned, Edson's battalion was already a trained commando force, and he desired to tweak Red Mike's suggested tables of organization only to add an 81mm mortar platoon so the outfit would have sufficient firepower to participate in a conventional amphibious assault. He formalized the new tables and promulgated them to both raider battalions. In a companion letter, he told Vogel that the resulting outfit would not only meet the Navy's earlier directive for a raiding force, but would also provide "a unit capable of participation in major operations." Three weeks later Holcomb made even clearer the source of his ideas about the raider concept. When Price asked for wide latitude to reorganize Carlson's unit, the commandant told him to let the current tables of organization stand, since they "were based largely on the recommendations of the CG, Amphibious Corps, Atlantic Fleet, as a result of actual operations with APDs for a period of six months."

Many historians have looked to the Donovan-Carlson-Roosevelt nexus as the source of the Marine raider concept. While these men did have an impact, they served more to accelerate a process already underway. Smith and Edson had created a battalion fully capable of raid duty long before the proposals of Roosevelt and Donovan stirred the pot in late 1941 and early 1942. The resulting controversy netted Carlson and Roosevelt a battalion of their own, and they would later break some of the shackles that Holcomb tried to impose on them. But they controlled only a few hundred men in a Corps that would grow to half a million. The guerrilla force they had envisioned might have been useful in the opening days of the war when the country was weak, but as the conflict progressed and American power increased, it became superfluous.

Barely two years later a new commandant would disband the raider concept completely without a whisper of concern from the White House. Even Smith's idea of a three-echelon assault went by the board as industrial developments provided the gear the Marine Corps needed to solve the problem of getting to the beach in a hurry under fire. The 1st Raider Battalion, designed for conventional battles as well as special operations, would prove its worth in the toe-to-toe slugfests to come in the Pacific. Edson, rather than Carlson, could lay claim to fathering every aspect of the initial raider concept except the name.

In February 1942 Red Mike's most immediate concern was Holcomb's levy to the West Coast, which cut a swath right through his battalion. He was to send one of his three rifle companies and an equivalent portion of machine gunners and mortarmen, a total of 7 officers and 190 enlisted Marines. It was a hard order to swallow since he had spent eight months molding these men, but there was nothing he could do about it. To Edson's credit, he did not comb the battalion for the weakest links, but simply selected Capt. Wilbur Meyerhoff's Company A. He assembled the officers and made a terse announcement; Lt. John Apergis thought Red Mike was having a hard time keeping his anger in check. The reaction of the handful of officers may not have helped; to a man they were excited at the prospect, since they expected the West Coast unit to see combat first and were eager for the fray. Now Edson had to get his outfit back up to full strength, train the newcomers, and undertake the "complete reorganization" authorized by Holcomb's acceptance of his recommended T/O.

Obtaining the required manpower was more than a simple question of numbers, which were no problem since the Marine Corps was recruiting as many as six thousand men per week in the aftermath of Pearl Harbor. The real sticking point was quality. With an elite image now bestowed on his unit from the highest levels, Edson was not about to settle for just anyone. He held a conference with the battalion's officers and they developed the formal standards: Every man had to volunteer specifically for the unit and its hazardous duty, be physically able to make long marches at faster than normal pace, and be a qualified swimmer. Red Mike was ready to make some exceptions. Captain Ira ("Jake") Irwin, the commander of Company D, pointed out that he could not swim, but that it would probably make no difference anyway given the heavy packs all men wore in the assault. The requirement remained, and so did Irwin.

Recruiting needs were raised even higher by the new standards, since there were many men already in the unit who might not meet the requirements. Edson formed the battalion, explained that the new designation meant a higher risk of combat and casualties, and informed the men that they would have to volunteer to stay on board. Red Mike interviewed those who did and rejected some of them. A few of those who did not sign up got to see the colonel, too; some changed their minds. More than a quarter of those remaining after Company A's departure opted not to stick around. For some the decision was based simply on the change in designation. Many had taken a great deal of pride in the heritage of the 5th Marines. Members of the unit still rated wearing the fourragère, a distinctive braided rope hanging over the shoulder that signified a French award for valor. The 1st Raider Battalion had no history at all, and a very uncertain future.

Edson did have two important things going for him. Due to the over-crowded conditions at the Parris Island recruit depot, the Corps was shunting many of the recruits up to Quantico to fire on the rifle range, the last stage of their transformation into full-fledged Marines. Since his battalion was the only infantry unit on the base, fifty of his men were serving as shooting coaches. These were often the first real Marines, other than recruiters and drill sergeants, the new men had seen. In addition to that free advertisement for the battalion, most of the recruits had joined in the wave of patriotic fervor after Pearl Harbor. They were easily drawn to a pitch that described the Raiders as a tough outfit, guaranteeing the earliest possible chance to fight the nation's enemies.

Edson's officers, and even the colonel himself, talked to assembled recruit platoons. The volunteers poured in. An officer interviewed each candidate and evaluated his capabilities. Sometimes the encounters were brief. Lieutenant John Antonelli asked only if Pvt. Herb Coffin could swim; the latter lied that he could and got accepted. Sometimes the officers were tougher. One captain liked to ask: "Do you think you can slit a Jap's throat with a knife?"

Red Mike's other ace in the hole was the high-level interest emanating from the president on down. Admiral King queried Holcomb on the status of the "Commando troops" on 9 February and ordered that they receive "first priority." Two days later the commandant informed Smith that the replacement of the 1st Raider's lost company "should be given the highest priority." Edson was quick to make use of this standing; the next day he sent out an appeal for several officers, naming the best he knew of in the Marine Corps.

The Raiders applied their hit-and-run skills to the rest of AFAF to flesh out their ranks with more experienced men. Captains Robert Brown and Ken Bailey went down to New River in early March and proceeded to "comb" the 1st Marine Division for suitable candidates. This added considerable insult to the injury that had hit the division when it lost 1/5. Coupled with the dual demands of creating new organizations and fleshing out others detaching for overseas assignments, the result was a bitter reaction to the Raiders among many senior leaders at New River. It "annoyed the devil" out of Vandegrift, soon to be the division commander.

If a number of Marine officers were upset with Red Mike, there was considerably more animosity toward Carlson, who was making much greater exactions on the 2d Marine Division. Even Edson had reason to be angry with his counterpart. On 17 February he received a private letter from Price. The general informed Edson that his Company A had made "a very bad impression," and that Carlson had accepted only a quarter of the men for his command. He then rubbed some salt in the wound. "I am trying to stop an official complaint on the case, not because I feel that one is not warranted but because I hate to see you get hurt over the matter." His readiness to take Carlson's side may have stemmed in part from his continuing concern that "this commando business is a hobby with high authorities in our nation and Capt. James R. is the Exec of the Battalion."

Price unwittingly put his finger on part of the problem: "Either there is an entirely different impression in the East as to what these men are to do and the types of men required effectively to do it or someone has made a serious bust." There definitely was a big difference between the two coasts. In addition to a focus on guerrilla tactics, Carlson was trying to impart a character to his unit that was an admixture of Chinese philosophy and Communist egalitarianism. Undoubtedly there was some culture shock for men trained under a more orthodox system such as Edson's. Price's offhand remark that Carlson was "building up a really handpicked unit" identified the other part of the problem. Red Mike had formed his battalion from whatever the Marine Corps had given him; only now was he getting the same opportunity as Carlson to pick and choose.

The "bust" became clearer when Edson received a letter two days later from Lieutenant Apergis, who had gone out to California with Company A. The 2d Raider Battalion had asked which of the men wanted to volunteer for a commando outfit; about half opted out, a phenomenon that Red Mike had experienced with his own unit. Those who did step forward were put through rigorous physicals followed by interviews with Carlson and his operations officer. Unlike the low-key affairs on the East Coast, these encounters were more like a "psychological test." They were conducted in a darkened room; occasionally a knife flew by and thudded into the wall, or firecrackers went off under the interviewee's chair. Few seemed to meet the intriguing standards Carlson had set.

General Price meant to forewarn Edson: "I am passing you this tip that you may know that the angel of wrath is abroad." It was an apt description, but he had applied it to the wrong person. Red Mike was livid when he received Price's condescending letter. Despite the gulf in rank, Edson wrote the general and expressed his "anger and disgust" over the situation:

> In my opinion, and in the opinion of others who have seen [my battalion] perform in the field and in maneuvers, it was, until I sent this detail to Carlson, the best battalion on the east coast and as good or better than any similar outfit in the 2d Division. . . . Whatever Carlson's so-called standards may be, his refusal to accept three out of four of these men only confirmed my opinion that the Marine Corps had lost nothing by his resignation a few years ago and has gained nothing by his return to active duty as a reserve major. . . . The statement in your letter to the effect that the men rejected by Carlson were distributed to units in the 2d Division 'where no one wanted them' is not so much a reflection upon the quality of men sent as upon the prejudicial attitude and ignorance of the officers under your command. It is true that Jimmie Roosevelt has connections with high officials in this country. It is also true that he is a reserve captain with very limited military experience as an officer in the Marine Corps. I have already stated my opinion of Major Carlson. I have given you many years of loyal, faithful and, I believe, efficient service. . . . If, as implied in your letter, you feel that an official complaint is warranted based on Carlson's report to you, I shall not ask you to withhold it on my account. I have no apologies to make nor anything to conceal in the transfer of this draft to the west coast.

The rebuke apparently caused Price to drop the matter. In an apologetic response he admitted the source of the problem: "The points at issue obviously involve two widely divergent points of view." That was not the end of it. Captain Meyerhoff wrote to Edson regarding the events that had transpired in California. He glumly described the "dissolution of A Company Reinforced" and noted that "the majority of the men were sorry to leave the First Battalion." That was not mere flattery. In mid-March Red Mike received another letter on the subject. "It is after a trial of one month that we, former members of the 1st Sep Bn sent to the West Coast to form the 2d Sep Bn but for personal or other reasons of the officers in charge of the 2d Sep Bn have not joined it and are in outfits which we cannot be satisfied with for many reasons. We would gladly pay our fare back to get into our former outfit again if such is possible." Twenty-seven men had signed the plea. Edson could do nothing to get them back, but it must have boosted his esteem at least a little to know that men were willing to pay to serve under him again. The loss, to no good end, of one-third of his hard-built battalion was not an easy blow to bear. Although rivalry between similar elite units would be normal, Red Mike would harbor a grudge against Carlson that would last even after the latter's death.

Despite the high priority accorded his battalion, Edson was often not able to get the people he wanted. Of the officers he asked for on 17 February, only one (Capt. Lew Walt) ended up in the battalion. Smith flatly turned down Edson's request for Krulak, still the general's aide. Red Mike eventually obtained some of his alternate choices. He went after Sam Griffith, now a major; in addition to experience as a commando observer in England, the young regular had written articles on guerrilla tactics and been a student at the Basic School under Edson's tutelage. One of the colonel's successful thefts from the 1st Marine Division was Capt. Justice M. Chambers. On at least one occasion the bureaucracy unwittingly frustrated the raider priority. The battalion dispatched a message requesting Capt. Herman Nickerson; HQMC issued the orders, but due to an error the recipient was Capt. Lloyd Nickerson, a reservist almost the same age as Red Mike. He reported aboard and ended up staying.

In addition to acquiring a large number of new officers and enlisted men, Edson had to get them up to proper standards as quickly as possible. Since most of the recruits coming direct from the abbreviated boot camp had the barest minimum of training, this was a daunting task. Even experienced men had to adapt to new equipment, as they exchanged heavy machine guns and mortars for light ones and picked up unusual weapons such as the Boys antitank rifle. Red Mike concentrated his efforts on four areas: physical fitness, marksmanship, individual skills, and small-unit tactics. The training day, which now began at 0500 and lasted till 2130 or later, opened with formation just after reveille. The troops ran a mile or so to the rifle range, did calisthenics, then ran back to the barracks for morning chow. The heavy emphasis on hiking continued. The Raiders strove to reach a pace of seven miles an hour, more than twice the normal speed of infantry. They did so by alternating periods of double-timing with fast walking. Rubber boat work in the Potomac in winter offered its own set of challenges; it required a lot of toughness to spend hours in the small craft soaked by freezing water.

When it came to individual skills, Red Mike wanted each man to know more than what was required in his regular billet. The goal was for every man to be able to shoot every weapon in the battalion. Specialists were supposed to learn how to fix their equipment as well as operate it. Edson sent a steady stream of men to school, for everything from ordnance repair to aerial photography interpretation. He also placed emphasis on speed of execution and the ability to do it silently and in the dark.

The communicators made a contest out of packing their gear, marching to a new point, setting up, and seeing who could make contact first. Another important skill was hand-to-hand combat. Red Mike sought out the acknowledged master, retired Col. Anthony Biddle, and arranged for him to instruct the battalion in bayonet and knife fighting. Edson was always ready to ask the experts for assistance; he went to the parachutists for help in designing his physical conditioning program, and to the Army engineers for instruction on defensive fortifications.

In terms of tactics, the Raiders concentrated on rubber boat work and night operations. In his letters home Pvt. Lee Minier provided the best contemporary account of raider training:

> We've been on the move nearly all week down here. Wednesday we were in the hills all day and covered about twenty miles. Thursday we had a maneuver or a problem as they call it. Covered another fifteen miles. Friday we were on the Potomac River all morning in rubber boats firing machine guns and getting wet. Then at 4:00pm we moved out and were on the move all night. Most of my moving was done on my stomach, crawling through brush and mud. . . . When we are on the march I carry a part of a machine gun on my shoulder, besides pack, bayonet, rifle, etc. The machine gun part weighs thirty-two pounds when we start but about the tenth or twentieth mile it has gained about fifty pounds. And about a fourth of the distance we run like the devil himself was after us. At a time like that I'd like to have that recruiting officer at the end of my bayonet. . . . Every morning we have physical exercise and every day we have school on the functions of the machine gun or some other subject. We also have gun drill every day.

Occasionally the Raiders got caught up in the usual mindless rear-echelon requirements. The base commander ordered the battalion to furnish fifteen officers to sit in the audience at the graduation ceremonies for the Marine Corps Schools. In late February the colonel and 381 of his men boarded a train for New York, where they participated in a parade kicking off a Navy Relief Fund Drive. They marched up 5th Avenue, passed in review before the commandant, and then served as a backdrop for a Marine Corps Band concert at Rockefeller Plaza.

Holcomb's antipathy to the raider issue was evident in his press conference prior to the parade. The reporters were very interested in Marine Corps efforts in the commando field, but the commandant chose not to mention the nature of the unit that would march that very day. Instead, he tried to convince the press that amphibious raiding was a principal function of the entire Corps and that all units were prepared to perform such missions. Soon thereafter he squelched a project by his own public relations bureau to play up the Raiders, much to the chagrin of the lieutenant who had been preparing the press release. "For reasons best known to yourself and Headquarters officials it has been decided not to publicize your battalion at this time. General Denig has met with the press and informed them that the Marines had such a battalion but that the information was confidential and was not to be publicized." A wide-ranging prohibition on the entire subject came into effect. Biddle wrote Edson that he "was authoritatively instructed not to compare the Colonel's command in any way with the commandos."

Whether or not they were successful in raising money for the charity, the trip was probably good for the welfare of those Raiders who participated. The city hosted the men to a hockey game and other diversions, and various hotels put them up for the night. Despite the temptations of New York, Edson could proudly report that every last man showed up at the train station on time the next day. If morale had been low during the difficult summer of 1941, that no longer was the case. By now the men of the raider battalion had developed a deep respect for their commander, even though he was very different from the officers under whom they were used to serving. Many Marine leaders were big, strapping fellows who had played football or other sports in college. Red Mike was small and physically unimposing. In fact, when the new helmets arrived to replace the old World War I versions, Edson's seemed to swallow up his head. The troops found the look humorous enough to give him a new nickname, "Eddy the Mole." On the march they discovered just how tough he could be; his efforts inspired the young men to try to keep up with someone old enough to be their father. He was equally impressive on the ranges, where he outshot nearly everyone in the battalion. Red Mike's demeanor also set him apart from most of his contemporaries. Too many leaders relied on hyperbole, volume, or vitriol to get their point across. Edson always spoke in a calm, low voice, no matter what the situation. He used words sparingly, each one carefully chosen and direct. During inspections he noted mistakes with the simple admonition, "Better get that fixed, son." If anyone doubted his resolve, a look into his eyes told them he was deadly serious. It was his habit to fix his gaze on anyone conversing with him; his eyes became the feature everyone remembered best.

Most important, though, he had a genuine interest in his men, not only as a group, but as individuals. He tutored his young runner, Pfc. Walter Burak, to help him advance in the Corps. He wrote the head of a promotion board about a mess sergeant previously prone to drink but now sober and hardworking after several months of marriage. When the wife of another man developed a lengthy illness, he offered to transfer him to a unit less likely to go overseas. It was the same sort of rapport that he had developed with an earlier generation. Private Minier summed up the feeling of the battalion in early 1942: "The Colonel is a pretty good egg."

Edson tried hard to instill the same dedication to leadership in his officers. He stressed constantly that their main role was not only to direct their men in combat, but to motivate them to fight as well. They could do neither if they themselves participated in the action. One young lieutenant found that out the hard way. He had gotten carried away during the Fort Story maneuvers and was busily engaged in firing blanks at a retreating Army unit. Red Mike walked up and rapped him on the helmet. The new officer never forgot the colonel's brief critique: "You've taken away the leader and added a single rifleman."

Red Mike looked after his men because he believed they were still the key to victory, a view not much in vogue at the time. The apparent dominance of planes and tanks on the battlefields of the world led many to denigrate the role of the infantryman. As Edson readied his Raiders for combat, one of his friends in the arms industry remarked that it was a machine age now and the rifleman was of little value. The colonel "quietly and patiently" explained to him that he was "dead wrong." He expected his Marines and others like them to be in the thick of the fight and to determine the outcome.

The 1st Raider Battalion did not have long to wait for a call to action. On 21 March the battalion passed from control of AFAF to the newly created 3d Marine Brigade. That outfit, built around the 7th Marines, 7th Defense Battalion, and assorted reinforcing units of the 1st Marine Division, was mounting out for Samoa. There was insufficient shipping to haul the entire force, however, so the 1st Raiders and 3/7 detached from the outfit within days and received new orders for independent movement to the Pacific.

The change was good news for Red Mike, since the brigade chief of staff was Watson, his old nemesis. There was a downside to the alteration in plans; the commandant decided to keep part of Edson's outfit in Quantico. The Navy apparently wanted to maintain some raider capability on the East Coast, a rationale borne out by a memo from Holcomb to Admiral King noting that part of the battalion "remains at Quantico for employment with the Amphibious Corps, Atlantic Fleet." Another possible explanation arose out of continuing pressure from the Navy Department on the commando issue. There were vague plans to stand up a third raider battalion, and the stay-behind element would make an excellent nucleus. Griffith, Company D, the entire 81mm mortar platoon, and a representative slice of Headquarters and the remainder of Company E (the weapons company) drew the assignment. Other Marine officers may have been upset with Edson for stealing their people, but he had no less reason to be unhappy with yet another amputation of his own command.

On the morning of April Fools' Day, 1942, the men of the 1st Raider Battalion turned out in formation on the parade ground across the street from their barracks. They knew they were boarding the long lines of rail cars on the nearby tracks, but they were unsure of the destination. In accordance with the date, many thought they were going south for training in Florida or the Caribbean. It was not until two days later, when they were headed west through Louisiana, that they realized they would end up on the Pacific coast. Meanwhile, Red Mike was not about to let the trip turn into idle time. He issued orders that each of the three trains should arrange a stop every day for exercise. The men duly turned out for calisthenics on a siding every twenty-four hours. Just after his group had formed up one morning, Edson walked to the front, yelled "Follow me!" and gave the signal for double-time. He led them across barren ground and up a nearby hill. Regrettably there had been no opportunity to warm up muscles stiff from 24 hours of enforced idleness in the cramped cars; the next day there was a trainload of very sore Marines. Captain Chambers took pleasure in finding that the colonel ached just as much as everyone else.

The battalion pulled into San Diego on 6 April and went into camp at the Marine base. Two days later they began to load their equipment and supplies onto the transport USS *Zeilin*. For most of the men, this was the first hint that they were going to leave the States. The officers had been aware of their destination since departing Quantico. Their written orders had a rather ominous tone for an otherwise bureaucratic document; they were detailed to "permanent duty beyond the seas." The phrase would end up applying all too literally to many of the Marines who clambered aboard the ship that April morning.

During the next few days Edson and Price took the opportunity to repair their strained friendship, with the general inviting his former subordinate to be his houseguest. The raider commander made the best of it; he got permission to flesh out his leadership ranks with two lieutenants from the 2d Marine Division. One was John Erskine, a Japanese language officer, and the other Henry ("Hank") Adams, Jr., a former FBI man and a crack shot with a pistol. Red Mike tried to hone his tables of organization, too. He submitted a lengthy list of recommended changes to equipment and personnel allowances the day after arriving at San Diego. Chief among them was a request to delete the 81mm mortar platoon, because the weapon and its ammunition were too heavy for rapid mobility on foot. Moreover, since Holcomb had grafted the platoon onto Edson's recommended T/O, there was no room for it on the APDs anyway. He also got a chance to talk to the commandant about the portion of his battalion left behind in Quantico. Holcomb was not entirely sympathetic, so Edson then made an official request via Amphibious Corps, Pacific Fleet, to obtain the return of his rear echelon.

The final night in town the officers, and probably many of the enlisted men, imbibed their last unlimited taste of stateside alcohol. On 13 April tugs pulled alongside the large transport and began to assist it away from the dock. It joined up with the cruiser *Honolulu* (CL-48) and set course for the west. The Raiders continued to train in whatever way they could within the confines of the transport. There was opportunity for the usual shipboard diversions, too. After the troops adjusted to their new quarters and seasickness, they spent time on deck enjoying the cool breezes, flying fish, and sunsets. On 22 April the ship held the traditional ceremony for crossing the equator; a tough rite of passage for the many first-time "pollywogs" in the Marine ranks. When things got too monotonous, a spate of submarine scares came along to inject a little tension into the trip.

Edson's major concern at this point continued to be the absence of a significant portion of his authorized strength. Not content to let the matter rest on his official request, he had another appeal ready to send off upon arrival at Samoa. This one was in the form of a personal letter to Col. Allen H. Turnage at HQMC. Edson argued that he needed his entire battalion (except the 81mm mortars) if it was to be "employed as fully and as aggressively as I believe it should be." The split in the battalion staff did worry Red Mike, as it essentially doubled the workload of key leaders. The operations officer with the forward echelon, for instance, was also the acting executive officer. Simple numbers were a concern as well. His fourth rifle company was not only an extra maneuver element in battle, but also a potential source of casualty replacements already schooled in raider methods.

Replacements were important because Edson anticipated that his battalion would sustain a lot of casualties. In early March he had asked HQMC to provide the Raiders with an increase from two Navy doctors to five. The troops were aware of the odds. They commonly referred to the battalion as "a suicide outfit," but they were still "anxious to get going." Edson was ready, too. He had honed himself and his unit to a fine edge. It was time to go to war.

Chapter 10

"First to Fight"

The *Zeilin* pulled into Pago Pago Harbor, Tutuila Island, American Samoa, on 28 April 1942. It was noontime, but it was raining so hard that visibility was nil. The next morning's sunshine revealed the picturesque bay in all its splendor, with towering mountains surrounding crystal blue water speckled with colorful native boats and pastel coral heads. The Raiders debarked, boarded trucks, and moved to the southwest coast near Leone Bay, where they set up tents in company encampments strung out along the single dirt road. The battalion did not expect to stay long, so little effort went into amenities. Even Edson had only a mat of palm fronds for a floor, though in deference to his rank he had an entire tent to himself. Mosquitoes were plentiful and bothersome, but not of the malarial variety. A short distance inland the ground rose from rough foothills into a range of jagged ridges up to fifteen hundred feet high. This last feature would be the one thing most Raiders would remember about the place.

After several weeks of physical inactivity during the move west, Edson reestablished a demanding regimen in Samoa. At reveille everyone from the colonel on down turned out for some form of exercise, though company commanders had flexibility to design their own programs. Hiking was still a favorite raider pastime, but the Samoan ridges added a new twist. The companies spent a lot of time moving up into the high ground, climbing more often than walking. They made good use of their toggle ropes—heavy manila lines about eight feet in length, with a wooden peg at one end, a loop at the other, and knots spaced in between. Each man carried one wrapped around his body. The steep trails seemed impossible during rainy weather, and high heat and humidity sapped strength when the sun was shining.

To simulate realistic conditions, the troops generally carried full combat loads, to include ammunition. Some of the men of Easy Company took to emptying heavy mortar rounds and machine-gun belts from their containers to save weight, but that backfired after one hump when Captain Chambers ordered a live fire at the end of a particularly arduous climb. As part of their penance, the troops had to make the same circuit again the next day. Edson discovered that he had to tweak the table of organization yet again to accommodate the crew-served weapons. He had reduced the standard machine-gun squad to five men in order to keep the battalion within the limited space available on the APDs. Now he upped the crew to seven so it could carry a realistic amount of ammunition into battle.

The battalion soon took great pride in its ability to scamper about the ridgeline. Edson made a bet with the island's commanding general that his Raiders could sneak up on a mountaintop radar post. They were successful after a long, stealthy approach, and then made off with some of the unit's equipment. A bit of raider doggerel penned in Samoa captured the battalion's increasing sense of strength:

> We've got up in the morning
> Before the break of day,
> When other folks were sleeping
> We were well upon our way.
> We've hiked o'er all the mountains;
> We've slept out in the rain;
> We've carried our guns and ammo
> To hell and back again.
> We've ached, grunted, groaned, and growled;
> We've wished that we were dead,
> Because the load upon our backs
> Would seem as though 'twere lead.

Despite the appearance of horseplay, there was a serious side to the night exercises on rough terrain. One Marine, Pvt. Daniel Toland, died after falling 150 feet off a cliff. Yelanich, Red Mike's old runner from the Coco River, also took a tumble that broke his back and put him out of action for a year. Other training was equally hard and dangerous. The men spent a lot of time paddling their small rubber boats out into the treacherous ocean surf and then coming back in for practice landings. They

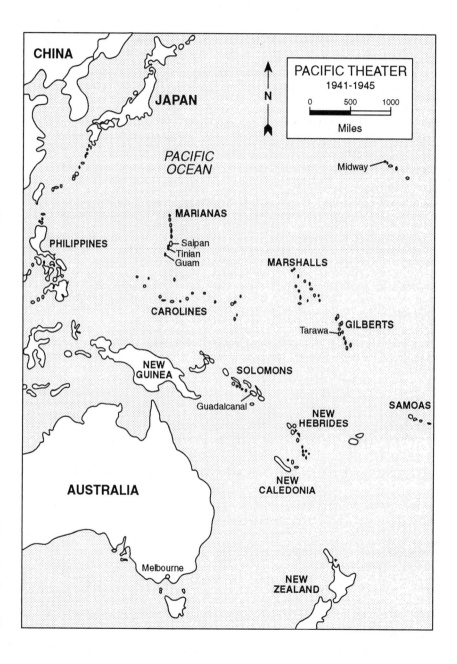

used large quantities of live ammunition, much of it for field problems rather than basic range practice. A second Marine, Pvt. Edward Chambers, died when he was shot in the stomach during one of the live-fire exercises. These incidents served as a reminder of what lay ahead.

Red Mike remained unfazed by training accidents or the prospect of combat losses. He wrote a relative of one casualty that her Marine "gave his life for his country fully as much as though he had died in battle." Edson's closing sentiment was the hope that "we, his comrades, display the same spirit of unselfish devotion to Corps and country as he did when we are called upon to make the same sacrifice." In a letter to Ethel he lamented the loss of Yelanich, but also recognized that "it is just one of those things to which we will have to become accustomed, I guess, as the war progresses." Edson loved his men as much as any commander, but he also knew that accomplishment of the mission came first. This readiness to accept casualties was not so common among senior officers; it would make Red Mike a valuable leader in the hard fighting to come.

The Japanese had not been resting as the Raiders made their way across the Pacific. On 3 May 1942 they landed on Tulagi, a small island that was the seat of British colonial government in the Solomon chain. The Japanese began setting up a seaplane base in the harbor. Since this southward extension of Imperial power threatened the maritime lifeline to Australia, American forces reacted rapidly. Planes from the carrier *Yorktown* (CV-5) struck the base the next day.

For a time it appeared that the Raiders would go into action as well. Admiral King had been prodding Admiral Nimitz, commander of the Pacific Ocean Area, to make some offensive move against the Japanese. On 28 May Nimitz proposed an operation by Edson's battalion against Tulagi. This message went to Gen. Douglas MacArthur, whose Southwest Pacific Area encompassed the target. MacArthur disagreed with the suggestion on the grounds that he had no forces to occupy the island once it was taken. King thought that a lack of land-based air support (there were no American airfields that put Tulagi in range of tactical aircraft) would also make it hard to hold onto the island. He approved only a raid to destroy facilities and disrupt Japanese use. This was the classic mission for which the Raiders were organized and trained, but in retrospect it was probably a good thing that senior leaders canceled the operation. Much as the later Makin raid would result in stiffened defenses on Pacific atolls, a hit-and-run attack on Tulagi might have drawn increased enemy attention to the area and dearly cost the Marines down the road.

As it was, the Japanese were slowly expanding their activities in the lower Solomons. They scouted the island of Guadalcanal for airfield sites in May and began construction of a dirt strip in June. Radio intelligence, coastwatcher reports, and aerial reconnaissance uncovered this effort. Then the Battle of Midway (4–6 June) struck a serious blow against the Imperial Navy's air power and opened the door for a more offensive American posture. On 24 June King ordered Nimitz to seize Tulagi by 1 August. Two days later the Joint Chiefs of Staff made a boundary change that put the lower Solomons into the Pacific Ocean Area. That same day Nimitz selected the 1st Marine Division as the ground assault force and assigned the 1st Raider Battalion and other formations as supporting units. The operation took on the code name Watchtower.

The advance echelon of the 1st Marine Division had only just arrived in New Zealand from the States on 14 June. Vandegrift, the commanding general, was under the impression that he would have at least six months to prepare his men for battle. He found out on 26 June that he would have less than six weeks. This would have been barely enough time for the best outfit to get ready, since more than half the division was still at sea, and all its equipment and stores needed to be off-loaded and then restowed on the ships in the proper order for use in an assault. Vandegrift's biggest problem, however, was the state of training within his command. Although the division officially stood up in February 1941, the rapid expansion in the Corps had wreaked havoc on its development. One entire battalion of the 5th Marines had been stolen to create the 1st Raider Battalion, of course. Periodically, the division had subdivided, almost like an amoeba, to provide cadres for other new formations. Training and unit cohesion suffered in the process; too few experienced Marines were trying desperately to pass on their knowledge to the mass of fresh recruits. Now two officers struggled to develop a plan for the unexpected operation. Luckily, Lt. Col. Gerald C. Thomas, the division operations officer, and his assistant, Lt. Col. Merrill B. Twining, were both strong leaders and brilliant staff officers.

The Raiders' stay on Samoa was coming to an end. Edson had foreseen that after the Midway victory. Captain Chambers recalled the moment years later: "I'll never forget Eddie coming to us and in one of the few times I ever saw him show emotion, he said, 'It was a clean sweep. They got all the Jap carriers and we'll be moving up.'" As if to indicate that the war was finally getting serious, Red Mike wrote his wife and asked her to forward his black leather pistol belt, the nonregulation one he had worn throughout the Nicaraguan campaign so many years before. The raider commander definitely was spoiling for a fight.

One other piece of information probably indicated that offensive action was not far off. On 7 June the rear echelon of the battalion saddled up in Quantico and boarded a troop train for the West Coast; they were finally going to rejoin the parent unit. They had been doing their own intensive training, to include an extended exercise with two APDs in the latter third of April (coincidentally at a place called Solomon's Island in Maryland). Griffith was bringing with him everything that Edson had asked of HQMC: Dog Company, the remainder of Headquarters, and the machine-gun platoon and 60mm mortar section of Easy.

Red Mike was undoubtedly pleased about the imminent arrival of these reinforcements, but there seemed to be a strained relationship between the commander and his executive officer. The first hint of it came in Edson's 28 April letter requesting reattachment of the rear echelon. While strenuously arguing for return of most of those men, he seemed unconcerned about the fate of the XO: "As much as I would like to have the services of Major Griffith, I realize that he may be of more value some place else." Griffith thought that Edson "was a very cold and unresponsive personality," an assessment most would have agreed with upon first meeting the reserved Vermonter. But Red Mike never warmed to his second in command as he did with most competent officers who served close to him. Years later Griffith would say: "I never felt I knew Eddie."

There may have been several reasons for this. Part of it was probably a difference in opinion over organization and tactics. Griffith objected to the setup in the 1st Raiders and wanted to adopt the arrangement then in use by Carlson's outfit, obviously not a model that would appeal to Edson. The head of the rear echelon went so far as to make proposals for this reorganization to HQMC, and he even spent two weeks of April observing the 2d Raiders in San Diego. In addition, Griffith expected in May 1942 that his group would become the nucleus for a third raider battalion. Although he may not have actively sought this role, he apparently did nothing to squelch it, a position in direct contravention of Edson's desire to reunite the unit. To the credit of both men, they never let these differences interfere with the performance of their mission.

On 3 July the rear echelon arrived at Pago Pago. The next day Edson and the remainder of the battalion joined their comrades on the transport USS *Heywood* (AP-12) and sailed the following day. On 10 July they arrived in Noumea, New Caledonia, where they disembarked and set up a tent camp. During the move Edson took the opportunity to make some final changes in the battalion. He had been trying to obtain an increase in the

T/O to accommodate a demolitions unit, and HQMC had finally given authorization. However, the staffers at headquarters had done so by substituting a demolitions platoon of two officers and seventy-four men for the 81mm mortar platoon of the same size. The problem was that Edson did not have those men available, nor could he obtain replacements. So he took the fifteen-man casual platoon of Headquarters Company, designed to be a casualty replacement pool, and designated it for the mission. In a series of personnel switches, Chambers took over Dog Company, Capt. George Herring got Easy, and Irwin became the quartermaster.

Activities on New Caledonia generally mirrored those on Samoa, except that this training area boasted an even higher set of hills. Edson also culled out several volunteers to prepare for a special reconnaissance mission. Informed of his attachment to the 1st Marine Division and the pending operation, the raider commander had offered to send small teams to the target by submarine to gather information and make contact with the coastwatchers.

The Raiders finally received definitive word on Watchtower around 20 July. Twining flew to New Caledonia from New Zealand with the orders. He briefed Edson, who in turn convoked a late afternoon conference of his company commanders to pass on the information. The objectives of the first American ground offensive of the war were Tulagi, the conjoined islets of Gavutu-Tanambogo, and the airfield on Guadalcanal. Intelligence was sketchy at best, though reports from the coastwatchers later proved rather accurate in terms of actual numbers. Division believed that there were several hundred men each on the smaller targets and a few thousand on Guadalcanal. The mistake was that most of the latter turned out to be unarmed labor troops. There was no real map of Guadalcanal, only a sketch based on aerial photos. For the other islands there was a hydrographic chart dating from 1910, which depicted some of the terrain contours.

❦ The division and its supporting units would be divided into two groups. Vandegrift and the majority of his men would attack and seize the airfield. Although this dirt strip, still under construction, had been added as a secondary target early in the planning process, it had now assumed priority. The American aircraft carriers of the invasion force were scheduled to remain in the vicinity of the lower Solomons for only a few days. When they departed, the Marines would be on their own in terms of air power; without that airfield, they would have no response to Japanese land-based aircraft coming down from the north. The landing force intended to complete the strip as soon as possible and fly in its own planes.

Since Tulagi was now a subsidiary part of the operation, it drew less attention. The remainder of the division, designated the Northern Group, would assault this objective and Gavutu-Tanambogo. Rupertus, now a brigadier general and the assistant division commander, headed the force of four thousand men, the main units being the 1st Raiders, the 1st Parachute Battalion, 2/5, and 1/2. What this command lacked in numbers it made up for in quality. Division rated the Raiders and Parachutists the best trained outfits, and Edson the best senior combat leader, closely followed by Lt. Col. Harold E. Rosecrans of 2/5. Although the planners considered these objectives to be less important than Guadalcanal, they realized that the small size of the targets relative to the number of defenders would increase the difficulty; hence Rupertus received the best forces.

The northern series of landings would begin with a company of 1/2 seizing a promontory on Florida Island that overlooked the landing beaches on Tulagi. The Raiders, followed by 2/5, would then go ashore on the latter island. The Parachutists would make the last assault of the day on Gavutu-Tanambogo, while portions of 1/2 grabbed another flanking peninsula of Florida and served as the reserve. Operations would commence just after dawn. Naval commanders slipped the date for the landing to 7 August to give the division more time to ready itself for the short-notice operation. That would be the fourteenth anniversary of the battle of Ililiquas. Before long Red Mike would take to calling that day "Lucky Seventh"!

Tulagi was a long, slender island, approximately four thousand by one thousand yards. Three-quarters of it consisted of a heavily wooded ridge, about 350 feet high, running from its northwestern tip down the central spine of the island. The southeastern tip was dominated by a rugged hill mass. In between was a patch of lower, generally open ground, some of it covered by coconut groves. Various government buildings (everything from the governor's residence to an insane asylum) were spread throughout this area; a small town and several sets of wharves occupied a section of the northern coast. The only suitable landing beaches from a purely hydrographic standpoint were those on either side of this saddle, since the rest of the island was fringed by coral formations. Aerial reconnaissance revealed, however, that the enemy understood this and had concentrated his defenses on these obvious approaches. Division planners thus chose a landing site about halfway up the western coast and designated it Blue Beach, though the adjective in this official title was hardly descriptive of reality. The Marines wisely decided to make the first American amphibious assault of the war against natural obstacles, not enemy gunfire.

Although the naval task force commander ultimately rejected Edson's offer to make reconnaissance patrols of the objectives, Twining did bring

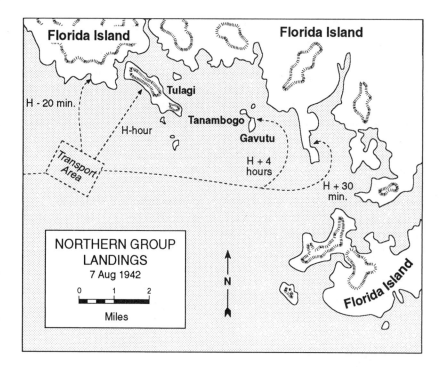

along three Australians, former colonial officials familiar with the target area. These men were attached to the Raiders, and they proceeded to construct a large sand table relief of Tulagi. Henry Josselyn drew two detailed maps that accurately depicted individual buildings and terrain features; these turned out to be an invaluable replacement for the lack of features on the issue map. The newcomers found themselves readily accepted by Edson. One of the officers noted that the raider commander's "light blue eyes, red hair and determined mouth bespoke a leader. . . . We took to him at once."

Based on their knowledge and the division directive, Edson developed his plan. The first wave ashore would consist of two companies, B and D. They would push directly across the island to the far side of the ridge, where Baker would capture the native village of Sasapi. Both would then wheel right and get on line. The second wave would follow shortly afterward and perform a similar maneuver on the near side of the ridge. Once the battalion was formed up (Companies B, D, A, and C, from northeast to southwest, with E in support), it would move down the length of the island and confront the Japanese in and around the southeastern tip. Division assigned 2/5 to land in trace of the Raiders, deal with any enemy in the northwestern quadrant of the island, and provide assistance to the main attack as required.

For a time, shipping limitations presented Edson with a dilemma, since there were only four APDs on hand, not enough to carry the entire battalion. He contemplated leaving one rifle company behind, but eventually higher headquarters made space available on another transport; Company E and elements of headquarters would ride to the target area by that means. On 23 July the battalion loaded on its ships from the rickety pier at Noumea under the guise of doing amphibious training. For the next couple of days the Raiders practiced embarkation and debarkation with their rubber boats, then one evening they just sailed away. A small detachment remained behind in camp to guard the gear and keep up the pretense that the rest of the force would return after a brief absence.

*   *   *

Sasapi

Cemetery

Blue
Beach

N

Phase Line A

Chinese
Quarters

208

281

D - Day

TULAGI
7 -8 Aug 1942

0   1/4   1/2

Miles

The flotilla of APDs and accompanying ships rendezvoused with the rest of the task force a few days later south of the Fiji Islands; the seventy ships of the fleet were an impressive sight. On 28 July the entire landing force conducted a less-than-impressive rehearsal on the tiny island of Koro in the Fijis. The practice operation was a success only in revealing a large number of deficiencies. The supporting fire of ships and planes was wildly inaccurate, and the Navy had great difficulty getting the Marines ashore due to mechanical breakdowns, unexpected coral reefs, and human error.

Vandegrift labeled the rehearsal "a fiasco." Griffith found it "shocking" and noted that it was "the only time in my life that I ever saw Edson despondent." Boats picked up the troops the next morning, and Rupertus had a conference with the Northern Group commanders on the transport *Neville* (AP-16) that afternoon. A second rehearsal on 30 July was much less ambitious. This time the boats closed to only two thousand yards from shore, then brought the men back to the ships. Following another meeting of commanders on 31 July, the task force set sail for the Solomons.

During the movement to the objective, the Navy went to work to fix what it could, while the assault units made their own last-minute preparations. Company commanders gave detailed briefs of the plan to their lieutenants, who in turn passed the word on to the troops. Some, such as Chambers and Walt, gave pep talks to the men. Erskine busied himself with teaching a few key phrases of Japanese to the Marines on his ship. As part of their camouflage routine, the men covered their helmets with squares of burlap daubed with paint to break up the telltale smooth surface of the metal domes. The colonel set the example; his helmet was "just as ratty looking as all the rest." Finally, Edson ordered all officers and senior enlisted men to pick two-word nicknames, which were then transmitted to the entire battalion. These would serve as a sort of recognition code in the upcoming operation. Anyone could authenticate the identity of a leader by challenging him with one part of his name and expecting the other half in return. The battalion commander had no difficulty picking his code name; he chose "Red Mike."

If the rehearsal had been disheartening, there was one order of business on the way to the target that must have cheered Edson. A further expansion in the authorized strength of the Corps, to three hundred thousand men, generated a requirement for more senior officers. A board selected Edson and sixty others for colonel on 17 July, with promotion to be made as the need arose. Edson did not have to wait long. Authorization went out just twelve days later, and the message reached the battalion at sea on 3 August. Red Mike was prepared for the event; he had already obtained a pair of colonel's insignia from Linscott, formerly of the Eastern Area of Nicaragua and now a staff officer with RAdm. Richmond Kelly Turner, head of the amphibious task force. The silver eagles were scarce items in the remote Pacific, and Edson ended up passing one on to R. C. Kilmartin of Rupertus's staff. Sam Griffith pinned the single eagle on his commander's shoulder on board USS *Little* (APD-4) just four days before the scheduled assault. Other Raiders had received promotions that summer; the XO made lieutenant colonel and several captains picked up the gold oak leaves of a major.

Those Raiders who had been able to sleep rose in the wee hours of the morning on 7 August 1942. They ate breakfast, checked their gear another time, and squeezed onto the crowded decks of the transports, all before first light. The raider battalion had pared the individual load of each man to the bare minimum: very little food, no shelter half, and none of the other items associated with a lengthy stay in the field. But the men were burdened with everything possible needed to fight: lots of ammunition, the ever-present toggle ropes, and even gas masks. The loads were heavy enough, but much lighter than those of other units carrying the full range of items. Their orders contemplated only a short stay for the battalion: "Upon completion seizure of Tulagi Island 1st Raider Battalion reembark at Beach Blue . . . prepared for further landings." Just about every Raider went ashore under the impression that it would be the type of quick operation for which they had trained; they would hit hard, capture the island, and be back on the ships in a day or so, ready for some new strike. Red Mike expected to take the objective in a single day.

After a period of heavy weather, D day dawned with perfectly clear skies, high temperatures, and smooth seas in the channel between Guadalcanal and Tulagi. Planes from the American carriers began striking various targets at first light; warships added the din of their guns. The destroyer *Monssen* (DD-436) prepped the landing site on Florida for Baker Company of 2/1, the very first unit scheduled to go ashore (at 0730). Its sister *Buchanan* (DD-484) and the antiaircraft cruiser *San Juan* (CL-54) pounded Tulagi. The latter, armed with sixteen five-inch guns, belched so much flame that some Raiders thought it had caught fire. Concussion waves rolled over the troops on the APDs and smoke boiled up from burning buildings and fuel tanks ashore.

In a twist from their normal routine, the Raiders clambered into Higgins boats rather than their rubber craft. Sailors manning machine guns in the bows sprayed the beach as the craft roared forward. Baker and Dog Companies touched down as planned at 0800, but not exactly where they wanted.

The coral heads, as expected, forced them to debark thirty to one hundred yards short of land. Marines jumping over the sides found the water at least waist deep and sometimes over their heads. They waded forward slowly against no enemy opposition; the heaviest resistance came from the sharp coral, which inflicted nasty cuts.

The beach was a narrow strip of sand that gave way almost immediately to the steep, wooded ridge, except in the center of the landing area, where there was a native cemetery, which "didn't add to any sense of well being" among the troops. As the first two companies moved out uphill, the second wave splashed ashore. The Marines, well briefed on the scheme of maneuver and the need for speedy execution, moved out so fast that they were initially disorganized. The tough climb up the ridge did little to help the situation. Many men quickly judged that their loads were too heavy, despite their commander's attempt to lighten it, and they took their own corrective action; apparently useless items such as gas masks soon festooned the landscape. Once Baker Company seized Sasapi, without opposition, Nickerson took a few moments to get his force organized in a proper combat formation. The unit then moved southeast down the coast, with a point and advance guard followed by the platoons in column. The other companies were likewise moving southeast, in more or less a rough line, though there was not always contact on the flanks.

The battalion commander had his own problems at first. Edson's boat departed the *Little* with those of Company A, but it broke down, and he reached the shore only after the second wave had landed and all companies had moved out. Red Mike caught up with his men by the time they reached Phase Line A, a control feature delineated by the southeastern end of the main ridgeline. Here the Raiders paused before launching their assault into the defended portion of the island, as air, naval guns, and the battalion's own weapons softened up the area.

When the attack kicked off again late in the morning, Baker Company ran into opposition on the left flank from enemy riflemen and machine gunners located in and around the village-wharf complex known as Chinese Quarters. In this small engagement the battalion took its first casualties, including a lieutenant and a Navy doctor. The company spent much of the afternoon rooting out most of the Japanese, then bypassed others and pushed on to the low hill occupied by the Residency, the colonial governor's official quarters. During Company B's delay at Chinese Quarters, Dog Company continued forward and temporarily pinched Baker out of the line. When the latter reached the Residency, the two units were now reversed in order, with Dog on the far left flank, near the sea, and Baker next in line to its right.

Stronger opposition developed on the far right flank, where Charlie Company came under fire from forces arrayed on the slopes of Hill 208, located just beyond the end of the ridge. After an hour of fighting with grenades and small arms, the Marines finally took the high ground and continued their sweep forward. Able Company and parts of Dog met increasing opposition from enemy holed up in caves and from prepared defensive positions. They had to blast out the Japanese or kill them one at a time with small arms when they showed themselves near an opening. At the same time, the Raiders began to take heavier fire from enemy positions on Hill 281, the ridge complex on the far side of the saddle. Edson called in naval gunfire on that location; the *San Juan* responded with a 280-round barrage. In the late afternoon Edson notified Rupertus that remaining enemy forces, estimated at five hundred men, seemed to be breaking contact and retreating to the tangled ridge at the end of the island.

As dusk fell, the Raiders took up positions for the night. Dog Company was well in advance of the rest of the battalion and hard up against the eastern slopes of Hill 281. As it dug in, it pushed its left flank down to the water and tied in its right with Company B. Baker faced southeast, still oriented in the original direction of attack. It was set in along a deep cut in the forward slope of the hill where the Residency was located. The vertical walls of this narrow defile served as a perfect obstacle; a single wooden bridge crossed it about in the center of Baker's position. Company A was on the right of Baker and dug in along an adjoining low hill overlooking the cricket grounds. Two platoons of Company C occupied the remaining frontage stretching to the beach in the west. The lead platoon of C Company had earlier lost contact with its parent unit and pushed ahead along the beach in the face of light opposition. It now occupied an isolated perimeter of its own at the extreme southern end of the island. Having met no opposition, 2/5 finished clearing the rest of the island, and elements of that battalion were now in place to the rear of the raider line.

Edson had set up his command post in the Residency by early afternoon. Along with the rest of the battalion, he had experienced occasional harassing fire all day from bypassed Japanese. He described the scene to a reporter just a few days later. "Snipers were everywhere, in the trees, in caves, behind rocks. Many times the snipers would let us go by and then open up on us from the rear. Some of their holes were natural caves. Others were blasted out of rock. The only way to get them was by dynamite and hand grenades." Despite the danger to anyone moving about, Red Mike spent most of his time ranging along his front lines. The acting sergeant major thought his commander was concerned because this was the first time in combat for most of the men. But this would become Edson's trademark—going to the scene of the action to view the situation for himself.

Chambers recounted one particularly vivid incident when his unit was clearing the area around the Residency that afternoon. They had come to some barbed wire, and the company commander sent one squad crawling forward to breach it while the others provided covering fire:

> I heard somebody say, "What's going on here?" I'm laying down of course, and I look up and here's Edson standing big as life, smoking a cigarette. I said, "Colonel, what are you trying to do, get me killed?" He said, "What do you mean?" I said, "I'm supposed to be ahead of you and those are the very front lines up there. We're crawling to cut those wires and we'll go right through." He said, "Keep them moving," and then moved on.

Chambers claimed that his multiple wounds, in this campaign and others, resulted directly from Edson's example; the junior officer thought leaders were supposed to unduly expose themselves to fire.

Edson had reason to be concerned about the course of the battle that evening. Two of his aggressive company commanders were now down with wounds. Major Ken Bailey of Charlie had been shot in the thigh after he had circled a machine-gun bunker, gotten on top of it, and tried to drop a grenade into the firing slit. Chambers had fragmentation wounds and two fractured wrists from a mortar blast. After translating captured documents in the Residency, Erskine confirmed that the heart of the Japanese defense was in the tangled ravines of Hill 281; there was tough fighting to come.

As darkness fell a commotion occurred in front of the Raider lines. The Japanese shouted and slapped their weapons to unnerve their opponents and draw the fire of machine guns to pinpoint their location. Edson called it their "noise campaign"; it was a tactic he had seen in China years before. The first attack began around 2200 and hit at the juncture of Companies A and C. This was the classic banzai assault, which would become so familiar to Marines in the Pacific war. The enemy came on at a dead run, screaming and firing on the move. They expected superior courage to carry the day, that the Marines would break and retreat under the show of moral strength. This first attack did in fact punch a hole in the line, but it petered out before doing more than that. A second assault, which might have exploited the gap, struck instead full against Able's front. The Raiders held this time.

Not far from Edson's CP, a few Marines pulled back when it became apparent that the Japanese were about to attack. Adams and some of his intelligence section were thus exposed in the house they had occupied. After fighting for a time, they withdrew and left the building to the enemy. Most of the Japanese activity that night consisted of infiltration. Small groups and individuals tried to make their way through the American defenses with stealth as well as brute force. In a variation of the noise campaign, one soldier would call out while others nearby stood ready to throw grenades if a Raider fired in response. Some of the infiltrators made it well into the rear of friendly positions. They drove Rosecrans out of 2/5's command post and attacked the aid station set up near Blue Beach.

As usual, communications broke down just when they were most needed. Edson could not get a report from Walt's A Company, so he decided to go there himself and get a firsthand look at the situation. He called for Lt. John Sweeney, in charge of CP security, and the two set out for the right flank. They moved along Company B's lines for a time, and got challenged every few steps by alert, nervous Marines. No one knew where Walt's CP was located. It became clear to Sweeney that the odds of reaching their objective were not good. After a brief halt and a reassessment, Red Mike decided to head back to his headquarters. The lieutenant was relieved, even more so when he found out the next day that another platoon commander had been shot that night while checking his lines, probably when his own men mistook him for an infiltrator.

Edson grew concerned at the chaotic conditions, and for a time considered calling for reinforcements, except that communications were nonexistent at the moment. Although they had "fully expected" the Japanese counterattack, the "viciousness and tenacity" of the assaults surprised Red Mike and his XO. Unlike on the other islands where laborers predominated, these were elite combat troops, members of the 3d Kure Special Naval Landing Force, the Imperial Navy's marines. At one point they fought to within fifty yards of the Residency; Edson later called this threat to his CP one of his "few exciting moments" in the Guadalcanal campaign.

Rupertus and his advance command echelon had tried to come ashore on Blue Beach at 2000, but they were driven off by sporadic fire (from Japanese infiltrators, or perhaps from fellow Marines, no doubt trigger-happy in the midst of their first night of combat). The Raider rear echelon ran into the same problem when it tried to land a few hours later. Both groups remained afloat in Higgins boats for the rest of the night, out of communication with the division and events ashore. Red Mike had no choice but to hang on with what he had. Although the Raiders gave up a little ground in places and had numerous enemy in their rear, they generally held firm over the course of the night. As the new day dawned, the situation looked less grim. Edson thought it just as well that he had been unable to talk to higher echelons.

In the morning the raider commander quickly got his forces on the move again. He ordered Adams to regain the house he had lost the night before. The intelligence officer led some of his small section against it under a heavy covering fire. They burst in the front door, only to discover that all the enemy were already dead: four inside, ten underneath among the stilts. Another ten Japanese lay sprawled on the slope of the hill leading up to their target. Able Company counted twenty-six enemy casualties in its front lines. At 0900 two companies of 2/5 passed through Dog's position, swept over the southern portions of Hill 281, and linked up with Company C of the Raiders on the western side. The remaining enemy were now isolated in a ravine in the midst of the Hill 281 complex. After a lengthy preparation barrage by the 60mm mortars of the Raiders and their heavier 81mm cousins of 2/5, elements of Edson's battalion and Rosecrans's Company G moved through this last pocket. They used dynamite and grenades to finish off the enemy fighting from caves and dugouts. At 1500 the Marines declared the island secure.

This did not mean that the battle was entirely over. Organized resistance was at an end, but there were still numerous Japanese hiding around the island. For the next few days Marine units searched the caves and made periodic sweeps to look for holdouts. This process began on 8 August while much of the action was still focused on Hill 281. The men of Company B discovered a large cave in the wall of the cut near the Residency. Erskine went out on the bridge and called to the occupants, urging them to surrender. He received no answer. Later some soldiers sortied from the entrance, one at a time, to be cut down immediately by a raider machine gun and BARs covering the entrance. These weapons were firing down the long axis of the narrow, high-walled cut, a virtual shooting gallery. The Japanese persisted in their attempts until the Marines used a large charge of TNT to seal the entrance.

For the next several days the Marines carried on the hunt for their enemy; each night, they hunkered down and waited for the inevitable infiltration attempts. Few of the Japanese had escaped to the caves on D day with any food or water, so it was only a matter of time before they came out searching for sustenance, if not battle. Much of the resulting combat was at close quarters, with grenades and knives, as exhausted men surprised each other in the night. The Raiders lost a few men in the process, but the two killed and two wounded on 10 August marked their last casualties in this phase of the campaign, and Japanese activity seemed to disappear not long after.

These minor engagements were not the main concern of the Marines.

From the very beginning Edson and other senior leaders expected the Japanese to make an immediate attempt to retake the lost islands. During the evening of 8 August, the raider companies deployed in defensive positions designed to repel any enemy amphibious assault. Like the Japanese before them, they expected it to come along the good beaches on either side of the saddle. Edson emplaced some of his men near the coast and arrayed others to cover likely inland avenues of approach. The threat was serious enough that Red Mike redeployed Company A after dark, even though the men were tired from a long day of fighting around Hill 281.

As the Raiders hunkered down on Tulagi on the night of 8 August, a cold rain chilled the men to the bone, an unexpected discomfort in the tropics. A 25 percent alert required that one man in four had to be awake at all times. Those Marines whose turn it was to stand watch had to keep one eye focused on the sea and the other on the lookout for infiltrators. The expected enemy riposte was not long in coming, though it did not include an amphibious assault. The Imperial Navy had launched a surface force south from the base at Rabaul in the northern Solomons almost as soon as they heard of the American landing. These ships—seven cruisers and a single destroyer—arrived in the waters between Guadalcanal and Tulagi just before 0200 on 9 August. They slipped past Allied destroyer sentinels and opened up with guns and torpedoes on the surprised detachment of cruisers guarding the amphibious force.

Raiders ashore heard the thunder of explosions and saw the star shells in the sky. They had no idea who was winning the naval battle, but when a single landing craft approached the coast, they assumed it was the awaited landing and started shooting. It turned and fled out to sea at about the same time the infantrymen recognized it as one of their own Higgins boats. In the morning, the Marines learned that the Allied force had suffered a stunning defeat—four cruisers and a destroyer sunk, other ships damaged, and more than twelve hundred sailors killed. The enemy had escaped with only minor losses. The Americans would soon come to know these deadly waters as Ironbottom Sound.

With the carriers already departing the area and his surface force decimated, Admiral Turner had no choice but to go ahead with a planned withdrawal of the transports, even though unloading was far behind schedule. They would sail on the afternoon of 9 August, and take with them more than half the supplies and equipment destined for the landing force. At the same time General Vandegrift received this bad news, he also got his first concrete word of the operations against Tulagi and Gavutu-Tanambogo via a personal brief from Rupertus in a meeting on *Neville.*

Prior to this time, radio reports from the ADC had diverged wildly from the truth. Based on initially optimistic messages on D day, division had already started planning to reembark the Raiders on the afternoon of 7 August. At 1645 Rupertus had claimed Tulagi secured; at 2125 he finally noted that there was still opposition on the island. Just after midnight he reported that the Raiders had suffered 22 percent casualties and the Parachutists more than 50 percent losses; he requested reinforcements. At 0500 on 9 August, the ADC could finally tell Vandegrift that all objectives had been taken with many fewer casualties than first reported. Reality was bad enough. During the initial seizure and following mopup, Edson's battalion lost thirty-eight men killed and fifty-five wounded, more than 10 percent of its strength. Other units on Tulagi suffered thirty-three casualties. In the process, the Marine force killed all but three of the 350 Japanese defenders.

The departure of the transports was a particularly serious blow to the Tulagi defenders, since the heavy fighting in the vicinity of the only suitable beaches and docks had prevented the unloading of supplies. Very little made it ashore before the fleet sailed, nor had the Raiders come prepared for a long stay. Red Mike rationed the meals to two per day, a familiar tactic from Nicaraguan days, though he thought things on Tulagi were never as tough as those lean times. Much of the food came from captured Japanese stocks. Potable water was also at a premium, and the men occasionally had to resort to catching rainwater in their ponchos. Dysentery began to crop up, but once the troops completed the grisly task of burying the dead and went into organized campsites, conditions improved.

There were occasional moments of excitement in the midst of the dull routine of garrisoning a conquered island. On 12 August a submarine chased three landing craft making the trip from Guadalcanal to Tulagi. Marine pack howitzers fired on the surfaced foe and forced him to retreat. On the nineteenth and again on the twentieth, a Japanese destroyer entered the sound in daylight and proceeded to bombard Tulagi from a distance. Although the ship was not in a position to be very accurate, it did send everyone scurrying for cover. Except Edson: He calmly went out on the veranda of the Residency, ordered everyone nearby to spread out, then went back inside. In the words of one observer, he was "just absolutely contemptuous of the Jap fire." Everyone who fought on Tulagi seemed to recall similar incidents. The citation for his second Navy Cross would later note "his gallant conduct" and his "courage." Richard Tregaskis, one of the combat correspondents who accompanied the Guadalcanal invasion force, put it a different way: "On Tulagi the legend was born that Edson was invulnerable."

This level of fearlessness was an important element in a commander, particularly in a situation where few of his officers and men had ever been in combat. His display of courage inspired his troops to go forward into the unknown. But Edson's value went far beyond bravery, a commodity in plentiful supply among his contemporaries in the invasion force, many of whom had demonstrated it on the battlefields of France as junior officers. What distinguished Edson from most of the senior leaders of the 1st Marine Division was his ability to command large formations and make bold decisions. Vandegrift soon noted this in a letter to Holcomb: "This man Edson is one of the finest troop leaders I ever saw. . . . Some that were awfully good in lower grades are not so good in higher ones in the field."

The swift progress of the raider battalion against stiff opposition on Tulagi was in stark contrast to what had occurred on the other side of Ironbottom Sound. The two regiments commanded by Colonels Cliff Cates and Leroy Hunt landed on Guadalcanal against no opposition. Despite the complete absence of enemy fire, both units advanced slowly and covered barely a mile of ground the first day. Vandegrift had to boot Hunt out of his CP and tell him to go forward in person and get his men moving. On the second day, the general got into a jeep and reconnoitered ahead of his sluggish forces. Thomas thought that some of the units were "not well commanded," especially Hunt's 5th Marines. The problem was not entirely due to leadership. There had been little opportunity for the regiments to train since their departure from the States months earlier, and an unexpected river obstacle had held up Cates's 1st Marines. Still, there were a number of senior officers who had become too cautious after twenty years of garrison life and peacetime maneuvers.

The same division between aggressive confidence and timidity seemed to hold true on Tulagi itself. Edson was only a battalion commander in the action, but he took charge of all forces engaged during the fight, a job that should have been done by Rupertus's Northern Group command element. This may have been due in part to the difficult assignment handed to the ADC, which placed him in charge of several landings. However, the brigadier had a propensity to follow operations "from a distance." He waited until the night of D day to head for Tulagi, an impossible time to set up a functioning command post and get the lay of the land. That island also seemed a strange choice inasmuch as he had earlier reported it secured, while on Gavutu-Tanambogo the issue was still in doubt and the battalion commander had been wounded and put out of action. The misplaced priorities of the group commander were apparent when he made a visit to the raider CP on the morning of the ninth, just after the island was secured, but with a counterlanding apparently imminent. His first reaction was to take the acting sergeant major to task for the "careless policing of the area," a place the Raiders had defended in hand-to-hand fighting not many hours previously.

Griffith "had practically no confidence in General Rupertus" and he was "sure Edson felt this way about him." The raider XO noted that Rupertus "relied almost entirely on Edson for recommendations, suggestions, this sort of thing." Edson wrote home, with no exaggeration, that 2/5 had been attached to him and under his command for the operation, as indeed it was for all practical purposes. His Navy Cross citation acknowledged as much: "Colonel Edson advanced the attack of his battalion and its supporting units with such skill, courage, and aggressiveness that he was an inspiration to the entire Combat Group and was directly responsible for the capture of Tulagi Island."

Tregaskis noted the disparity between Rupertus and Red Mike when he interviewed them during a visit to Tulagi on 12 August. The general "lamely" described the battle as "the most wonderful work in our history." Edson, on the other hand, quietly and coolly summarized the action and highlighted the feats of his men. His "talk was all about his Raiders, nothing about himself." On learning of Red Mike's own deeds, the reporter pronounced him "a first-class fighting man."

On 28 August the commanding general called Edson to Guadalcanal for a conference. There had been no significant Japanese efforts against Tulagi, but the Imperial Navy had been making nightly runs to drop reinforcements on the coast of Guadalcanal. Vandegrift thus had a need for more men, and the only ready source was the underutilized garrison on the smaller islands. He told Edson that his men and the Parachutists would be brought over, and that the paramarines would now be attached to the Raiders and under Red Mike's command.

At the prospect of a transfer to Guadalcanal "spirits revived," because the Raiders had heard that food was more plentiful there. However, the enemy was also more of a threat. As if to remind the Raiders of that, Japanese bombers attacked *Colhoun* (APD-2) on 30 August and sent it to the bottom just after it had delivered some of them to Guadalcanal. Other ships got the rest of the battalion and the Parachutists safely to the big island. The combined units set up a bivouac in a pleasant coconut grove near the Lunga River about one mile from the coast at Kukum. For a few days this seemed like another stint of occupation duty, the same slow life they had come to enjoy during the latter period on Tulagi. "But those who knew Edson better were uneasy." They were certain he had not brought them there to rest.

Chapter 11

"And Never Lost Our Nerve"

The Raiders had little opportunity to enjoy their new quarters in the coconut grove. The division was on the defensive, but Red Mike was determined to employ his force in the aggressive fashion contemplated by its name. Griffith later said that "Edson had not been on the island an hour before he began to urge the need for reconnaissance in force toward either Esperance or Taivu." Jerry Thomas, the D-3, was also disposed toward an offensive posture and therefore inclined to listen. His knowledge of Edson's reputation was bolstered by Griffith, a friend from China days, who affirmed that Red Mike was an outstanding tactician. In the weeks of combat to come, Edson and Thomas, two like-minded, stouthearted Marine officers, would form a strong bond of friendship and mutual professional admiration that would last for the rest of their lives and influence the direction of the Corps for the next several years.

The first product of this collaboration was a large combat patrol to Savo Island. Intelligence reports indicated that a small number of Japanese located there were using it for a radio station and observation post. Griffith and two raider companies landed on the island on 4 September and scoured its volcanic slopes for ten hours, but returned empty-handed. While half the battalion was thus employed, Edson was planning a similar operation against Cape Esperance for the next day. Since the two APDs carrying the Savo patrol returned late in the afternoon, the colonel radioed Griffith to keep the men on board in preparation for the next move, but the message did not make it in time. When Edson went down to the beach to embark for the planned raid, he saw that one company was already moving ashore, while the second had just gotten in the boats and was preparing to shove off. Rather than countermand that activity, he decided to delay the Esperance move for twenty-four hours and let the troops finish coming ashore. This intervention of "Old Lady Luck," as Red Mike later characterized it, prevented a potentially tragic loss. *Little* and *Gregory* (APD-3) tangled with Japanese destroyers of the Tokyo Express that night and both were sunk.

That small naval action on the night of 4 September resulted from an ongoing effort by the Japanese to build up an assault force east of the Marine perimeter. For several nights destroyers and barges had been landing the men of Maj. Gen. Kiyotaki Kawaguchi's army brigade around Taivu Point. As information of this buildup filtered back to Marine headquarters from native scouts, the division staff's attention shifted from Cape Esperance to the new threat. Edson, Thomas, and Twining talked about the possibilities on the morning of 6 September, and all agreed that a raid to the east would be useful. They selected the village of Tasimboko, the apparent Japanese staging area, as the target. Vandegrift accepted the suggestion and Edson found out that evening that the operation would take place on the eighth.

After the loss of *Little* and *Gregory,* shipping was at a premium. Two converted tuna boats, designated as YPs (patrol craft), would supplement the remaining APDs, *McKean* (APD-5) and *Manley* (APD-1). The addition of the 1st Parachute Battalion brought Edson's force up to about 850 men. Bolstered in manpower and short of transport, he would have to make the move in two echelons. In order to fill up holes in the depleted line units, he also decided to transfer most of the men from Dog Company into the other three rifle companies. Captain John Antonelli would command Company A for this operation while Walt recuperated from malaria.

Intelligence was sketchy. Initially there were supposed to be only a few hundred Japanese troops. Then reports from native scouts increased this figure to between two and three thousand men, but division believed that either the estimates were excessive or the force was starving and poorly equipped. In either case, the odds appeared manageable, though risky. Since the scouts said that the enemy had oriented his defenses west toward Marine lines, Edson planned to land beyond the village at Taivu Point itself. Hopefully this beach would be undefended and the Raiders could get organized ashore and move in from the rear. The landing would be made at night to achieve surprise. Able, Baker, and Charlie Companies and the remainder of Dog would make up the assault echelon, with the rest of the battalion and the Parachutists serving as the reserve back at Kukum.

The Marine force launched the operation on the morning of 8 September, but it did not achieve the surprise it had hoped for, since the Japanese

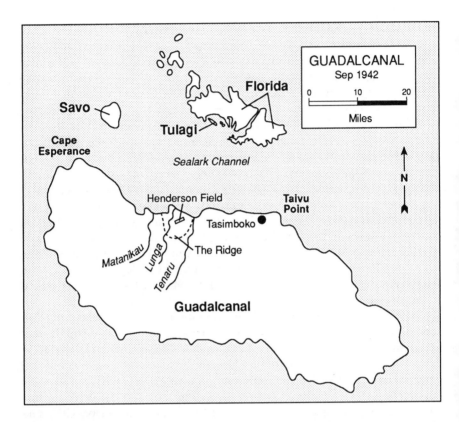

detected the landing. However, a passing American convoy apparently made the enemy think that a major assault was in progress, so most of the three hundred troops in the area filtered away into the jungle. The main part of Kawaguchi's brigade was then far inland and unable to respond. Able and Baker Companies landed as planned at 0520, just before dawn, and for the second time in the campaign the Raiders got ashore without opposition. The landing craft returned at 0615 with the second wave. In the dwindling darkness the force assembled for the attack and was ready to move out at 0655. Edson, as usual, was out on the front lines making his presence known. As one Marine crouched behind a sand dune, Red Mike quietly walked up and corrected him: "Mallamas, move up to the top; you have no field of fire there." In one brief encounter Edson instilled confidence by his demeanor, reinforced proper combat techniques, and demonstrated his uncanny ability to recognize his men.

Edson and most of the first wave pushed directly along the coast toward Tasimboko. Dog Company, little more than a platoon of thirty men, secured the beach. At dawn, planes from Henderson Field made bombing and strafing runs, and the APDs headed back to Kukum to load the reserve force. The troops uncovered ample evidence of enemy strength as they moved forward. The large numbers of foxholes, infantry packs, and life preservers indicated that the enemy force was considerably larger than a few hundred men. They also discovered abandoned 37mm antitank guns, proof that the Raiders had forced a hasty withdrawal.

Thomas, concerned about the outcome, stayed by the radio all morning. Earlier in the campaign he had sent a small patrol down the coast against a weak enemy allegedly ready to surrender; the patrol had been ambushed and nearly wiped out. Thomas had misgivings that he might have again underestimated Japanese strength. To compound his anxiety, communications were not that reliable. The raider assault force had a single TBX radio, a 120-pound behemoth that required a three-man crew to carry and set up. Its range was limited, so the battalion's other TBX stayed on the *Manley* and served as a relay station back to division. Every time the command element moved, the radio crew had to spend several minutes tearing the set down and a like amount of time putting it back into operation.

The TBX initially went with Griffith, until Burak, the colonel's runner, brought word that Edson wanted it at his location. The exhausted crew had its hands full trying to keep up with the movements of the two raider leaders. They finally gave up trying to pack the set for each move and just dragged the twenty-four-foot antenna from place to place.

Their initial transmissions gave Thomas more reason to worry. Edson passed on the news that he had "landed in the rear echelon of a sizable Jap force." He reported the capture of several field guns and the presence of more than a thousand life preservers. He was soon calling for more air support and a speedy arrival of his second echelon. The Japanese rear guard recovered and began to put up resistance as the Marines advanced through a coconut grove. In addition to machine guns and rifles, the defenders brought to bear 75mm field guns, which they used in a direct-fire mode down the lanes between the trees. Although the crash of the firing and the whistle of the shells sounded fearful, most of the rounds landed to the rear and caused few casualties, though one burst killed one man and severed the arm of another unlucky Marine. Edson moved rapidly along the front to steady the men and keep the attack pressing forward. He then ordered Griffith and Company A to swing out to the southwest with the objective of coming in on the enemy from his southern flank. Two of coastwatcher Martin Clemens's scouts led the way.

Major Nickerson's Company B continued to lead the attack along the coast. Edson, "irritated" by the slow pace of the major's advance, remained close at hand to press for more "aggressiveness and speed." A rainstorm swept the battlefield and made things more uncomfortable for both sides. The planes were having difficulty identifying troops on the ground, and then the weather caused them to head home, but the APDs soon returned with their second load and added their fire support to the din. At 1045 Red Mike asked if troops could be landed to the west of Tasimboko; apparently he hoped to break the stiff resistance with an attack in what was now the enemy rear. The last part of the message had an ominous ring: "If not, request instructions regarding my embarkation." Division headquarters responded in ten minutes that an additional landing was impractical and ordered the Raiders to withdraw. At 1130 Edson again asked for another landing and more air support, and division repeated its order for him to reembark. Despite his earlier apparent willingness to call off the operation, he now ignored the order.

Edson's decision worked out for the best. Shortly after noon, Japanese resistance seemed to melt away, and the raider main body covered the last few hundred yards into Tasimboko in short order. Griffith and his flanking unit arrived there at just about the same time. Appropriately, the sun came out to greet their success. The area was stockpiled with large quantities of food, ammunition, and weapons ranging up to 75mm artillery pieces. Red Mike labeled this one of the other "exciting moments" of the campaign: "All the signs indicated there were five to ten Nips in the area to every one of us and the lack of opposition looked like a trap." He realized that the main enemy force, clearly much larger than his own, might return and attack at any moment. Vandegrift radioed a "well done" and repeated his order to withdraw.

The raider commander chose to stay put for the time being, and his men set about destroying as much of the cache as they could. Troops wrecked a powerful radio station, bayoneted cans of food, tore open bags of rice and urinated on the contents or spilled them on the ground, tied guns to landing boats and towed them into deep water, and then finally put the torch to everything that was left. Tregaskis, one of the reporters along for the raid, gathered all the documents he could find, which vexed the raider intelligence officer. As the sun went down, the last men boarded the APDs and YPs and headed for the perimeter, all of them a little bit heavier with liberated chow, cigarettes, and alcohol. Another combat correspondent aptly captured the mood of the moment: "Just finished a first-class job of arson. . . . It was fun."

*   *   *

The Tasimboko raid was a minor tactical victory in terms of actual fighting. The Marines counted twenty-seven Japanese bodies and estimated that they had killed a total of fifty. Their own losses were two dead and six wounded. But the battle's importance went far beyond a simple body count. Griffith later called it "one of the really very successful small operations of World War II." Edson believed that it had "much to do" with the outcome of the developing enemy offensive. Many of the Marines who participated thought that they had seriously hurt Kawaguchi's brigade in terms of logistics, fire support, and communications. Although the Japanese did sustain significant losses in all three of these areas, that probably did not have much impact on later battles, given the type of assault Kawaguchi planned to make.

🕆 Two other results were of critical importance. First, the trove of documents captured by the Raiders and Tregaskis revealed substantial information about the size and intent of the Japanese force. Armed with this knowledge, the division could better prepare itself for the coming storm. Second, and possibly as significant, was the effect on morale. The men of the Japanese main body, already suffering in their difficult march through the jungle, found it "maddening to be the recipients of these daring and insulting attacks." If they had harbored illusions about their superiority in courage and boldness, the Tasimboko raid must have dispelled those notions and replaced them with the certain knowledge that the Americans also could fight well. For their part, the Raiders had defeated the Japanese yet again, and literally were feasting on the fruits of victory. They had every reason to be confident about the future.

Edson went to the division CP upon his return from the raid and briefed Thomas and Vandegrift on the action. He concluded that the force represented by the supplies at Tasimboko was "no motley of Japs," but a substantial unit preparing for an attack. The handful of Japanese-speaking Marine intelligence officers reviewed the captured documents later that night and confirmed that analysis; more than three thousand Japanese were moving southwest from Tasimboko. Edson firmly believed that they planned to assault the nearly unguarded southern flank of the American perimeter. Given their limited resources, the Marines could not defend everywhere in sufficient strength to stop a thrust; but division had to make some sort of decision where to deploy its forces.

On the morning of 9 September, Edson, Thomas, and the operations section pored over available maps and photos of the southern perimeter. After much discussion, Red Mike pointed to a ridge on an aerial photo: "This looks like a good approach." Located directly south of the airfield, its bare slopes stood out amidst the surrounding tropical growth. Edson's choice was based on his years of combat experience. He was certain that the attack would take place at night; that had become a Japanese trademark, and that was the only time they could get fire support from the sea. In addition, in the dark they would not stand a chance unless they made their attack along a well-defined avenue of approach, preferably one free of heavy growth. The ridge met both those criteria, and pointed straight at the airfield less than a mile away. Red Mike had remembered his lessons from the Coco Patrol.

Thomas and Edson tried to convince Vandegrift that some provision should be made to protect that open flank. This was not an easy task, since it would involve a major shift in the current defensive dispositions. Moreover, the general was just about to move his CP into newly constructed and more comfortable quarters located in the lee of the ridge, away from the daily Japanese bomber raids on the airfield. Edson, characteristically unafraid to speak his mind, informed his commander that he had chosen a bad spot for the new headquarters. Vandegrift, tired of the constant near misses, refused to believe his subordinates and continued preparations for the displacement.

Thomas and Edson then tried a new tack. The CP would require some sort of security force once it moved out on the edge of the perimeter, and the raider/parachute battalion was in need of some easy duty after a month of hard fighting and patrolling. Their current bivouac was also too close to the airfield for comfort and they had taken their share of occasional misses from Japanese bombers. Vandegrift accepted the suggestion that they go into a reserve position on the ridge, although he still did not acknowledge the scale of the potential threat. As far as he was concerned, the basic defense plan would remain oriented toward the coast.

Edson returned to the battalion bivouac in the coconut grove and informed his staff and commanders that they would soon be displacing up to the ridge to "get out of the V-ring" near the airfield. The word filtered down to the troops in short order that they would be moving to a "rest area," but the colonel's preparations for the shift to a quiet sector seemed rather odd. He and Griffith personally accompanied patrols that scoured the vicinity of the ridge.

On the morning of 10 September the Raiders ate a typical field breakfast of soggy rice and dehydrated potatoes (no doubt fortified from personal stocks of Japanese chow). The battalion then packed its possessions and humped the short distance to the grassy high ground, with interruptions for the daily air raids. When the troops arrived, they soon learned that the title to their new home might be in dispute. Orders came down to deploy in a defensive stance and improve the positions as quickly as possible. The men broke out their entrenching tools (undersized affairs adequate only for flower gardening) and set to work. A shortage of all forms of engineering material hampered the effort. There were no picks or shovels, and only meager quantities of barbed wire and sandbags. Marines had to use their bayonets to clear brush for fields of fire. Those on top of the ridge found the digging tough going; once they got through the shallow topsoil, they hit coral. The weakened condition of the men made the labor that much harder. Many suffered from dysentery and other illnesses, and the poor quality of field chow did little to maintain health.

Casualties and illness had taken their toll on the chain of command, too, though there were some positive changes in key billets. Bailey had recuperated sufficiently from his wound to make an early and unauthorized departure from the hospital in New Caledonia and return to Guadalcanal and his Company C. Nickerson was ill, as was his XO; Red Mike took advantage of that to place newly promoted Captain Sweeney in command of Company B. Walt was still sick, which left Antonelli in charge of Company A. Both were strong officers, but Antonelli was comparatively new to the job. Many other leadership slots, particularly at the platoon and squad level, also were filled by men fleeting up from lower positions.

During the next two days, Japanese actions put to rest any doubts about the need for the defensive preparations. Twenty-six bombers came over on 11 September and dropped their loads on and around the ridge. Since the sky was clear, and this was far out of the normal pattern of attacks against the airfield, it could hardly be an accident. The Japanese obviously thought that the ridge was important. The bombs inflicted several real casualties, in addition to killing any last hopes about a rest area. Soon after, raider patrols discovered an enemy force less than a mile south of the ridge. Native scouts confirmed that it numbered three to four thousand men. The only relief from the increasing tension was the first delivery of mail since the battalion had landed in the Solomons. Bailey had thoughtfully brought it with him from New Caledonia.

As the Raiders and Parachutists braced for an assault, a debate raged at the CP over defensive dispositions. Thomas, more certain than ever that the Japanese would hit somewhere along the exposed southern sector, argued for increased attention toward that threat. At a staff conference on 10 September, Edson weighed in on the side of the operations officer. He stated that the enemy, past masters of infiltration tactics, would easily pick their way through the thin outpost line then guarding most of the inland portion of the perimeter. Patrol reports and the bombing of the ridge on 11 September finally swayed the general. He approved Thomas's recommendations, which included redeploying a battalion along the inland stretches of the Tenaru River, moving 2/5 into a reserve position between the airfield and the ridge, and relaying some of the batteries of the 11th Marines so that they readily could fire missions to the south. Artillery forward observers joined the men on the ridge and registered the guns on likely target areas.

Edson faced a difficult tactical situation. Although he believed that the enemy advance would come down the long axis of the ridge, it would also be possible for them to infiltrate through the jungle and bypass his flanks if he concentrated his force on the high ground. To extend his lines far into the jungle on either side was equally dangerous. There were no forces for him to tie in with in any case, so he would still have open flanks. He also would be relying on a long, thin line with little depth, which the enemy could break anywhere in a concentrated attack. The Raider commander tried to make the best compromise he could between the two options.

He chose the spine of the ridge as the dividing line between his two battalions. As he faced south toward the enemy, he put Baker Company of the Parachutists on his left (the east side of the hogback). Its lines extended down the slope and into the jungle for a short distance. To its rear were the two remaining parachute companies, Charlie and Able. They added depth to the front in case of a penetration and held the rest of the ridge against anyone seeking to flank the main line from the east.

On his immediate right he placed Baker Company of the Raiders. Its left flank tied in with Baker Company of the Parachutists; its right likewise trailed down the ridge and into the jungle at the bottom, where it anchored on a lagoon. Charlie Company closed the gap between the lagoon and the east bank of the Lunga River. To their rear was Able Company, the remnants of Dog, and the Easy Company mortarmen. The machine gunners were attached to the line units. Elements of the 1st Pioneer and 1st Amphibious Tractor Battalions occupied strongpoints on the western side of the Lunga. To the east was nothing but a mile of empty jungle until one reached the positions of the 1st Marines near the Tenaru.

Edson set up the raider battalion headquarters in a draw on the western side of the ridge, several hundred yards from the front lines. Here he placed his communications net, the aid station, and most of the intelligence section. A little farther to the rear was Vandegrift's command post. Edson located his advance CP, the place from which he would fight the battle, on the crest of Hill 120 about five hundred yards behind his front lines. As usual, he wanted to be "up and to the front," where he could observe the action firsthand and influence the battle in person rather than

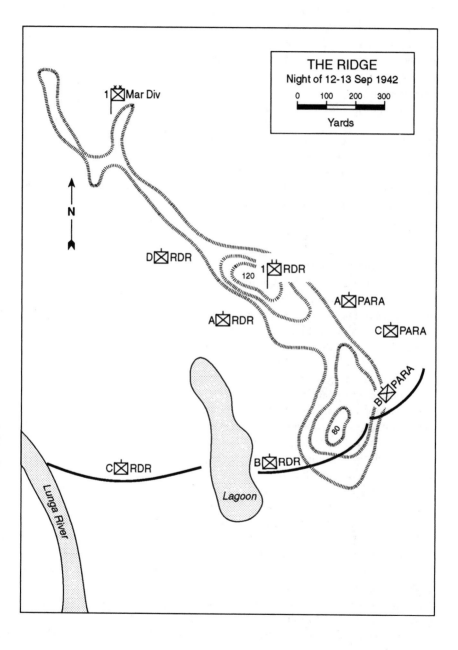

THE RIDGE
Night of 12-13 Sep 1942

0   100   200   300

Yards

1 ⊠ Mar Div

N

D ⊠ RDR

120

1 ⊠ RDR

A ⊠ PARA

A ⊠ RDR

C ⊠ PARA

B ⊠ PARA

80

C ⊠ RDR

B ⊠ RDR

Lagoon

Lunga River

over a telephone or radio. His command group consisted of himself, Maj. Robert Brown (the operations officer), 1st Sgt. Jim Childs (the acting sergeant major), Sgt. Pete Pettus (chief of the intelligence section), and a handful of forward observers, runners, and communicators. Their post was a scratch in the shallow soil and a few telephones and walkie-talkies.

Kawaguchi was, in many respects, in a worse position than his opponent. He had been having difficulties, some self-imposed, in marshaling his forces for a concentrated assault. First, earlier American efforts to intercept the nightly runs of destroyers and barges had inflicted many losses and forced an entire battalion to land west of the Marine perimeter. Kawaguchi tried to make the best of this bad situation by scheduling the unit for an independent attack against that flank. This might at least draw attention and reserves away from his primary objective. He then left three hundred men to defend the Tasimboko beachhead, with the results already noted. Of the four remaining infantry battalions, one would make its assault against the eastern Marine defenses along the Tenaru. The other three units, totaling about twenty-five hundred men, would attack down the ridge and seize the airfield. All three prongs of the offensive were to make a coordinated attack on the night of 12 September. Since Kawaguchi believed his main avenue of approach to be undefended, he might be forgiven for such a complex plan. Like Wolfe at Quebec, he no doubt expected to achieve total surprise by attacking where geography seemed to make offensive operations impossible.

There were two problems with the Japanese plan: The Marines knew they were coming, and the inland march to the assembly area proved much more arduous than Kawaguchi had expected. The troops had to cut a trail through thick undergrowth and negotiate the steep, slippery slopes of numerous ravines. Each man struggled forward under a staggering load: a weapon and equipment, ammunition, and several days' supply of food. There was no possibility of bringing supply trains or artillery along this tortuous route; even weapons that packed a comparatively light punch, such as mortars, proved extremely burdensome when the heavy, bulky rounds were parceled out among the line units. One can imagine the average Japanese soldier, exhausted by each day's laborious efforts, trying to find some sleep at night in a rough niche in the muddy, mosquito-ridden jungle.

As the appointed hour for the attack approached on 12 September, Kawaguchi realized that the forbidding terrain had thrown off his entire schedule. Only one battalion had reached its assigned jump-off point, and then so late in the day that it was unprepared to move forward on time. The other two units were still struggling through the jungle. He wanted to delay the operation, but communications failed and he could not pass the necessary orders. He later lamented that "the Brigade was scattered all over and completely beyond control. In my whole life I have never felt so helpless." As the battle opened, he commanded only a half-dozen men of his personal staff. Given the delays, Japanese scouts also had failed to reconnoiter and establish exact routes for the night attack. Behind schedule and without guides, the battalions hastily blundered forward, only to break up into small detachments as they fought their way through the black-green hell of tangled growth. Kawaguchi's master stroke was fast deteriorating into a series of confused, random jabs.

On the ridge, tired Marines settled down for another night of watching and listening. They knew that the enemy was coming—if not this evening, perhaps the next. Iguanas and other small animals scurried about, vegetation rustled, and shadows seemed to move in the gloom. The defenders strained their senses to distinguish the Japanese from the normal nocturnal activities of the jungle. Weariness made the difficult task even harder. At about 2200 a Japanese floatplane dropped a series of green flares over the perimeter. Then a cruiser and three destroyers of the Tokyo Express opened up on the Marines. These were common occurrences, except that this time the naval gunfire was targeted at the ridge instead of the airfield. A ship's searchlight turned the night into day on the high ground.

The bombardment lasted only a short while, perhaps twenty minutes, and most of the shells soared over the ridge and fell into the jungle beyond, where they occasionally struck the Japanese infantry they were to support. When the ships quit firing, more flares burst in the sky, though these were smaller ones launched from the jungle below. With that signal, the first of Kawaguchi's piecemeal attacks began. Edson had "called the turn almost to the hour."

The Japanese assault concentrated largely on the right of Edson's line, around the lagoon, in between the ridge and the bank of the Lunga River. This may have been an attempt to find an open flank around the American position, or possibly just the result of lack of familiarity with the terrain. Some of the Japanese began "jabbering and shouting" in their usual style. The Raiders, veteran fighters by this point in the campaign, did not fall for the trick. "We remained silent," Edson later said, "waiting for them to advance." As knots of Japanese moved forward, some of their machine guns and mortars opened up in support. Given the overall lack of coordination in the attack, this fire was comparatively weak and sporadic. The periodic rushes met with a strong response from raider weapons and the heavier guns of the 11th Marines. The artillery fired concentrations on likely assembly areas but not close enough to the Marine front to be of immediate assistance there.

The Japanese had hit the American line at the best possible point (from the Japanese perspective). In the thick jungle of the low ground, the Marine advantage in firepower counted much less than it might have, and small groups could readily slip through the raider positions, which were platoon-sized strongpoints rather than a continuous line. The Charlie Company platoon located nearest the lagoon took the brunt of this infiltration. It was soon cut off and surrounded. Attacks nearer the river then dislodged the remainder of Company C. The isolated platoons withdrew in good order, though some men had to fight through to the ridge. In the bitter, close-quarters combat, Charlie Company left seven of its number unaccounted for on the battlefield. The Marine units on the ridge itself remained nearly untouched.

Kawaguchi's effort, long on offensive spirit and short on preparation, ran out of steam as the night wore on. With daylight, infiltration became impossible and the attacks ceased altogether. His officers began the slow process of regrouping their units, now scattered over the jungle and totally disoriented. They disengaged from immediate contact with the Marine lines, but held on to most of the ground they had gained. They proceeded to rest and ready themselves for the next night.

Had the Japanese been better organized, they might have exploited their penetration and created a grave threat to the airfield. Company A was still in reserve for the Raiders but not in position to block the corridor between the ridge and the Lunga. However, Kawaguchi's men would have faced a long push through the jungle and would not have reached the open plain until daylight, only to find 2/5 waiting there with ample fire support. And the remaining Raiders and Parachutists would have been sitting astride the open flank and rear of the Japanese. Thomas and Edson had organized a sound defense.

❧ Red Mike's first reaction in the morning was to order a counterattack by his reserve companies to restore his lines. Raiders and Parachutists moved forward, but the former soon encountered stiff resistance from the more numerous Japanese. In some places the attack regained lost positions, but in other areas strong pressure drove the Marines back to their starting point. With the effort bogged down, and his own men in need of rest and reorganization, Edson decided to break off the action.

In midafternoon he called his company commanders together and issued new instructions. As he spooned cold rations out of a can, he expressed his opinion that the previous night's activity had been merely probing attacks. "They were testing. Just testing. They'll be back." If intelligence was correct and there were three thousand Japanese out there, they had the potential to hit much harder. If that happened, Edson's present dispositions would not work; Baker Company was in an exposed position, with strong enemy forces on its right flank. Company C also had borne the brunt of the night battle and was not ready for another stint on the line. Since Edson could not restore an unbroken front, he opted to withdraw to his reserve line and establish a new defensive posture. This had the added benefit of forcing the enemy to cross more open ground between Marine lines and the edge of the jungle at the end of the ridge.

In the late afternoon both Baker companies pulled back and anchored themselves on the ridge midway between Hill 80 and Hill 120. Able and Charlie of the parachute battalion withdrew only slightly and thus bulked up the left shoulder of the line. They now constituted more of a refused flank than a reserve. Antonelli's Company A anchored the right flank on the bank of the Lunga. Since this rearward move actually extended the territory to be covered by five hundred yards, Edson brought in a company of the 1st Engineer Battalion, then engaged in division CP security, to plug the gap between the Raiders of Able and Baker. The remainder of Edson's battalion assumed a reserve position on the western slope of the ridge, just behind Hill 120.

The commander kept his CP at the highest point on the ridge, but now he was only about two hundred yards from the front lines. He ordered the raider battalion headquarters to displace to the eastern side of the ridge, where it would be out of the line of another attack from the west. Aware that he could not exert on the distant right flank the personal leadership he deemed so important, Edson put Griffith in charge of Company A and the engineers. Vandegrift and Twining visited the front during the day. Edson repeated his "just testing" evaluation and asked them to bring the reserve battalion closer. The general agreed and 2/5 moved up onto the northern edge of the ridge. The company commanders reconnoitered routes forward should they be called to reinforce.

Edson's men were worse off now than at the start of the battle. A night of defense and a day of counterattack and withdrawal had left them physically exhausted and emotionally spent. The sun stared down on those men stuck on the ridge with no shade and sapped even more energy and will. Twining thought that the troops and their commander displayed every evidence of being totally played out. Edson visited at least some of his units and tried to buck them up for another long night. He put the issue bluntly to

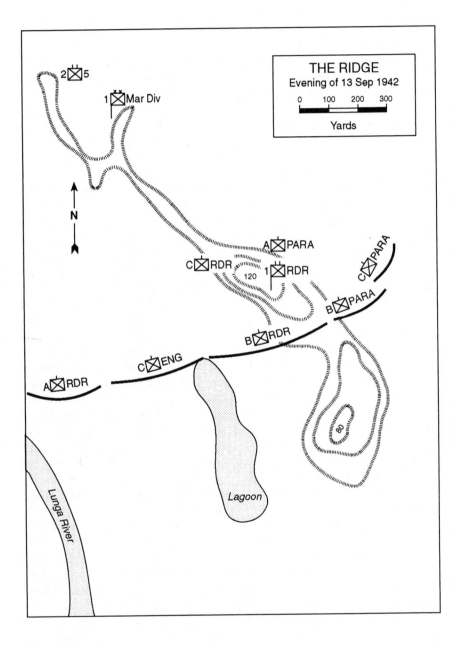

his headquarters group in the rear: the Marines either held the ridge or they would be the ones out in the jungle eating lizards. He passed a similar warning to Sweeney.

The Japanese made good use of the daylight hours. The battalions reorganized, oriented themselves to the terrain, and prepared to launch strong attacks. This time Kawaguchi would not make the same mistake of getting bogged down in the jungle; he would follow the tactics Edson had originally expected and concentrate his efforts on the open ground of the ridge.

The Kawaguchi Brigade kicked off in the attack just after darkness fell, at about 1845. The initial blow hit Baker Company's right flank, near the lagoon. The mad rush of screaming soldiers drove a weakened raider platoon out of position. There was hand-to-hand fighting, but the small, understrength unit managed to break free, fall back on the ridge, and link up with Company C. Some members of the Japanese assault force then worked their way behind the remainder of Baker Company. Inexplicably, Kawaguchi did not attempt to follow up this effort and exploit the gap he had created. Quite possibly, the maneuver had been a diversion from the start, designed to draw Marine reserves off the ridge and out of the way of the main effort.

The Raiders and Parachutists were in a precarious situation. If Edson attempted to plug the gap with Charlie Company, he would have little left to deal with any other penetration. If he did nothing, the center of his line might be quickly encircled and destroyed by the next assault. The enemy provided an answer. By 2100 the Japanese were massing around the nose of the ridge forward of the Baker Companies, making their presence known with the usual barrage of noisy chants. They were going to launch a frontal assault on the center of the line. Edson ordered Able Company of the Parachutists and Charlie Company of the Raiders to form a reserve line around the front and sides of Hill 120. He bolstered them with a handful of spare headquarters personnel from his CP. These were the only units with which he had secure communication. (In the last-minute redispositions that evening, there had been no time to run phone lines to the front.) He could still contact the frontline units by radio, but the enemy was listening in and trying to disrupt that link.

Clouds of smoke, apparent in the glow of flares, boiled up from the enemy lines, and many Marines thought they heard Japanese shouts of "gas attack." A heavy mortar barrage swept the defenders. The Marine forward observer called in artillery on suspected enemy assembly areas at 2100 and again at 2130. He brought more guns to bear when the assault waves surged forward at 2200. The attack, on a front all across the

202 ONCE A LEGEND

ridge, immediately unhinged the Marine center. Japanese threatened to swarm around the jungle flank of the left Company B; Capt. Harry Torgerson, the parachute battalion XO, ordered a withdrawal. As these men moved back under the heavy pressure, their fellow Parachutists in Company C did likewise. Torgerson gathered the two units in the rear of Company A's position on Hill 120.

The situation, once difficult, was now desperate. The Japanese had broken the entire left side of the main line of resistance and had punched a large hole on the right. Two platoons of Raiders, the remnants of Baker Company, were now isolated in the center. Edson had no secure communication forward to them; his telephone lines to the rear had also been cut by the enemy's mortar fire. The remaining units on the old front, the engineers and Able Company, were effectively out of the battle; they were not under attack, but they also were not in a position to lend a hand on the ridge. Two weak companies manned the hastily formed position around the knoll, while the two disorganized parachute units now constituted the only reserve.

At this point, the Japanese seemed to take a breather. Their mortars and machine guns still raked the ridge, but they did not immediately follow up their initial success. The Marines knew that the respite would not last for long, and they made full use of the opportunity. Edson ordered Sweeney to get his rump company back to the knoll. He did so by having Burak shout out the command using the raider code names. The runner called out: "John Wolf, do you hear me?" When Sweeney yelled back in the affirmative, Burak replied: "Red Mike says it's okay to withdraw." As those sixty men moved slowly to the rear, other Marines intensified their fire to cover the movement. Burak then braved heavy fire and infiltrators to run a phone line back to the raider headquarters, which was tied in with the division CP. Over this line Edson reported that he had only about three hundred men in position to defend the ridge, those few arrayed around Hill 120, and he arranged for fresh artillery concentrations to keep the enemy at bay.

There was some danger that the withdrawal might degenerate into a rout. As a few men around Hill 120 began to filter to the rear, the colonel took immediate steps to avert this possible disaster. From his CP, now just a dozen yards behind the front, he made it known that there would be no more backpedaling. Word passed among the troops that this was the "final stand." "Nobody moves, just die in your holes." Major Bailey, an extrovert by nature, raised his voice above the din. The Charlie Company commander went up and down the new line encouraging everyone, breathing life into those on the verge of giving up, and "rendering valuable

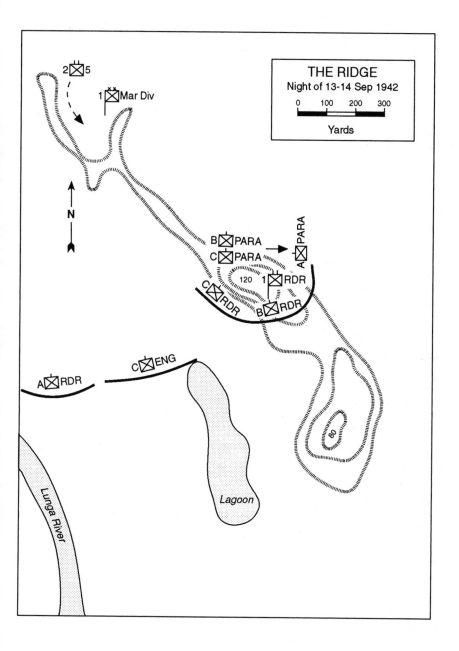

assistance to the Battalion Commander in stemming the retreat." The commander of the parachute battalion was evidently not up to the task of controlling his men, many of whom were confused in the absence of direction from above. Edson relieved him on the spot and put Torgerson in charge.

By 2400 Company B had made it safely to the knoll. "From then on," Edson would later say, "we had them licked." The outcome was probably not so clear at that moment. The Raiders and Parachutists had the semblance of a new line now in place, though it was bent like a horseshoe around the hill and covered nothing but the bare slopes of the ridge. Edson directed the artillery to maintain a continuous barrage close along his front. Then enemy mortar fire or infiltrators again cut the telephone lines. One forward observer raced back along the ridge to the division CP, where he passed on new adjustments to bring the rounds another fifty yards closer to Marine lines. A runner, probably Burak, followed a little later to confirm the accuracy. "It's right on. It's knocking the hell out of 'em." When the indomitable corporal observed that division communicators were making no effort to restore the line, he grabbed a spool of wire and made another trip along the fire-swept high ground back to Edson's post.

The Japanese were again coming on strong. The attack was not continuous, but periodically a new wave of Imperial soldiers came boiling out of the jungle and along the ridge. Each time, they met a rain of steel from Marine batteries, as well as flickering fingers of tracer bullets stabbing out of machine guns, automatic rifles, and submachine guns. With all that firepower erupting along the front, most ordinary riflemen (still armed with bolt-action Springfields) felt impotent. They had a hard time picking out targets, and an even harder time trying to hit anything with a single shot. Most gave up the effort and simply tossed grenade after grenade at whatever shapes or sounds appeared. As the night wore on, supplies of ammunition dwindled rapidly. Edson called Thomas and asked for more grenades and belted machine-gun rounds.

One of the Japanese assaults, probably avoiding the concentrated fire sweeping the crest, pushed along the jungle edge at the bottom of the slope and threatened to envelop the left flank of the Marine line. Edson ordered Torgerson to launch a counterattack with the two parachute companies that he had withdrawn and reorganized earlier in the evening. These Marines advanced, checked the enemy assault, and then extended the line to prevent any recurrence. This fighting was particularly heavy and resulted in 40 percent casualties for the two units. Edson thought this attack was "a decisive factor in our ultimate victory."

The Marines were holding, but the Japanese kept coming on and the shortage of ammunition grew acute. Getting those supplies to the men who needed them became the heart of the battle. Captain Clarence R. Schwenke of the division staff, Captain Irwin, and 1st Sergeant Childs led the effort to move the stuff forward. A truck brought a load part of the way, but the heavy boxes had to be carried the last few hundred yards through a gauntlet of fire from the enemy's heavier weapons and from innumerable snipers who had infiltrated the flanking jungle. Once the ammo reached the knoll, men had to move it along the lines. Bailey and others crawled along the ground, dragged the boxes behind them, and distributed the precious contents.

At 0400 Edson asked Thomas to commit the reserve battalion to bolster his depleted line. A company at a time, the men of 2/5 filed along the top of the ridge, past the division CP, and into place beside those who had survived the long night. By this time the Japanese were largely spent. Kawaguchi sent in two more attacks, but they were hit by artillery fire as the troops assembled and never presented much of a threat. A small band actually made it past the ridge and reached the vicinity of the airfield; the Marines providing security there dealt with them.

The onset of daylight brought an end to the assault though not to all enemy activity. Numerous Japanese were scattered throughout the jungle fringing the division CP and the rear of the ridge. Some might have purposely infiltrated the area; others were no doubt the flotsam of the night attacks. These men fired at any movement in the open, and a sword-wielding officer even led a three-man assault on Vandegrift's headquarters. A machine gun riddled a truck carrying raider wounded and killed the occupants, among them Major Brown. Squads began the long process of rooting out the snipers.

Other Japanese troops still clung to the southern end of the ridge, where they were in defilade, out of the reach of Marine weapons on the knoll. Edson, no doubt considering the present state of his men and the abortive counterattack of the previous day, assigned Major Bailey to coordinate an air strike on the position. A flight of P-400s responded to the call and strafed the enemy in the now-exposed position. By early afternoon Kawaguchi admitted failure and ordered his tattered brigade to retreat. He left about seven hundred dead on and around the ridge. Of his five hundred wounded, most would not survive the long, terrible trek back to the coast. His troops had long since exhausted their supplies of food, physical energy, and fighting spirit.

The Raiders and Parachutists walked off the ridge in the morning and left 2/5 to mop up the battlefield and bury the Japanese dead. The two exhausted battalions had sustained heavy casualties. Griffith placed raider losses at 135 men, and those of the Parachutists at 128. Of the total, 59 Marines were dead or missing in action. A more detailed survey of Edson's battalion listed losses from 12 to 14 September as 34 killed in action and 129 wounded, though this might have included those hit in the air raids prior to the ground battle. Coupled with earlier combat actions, the Parachutists had now suffered a 55 percent casualty rate; the Raiders had lost more than 30 percent of the men they originally brought to the Solomons. Victory on the ridge had not been cheap.

This battle, by far the most serious up to that point in the land campaign, quickly became a legend, with considerable justification. As Twining put it, the ridge "might have ended as a ghastly defeat, had it not been for Edson and those who stood with him." Over the course of time, however, the scale of the already-heroic deeds grew with each telling. In a 1948 manuscript, a participant said that the ridge was held for a time by just sixty men. By the 1950s Lew Walt would describe the numerical odds as having been fifteen to one in favor of the enemy.

There was some basis in fact for these assertions, if one looked at the brief stand by Sweeney's Company B or added all the Japanese forces available to Kawaguchi and ranged them against the three hundred or so Raiders and Parachutists on the knoll at midnight. But, like Edson's forces on the right flank, out of the battle and thus out of the counting, one must also subtract significant numbers from the Japanese figure. Although there were about forty-five hundred soldiers in the Kawaguchi Brigade, the general split off more than a third to perform independent missions. He began the attack on the ridge on 12 September with twenty-five hundred men, but surely lost a significant number in the fighting that night. During the climactic engagement on 13 September and into the fourteenth, his reserve battalion remained largely out of action, much like Edson's companies on the right flank. The raider commander and Thomas both estimated the enemy force at two thousand men in the immediate aftermath of the battle. It seems fair to say that the few hundred Marines on the ridge that night faced about fifteen hundred Japanese soldiers—difficult odds under any method of calculation.

Several factors contributed to the American victory over a numerically superior foe. One important aspect was the availability of firepower. Although the Japanese had brought artillery ashore, there was never any practical hope that they could bring it to bear in direct support of the main force. (Some pieces did participate in one of the attacks on the flanks of the Marine perimeter, but even here terrain placed great limits on their effectiveness. The awkward guns and heavy ammunition just could not be hauled forward over the rough trails cut by Kawaguchi's men.) The bombardment by naval guns was equally irrelevant. The batteries of the 11th

Marines, on the other hand, undoubtedly inflicted a substantial proportion of Japanese casualties. Without that virtual wall of steel to their front, it might have been impossible for the Raiders and Parachutists to stop the onrushing enemy.

The infantry was absolutely necessary to the equation, too. No amount of indirect firepower would have won the battle without someone on the ground confronting the enemy face to face. Otherwise, the Japanese could have easily filtered through the jungle around the edges of any barrage, or charged through it with bearable losses. But a fence of Marine infantrymen held up each attack, forced the enemy to prolong his stay under the thunder of concussions and rain of shrapnel, and then caught any who made their way through the belt of fire. The automatic weapons and grenades of the infantry also contributed their share to the carnage. But one thing, above all, kept those Marines in place and allowed the firepower to do its deadly work—the leadership of men such as Edson.

It is difficult to reconstruct exactly what Red Mike said or did during the battle. It was rare for any infantry battalion to keep detailed combat records in the early days of the war, and the spartan nature of the raider field CP made no provision for a journal clerk or message files. Of the small handful of officers and men who served next to the colonel during that period, many died later in the war, several within just a few days.

As with the battle itself, stories of the raider commander's deeds grew to mythic proportions. Thomas would later say that he could hear Edson's shouted commands and exhortations "all night long," from all the way back at the division CP, a distance of several hundred yards. According to one account, the colonel "strode up and down [his] lines time and again, cajoling, correcting." When morale was lowest and a rout appeared imminent, he supposedly shamed the weak Marines by comparing them with their enemies. "Go back where you came from. The only thing they've got that you haven't is guts."

His specific words or acts are unimportant, for there is no doubt that Edson was the catalyst of victory that night. He described himself as having been "lucky in being at the right place at the right time and getting away with it." But his "tactical nose," as one fellow officer described it, ensured that the Raiders and Parachutists were in that position in the first place. The Tasimboko raid, which he had inspired and executed, made that possible. His interpretation of the evidence and his assistance in convincing Vandegrift were critical, too. "Although it may have caught some by surprise," it was Edson who "G-2'd the Nips would come that way." After the battle was over, the only thing he was ready to "brag about" was his reading of the enemy plan. Edson's second contribution was his skill as a tactician. In planning the defense he used the terrain and his small force in such a way as to minimize the disadvantages of both. Once the fighting began, he responded to each new crisis with sound decisions on the placement of companies and the employment of firepower.

Finally, he demonstrated a level of bravery that bolstered the will of those around him when the situation appeared most desperate. Everyone who saw him on the ridge agreed on one thing—his absolutely fearless disregard for his own safety. At the height of the battle, with friendly artillery shells landing just seventy-five yards to the front and enemy bullets and mortars sweeping the knoll, Edson never took cover. He stood erect in his CP, maintained the best possible field of view of the action swirling around that spot, and calmly relayed orders and information over the phones and radios or passed instructions to his staff, most of whom were hugging the ground. He may have "barked" words of command and encouragement (though probably not loud enough for Thomas to hear). It is certain that Edson's calm behavior helped others overcome their own fears and do their jobs in spite of the danger. Just as important was the tremendous reservoir of trust and confidence in their commander that the men had built up in months of training and fighting. Men such as Bailey and Burak could perform their heroics secure in the knowledge that the overall direction of the battle was in capable hands.

Edson's Medal of Honor citation accurately described his role in the victory:

> During the entire battle Colonel Edson, continuously exposed to hostile fire of great intensity, personally directed the defense of his position. He displayed such a marked degree of cool leadership and personal courage that the officers and men of his command were constantly inspired by his example, and his personal influence over them kept the men in position throughout the night in the face of a fanatical enemy of greatly superior numbers despite the severest casualties to his own men.

Tregaskis personally verified that Red Mike had a few close calls. Shortly after the battle he had occasion to note the bullet holes in the colonel's collar and the side of his shirt. Edson admitted that "the stuff buzzed around like a bunch of hornets." How did he carry on in the face of such grave danger? Admiral Raymond Spruance, another leader of demonstrated courage, once said: "Some of us have steeled our nerves, to a certain degree, to be brave." Bailey, who finished the battle "beaming like a kid on the night before Christmas," represented another sort of courage. Some men got caught up in the excitement of the moment, almost as if in a football game, and they simply forgot about the danger.

Edson seemed to fit neither of those categories. One of his men described the colonel's attitude as being almost that of a religious martyr, someone who simply had no fear of dying, who actually looked forward to the prospect. There was undoubtedly some element of truth in that evaluation. In describing the maelstrom of steel that night, Red Mike told his wife: "I am firmly convinced that it is all in the hands of God, anyway, and so one should not worry too much about such things." This would not be the last time Edson would dare death to take him—dare it in a way no man who wanted to live ever would.

Chapter 12

"We Fight Our Country's Battles"

As the haggard men of the raider battalion stumbled back to their old bivouac near Kukum, Edson dropped into the division command post to make his report of the action. Tregaskis was particularly glad to see him in the rear, since it meant that the tough struggle of the past two days and nights was successfully concluded. One division staff officer indicated how close the battle had been when he whispered to another reporter: "We didn't know whether we would see [Edson] this morning or not." Thomas lavished praise on the Raiders, calling them "the best gang of cut-throats you could find anywhere in the world."

Edson readily acknowledged the vital assistance of the artillery and gave it ample credit for many of the Japanese casualties. He also cited the bravery of his men, collectively and individually. Tregaskis later gathered stories from others who attested to the colonel's own courage. After inspecting the scene of the battle the next day, the correspondents christened the place "Edson's Hill" in their dispatches. The name did not entirely stick. Some Marines called it Bloody Ridge, others Raider Ridge, but among those who fought there, it generally became enshrined as Edson's Ridge.

At the moment, however, the Raiders were concentrating on other things. After several days of hard fighting and no sleep, they were utterly exhausted. The physical effects of poor nutrition and insufficient rest were accumulating into rampant illness—malaria, dengue fever, gastroenteritis, and dysentery ravaged most of the men, oftentimes in combination. Even the exhilaration of victory and survival was tempered by the loss of numerous comrades. In testimony to the increasing psychological rigors of the campaign, the battalion registered its first cases of shell shock and combat fatigue. Division assigned the battalion to a reserve role and some well-deserved rest.

Good news seemed to come on the morning of 17 September. An American convoy sailed into view off Lunga Point and disgorged the 7th Marines. The parachute battalion, reduced to ineffectiveness by heavy losses, boarded the empty transports. Rumors swept the raider ranks that they would be going home very soon, too. After all, they had fought just as hard as their elite comrades and suffered their own share of casualties. The addition of the 7th Marines, a fresh force thoroughly trained by experienced leaders such as Lt. Col. Lewis B. ("Chesty") Puller and Lt. Col. Herman Hannekan, seemed to make the Raiders less necessary. Many Raiders thought it was high time the battalion, a hit-and-run unit, got back to the base camp in New Caledonia.

Edson, an old hand at squelching similar sentiments along the Coco, made short work of this spate of wishful thinking. He went from company to company, gathered the men around him at each site, and spoke briefly about their future. No one recorded his exact words, but everyone remembered the gist: "He was all business and very blunt about it." There were references to a long war yet to be fought, about going all the way to Tokyo, and, in a phrase reminiscent of Christmas presents to Poteca, a desire to "eat Thanksgiving dinner in Bougainville" (an island farther north in the Solomons chain). The speech was a real blow to morale, but it produced the desired effect: The men steeled themselves to the prospect of further combat. By the time it arrived they had forgotten the rumors and focused their minds on the business at hand.

The next opportunity to fight was not long in coming. In the immediate aftermath of the battle of the Ridge, the division was too weak to exploit its victory over the Kawaguchi Brigade and pursue the defeated Japanese. Vandegrift and Thomas did send out large patrols in that direction on 14 and 17 September to ensure that the threat had subsided, but these met resistance and withdrew after taking casualties. On the afternoon of the nineteenth, division assigned the Raiders to make a reconnaissance in force to the south of the ridge and break up any remaining enemy concentrations. The battalion left its bivouac that afternoon and went into attack positions not far from the perimeter, now strongly held by the 7th Marines. The Raiders slept by the side of the road so they could move out at 0430 the next morning. They would take the east side of the river, while elements of the 7th made their way up the other bank.

The path of the patrol the next day was torturous. It alternated between arduous climbs up steep, sun-beaten ridges and equally tough going through dense, muggy jungle lowlands. The lead company had not gone far when it began to encounter signs of the Japanese retreat; the foe had abandoned equipment, weapons, ammunition, and even the dead. Although the enemy was already beaten, Edson was cautious in his tactics. Forward observers called in artillery on suspected enemy locations, and when his men finally made contact, he brought to bear all his machine guns and mortars before ordering the infantry forward. He moved along the line of gunners arrayed on a ridge and personally directed their fire. After capturing a dismantled field howitzer and killing at least nineteen enemy (at a cost of three wounded), Edson ordered the battalions to head back to the perimeter. They had accomplished their mission of scouring the area. The greatest point of danger in the operation turned out to be the return trip. As the patrol neared friendly lines, the jittery new arrivals of the 7th Marines opened up on the Raiders. Luckily no one was hit.

Although they had been gone for only a few hours, the Raiders returned to a division with new leadership. The process had begun with the early August promotions of Edson and five other lieutenant colonels in the outfit. Then Commandant Holcomb had asked Vandegrift on 8 September to send home his excess colonels for employment elsewhere. The commanding general used this as an opportunity to clean out the senior officers who had performed poorly, in particular Hunt of the 5th Marines, as well as those who simply did not mesh well on a personal level. Red Mike had been a colonel for only a few weeks, but he had proven himself to be the most audacious and competent combat leader in the division, so he received command of his old regiment. Thomas later claimed a role in the decision. He recalled a session in which the general complained of problems in the 5th Marines. "Well, I had no hesitation. I said, 'Take Merritt Edson of the Raiders and put him in command.'" By this time the operations officer exerted considerable influence on his commander, to the point that Vandegrift also sent home Col. Capers James, his chief of staff, and gave the position to Thomas. In the process, he secured a temporary promotion to colonel for Thomas. Twining moved up to head the operations section.

These four men—Vandegrift, Edson, Thomas, and Twining—formed the heart of a "Guadalcanal mafia," which would come to dominate the Corps until 1948. Vandegrift, by virtue of his close association with Holcomb and his command of the first successful American offensive of the war, would rise to the commandancy. He would take Thomas with him along this road to the top and lean heavily on his subordinate's wealth of personal strength and wisdom. Thomas, in turn, made ready use of the valuable skills of the other two: Twining, the brilliant thinker; and Edson, the courageous leader, proven tactician, and able staff officer. They were not all friends. Twining was too junior and too outspoken to suit Vandegrift's tastes, and the courtly southern general never fully warmed to the flinty Yankee from Vermont. But he valued both for their superior skills demonstrated in the crucible of combat.

⚫ Thomas and Edson were kindred spirits in many respects and did become close friends. Their hard-bitten emphasis on performance engendered mutual respect, whereas some of their colleagues viewed this trait with distaste, as a manifestation of ambition or poor fellowship. Undoubtedly both men were ambitious, though they moved ahead by their own efforts, not by intrigue or back-stabbing. Vandegrift fit more into the "go along–get along" school. Even though he had relieved Hunt and James for mediocre performance, he had disguised the move as part of the response to Holcomb's request, and he soon recommended each for promotion to brigadier general. Hunt and a few other officers with equally spotty records would make the grade, to the detriment of men such as Thomas and Edson, who assumed increasing authority but found little room for advancement in rank.

The transfer came so suddenly that Edson did not even hold a battalion formation to say farewell. He did issue a written statement that expressed his feelings to the men. He began by noting that the "honor and praise" heaped upon the Raiders had been far out of proportion to their relative size within the Corps. He then recounted the unit's achievements up through the patrol of the previous day and averred that the battalion was "among the best of the fighting organizations that the Marine Corps has ever produced." For the colonel, it had been "a pleasure and a great honor to have the privilege of commanding" the Raiders. That sentiment was genuine: He had created the unit and given it its character, this had been his first major combat command, his fame was inextricably tied with that of the unit, and he would hold the battalion and its members dear to his heart for the rest of his life. Later in the war he would privately say that the Raiders were his "first and naturally best love."

His men had mixed emotions at his departure. On the one hand, the troops revered him because of his demonstrated courage. He was not only a hero to the outside world but to them as well. They also hated to lose a leader whom they could trust in the thick of a fight. Finally, he was the type of officer who set the example and never asked his men to do anything he was not willing to do himself. But that was the crux of the matter, because the fearless commander was often ready to do more than many men could endure. After the Ridge, a few of the officers and men had developed a new nickname for their commander, one that expressed their ambivalence over his willingness to risk not only his own death, but theirs as well; they called him "Mad Merritt the Morgue Master."

Sometimes, Edson's desire to fight seemed to border on callous disregard for the lives of his men. One Marine was upset when he saw his commander sitting on a log, casually sipping from a canteen, with a dead Raider sprawled nearby. Griffith registered a similar feeling about Red Mike: "I think he was in many ways a pretty cold man; I don't know how truly capable he was of loving his fellow man. . . . That sounds pretty harsh, but I don't mean it to be, that's just the way he was made." Edson would have accepted that assessment without complaint. Within days the new commander of the 5th Marines would provide a brief lesson in battlefield philosophy to a subordinate who could not get his men to move forward. "You've got to take a chance on getting hurt," he told him. Red Mike knew that casualties were unavoidable; he tried to lower them by ensuring a quick victory, not by avoiding combat.

Many of the Raiders were glad to see him go, because they believed they could not survive many more fights like the ones of the past few weeks. As time passed, they forgot the danger and remembered only the positive aspects of Edson's tenure. At the end of the war, despite a succession of outstanding commanders, the former members of the battalion would choose to name their unit association after their founder.

The reassignment placed Edson in one of the most difficult situations of his life. In addition to the increased responsibility, he had to adapt to an entirely new unit, one that had a reputation of failure, and he had to do this in a combat environment where victory or defeat hung in the balance. There was no margin for error. To top it off, Hunt had been well liked by his officers and men, and the nature of his relief gave them no hint that their performance had been less than adequate.

Red Mike knew exactly what he had to do to get things on the right track. His focus would be on leadership. Unlike Hunt (and Vandegrift), Edson would not suffer the shortcomings of poor performance by subordinates, but would move quickly to identify those who could do the job and put them in charge. To make that task easier, he brought a few trusted people with him from the Raiders. Walt took over as regimental operations officer; Hank Adams assumed the intelligence billet. Burak came over as well to continue as Edson's runner. Beyond these formal transfers, Edson also temporarily borrowed the services of other Raiders, such as Lt. Jim Blessing, who would train the regiment's demolitions personnel. Griffith, already shorthanded due to casualties, protested the raid on what was now his battalion. The division staff gave him short shrift; the 5th Marines needed a "builder," someone who could steal a few people and turn an organization around.

As if to illustrate his focus on leadership, Edson made no significant changes in policy, no bold pronouncements upon his assumption of command—unlike most new commanders, who feel compelled to alter their predecessor's routine. The junior officers and men saw no discernible difference in the regiment, at first. One of Red Mike's initial acts, however, was to relieve the inept commanding officer of 3/5 and elevate the XO to the job. Thereafter, he took every opportunity possible to encourage the development and exercise of good leadership. He had to train the troops as well, since much of the regiment had spent little time in the Corps prior to Guadalcanal, and the movement of the division from the States to the target area had left little time for the task. He got the effort under way by touring the front lines, making corrections to the defensive dispositions, and demonstrating the proper way to do things.

This gave him his first opportunity to foster a new leader. One young officer transferred into the regiment shortly thereafter and immediately complained about the location of his company's machine guns. Told that the regimental commander had made the decisions about placement, Capt. Victor Croizat took his concerns to Edson. Red Mike responded, "Let's go take a look." The two officers spent the afternoon in front of the battalion's lines "looking at potential fields of fire from the direction of the enemy." Edson demonstrated again and again this desire to encourage junior leaders. Later in the campaign an Army team interviewed members of the 5th Marines to compile a pamphlet on combat lessons. One corporal mentioned that his platoon was the best in the company because the lieutenant had honed it like a good coach would a baseball team. The interviewer later recounted: "When I read this to Colonel Edson at the end of the day, he was so delighted that he sent a runner to find out who the corporal's platoon leader was."

Red Mike was no stickler for the rules, if common sense worked better. During his first night in the 5th Marines CP, he quietly chided a staff officer who spoke on the phone without using proper authentication procedures. The captain defended himself by arguing that no Japanese could imitate the distinctive accent of the man on the other end of the line, Capt. Walter McIlhenny, a Louisianan whose family was famous for its Tabasco sauce. Edson grinned and let the subject drop.

Despite his hard-earned reputation as a warrior, Edson did not assume that his new subordinates would automatically revere him. Instead, he set about building the same sort of confidence among the 5th Marines that he had within the Raiders. Some feared he might be a glory hound ready to sacrifice their blood to further his career. His actions soon destroyed that view. Those who heard him issue an order for an operation came away amazed at how he dictated the situation and mission without reference to notes. His precise, controlled, quiet presentation belied the firebrand leader they had expected. He exuded confidence in himself and his decisions, and that boosted the confidence of others. As time passed, a belief in the regimental commander's competence percolated down through the ranks.

To bolster that positive view, Red Mike continued to demonstrate leadership by example. One lieutenant thought him "omnipresent." "Any time you were in a fire fight you could rest assured you'd be looking around and the regimental commander would *be* there." Although in charge of a much larger unit, Edson still believed in the "principle of the Command Post up and to the front." The 5th Marines developed its own set of stories about his courage. In one instance, the headquarters group had just settled in a clearing on the bank of a river when a machine gun opened up from the opposite bank. Everyone dived for cover, except for the colonel, who continued to sit on a tree stump and read the messages in his hand. To the pleas of his staff he responded: "Hell, even if they aimed at me they couldn't hit me." The tale was probably apocryphal, but the pervasiveness of similar accounts seems to prove that Red Mike demonstrated his bravery often enough to convince everyone in the regiment.

Edson's first test as a regimental commander came very quickly. With the arrival of the 7th Marines, division now had adequate strength for limited offensive operations. Twining felt that a first priority should be the expansion of the perimeter east and west to prevent Japanese artillery from reaching the airfield. Although the division could not permanently man such an extended front, the planners decided on a compromise effort in the direction of the Matanikau River. Puller's 1/7 would clean out any Japanese units between the present western flank and the far side of the Matanikau. The 1st Raider Battalion would then set up a patrol base near Kokumbona to ensure that the area remained sanitized. The effort, which commenced on 23 September, ran into early difficulties. On the twenty-fourth Puller's men surprised a Japanese force eating their evening meal; they dispersed them but lost seven killed and twenty-five wounded in the process. Division sent out 2/5 as a relief force and the two units linked up the next day. Puller sent back his casualties with an escort of two of his companies, then continued on with a task force composed of his one remaining rifle company and 2/5. This odd concoction would characterize the rest of the battle, which would become known as the Second Matanikau.

Puller and his force reached the river on 26 September near a single-log bridge. According to the original plan, they were to cross here, but

Puller decided to proceed down the east bank. The Marines received harassing fire from mortars on the far side, and then ran into heavy resistance when they tried to cross the sandbar at the river's mouth. A Japanese company blocked the way here and, unbeknownst to Puller, another enemy company occupied defensive positions on the eastern end of the single-log bridge upstream. Division ordered the Raiders forward in support, and late in the afternoon placed Edson in overall charge of the situation, with Puller to act as his assistant.

The two leaders devised a new plan that evening. In the morning the Raiders and Puller's Company C would move upriver, cross at the bridge, and then come back downriver on the far bank to take the Japanese at the river mouth in the flank. So far, this was nothing more than a rerun of the earlier battle of the Tenaru. To ensure that the enemy force did not retreat out of the trap, 2/5 would pressure them with its own attack across the sandbar. This was the Tenaru in reverse, with American forces assaulting in the open against a strongly entrenched enemy. Finally, the other three companies of 1/7, then in the perimeter and under the command of the executive officer, would execute an amphibious landing beyond Point Cruz, advance along the coast to the east, and slam shut any possible escape route. The ambitious plan received division's blessing.

After a heavy rain that night, things started to go badly the next day. A morning assault by 2/5 failed to establish a hold on the far side of the sandbar. The Raiders advanced upriver, but soon found themselves in a narrow area between the river and a steep ridge. Japanese infantry, machine guns, and mortars put a tight stopper in the bottle, and no amount of courage could break the impasse. Bailey, already recommended for the Medal of Honor for his heroics on Edson's Ridge, died trying to force his way forward. Griffith fell wounded after leading part of the unit up onto the ridge in an effort to flank the Japanese. The enemy had that approach well covered, too.

Poor communications made things worse. Both division and Edson thought that the Raiders had indicated they were across the river, so the regimental commander again launched 2/5 in the assault. He had brought up mortars and 37mm antitank guns for added fire support, but with no help in the enemy's rear that frontal attack also failed. Meanwhile 1/7 went ashore as planned. The unit moved inland to high ground, only to be surrounded by a strong Japanese force bivouaced in the vicinity. Since the three companies had no radios, they had to use undershirts as air panels to signal their plight to supporting aircraft.

Edson called off 2/5's attack across the sandbar to avoid further wasteful casualties, even though Puller insisted that it continue as a diversion to

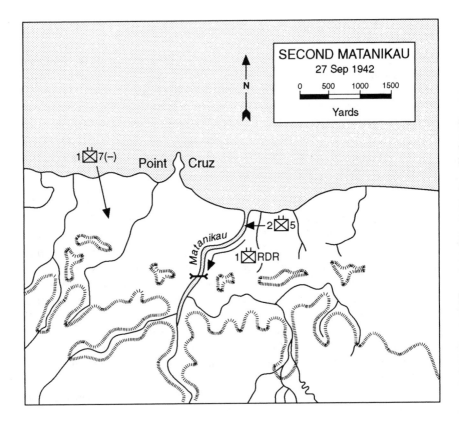

assist his beleaguered companies near Point Cruz. The angry lieutenant colonel then raced back along the coast, boarded a warship, and oversaw the extrication of his men. That was accomplished by naval gunfire and old-fashioned semaphore flag communications. The Raiders likewise broke off their attack and retraced their steps to the coast, at which point they and 2/5 withdrew to Marine lines. The entire operation had cost 67 men killed and 125 wounded, most of them on the last day, and had inflicted an unknown but insignificant number of casualties on the enemy. Moreover, division had not achieved its objective of clearing the Matanikau region.

The official Marine Corps history of the Guadalcanal campaign could not bring itself to call the battle a defeat, though it did acknowledge that it came the closest of any ground action. Edson was not so squeamish; he referred to it as the "abortive Second Matanikau," though he almost never spoke of it afterward. The 1st Marine Division's report tried to salvage some good from the admitted debacle: "But for the good judgment of senior commanders present our losses might well have been much more severe." The fight proved unimportant in the course of the war and provided no advantage to the Japanese. Casualties were not great, though even small numbers loom large when suffered for no gain. It would be easy to gloss over the encounter and move on to more spectacular events, but this was Edson's only defeat in an otherwise spotless combat career. Moreover, it sullied the reputation of several outstanding units and commanders.

Among the participants, there was a readiness to assign blame elsewhere. Griffith accused Edson of needlessly dispersing his force and Vandegrift of allowing him to do it. Puller was apparently disgusted with the whole thing and ready to disparage the Raiders and their former commander. Twining blamed Puller for failing to cross the upper river in the first place, as the plan directed him to do, and claimed that Puller and Edson had authored the bungled supplementary plan of 26 September. The division operations officer accepted responsibility to the extent that he had gone along with the poor scheme. Thomas was apparently against the whole idea of offensive operations along the Matanikau; it was Twining who wanted to expand the perimeter and he who convinced Vandegrift to launch the operation. Only Edson remained silent on the issue.

Red Mike could have made many excuses. He had been in command of his regiment for only a week and could hardly be expected to know all its strengths and weaknesses in so short a time. However, he was intimately familiar with two of the three battalions engaged, so the handicap was minor. Next, the composition of the force and the chain of command were so contorted as to make operations difficult. Instead of sending a regiment to do the job, division assigned three unrelated battalions to work together. Edson was clearly placed in charge, but Puller and his command group were somehow grafted onto the 5th Marines staff. Moreover, the rump of 1/7 went into combat under the XO and a makeshift staff, with no opportunity for Edson to brief the acting commander in person. Although such actions would normally be considered poor procedure, they seemed to be standard practice on Guadalcanal. Red Mike had intermingled parts of 2/5 and the parachute battalion into the Raiders in past engagements, and similar lash-ups would fight many of the battles to come.

Another problem was that Edson had come on the scene late and hastily grafted a new scheme of maneuver onto a plan that had already come apart at the seams. This was a tough chore but not unlike many he had faced before. There had been little time to prepare for the Tasimboko raid or the Ridge. It is not even clear that the plan was Edson's, but he bore responsibility for it nonetheless in his role as commander. Finally, poor communications had made a bad situation worse. Some of this was fortuitous, due to bomb damage inflicted on the division radio net during the operation. Some of it was due to Puller's propensity to ignore the importance of communications, as Twining later noted. "Edson was meticulous about the way he worked up his communications. He was always in touch with us. But Puller never told us anything. He wouldn't even use his radios."

Since Red Mike made no attempt to assess blame elsewhere, one can speculate that he meant to accept it himself. Certainly he had made some errors. He widely dispersed his force and put each element out of supporting range of the others. He kept no reserve with which he could influence the battle; when the Raiders and 1/7 got stuck, they could not seek help elsewhere. But the biggest shortcoming—one that pertained to every leader involved—was a failure to obtain adequate intelligence before launching the original operation and its permutation. Griffith's assessment did mention the lack of knowledge of terrain and the enemy. The official history ascribed this to the fact that the battle ranged far beyond the bailiwick of normal defensive patrols and to the inability of aerial reconnaissance to observe activity under the jungle canopy.

Martin Clemens, the chief coastwatcher on Guadalcanal, probably provided a better explanation. The natives of Kokumbona, the only village in this otherwise uninhabited stretch of the coast, had evacuated that location early in the campaign and had not returned. Without this source of local intelligence and support, his scouts were severely handicapped; the best means of gathering information on the island simply did not exist. As a consequence, a force of just over two thousand Marines had tried to subdue a well-entrenched Japanese force about twice their size. The inevitable result was a fiasco. The best that can be said about Second Matanikau is that there was blame enough to spread around among many men.

Three days after that failed operation, Admiral Nimitz, the theater commander, made his first visit to Guadalcanal. He toured much of the perimeter, to include a walk over Edson's Ridge guided by its namesake, an event that "particularly impressed" him. The next morning the admiral held an awards ceremony and decorated about two dozen Marines with the Navy Cross, the highest medal he could give on his own authority. The awardees included several of the most successful pilots, a sprinkling of enlisted men, and most of the major commanders. Edson was among the group, due to his efforts on the Ridge.

The ceremony was simple: two lines of men in front of the division CP, a handful of onlookers, the occasional raucous routine of camp life going on in the distance. This was the middle of a campaign—no place for troop formations or elaborate ritual. For Edson, the second Navy Cross apparently did little to boost a morale that seemed to be at low ebb. He wrote home just three days later and mentioned both the Navy Cross and a recommendation for the Medal of Honor, but in a matter-of-fact way. He seemed more concerned about the fate of Bob Brown and Ken Bailey and told Ethel they "had bad luck recently about which I feel extremely sorry." This was a rare admission of sympathy from a man who was generally hardened to the death of fellow Marines in the course of war.

The failure along the Matanikau may have been weighing heavily on his mind. In addition to the defeat itself, it had cost his old raider battalion the last of its senior officers and further reduced them to just a shadow of their former selves. As one Raider put it: "A more sickly, bedraggled, miserable bunch of Marines would have been hard to find." The defeat had also soured Edson's relations with Twining and created friction between the regimental commander and elements of the division staff. Red Mike, like most everyone on Guadalcanal, was worn down after two months of tough campaigning.

Following the defeat of late September, the 5th Marines made patrols to the west of the perimeter that revealed the Japanese were building up their forces there. Other intelligence indicated that the enemy was preparing to launch a large offensive in the near future. Division decided to hit first to secure the crossings over the Matanikau and keep the foe's artillery out of range of the airfield. In a plan reminiscent of the Second Matanikau, a Marine sweep would clear the area beyond the river and a battalion would take up permanent positions at Kokumbona. The scheme of maneuver was also similar, only this time the forces would be stronger.

According to the plan, two battalions of the 5th Marines would move down the coast road, seize the near bank of the Matanikau, and fix the attention of Japanese forces on the far side. A composite force of division scouts and 3/2 under the command of Colonel Whaling would cross the river above the log bridge and attack north toward the sea. Two battalions of the 7th Marines would follow in trace of the Whaling group, also cross the river, and attack in the same direction, only at intervals farther west. The result would be three battalion-sized elements moving abreast against enemy forces located on the west bank of the Matanikau. If that attack was successful, the 5th Marines would then cross the river at its mouth, pass through the other battalions, and continue down the coast to Kokumbona.

In addition to strengthening the forces engaged and having better knowledge of the terrain and enemy, this time division provided a reserve (the Raiders and 3/1) and ample artillery support in the form of three battal-

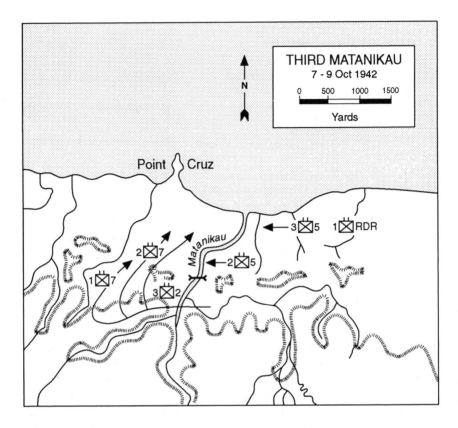

THIRD MATANIKAU
7 - 9 Oct 1942

0   500   1000   1500

Yards

Point Cruz

Matanikau

ions of the 11th Marines. Command arrangements seemed typically haphazard, however. Division may have established a formal command structure for the operation, but afterward there was considerable dispute about who was in charge. Some sources indicate that division maintained control over the battle; others acknowledge Edson as the field commander. To complicate matters, Vandegrift spent most of the period forward with Edson and took such a detailed interest in events that Red Mike's influence on the overall outcome may have been nominal at best.

The American forces were to move into position on 7 October with a view to actually launching the attack across the river on the eighth. One problem developed immediately: The Japanese had planned their own operation in the same area. The Tokyo Express was in the process of delivering strong reinforcements, to include heavy artillery pieces and tanks, for a push against the Marine perimeter in mid-October. The enemy commander on the island thus ordered units to seize two bridgeheads on the east bank of the Matanikau in preparation for the coming attack—one at the mouth of the river, and the other near the log bridge. This would secure a crossing point over the sandbar for the armor and room for the artillery to deploy. Those advance elements were in place by the time the Americans launched their offensive.

When the 5th Marines moved up on 7 October, they ran into a Japanese company dug in on the near side of the river by the sandbar. Edson's 2d Battalion managed to secure most of its assigned frontage farther upriver, but his 3d Battalion was unable to break the enemy resistance centered on a trench-and-bunker complex just inland from the mouth. Red Mike committed Company L, 3/5, to the battle and then radioed division for reinforcements so he could reconstitute a regimental reserve. Company A of the Raiders soon marched down the coast road and into a bivouac next to his CP. The company numbered less than a hundred men, and not one of Able's officers on 7 August was around now; the rest of the battalion was worse off. Spirits were high, though, as rumors were rife again of impending withdrawal from the island. Most Raiders thought their reserve role would bring no fighting.

Of course, being next to Edson's command post practically put one in the midst of the battle. He was located about four hundred yards from the mouth of the river; his CP was "a foxhole and a field telephone slung on a coconut tree." Red Mike liked to stay near the front not only to encourage his men, but also to obtain solid information regarding the course of the battle. He later told an observer: "The offensive is the most difficult to support, as you cannot tell exactly where your troops are." Both these points would be fully demonstrated on the second day of the Third Matanikau.

At the moment Edson was very unhappy. His troops were moving forward at a crawl, and he complained to a nearby correspondent: "Every time a Jap fires a shot they dig a hole in the ground and stay there." He called one of his subordinates on the phone and told him he had to clear the near bank of the river or the unit would "be in for a hell of a lot of trouble tonight." Displeased with the response he received, Red Mike gave the officer a brief lesson in battlefield philosophy. "You've got to take a chance on getting hurt. Somebody has to get hurt in these things. I want it done!"

That night the Japanese on the near side of the river probed the lines of 3/5 and mauled the company nearest the sandbar. Early in the morning of 8 October, Edson decided to commit Company A of the Raiders to the task of reducing the Japanese pocket. He placed Walt, the unit's former commander, in charge of the effort, but the interlocking fire of the concealed Japanese positions stymied the Raiders, too. Meanwhile heavy rains during the night and continuing into the day caused division to delay the move across the river for twenty-four hours, till 9 October. At the same time, intelligence sources indicated that a strong Japanese reinforcement effort would approach the island in the near future, possibly to conduct a direct amphibious assault on the perimeter. Vandegrift decided to compress his original objectives to a quick envelopment of the west bank of the Matanikau followed by a complete withdrawal into the original perimeter in preparation for the enemy offensive.

Based on these changed circumstances and his own observation at close range of Company A's predicament, Edson halted the attack on the Japanese strongpoint. His 3d Battalion would continue to encircle most of the enemy position, while Able Company went into the defense on their right flank. The position of the latter was shaped like a horseshoe, with the left linking up with 3d Battalion and facing south toward the bunker complex, the center facing west toward the sand spit, and the right facing north toward the sea. The Marines expected an assault across the sandbar to relieve the enemy company, so they strung barbed wire across their western front.

The Japanese had other plans. Just after dusk on 8 October they came pouring out of the strongpoint in an effort to break through to their own lines. They quickly overran the weak left flank of Able and hit the center of the line in the rear. Those who broke through the heavy fighting in both locations then ran headlong into the wire, where Marine fire cut them down. Lieutenant Robert Neuffer, then in command of the raider company, tried to recover from the confusion and establish a fresh line farther back along the coast road in case the expected attack across the river still developed. The young officer reported by phone to regimental headquarters that most of the company had been destroyed. Edson, aware that things generally seem much worse than they really are, calmly ordered him to hold the position. In the morning there was some more fighting with the remnants of the Japanese force still wandering the battlefield, but these were soon wiped out. Patrols occupied the abandoned Japanese position, which consisted of trenches and bunkers connected by underground tunnels to a central command post. The Marines counted fifty-nine bodies stacked up against the wire and strewn about the perimeter.

Edson's 2d Battalion had its own problems during the course of 8 October. Two companies were ordered to cross the river to support the operations on the far bank. John Hersey, a reporter, accompanied the weapons outfit, Company H. As that unit moved down the ridge and into the valley of the Matanikau, the Marines came under heavy fire from a Japanese battalion holding the opposite bank. When it seemed too much to bear, the word began to circulate that they were to withdraw, and men soon began a rapid movement to the rear. The company commander, Capt. Charles Rigaud, stood up in the midst of the confused rout and quickly reestablished control by his cool presence and a few well-chosen words, capped by the shaming observation, "and they call you marines." The captain may not have learned such skills from his regimental commander (the battalion had been well led from the first, though it had seen much service with the Raiders), but it was exactly the type of personal leadership that Red Mike tried to instill in all his subordinates.

An incident the following day highlighted the other reason Edson liked to be near the front lines. The enveloping force had finally crossed the river and begun its sweep down to the sea. The 1st Battalion, 7th Marines, was moving north on the left flank when it uncovered a large Japanese force in a ravine to its front. The Marines held the high ground overlooking the enemy position and dominating any avenue of escape. The battalion called in artillery fire and used its own mortars to wreak havoc in the jungled lowland, then covered the grassy ridges bordering the area with machine guns. They slaughtered the Japanese. In the midst of this action, Col. Amor L. Sims, the regimental commander, radioed Puller to avoid any major contact and make a reconnaissance in force along the coast road. Puller ignored the order and expressed his exasperation at a commander who tried to lead from a position well to the rear: "If you'd get off your duff and come up here where the fighting is, you could see the situation." Puller disagreed with Edson on many things, but he would have had no complaint in that area; Red Mike also believed in observing the action firsthand.

Staying near the sound of the guns could be costly, of course. On 9 October Edson and his runner had been moving along the front in the middle of the afternoon and had come under small-arms fire, which they ignored. An hour later, Edson wanted to assemble his commanders for a conference before sunset. One could not be reached by telephone or radio, so he sent Burak off to find him, over the same trail the two had recently used. The young corporal who had served Red Mike so faithfully for more than a year was killed by a burst of machine-gun fire before he could complete the mission.

Word went round that Edson cried when he was told of Burak's death. That Edson was indeed shaken by the event might be deduced from his actions the next afternoon. With the operation complete, the battalions on the western side of the river crossed at the sandbar and headed back toward friendly lines. Once they were past, the 5th Marines began their own pullback. A Marine later reminded Red Mike what happened next:

> I substituted temporarily as your runner after the unfortunate death of your runner. I must confess Sir, you gave me the scare of my life later in the day when you decided to withdraw our troops and leave

the Matanikau. I remember you stood with Lou [sic] Walt while your Raiders passed leaving a machine gun platoon to cover our withdrawal, and even when that platoon had cleared you stayed until I thought you would never leave. It was a feeling of great relief to me when you turned down the trail.

Despite the personal loss to Edson, Third Matanikau was a success. The 5th Marines had wiped out the Japanese bridgeheads on the east bank of the river, while Puller's force had nearly destroyed an entire Japanese battalion on the opposite side. The Marines had killed more than 700 of the enemy at a cost to themselves of 65 dead and 125 wounded. The offensive did not achieve its goal of establishing an outpost to prevent further Japanese moves into the region, but the operation had disrupted enemy plans for their own attack against the perimeter. As the Imperial Navy tried valiantly to replace the army's losses and build up additional forces for an offensive, the Marines received their own reinforcements. On 13 October a convoy delivered the 164th Infantry, an army regiment, to Guadalcanal. The same ships embarked the Raiders, who had suffered 34 more casualties during Third Matanikau and were left with about 200 effectives. Edson walked down to the beach from his nearby headquarters and saw them off.

The Raiders departed just in time, for later that day the Japanese elevated their efforts to retake the island. Two 150mm guns emplaced west of the Matanikau opened up on the airstrip at dusk, the first time that Henderson Field had come under artillery fire. The Americans had nothing that could respond to the long-range pieces. After midnight two Japanese battleships commenced a bombardment with their fourteen-inch guns. More than an hour and nearly a thousand shells later, the field was in ruins, most of the aviation fuel was in flames, and a substantial number of aircraft were damaged or destroyed. A handful of planes managed to get off the ground the next day, but could do little to stop two air raids, more artillery shelling, and the arrival of a large convoy. Two cruisers pounded the field again on the night of 14 October, and another two repeated the feat the following night. The transports suffered damage from desperate American air attacks and were forced to withdraw, but not before depositing 4,500 troops and large quantities of supplies. Further operations of the Tokyo Express brought another 2,150 soldiers to the island in succeeding days.

Things looked bleak for American forces on Guadalcanal, and the government began providing the press with gloomy assessments that seemed designed to prepare the public for possible defeat. The men fighting the campaign expected eventual victory, but even they occasionally wondered about the outcome. Thomas let "notes of doubt creep into his letters home." Edson wrote a positive appraisal for Ethel on 22 October. "We are girding our loins for what will probably be the show-down here and may be a deciding factor so far as the length of the war is concerned." He praised Vandegrift and the aviators and castigated those who were spreading defeatism at home: "In my opinion, the present headlines should never have been printed because they could have been avoided by proper action by others than the officers and men here." He seemed unruffled at the current state of affairs and closed with a discussion concerning whether they should buy or lease a house in Washington.

The awaited Japanese ground offensive began on 20 October. Elements of the 1st and 7th Marines had taken up positions along the Matanikau, the same area cleared by the 5th Marines and Raiders two weeks earlier. Enemy artillery fire struck them that evening, and a series of Japanese attacks by infantry and tanks occurred over the next four days. This action was a feint to cover the main Japanese effort—another attack on Henderson Field from the south. That assault went in on the nights of 24 and 25 October. Initially 1/7 defended the area, but division quickly fed an Army battalion into the lines to assist. Although the fight raged over Edson's Ridge and points east, the situation had changed considerably from the time of the first battle. Well-prepared defenses included fire lanes cut through the jungle, strong barbed-wire obstacles, well-constructed fighting positions, and heavier firepower. The enemy, suffering from the same difficulty of getting through the jungle, again took severe losses. Edson's regiment guarded the perimeter in the vicinity of the Lunga River and saw no action in this series of battles; it was the only significant fighting Red Mike missed during his stay on Guadalcanal.

With the late October victory in hand and more reinforcements on the way, division decided to launch yet another offensive across the Matanikau. The goal again was to reach Kokumbona and push Japanese artillery out of range of Henderson Field. Vandegrift selected Edson's 5th Marines to lead the attack, and Red Mike made a two-hour aerial reconnaissance of the area west of the river on 25 October. In a unique turnaround, this plan would be a simple one. Two battalions of the regiment with one in reserve would cross the Matanikau and advance abreast up the coast. A new Whaling group (the division scouts and 3/7) would extend the line farther into the interior. Two battalions of the 2d Marines would serve as the operational reserve. Heavy fire support, to include a strike by B-17 bombers, would soften the enemy positions in advance of the attack. Division issued the order on 30 October.

At 0630 on 1 November the lead infantry formations began crossing the river. Walt, now commanding 2/5, met little resistance in the center of the line and Whaling's men were doing well on the left flank, but 1/5 ran into strong opposition at 0830 near the coast. Counterattacks by the single reinforced Japanese company entrenched there actually drove the Marines back for a time, until Edson fed in 3/5 to bolster the line. Edson, Thomas, and Twining conferred late in the day and decided to focus the 5th Marines on clearing Point Cruz the next day. The 2d Battalion would move toward the coast to the west of the point and seal off any retreat, while the remaining two battalions of the regiment cleaned out the pocket. The 2d Marines would fill in for the 5th Marines and continue the attack along the coast beyond Point Cruz. In the evening, the Japanese inserted additional forces—a well-armed antitank battalion and some labor troops—into the point area.

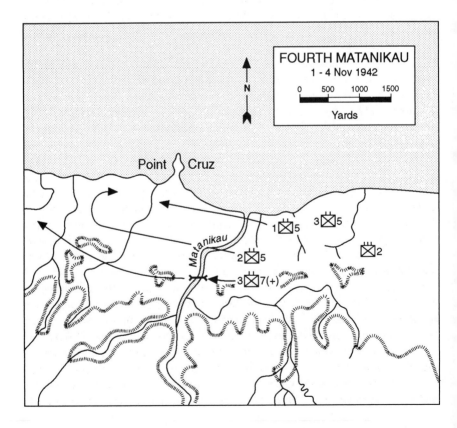

The division operations section, headed by Twining, continued to be unimpressed by the capability of the 5th Marines. To an extent these staff officers were correct: The regiment was not up to the standards of the Raiders or even the 7th Marines. However, the mission of training troops and weeding out weak leaders in the middle of a campaign was not an easy one. The poor state of training in the regiment, even at the highest levels, was demonstrated early in this push. Red Mike ordered his XO to select a new CP site forward of the Lunga perimeter so the regimental headquarters could be nearer the action beyond the Matanikau. When Edson arrived at the location he could not conceal his disgust. The lieutenant colonel had placed the command post on the side of a ridge facing *toward* the enemy, a perfect target for Japanese artillery.

Twining did admit that the regiment had gotten better under Edson, a conclusion bolstered by Vandegrift's repeated offensive use of the 5th Marines while the 1st Marines seemed to languish on the defensive for most of this period. The regiment's improvement also was borne out by the advance beyond the Matanikau. Although 1/5 had trouble handling the Japanese counterattack of 1 November, the battalion held its own, and by the end of the day it had nearly wiped out the enemy company.

The reviving 5th Marines had a successful day on 2 November. Walt's battalion quickly achieved its objective of reaching the beach and sealing off the area. The 3d Battalion then led the effort to root out the enemy reinforcements emplaced in a cave-pocked ravine near the base of Point Cruz. Red Mike took pride in episodes that epitomized the type of leadership he was instilling in the 5th Marines. A platoon commander in Company G, 2/5, was hit and his position taken by the unit's XO, Capt. Willard Keith, Jr. The captain personally led a flanking attack until he was mortally wounded. His men pressed on and drove the enemy out of their prepared position. Another captain, Erskine Wells of Company I, 3/5, led a bayonet charge that broke through the enemy line and established a linkup with 2/5. By the end of 3 November the 5th Marines had cleaned out Point Cruz, killed more than three hundred enemy soldiers, and captured numerous heavy weapons.

As the offensive to the west progressed, a new situation developed to the east of the perimeter. The Japanese were landing fresh forces near Koli Point. A battalion of the 7th Marines sent out to stop them ran into heavier than expected resistance and fell back. On the morning of 4 November Edson attended a conference at the division CP to discuss the new situation. Twining advocated a continued advance to the west. Edson, unusually cautious, argued that each ravine might hold enemy pockets like the one his forces had just reduced at heavy cost. Moreover, the American left flank hung in the air in the inland ridges, with the possibility of extensive Japanese infiltration in the rear of the attacking force. Vandegrift and Thomas, not willing to disperse their forces in the absence of hard information on enemy intentions and capabilities, decided to put further operations in the west on hold. Vandegrift called the 5th Marines back to the perimeter.

Red Mike and his regiment had one month left on Guadalcanal, but this was their last combat action. Thereafter they stood guard duty on the perimeter and functioned as a division reserve unit. Edson exaggerated the situation when he wrote Ethel: "My outfit has had so little to do that they have become fat and lazy—but not too fat." Although this lack of activity might be explained in part by the operations section's disdain for the 5th Marines, the truth was that the outfit was nearly played out. It had fought several battles since the initial landing on the Solomons in early August, the 2d Battalion even more than the rest of the regiment. In addition to casualties, disease and sickness had taken a heavy toll. Most of the men had been under treatment for malaria at one time or another during the campaign. Fresh regiments were now arriving on a regular basis, which alleviated the need to send worn units such as the 5th Marines back into the meat grinder. Despite the flow of reinforcements, the veteran outfits received no replacements until mid-November. Even then, after assimilating several hundred new men, one-third of the regiment was listed as unfit for combat.

One of the new units to come ashore late in the campaign was the 2d Raider Battalion. Carlson's men landed at Aola Bay on 4 November and made a combat patrol westward toward the main position around Henderson Field. They successfully engaged several enemy units and moved well in the rough country, in large measure due to the aid of a substantial contingent of native bearers to carry supplies. Thirty days later they approached the Lunga perimeter and Edson went out to meet them. Red Mike gave Carlson a cool reception but provided a hearty welcome to those men who had served in his original Company A before their transfer to the West Coast.

By the middle of November the Americans on Guadalcanal were certain of victory. The U.S. Navy had wrested control of the sea in the lower Solomons from the Japanese; planes from the several American strips now on Guadalcanal dominated the skies; and troops continued to flow onto the island. Marine leaders felt more secure, and Edson could write home in a jocular vein: "I have the finest collection of field mice in captivity right in my tent. If you hear me stomping my feet, it is because I am trying to keep them from running up my trousers legs."

Edson was confident about the outcome of the war, too, though he expected another four years of hard fighting. He respected the "Indian warfare" methods of the Japanese, who used stealth and ruses to good advantage. A reporter quoted Edson as saying: "They're good all right, but I think we're better." Red Mike thought that comment "need[ed] interpretation—for in conservative Vermontese—it was equivalent to 'We're a hell of a lot better.'" He acknowledged the enemy might still have an edge in experience, but "with proper training, our Americans are better, as our people can think better as individuals."

The 5th Marines were not fighting during this period, but they had another contribution to make to the war effort. An Army team was interviewing experienced units on the island for a pamphlet on the lessons of jungle warfare. Much of their information came from the ranks of Edson's regiment and its commander, so his emphasis on leadership appeared throughout the resulting document. The colonel stressed the importance of leadership at every level, but in his eyes, training needed to focus on the squad and platoon rather than higher units. It was obvious that he had thoroughly imbued his philosophy in at least some of his officers; the interviewer noted that he talked to Walt for "over twenty minutes before I was able to make a single original note as his ideas seem to echo Colonel Edson's."

The veteran of the Coco Patrols reiterated some of the same logistical shortcomings that had plagued him years before, to include the unsuitability of the current field shoe. Edson dwelt at length on tactics, particularly the offensive. He argued for use of lighter weapons in the assault, such as the light machine gun and the 60mm mortar, though units should also have the heavier versions for employment in the defense. His reasons were practical: The added weight of weapons and ammunition was just too much to carry in rough terrain. To beef up firepower, he suggested the issuance of additional BARs and the adoption of a grenade launcher. To keep up momentum, he drilled into the troops that "the best way to aid a wounded man is to push ahead so that the wounded man can be cared for by the corpsmen." In terms of training, he recommended "maneuvers with ball ammunition where possible, even if you get a few casualties."

Walt added comments on communications and the use of the reserve. The 5th Marines maintained wire links between regiment and the battalions even in the offensive, and battalions were expected to run phone lines to the companies as soon as they went into static positions. Wire provided a more reliable and secure means of communication than radio, which frequently suffered from equipment failure or enemy interference. The major also noted that it was regimental practice to keep the best company in battalion reserve but close to the front. To speed employment, the reserve commander kept apprised of the situation through continual reconnaissance.

Edson's contributions to the victory on Guadalcanal had been immense. Many observers thought his success on the Ridge had saved the vital airfield from one of the most critical threats in the campaign. Nearly all of those who served under him during this period came away believing he was one of the best combat officers they had ever seen. Captain Gordon Gayle, one of his operations officers, rated him the second greatest genius he knew in the Corps (the first being Twining). Gayle thought Red Mike's strongest asset was that he always thought at a higher level than just his unit. Correspondents universally ranked him high as well. In early 1943 Tregaskis wrote: "If there were more leaders like Col. Red in the service, we'd be in Tokyo by this time."

On 8 December a convoy brought the 132d Infantry to Guadalcanal, and the 1st Marine Division officially turned over command of the island to the Army. The 5th Marines embarked the next day as the lead element of the 1st Division's withdrawal. Some of the men were so worn out that they needed help to make it up the cargo nets onto the transports. But even as they headed for the rear, Edson published a notice to the troops to keep their minds on the next battle. "The primary objective before us is to refit, reorganize, and train for further offensive operations in the Pacific area. . . . It is my intention that this regiment become the best disciplined, the best appearing and the best trained regiment in the Marine Corps. Only by doing so will you become the best and toughest fighting regiment in the Corps."

Chapter 13

"In Many a Strife We've Fought for Life"

The destination of the 5th Marines and the following echelons of the 1st Marine Division was Brisbane, a city midway down the east coast of Australia. Here they would refit, absorb re-placments, and train for future employment. The division's new home was Camp Cable, a tent city twenty-five miles south of Brisbane. It had little to recommend it. The wooded, marshy area was a haven for malarial mosquitoes. Since extended periods of leave prevented enforced daily doses of atabrine and quinine, the incidence of the disease soared. In addition, there was only a single scheduled train to transport troops on liberty from their spartan quarters to the distant town. Even the officers found it "more like a penal colony" than a rest area. Eventually MacArthur's Southwest Pacific command allowed the Marines to move to a better clime and place. By early January 1942 the lead elements of the 1st Marine Division, to include Vandegrift and his staff, were on their way to Melbourne and the cooler latitudes of southeast Australia.

Since the 5th Marines were the last unit scheduled to leave, Vandegrift placed Edson in charge of the rear echelon—about nine thousand officers and men. Just three days later an unexpectedly large transport became available to carry the remaining troops, so the 5th Marines and other units embarked with less than twenty-four hours' notice. As the division fled Camp Cable, an Army unit moved in and found a horrendous mess: ruined food, unsanitary conditions, discarded serviceable gear, and even abandoned weapons. The commander of the new tenants called in press representatives and wrote a scathing report to the Army general responsible for the area. Red Mike made an immediate and successful effort at damage control. He cited flooded roads, the Army's unwillingness to accept excess property into its dumps, and the new unit's insistence on moving in before the area was released to them ("a gross violation of military courtesy"). Following a long meeting, the Army general decided to make no official inquiry and even agreed to censor any media accounts of the incident.

Edson then made his own report to Thomas. The man who had cut his Marine teeth on the duckboards of Smedley Butler's Camp Pontanezen admitted ruefully that the Army's complaints were justifed: "I have never seen a worse mess in my twenty-five years of service." He called it "a disgrace to any service" and recommended that commanding officers "be burnt plenty" and that troops should pay for any shortages of individual gear. He thought the "wanton destruction" was "an indication of the state of discipline in the outfit that . . . is sickening to think or talk about. . . . Even the Bonus Army of 1931 was less of a mob." Even his own regiment was at fault. "The officers, of course, are primarily responsible and any action that the General may take after my report has been submitted cannot be too drastic. Unless they can be made to realize that they have responsibilities as well as privileges with their rank and pay, we are going to get a terrible awakening one of these days and all the credit we have won during the past six months will be lost in the period of a few hours."

The only strange thing about Red Mike's letter was his reference to the officers of the division as "they," by which he apparently meant the junior leaders at the company and battalion level. Although they were in immediate contact with the troops, Edson seemed to overlook the culpability of himself and the other senior officers. The colonels had been ensconced in the comparative comfort of a downtown Brisbane hotel and obviously they had made little effort to supervise the departure from the distant camp. A certain amount of laxness was inevitable in the aftermath of a tough campaign, but this pervaded all ranks, to include the division's top leaders, who were in no position to cast stones at their subordinates. This apparent lack of attention to detail, unprecedented in Edson's career, would bring him more trouble before the Australian interlude came to an end.

After supervising the cleanup of Camp Cable, Red Mike flew south to rejoin the division on 30 January. The new location was an improvement, but the organization was now spread out: Division headquarters and the 1st Marines took up residency in the city center at the cricket grounds, the 5th and 7th Marines were thirty miles to the south at Camp Balcombe on the shores of Port Phillip Bay, and the 11th Marines were sixty miles to the west at Ballarat. Although the climate was more hospitable here, the mosquitoes had long since done their work and malaria continued to be a major problem. It took weeks for the division to recover enough to begin training.

In addition to the medical problems, the commotion of the transfer, and the geographic spread of the camps, the division suffered from a lack of direction from the top. Soon after their arrival in Melbourne, Vandegrift, Thomas, and others were called back to the States by HQMC, largely for the purpose of parading successful war heroes before the public. During their two-month absence, Rupertus was the acting commanding general. Although Edson found him "a fine fellow personally," he did not think he was much of a leader. Red Mike did not make the trip home, so he was elevated to the position of acting assistant division commander. He remained at distant Balcombe, however, and also continued to fulfill his duties as regimental commander and as the officer in charge of all Marine units in that encampment. Given the competing demands of his multiple jobs, he did not feel he did "real justice" to any of them. In accordance with his usual practice of stealing good subordinates, though, he was successful in obtaining Lt. Col. Leonard B. Cresswell as his regimental XO, and that fine officer took a lot of the weight off his shoulders. Red Mike looked forward to the return of Thomas and the other "wheelhorses of the division."

Edson's busy schedule was only partly due to the actual requirements of running the division. As one of the few available senior leaders of the famed 1st Marine Division, Melbourne society placed great demands on his time. His status was probably enhanced by his receipt of the Medal of Honor for the Ridge. On 3 February 1943 Rupertus hung the medal around Red Mike's neck during a "very impressive ceremony," a sunset parade before the assembled officers of the division and "many of the local big shots." The tough social schedule did more than impinge upon the time of a busy colonel; Edson bewailed his returning paunch, which made him "look again like a banker."

Although Red Mike was not accorded the triumphal tour that Vandegrift experienced in the United States (the general received his Medal of Honor from President Roosevelt at the White House), he was the subject of an increasing amount of attention. The *Marine Corps Gazette* featured his picture and citation, he made it onto the pages of *Life* magazine, and books about Guadalcanal began to appear in print. Many of these works, such as Hersey's *Into the Valley,* lionized the colonel. Tregaskis sent Edson a copy of *Guadalcanal Diary* inscribed to "the only really tough guy I've ever met—as I've tried to point out in this book." Edson frequented the company of personalities such as Douglas MacArthur, the governor general of Australia, the American ambassador, and the prominent citizens of Melbourne. He had been a colonel for just a few months, but some officers began to suggest that it was time he be promoted to brigadier. It must have been heady stuff for a man who not many years earlier had spent his free time operating a chicken coop in his backyard to make ends meet. He had gained notice during the Coco Patrols, but that had been a small operation in a small war; now he was a prominent figure in a conflict that engulfed the world. An element of vanity began to creep into his personality. In writing Ethel about the Medal of Honor, he noted that he was still hoping to get an award for the Tulagi operation, as well as a British decoration for his work in the Solomons. Where once he used to deprecate his performance, he now seemed to delight in describing his newfound prominence, at least in private to his wife. For public consumption he could still retain a humble face, as he did in responding to Tregaskis's high praise. "I cannot but feel that my capabilities have been grossly overrated not only by you but by many others. . . . The worst of it is that you have set a terribly high standard for me to live up to. I only hope that I may never disappoint you."

This was indeed a pleasant time for Edson. Balcombe was situated in what had been a prewar resort area. He found it an "ideal campsite" that overlooked a huge bay, with the ocean not far away. For his quarters he had a big brick country home with spacious rooms and first-class furnishings. He took the unusual step of inviting his principal staff officers to live with him, which gave him a steady supply of partners for card games, chess matches, and conversation. The close-knit group included Cresswell (his XO), Hank Adams (intelligence), Gordon Gayle (operations), and Capt. Charles McAuliffe (personnel).

Despite the inviting surroundings, Red Mike spent little of his free time at Balcombe. The officers' club was in downtown Melbourne, conveniently located near the quarters of the division staff and Edson's contemporaries and friends. Senior officers received complimentary memberships to the elite clubs of the city and made the rounds of frequent events hosted by leading families. Edson rated a sedan and driver, so he generally made the hour drive into the city each evening and returned after midnight. In the course of this whirlwind of social activity, he met an Australian divorcée and developed a strong attachment to her. The two spent a great deal of time together and he lavished "Bibs" with small gifts and attention. He enjoyed the company of her young son, too. In some respects they may have represented the happy family life that had disappeared in the 1930s. His letters to Chicago, once prolific, dropped off markedly.

At the moment his real family was scattered to the winds. Ethel had taken a job in the weather bureau after his departure for the Pacific, so she sent Bobby to live with her mother in Maine. Austin had joined the Marines in October 1942 and was now enrolled in the V-12 officer program at Villanova. (He had needed a waiver for eyesight and insufficient weight, but the commandant had personally authorized it.) Red Mike was pleased, since his son had earlier shown no inclination to follow in his father's footsteps.

Edson's relationship with Ethel seemed to be somewhat better during this period, despite his flirtation with the Australian. His letters to her were not frequent but were newsy and friendly. At one point he even spoke of hoping to get home to receive his Medal of Honor, though he soon reiterated his desire to stay in the Pacific until the war ended. He cajoled her about her dreary routine of working hard, keeping house, and pinching pennies. "You should try enjoying life for a change. Worrying does no good. One's span of life is marked from the day of birth and there is nothing one can do to change it, so why not enjoy what is left of it?" He certainly seemed to be following his own advice in that regard.

Australia was far from being all play and no work. Red Mike may have been burning the midnight oil of a tough social regimen, but when it came to preparation for the next campaign he was still all business. In January he began to advocate that it was "time we started active training once more," but malaria and a lack of replacements prevented any serious work through March. It was not until a month later that he got his regiment out in the field for an extended operation. From there things finally began to get "intensive" enough to suit his tastes.

Red Mike divided his attention equally between his officers and the men. Soon after the arrival at Balcombe the colonel decreed that there would be a single regimental officers' mess instead of the usual battalion-level establishments. The junior officers did not care for the change in routine; it was only later that some of them realized this was just the first step in melding them into a regiment. When it came to decision making, Edson maintained his habit of posing problems to his staff and asking them to develop solutions. He found good people and gave them authority irrespective of rank. Gayle, a junior captain who had been a battalion operations officer, fleeted up to the same billet at the regiment, a position normally held by a much more senior officer.

The training program was vintage Edson. He emphasized night work, physical fitness, and marksmanship. He spent little time in his office, but instead got out among the troops. He especially liked to go to the range, where he delighted in talking to the men on the line, borrowing a weapon, and firing a round (which invariably hit the bull's-eye) from the difficult standing position. He took the same interest in the men's liberty and ensured that there was a steady schedule of organized dances to get them acquainted with the locals and to keep morale sharp. Twining, ever the tough critic, gave the 5th Marines its due when he assigned that outfit to make a demonstration amphibious landing for the Australians. "I selected them as more or less a tacit tribute to how far back on the road he had brought that regiment, and he had."

In addition to looking after his own unit, Edson continued to think and act beyond the confines of his billet. He took the time to ship a captured Japanese grenade thrower to the Army ordnance people at Aberdeen Proving Ground along with an analysis of its weaknesses and possible improvements. He thought a similar weapon would be a lightweight but powerful addition to infantry firepower. In March, when training was nearly at a standstill due to malaria, he wrote to a friend at HQMC about the issue of replacements. He thought it more expedient to maintain a veteran organization such as the 1st Marine Division at full strength so it could train and thus be available on short notice for operations. Instead, the planners in the States were diverting the manpower flow to create new units, which would not be ready to fight for some time, on the assumption that malaria cases would eventually return and flesh out the ranks of the division. Edson argued that fresh men now would allow the command to train, while the eventual return of the sick would provide a pool of ready replacements for use in the next campaign. This would prevent a recurrence of the situation on Guadalcanal, where a lack of on-hand replacements left units too weak to fight after a few battles. "I think that these things should receive a most careful consideration by the people back in Headquarters."

The day was not far off when they would be so received. In early July Holcomb ordered Vandegrift to take over command of the I Marine Amphibious Corps (IMAC), which would temporarily delay the handover of the commandancy between the two men. Initially an administrative command, IMAC had begun to assume increasing operational responsibility, and its present commander was not up to the task. Vandegrift would get the organization on its feet in a few weeks and then take over the reins of the entire Marine Corps. Thomas and Twining flew off to Noumea with their boss; from there they would accompany him to Washington, where Thomas would become the director of Plans and Policies, the principal staff officer for the whole Corps. When Edson recommended something to HQMC in the future, he would have the sympathetic ear of a friend in a high place.

Edson got his own orders not long after. On 1 August 1943 he reported to the 2d Marine Division in Wellington, New Zealand, for duty as the chief of staff, the third senior officer in the organization after the commanding general and the assistant division commander (ADC). Edson was ambivalent about the change. On one hand he "would naturally prefer to fight any regiment than be on any staff." However, he bragged to his wife and mother that "the success or failure of the division will lie largely in my hands" and "this was handed to me because the big boss considered I was the one man to do it." Up to this point he had not given much credence to the rumors that he would soon be promoted, though he had taken a close interest in the latest board, which had considered the records of many of those sent home early from Guadalcanal. (He had assumed that the relief from duty would "make no difference in the majority of cases," and the board proved him right.) Now he saw his present move as "a step up, with the silver star [of a brigadier general] a possibility in the offing." He expected long days of work ahead: "But it should be fun and I am looking forward to it all."

He found the swift course of events a little mind-boggling at times. "It is hard to realize that a few days from now will see the anniversary of our landing in the Solomon Islands. That a year ago tomorrow I was putting on the eagles of a full colonel for the first time. That a year ago next Saturday we were fighting desperately for possession of Tulagi." The awards were still arriving for those deeds. During a brief visit with the IMAC staff in Noumea, Edson had gotten word that an American medal was assured for the Tulagi operation. On 7 August the British ambassador presented Ethel with her husband's Distinguished Service Order (DSO) in a ceremony at the embassy in Washington. A newspaper pictured Red Mike as "overjoyed" upon receipt of the news of the DSO: "His face broke into a boyish smile as he happily showed the cutting to his fellow officers." The future looked rosy.

His Australian escapades soon came back to haunt him, though, and bring him back to earth. Colonel John T. Selden, the new commander of the 5th Marines, discovered a mess at the regimental laundry soon after Edson's departure. In the middle of the formal investigation into conditions there, the sergeant running the facility disappeared and investigators discovered there were large debts to civilian firms as well as an even larger sum of missing money. Moreover, the very existence of such a Marine-run business violated Corps regulations.

In a personal letter to Cresswell, Edson acknowledged that he had been aware of the facility, but blamed the entire situation on a Navy officer assigned the additional duty of regimental laundry officer. Red Mike wrote Thomas, admitted his responsibility as a commander and his failure to inspect, but argued that he should not be held financially liable for the thousands of dollars involved. He also asked his friend to intercede to prevent any record of the matter from reaching official files at HQMC. "This is the first time that I have ever been caught napping in a thing like this and I can assure you that I do not believe it will ever happen again."

With the help of Thomas and the commanding general of the 2d Marine Division, the affair blew over. But this was not the only hint of scandal to trail Red Mike out of the land down under. While still there he had had to defend himself against charges that his regimental dances were drunken brawls frequented by prostitutes. He also had gotten into a verbal "altercation" with a military policeman who had stopped him at 0300 one morning for speeding and carrying unauthorized civilians in his government sedan. He had taken the offensive on that incident and written a formal report accusing the MP of improper conduct: "I have nothing but contempt for a military policeman who believes that his function is to pry into the private affairs of officers and men of this division." Later on Edson would face a new problem regarding alleged violations of the censorship rules.

The accusations of impropriety seemed to be unfounded or blown out of proportion, but the frequency of problems and the constant connection to Australia highlight his apparent failure to concentrate on his duties during that period. He undoubtedly was distracted by his social life, particularly his attachment to Bibs, which remained strong even after his departure for New Zealand. He wrote her nearly every day, sometimes more often, and arranged for a florist to make regular deliveries to her. He even gave her a power of attorney to handle personal details after his departure.

Red Mike later described her as nothing more than a friend, but at a minimum he was certainly guilty of emotional infidelity. During a period in which he wrote hundreds of letters to her, he sent barely half a dozen to his wife. He addressed Bibs in affectionate terms such as "darling," which he studiously avoided in letters home. Bibs was certain that he would divorce his wife and come back at the end of the war to marry her. He just as conveniently lost his former passion for the woman in Chicago, a pattern he would repeat in the future; he seemed to practice fidelity of a sort by maintaining only one love at a time.

If Edson was a less than perfect husband, he at least learned a professional lesson from the Australian problems. There were ample distractions in New Zealand, and the Kiwis were just as cordial, but now he kept his focus in the right place. The unusual lapse in attention to duty, however slight, disappeared, and he returned to his old form with the 2d Marine Division.

He found plenty of work to keep him busy. The division had stood up on the West Coast in 1941 and had suffered even greater birth pangs than the 1st Marine Division. In addition to the problems of rapid expansion, the 2d Division lost its best regiment in spring 1941 when the 6th Marines sailed off for garrison duty in Iceland. The 8th Marines departed in early 1942 to perform a similar function on Samoa. Then the 2d Marines temporarily joined the 1st Marine Division for the Guadalcanal operation in August. The entire division did not concentrate on that island until late in the campaign, but the 2d Marines soon sailed off as one of the veteran organizations being relieved. The first opportunity for rear area training as a division thus did not come until the rest of the organization was withdrawn to New Zealand in February 1943. There they had to go through the same period of recuperation from combat and rampant malaria as their comrades in Australia.

Major General Julian C. Smith had taken command of the division in May 1943. Leo D. Hermle, a freshly minted brigadier, had moved up from a regiment to be the ADC. Smith had carte blanche to bring in anyone he wanted to flesh out the staff; he asked for Edson, his former assistant from the 1930 rifle team. This was a surprising choice, since Smith thought of Red Mike as a field commander rather than a staff officer and only later realized the versatility of his new colonel. There was certainly a need for Edson's organizing skills, since his predecessor in the chief of staff billet had not performed well. Up until Edson's arrival, most of the work had been done by the operations officer.

In many ways Smith and Edson were similar. Both were outwardly quiet and unassuming, though one keen observer was quick to note the difference in their smiles. Smith's face seemed to light up with a genial glow; Edson's "pale blue eyes gleamed with the impersonal menace of pointed pistol muzzles." Whereas Smith projected a fatherly image of the benign leader, Red Mike would provide the iron will necessary to ramrod the division into shape. Smith himself later referred to his chief of staff as the "relentless" one who "spurred on" the regiments in training.

At first Edson missed the 5th Marines and the prospect of more opportunities to lead men in battle. "There is nothing that can quite compare with the thrill—the exhilaration—or the satisfaction of fighting one's battalion or one's regiment in battle, pitting one's wits and leadership against a tenacious and aggressive hostile force until he is out-maneuvered, out-fought, and completely defeated." But he was glad to leave the 1st

Marine Division now that it was under the command of Rupertus, who knew only too well what Edson thought of him. And Red Mike did look forward to the new challenge, a job "infinitely bigger and more important—for the work done here, the decisions made, the vision and foresight to prepare for the future, may well mean success or failure—not of a single battalion or a single regiment—but of the entire division—and the quality of leadership displayed will affect not just one regiment, but several regiments and all of the attached units that go to make up the whole."

In describing these feelings to his wife he noted "so many things I see to be done that I scarcely know where to begin," but then he quickly answered his own rhetorical question. "With no spirit of braggadocio, I know that that regiment when I left it was the best in the M.C.—not so much by what I did—let us say in spite of and not because of me—but because I gathered around me for my staff and battalion commanders the best men I could possibly find. Now comes the task of starting all over again—of learning new people—learning how to work with them as individuals and as a team—building up a group in whom I have the utmost confidence and who, in turn, have the same confidence in me." He tried hard to pry topflight officers such as Brute Krulak and Hod Berry out of the States, and to steal Walt, Adams, and McAuliffe from his old regiment, but he "didn't have as much drag" as he had thought. After much effort and many months, he got only his driver, Clarence Kempkes, and his stenographer, Albert Tardiff, from the 5th Marines. But he soon found some new stalwarts in the ranks of the 2d Marine Division, such as Lt. Col. David Shoup, the capable operations officer, and he rediscovered others, such as Jesse Cook, now a lieutenant colonel and the logistics officer.

Edson and the rest of the division were focusing their effort on Tarawa Atoll in the Gilbert Islands. The decision to attack the Gilberts came out of the high-level debate over Pacific strategy between MacArthur, Nimitz, and the Joint Chiefs of Staff (JCS). Once the Navy won the right to launch its desired offensive in the Central Pacific in competition with MacArthur's Southwest Pacific drive, the Gilberts surfaced as a natural starting point. Their capture would reduce the threat to Samoa, uncover a more direct logistics route to Australia and New Zealand, provide air bases for future operations against the more important Marshall Islands, and allow the Central Pacific campaign to get underway against what were initially thought to be comparatively weak defenses.

On 20 July the JCS ordered Nimitz to plan the seizure of the Gilberts; he in turn assigned the task to VAdm. Raymond Spruance's Fifth Fleet. The other forces were RAdm. Kelly Turner's V Amphibious Force and the soon-to-be-created V Amphibious Corps (VAC) under Holland Smith. The latter consisted of the 2d Marine Division and the Army National Guard's 27th Division (commanded by Maj. Gen. Ralph C. Smith). Spruance came to Wellington in August and informed Julian Smith that his division would play a major role in the operation, code-named Galvanic. Planners eventually settled on 20 November for D day.

The Tarawa Atoll consisted of a series of coral reefs roughly aligned like a right triangle. The southern, bottom line and the northeastern, diagonal line were topped with small islands of sand resting on the coral beds. The vertical line, facing to the west, barely rose to the surface from the ocean floor. There was a breach in the chain of coral in the southwest corner. Just below that passage to the interior of the lagoon and anchoring that corner of the triangle was the island of Betio. This half square mile of sand was shaped like a long-tailed bird lying on its back, with its beak pointing to the north and its tail to the east. It was a little more than two miles long and measured just half a mile at its widest point. The highest spot on the island was about ten feet above sea level. Betio's importance, like that of Guadalcanal, lay in the airfield that covered much of its surface.

◎ Information on the enemy was much more complete for Galvanic than it had been for Watchtower. Aerial photographs pinpointed most of the defensive installations and allowed a very accurate estimate of manpower, believed to be no more than 2,750 men, of which 2,300 were thought to be combat forces (mainly Special Naval Landing Forces). (The figure for combat forces turned out to be nearly correct, but the laborers numbered about 2,000, many of whom would end up fighting, too.) In addition to typical infantry weapons, the defenders had eight large coast defense guns, twenty-nine medium or heavy antiaircraft guns, and numerous machine guns and light antiboat guns. The forces were well entrenched in prepared positions and fortified bunkers. The western and southern approaches were covered by underwater antiboat obstacles of coconut logs and concrete, minefields, and barbed-wire barriers. The northern approaches were similarly protected but in much less strength.

The greatest uncertainty lay in the tides, for which there were no reliable records. Former British residents of the area gave varying estimates, most of which indicated there would be five feet of water over the reefs at high tide, enough to allow normal landing craft (with three and a half feet of draft) to reach shore. The initial waves would go in on amphibious tractors (LVTs) that had the capability of crossing the reefs no matter what the water level, but subsequent reinforcements would be in boats due to a shortage of the relatively new vehicles.

The division was largely on its own when it came to planning the Tarawa operation. Spruance did not even get his new Fifth Fleet staff formed and working until September, and thereafter concentrated as much on the Hawaiian social life as the coming battle. Holland Smith, a much tougher taskmaster, arrived in Pearl Harbor at about the same time to create his corps staff. These higher headquarters also were preoccupied with debates over campaign objectives and the employment of the 27th Division. As late as early October the 2d Marine Division had to make assumptions about its mission since it had as yet received no formal order.

The planning got serious after Julian Smith, Edson, Shoup, Cook, and two other staff officers of the division flew to Hawaii in late September for meetings with the commanders and staffs of VAC and Fifth Fleet. In a 2 October conference Julian Smith and Edson presented their preliminary ideas to Holland Smith. Conversations between the two staffs resulted in the division's "Estimate of the Situation," published on 5 October, which laid out the options available to the enemy, their expected plan, and possible American courses of action. The document was signed by Edson and approved by Julian Smith.

The estimate anticipated that the Japanese would concentrate on the defense of Betio, since it contained the main prize, the airfield, and also commanded the other islands in the atoll that were large enough for alternate airfields. Intelligence seemed to confirm this belief; the enemy had put all his efforts so far into fortifying Betio. In developing the division's options, the time factor hung heavily over the possible courses available. Initial landings on the other, undefended islands of the atoll could provide a base for Marine artillery and the chance to soften up Betio's defenses at close range prior to an assault. However, the Navy would not tie its carriers and gunfire support ships to the operation for an extended period of time. Still traumatized by the bloodletting around Guadalcanal, the admirals feared that a prolonged land battle that kept them in the vicinity of the atoll would result in heavy naval losses from submarines, land-based planes, and surface task forces. Thus the airfield had to be taken immediately so that the ground forces could supply their own air support as soon as possible and free the fleet for employment elsewhere.

Holland Smith also designated the 6th Marines as corps reserve, which meant that the division had just two infantry regiments for the job. Stripping out the supporting elements of the division that could not actually fight in a landing left just over six thousand men for the assault, a bare superiority over the defenders of two to one. Since doctrine dictated a ratio of three to one for a successful assault, division planners felt they were already well below acceptable margins for error and could not divert any of their limited strength to supporting or diversionary landings. Had the division maintained control of its third regiment, it would have had the forces to seize the other islands first for artillery bases to support the main landing, a plan Edson had championed throughout the staff debates. The Navy also scotched a Marine request for a feint on the southern coast; naval planners said they could set up a second transport area only at the cost of using 50 percent of the scheduled gunfire support destroyers to cover the additional area against submarines.

Given the strong enemy defenses and the small size of the objective, there was no other way to get ashore on Betio except into the teeth of enemy fire. The division's leaders believed they had no choice but to employ the most costly tactic, a frontal assault. To make it clear that he felt higher headquarters was forcing him into this unpalatable option, Julian Smith demanded that Holland Smith put into writing the order to land first on Betio. The only discussion then concerned which beach to attack, and that quickly came down to the northern coast, which had the best hydrographic conditions and the weakest defenses.

Edson and the others returned to New Zealand on 11 October, where they continued to mull over the tough task ahead of them. In his position as chief of staff, Red Mike normally would not have played a vital role in operational planning, but the situation in the 2d Division brought his tactical expertise to the fore. Julian Smith had not yet fought the Japanese, and Shoup had been in combat with them only as an observer. Although Shoup is generally credited with being the primary architect of the Tarawa plan, Red Mike had more of a hand in it than just signing off on documents produced by the operations section. He was so concerned about the situation that he wrote a series of personal letters to the VAC chief of staff, Erskine, which outlined his thoughts on the matter and registered his apprehensions. He focused largely on the efficacy of the air and naval gunfire that would provide the prime source of fire support for most of the battle.

In his initial letter Edson stressed the low ratio of attackers to defenders in a way that Shoup could not have: "I am basing this opinion on my observations of the fighting qualities of the Japs in Tulagi and Guadalcanal, as well as my observations of the effect of aerial and naval bombardment against hostile installations and on our own installations by the Japs on those islands." Erskine responded that the ratios of strength gave little weight to the American preponderance in air and naval gunfire support, which would at least neutralize most of the defenses. This overconfidence in supporting arms was the prevailing viewpoint of the higher staffs. Spruance's gunnery officer, for instance, actually spent most of his time updating the admiral's plotting board with ship locations. Vice Admiral John H. Towers, head of naval aviation in the Pacific, thought Spruance was using too much firepower—in his words, employing a "sledgehammer to drive a tack."

Red Mike took issue with that position and reiterated that his personal experience with air and naval guns provided him with much less confidence in their effectiveness: "We should base our estimate upon past experience rather than upon an unknown future component." Although he expected the supporting arms to take out the larger caliber guns, he anticipated that many of the enemy's automatic weapons would still be in operation at H hour. In a final letter just days before the assault, he noted with some irony that the corps reserve would ultimately be used to mop up the other islands of the atoll after Betio was taken, "the reverse of the secondary landings which I would have liked to have made prior to the attack on HELEN [Betio]."

The division chief of staff expressed his confidence in the final outcome, but he worried about the cost. In a prediction of casualties to come, he asked HQMC to make available at least two replacement battalions (a thousand men each) by D+15. Just prior to the operation Edson attempted to forewarn the accompanying correspondents, whom the Navy had filled with rosy predictions of the destruction to be wreaked by the preparatory fires. Robert Sherrod was one of those who expressed "more-than-mild surprise" at the colonel's cautionary declarations, but he listened respectfully to the "best-known" Marine in the division. In an hour-long session with the press, Red Mike briefed them on the details of the plan and told them to expect tough fighting. "We cannot count on heavy naval and air bombardment to kill all the Japs on Tarawa, or even a large proportion of them. Neither can we count on taking Tarawa, small as it is, in a few hours. You must remember the inevitable slowness of ground action. Some of the battalion commanders think we can take it in three hours, but I think it may take a little longer. These Nips are surprising people." Erskine's last letter to Edson had ended with the sentiment: "I would give my left leg to be able to go with you." Many Marines would give that much and more in the desperate fighting to come.

The division completed combat loading the transports at the end of October 1943 and sailed on 1 November under the guise of amphibious training elsewhere in New Zealand. The force arrived in the New Hebrides on 7 November and conducted landing rehearsals off Efate Island that day and on the ninth. During that process Julian Smith replaced the commander of the 2d Marines with Shoup. A New Zealand army adviser, Maj. F. L. G.

Holland, made it known during the rehearsal that he thought there would be less than three feet of water over the reef on D day; his earlier estimate of five feet had been based on flood tides, because he had never dreamed that anyone would attempt a landing during the neap tide. The other advisers conferred again and reiterated their belief that there would be enough water. Since the primary assault waves were embarked in tractors anyway, and it was too late to make substantial changes in the plan, the Marines decided to continue on the original course. H hour was scheduled for 0830, which would allow the follow-on waves of landing craft to cross the reef at high tide at 1000.

Julian Smith and his command group were embarked in the battleship *Maryland* (BB-46), which would form part of the Navy's fire support force. By D⁻1, Edson and the other staff officers had done all they could; he sat down at his desk in a cramped, hot, below-decks stateroom and wrote letters. He was still concerned about the tough situation the division faced. "Tomorrow by this time we shall have learned whether all the work and planning that has taken place since I joined this division has been worth the effort or not. For the sake of the boys who have to bear the brunt of it all, I hope that the things we have done are the right things." To his wife he lamented his unaccustomed status as part of the rear echelon. "For the first time since this war started, I shall probably not be in the thick of it, but setting back in comparative safety waiting for the progress reports of others. In many ways, this is the more difficult job." He also expressed the negative fatalism that increasingly marked his rare pronouncements on his own future. "In any event, you need not worry. I am sure that I shall be all right. If not, it would not matter anyway, especially so far as I am concerned."

Not long after midnight, the impressive American fleet steamed up to Tarawa Atoll; with the moon rising at 0058, the target was plainly in view. Fire support ships took their stations and the transports entered the lagoon, but the Japanese apparently did not observe the arrival of their unwelcome guests until 0441, when they fired a signal rocket. Twenty minutes later their shore batteries opened fire on the nearest ships; an early enemy salvo landed just a hundred yards off the *Maryland*. From that point on, things developed badly for the attackers. Naval guns ceased fire for twenty minutes while awaiting a tardy air strike. The transports, which had taken station too close to the beach and had already moved once, came under fire and had to move again. These shifts and the slower-than-expected speed of the LVTs caused two delays in H hour, which slipped to 0900, thereby cutting into the precious period of high tide. The planes scheduled to strafe the beach just prior to the landing did not get the word on the change and went in as scheduled at 0825. Gunfire and bombs created so much smoke and dust that the ships gave up searching for specific targets and switched to less-effective area fire.

The prearranged bombardment was partially successful. It destroyed most of the larger targets, such as the coast defense guns, and neutralized or wiped out many of the less heavily shielded installations, such as antiaircraft guns. It also shredded the Japanese wire communication system, a factor that would loom large in the battle because they had no tactical radios. But the vast majority of smaller weapons—the machine guns, automatic rifles, and small direct-fire cannon emplaced in thickly covered bunkers—survived. Friendly fire support shifted off the beaches just prior to the scheduled 0900 H hour, but the leading waves of LVTs were late; they came under a withering fire during the final run to the shore.

The first troops got ashore at 0910. Major Henry P. Crowe's 2/8 landed largely intact on Red 3. The two battalions of the 2d Marines fared less well. Despite the heavy opposition, casualties were initially low, because the tractors absorbed much of the punishment and got their occupants onto the beach with minimal loss. But the units were disorganized and out of position, as LVT drivers sought to avoid the fire or obstacles and lost any semblance of order; squads were separated from their platoons, units from their commanders. The plan called for the tractors to carry the first waves

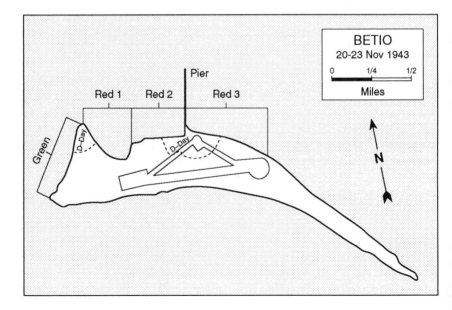

inland while subsequent waves mopped up resistance on the beach, but only two LVTs actually carried out that order, and the troops they dropped off had to retreat to the beach before being cut off. The fire from interlocking machine guns was so intense that few troops could make it off the beach and over the low coconut-log seawall that bordered the island.

If things appeared bleak on shore as the initial waves hugged their few yards of hard-won sand, they were worse out to seaward. Even as the first LVTs roared toward shore, aerial observers reported that water levels were much lower than expected and parts of the reef were exposed. The Marines had run into the worst luck—a dodging tide that deviated significantly from the norm. No boats could get into shore even at high tide. Although the division had accounted for this possibility (LVTs were to pick up troops at the reef and ferry them to the beach), the plan quickly broke down in actual practice. Most of the tractors had survived their first run into shore, but as they turned seaward and the fire increased from defenders recovering from the preparatory bombardment, equipment losses mounted rapidly, and there were soon too few LVTs to make the shuttle service work. Boats that hung up on the far edge of the reef made inviting targets and began to absorb hits.

Many of the men, unable to ride to shore, clambered out and began the long wade across several hundred yards of shallow water. They were exposed throughout to heavy fire from machine guns and mortars. Losses here were extremely heavy, and those men who made it ashore represented disorganized stragglers rather than combat-ready reinforcing units. Red Mike would later cite Marine adaptability in this regard as a key factor in the outcome: "It is my opinion that the reason we won this show was the ability of the junior officers and noncoms to take command of small groups of six to eight or ten men, regardless of where these men came from, and to organize and lead them as a fighting team."

On board the flagship the situation looked just as muddled. There was little information coming from the shore, partly due to disorganization, but largely to water-soaked radios. Communications were none too good even at sea, since the concussion of the battleship's big guns played havoc with the fragile radios of the embarked Marine headquarters. Julian Smith and Edson had to rely heavily on the reports of an airborne naval observer who only dimly understood what he was looking for on the ground (in spite of Red Mike's attempts during the cruise "to make a Marine out of him"). The first cryptic radio message from shore said, "Issue in doubt." At 1000 Shoup ordered his regimental reserve (1/2) to go ashore at Red 2; division released half of its reserve (3/8) to Shoup with similar orders. These units endured the same gauntlet from the reef to the beach as had earlier boated waves. The commander of the 2d Marines made it onto the end of the pier at 1030 and reached the center of the beachhead by noon, where he established his CP. His request for situation reports elicited a short reply from 2/2. "We need help. Situation bad." Early in the afternoon Julian Smith requested VAC to release 6th Marines for use on Betio and ordered his ADC to go to the pier and gather an accurate picture of the situation.

Holland Smith released his reserve to the division at 1525, a decision rendered easy by the lack of tough opposition on Makin. With that boost in strength, Julian Smith ordered the 8th Marines headquarters and 1/8, the last of his original six battalions, to land to the east of Red 3. From there they were to attack to the northwest to create a diversion and flank the defenses commanding the beachhead. He also radioed an order to Hermle to take command of all forces ashore; Shoup had been running the activities of all battalions insofar as he could, given the chaotic situation.

Communications snafus continued to hinder operations. The ADC never received the message to take command; he eventually departed the pier for a ship from which to make his required report. The transport carrying the 8th Marines received the message regarding the landing of its embarked units, but they were already in boats at the line of departure and the word did not get passed on to them. In an effort to work around the poor communications, Edson contacted Jesse Cook, now aloft in a *Maryland* floatplane, and asked him to report on the movement of forces toward shore. As it happened, a wave of boats carrying a battery of the 10th Marines headed for Red 2 at this time. Cook erroneously reported that this was 1/8, apparently moving toward the wrong beach. As Edson later described it to the Marine Schools: "We cursed and tore our hair and wondered what was wrong—but there was nothing we could do about it and so we plotted on the operations map 1/8 in here [Red 2]." Only at midnight did the division CP discover the battalion still afloat at the line of departure awaiting orders.

The situation ashore was precarious at best that night. The two battalions of the 8th Marines held the left flank of a Marine bulge around the base of the pier while the remnants of 2/2 and 1/2 held the right. The beachhead was perhaps 250 yards deep and 750 yards long. There were no organized defensive lines held by specific units, just small groups of men occupying shell holes and hastily dug fighting positions at irregular intervals. The 3d Battalion, 2d Marines, and stragglers from the rest of that regiment held a small perimeter of about 300 yards in depth and width on the bird's beak. Most of Red 1 and half of Red 2, an interval of about 800 yards of beach, remained in enemy hands. All supplies—but particularly ammunition, water, food, and medical kits—were critically short. With few LVTs still running, most items had to be manhandled ashore from the reef across the fire-swept shallows.

The night was bad enough for the men on Betio, but it seemed infinitely worse on the *Maryland*. Red Mike had prophetically described the situation to his mother a week earlier. "I would much prefer to have command of a company, of a battalion, or of a regiment, for those are the boys who really do the work, and who have little time to worry and think about the outcome. Things happen rapidly with them, while here [at division level], once the action is joined, the picture builds up slowly and there is so little that we, as individuals, can really do to influence the action of others." The division staff awaited with some trepidation the standard Japanese banzai assault that night. The Marine perimeter was weak and shallow and the fire support situation was poor; very little artillery had yet made it ashore, and poor communications would hamper the use of naval gunfire in a confused night battle.

Apparently the Japanese were just as disorganized. The Americans had landed where the defenders least expected them, and there was no communication between the many small groups isolated in bunkers. There were occasional struggles in the night with infiltrators, but not the mass charge that might have driven the Marines into the sea. The division's fire discipline was excellent, too, a source of great relief to Edson and the others who knew that no noise meant no Japanese counterattack.

By first light the 10th Marines had several 75mm pack howitzers established ashore. These began to take on the enemy at point-blank ranges of as little as seventy-five yards. The 1st Battalion, 8th Marines, which had spent the night in its landing craft, finally started for the beach. The delay had given Shoup time to influence their use. He requested that they come ashore near the pier, where there was some protection from the still-heavy enemy fire. However, another communications failure brought the boats to the reef near the junction of Red 1 and 2, "the worst possible place they could have picked." The men eventually waded toward the pier and thence inland, but they suffered heavy casualties in the process. In response to a late-morning division request for recommendations on the use of 6th Marines, Shoup responded: "Situation does not look good ashore."

Confusion still reigned throughout the battlefield, and division received reports of its own troops being hit by fire from friendly air, naval guns, and tanks. Elements of 1/2 and 2/2 did manage to cross the airfield and seize a portion of the south shore, thus cutting the island in half. The Marines on the western end of Red 1 attacked south along the western coast, took many of the emplacements facing the sea from the flank and rear, and succeeded in clearing Green Beach of the enemy. Division received reports of Japanese soldiers crossing the shallows to Bairiki, the next island in the chain. At 1700 Shoup's situation report closed with his first positive summary: "Combat efficiency, we are winning."

The Marines ashore were slowly but surely reducing the Japanese defenses. Tanks, half-track–mounted guns, and the pack howitzers played a role, but most positions fell to infantrymen and engineers working with demolitions and flamethrowers. As they reduced each bunker, the enemy's fires slackened. When it became clear that defeat was likely, some defenders also began to commit suicide, often blowing themselves up with grenades or shooting themselves in the head. With Green Beach cleared of Japanese direct fire, 1/6 went ashore there in the evening. It was the first unit to land with its organization intact and minimal casualties. The 2d Battalion, 6th Marines, was to follow it ashore, but at the last minute division diverted them to Bairiki to close off any Japanese escape route.

With the situation visibly improving, Julian Smith took steps to establish division control ashore. Perhaps because Hermle had spent the night of D day on the pier trying to gather information, and because Red Mike volunteered for the mission, the general assigned Edson to take charge of setting up a forward command post. Shoup had done an admirable job, but he was exhausted after thirty-six hours of continual combat, and the number of units ashore was mushrooming far beyond the ability of a regimental headquarters to handle effectively. Red Mike departed the *Maryland* at 1750, the boat dropped him at the end of the pier, and two and a half hours later he had covered the half mile to the 2d Marines CP, still located in defilade behind a Japanese bunker on Red 2. Shoup briefed him on the situation and the two colonels made their plans for the night and the next day. The 3d Battalion, 2d Marines, backstopped by 1/6, now held all of the western end of the island to a depth of about two hundred yards inland. The 1st and 2d Battalions of the 2d Marines held a perimeter a few hundred yards in length and bounded by the beach on the south and the airfield on the north. On the far side of the runway, the 8th Marines held basically the same bulge around the pier that had been in American possession the night before.

Edson issued orders to 3/6, the only remaining uncommitted battalion, to be prepared to land at Green Beach the next morning when directed. These orders went out by radio at 0359. As the communicators performed that chore, Red Mike personally briefed Shoup and the commander of 8th Marines, Col. Elmer E. Hall, at the Red Beach CP site. To ensure that 1/6 got the word, he sent the assistant operations officer to that battalion's location. A small number of Japanese bombers came over about this time and indiscriminately dropped their loads over the island on friend and foe alike. None hit home near the CP. The defenders on the island also let another night slip by without their trademark counterattack.

The plan of attack for the next morning would have received a failing grade at the Senior Course, but Edson had little choice given the terrain and the fragmented dispositions inherited after two days of battle. The 1st Battalion, 6th Marines, was to pass through 3/2 and attack east along the south coast to link up with the rest of 2d Marines. The 1st Battalion, 8th Marines, would attack in the opposite direction along the north coast and wipe out the Japanese still holding portions of the original landing beaches between the perimeters of 3/2 and 8th Marines. The remainder of 8th Marines would attack east along the north coast and link its flank with the 2d Marines to the south. If successful, these operations would finally consolidate Marine lines and compress the enemy into the narrow eastern tail of the island.

To augment these operations, Edson and Shoup arranged for strong supporting fires. They scheduled four twenty-minute bombardments by ships and planes combined against the eastern end of the island at 0700, 0830, 0930, and 1030. Edson asked the 10th Marines to land two batteries on Bairiki, where they would be in excellent position to fire on Betio. If the division could not get its supporting landing prior to the main assault, it at least had it now to help make the end of the battle easier. More guns continued to land on Betio itself; by the middle of that day (D+2) there would be a total of two battalions of artillery in place on the two islands.

With these preparations complete, Red Mike was reduced to waiting and watching again. He stood amongst the shattered palms and provided some analysis of the battle to Sherrod, an Alpha Tau Omega fraternity brother. "This is the first beachhead they have really defended. They had no choice but to defend here—they had no interior position to retreat to; it was all exterior." He closed with a bit of a smile and his characteristic Vermont understatement: "Anyway, it won't last as long as Guadalcanal." Carlson, an observer from the 4th Marine Division, sat nearby and marveled at the beating 1/8 and 3/8 had taken during their wade to the beach.

In the ensuing attacks, 1/8 did not gain much ground against the Japanese pocket on Red 1 and 2, but the assault did destroy additional bunkers and erode enemy strength. The attack of 1/6 progressed rapidly and made an early linkup with the 2d Marines to the east. With that success in hand, Edson called the commanders to his CP to arrange a further advance. He ordered 1/6 to pass through 1/2 and 3/2 at 1330 and push toward the tail. The 8th Marines (less 1/8) would continue its attack to the east and remain on line with 1/6. Colonel Elmer Hall, CO of the 8th, told Edson that his men had only one assault left in them, so Red Mike promised eventual relief by 3/6, which he had brought ashore on Green Beach that morning. The 1st Battalion, 8th Marines, was to continue working on the Red Beach pocket following an air and naval gunfire bombardment to be arranged by the division CP.

All attacks progressed well in the afternoon. By early evening both 1/6 and the 8th Marines had reached the far end of the airfield. Company C, 1/6, shifted to the area north of the runway in support of 8th Marines, while Able and Baker split the southern flank. Machine guns covered the flat expanse of the airfield itself. The 1st Battalion, 8th Marines, further reduced the enemy holdouts on Red Beach and established a strong perimeter around them by nightfall. Julian Smith had come ashore at Green Beach just before noon that day, then decided to set up his shop at the well-used 2d Marines CP. During Smith's movement to the new location, his amphibious tractor ran into heavy fire off the south shore from the Japanese position bedeviling 1/8. The enemy knocked out the general's LVT; the command party remained stranded behind it until another came up to rescue them. Smith finally made it to Edson's location after 1300 and formally assumed control by 1400. Red Mike had been in charge of the fighting on Betio for twenty hours.

Julian Smith's initial impression was that the battle would continue for another five days due to the difficulty of reducing the dug-in enemy and the disorganization resulting from heavy casualties among the division's officers and NCOs. That night, however, the Japanese finally launched the long-awaited banzai assault. A small attack came in at 1930 and two more at 2300, followed by a larger attack of about two hundred men at 0400. Only the first made any penetration; increasing amounts of Marine artillery and naval gunfire caused heavy casualties to the enemy, now exposed above ground in large numbers for the first time in the battle. This last-ditch effort seemed to break the remaining strength of the Japanese and use up most of those troops who still had the will to fight.

❧ The next morning, after a heavy preparatory bombardment by air, naval guns, and artillery, 3/6 passed through the lines of 1/6 and attacked to the east. Progress was rapid and the Marines reached the tail end of the island at 1300. The 1st Battalion, 8th Marines, and 3/2 resumed operations against the Red Beach pocket that morning and finally occupied the last enemy territory in that area at 1300 as well. At 1330 Julian Smith announced that organized resistance had ceased, though Marines would be cleaning out snipers and bunkers for several days to come. Elements of the division also had to secure the rest of the atoll and seize nearby Abemama. Those operations met little or no resistance, except for a tough fight when 2/6 cornered the last 150 Japanese at the northern end of Tarawa.

The cost of the operation had been high. It was impossible to immediately establish an accurate count of casualties because of the thorough disorganization of the units that landed on D day and the rapid reembarkation of the 2d and 8th Marines on 24 November (D+4, the day after the island was declared secure). Initial estimates placed American dead at 1,026 and wounded at 2,600 (final figures were somewhat less than that). The reaction back home was extremely negative. The losses were about the same as those sustained on land at Guadalcanal, but being compressed into four days rather than six months made them much harder to bear. The public was shocked, and some editorial writers and congressmen reacted with diatribes against those who had ordered the slaughter.

A few Marines, Edson and Julian Smith principally among them, were not surprised at the casualties; they had expected the worst from the first and had swum against the tide of optimism prevalent before the operation. Red Mike, "considered very much a pessimist aboard ship," later related one indication of the division of opinion. The Navy's air support commander bet a bottle of scotch with the colonel that the naval officer would be able to walk ashore before darkness on D day. The man finally made it on D+4, only to be shot at by a sniper. The differences in outlook, of course, centered on rival evaluations of the effectiveness of air and naval gunfire support. The debate was not forgotten in the heat of battle. On the evening of D+2 Smith's summary of the situation noted that bombardment was insufficient to destroy the enemy's fortifications. Anxious to demonstrate to the Navy the need for stronger support in the future, the general also sent a message to the task force commander just before declaring the island secure: "Strongly recommend that you and your chief of staff come ashore this date to get information about the type of hostile resistance which will be encountered in future operations."

A large percentage of the casualties were also due to the lack of sufficient amphibious tractors for all of the assault and reinforcing waves, which caused many men to wade hundreds of yards across fire-swept waters devoid of cover. Ironically, on the day the island was secured, tides returned to normal heights and there was sufficient water over the reef for landing craft to reach the beach. Press reports in the States highlighted the tide issue; some accounts left the impression that it was the result of a mistake on the part of the planners. The photographs of Marine bodies floating in the lagoon indelibly stamped the idea into the public mind. The Marines, and their amphibious counterparts in the Navy, soon ended up in a debate about the ability of American forces to successfully seize such heavily defended targets. Edson would find himself caught in the center of that argument.

Julian Smith and Edson played host to several important visitors in the immediate aftermath of the battle. Holland Smith arrived for a tour of the island on 24 November and Admirals Nimitz and Spruance on the twenty-seventh. Red Mike accompanied the official parties as they walked over the battle-scarred landscape. Marines were still dealing with snipers and burying corpses; the smell of death, heightened by the equatorial heat, was thick enough to cause many men to vomit. The focus of conversation between the two Smiths was the heroism of the men who had taken the island, but Holland also discussed the future of Julian's chief of staff. The corps commander told the division commander to recommend Edson for promotion to brigadier general.

Julian Smith initiated the action the next day on the basis of Red Mike's "extraordinary heroism and outstanding performance on the field of battle." His letter then outlined the chief of staff's contributions to the victory. "Colonel Edson's sound tactical judgement and untiring efforts during the planning stages of the operation were invaluable. During a critical period when it became necessary to establish a coordinated command on shore as well as to continue command afloat, he volunteered to assume this responsibility and continued to do so until the situation permitted the Division Commander to come ashore." Holland Smith attached an even more glowing endorsement to the message just a few days later. He considered Edson and Shoup to be "primarily responsible" for the victory.

The generals did not have to worry about the reception the request might receive when it passed through the hands of the commander of the Pacific Fleet. During his visit to Betio, Nimitz must have been as impressed by Edson as he had been during a similar tour of the Ridge on Guadalcanal. In a congratulatory message sent the next day, he lauded the operation as an "all time high" in the history of the Corps and cited just two individuals by name. One was Lt. W. D. Hawkins, the scout platoon commander who fought gallantly on D day, earned a posthumous Medal of Honor, and bequeathed his name to the Betio airfield. The other was Edson, of whom Nimitz said, "I strongly recommend [his] immediate promotion to brigadier general . . . for outstanding performance of duty in GALVANIC."

Admiral Harry Hill, the task force commander who had predicted that Marines would walk ashore without opposition, seemed to think the promotion was guaranteed. He sent his congratulations on 30 November with the notation, "We're all cheering."

The potential promotion would not be Edson's only reward for the operation. Speculation about medals arose practically before the shooting was over. During the tour by Holland Smith, the division commander informed his boss that his first recommendation for the Medal of Honor would be for Hawkins. Shoup, the valiant commander during the first two critical days ashore, would get the second of four awarded for the battle. In retirement many years later, Julian Smith told one interviewer that Edson was upset when he discovered that he would not be so honored along with Shoup. The chief of staff, "bone-weary" in the immediate aftermath of the fighting, is supposed to have protested: "General, that's my damn medal you're giving him."

The story could be true: Red Mike was beginning to take some pleasure in acquiring new honors and awards, and he was willing to stand up for himself if he thought he was cheated in that regard. It is harder to credit the allegation that Red Mike felt he deserved it more than Shoup. In a private letter a few weeks after the battle, Edson praised the commander of the 2d Marines and cited him as "largely responsible for the winning of Tarawa." Two Marine officers who survived the battle may have summed up the situation best in answer to a question from war correspondent Robert Sherrod. "We were talking about medals. We decided nobody should be recommended because everybody should have one."

For Tarawa, Edson would receive a Legion of Merit, the same award issued to all the primary staff officers of the division, although Smith had recommended him for the higher Distinguished Service Medal. If the medal was not necessarily the most appropriate one, the citation certainly captured the essence of his contribution to the victory. "Schooled by grim experience in the art of countering Japanese strategy, Colonel Edson directed his division staff in a meticulous intelligence study of Tarawa Atoll, subsequently preparing a carefully evaluated estimate of the situation upon which the Commanding General based his decision to attack on the North Coast. Landing at Betio on D-Day plus 1, he quickly established an advance command post and . . . effected sound solutions to direct problems encountered during critical stages of the operation and prepared tactical plans for the final attack and for clearing the entire Atoll of Japanese positions."

Edson had reason to be pleased with the results of his efforts, as he indicated in a letter to his wife. "This division did a splendid job, and I am proud to be associated with it. I believe also that it is equally glad to have me." In addition, the long-hoped-for general's star seemed near at hand. His sense of satisfaction was no doubt tempered by the news of his father's death on 25 November, but that had not been unexpected. For now, Red Mike would remain with the division, with the prospect of another battle, and that was all he wanted at the moment.

Chapter 14

"In Sunny Tropic Scenes"

A s a consequence of the 2d Marine Division's shift to Nimitz's command for the Tarawa operation, it would not be returning to New Zealand but was instead destined for Hawaii. Its base camp would be a portion of the Parker Ranch, a huge cattle outfit on the big island of Hawaii, about two hundred miles from Pearl Harbor and Oahu. The location on the slopes of Mauna Kea volcano was cool, a welcome relief after the torrid heat and charnel house smells of Betio, but the facility was otherwise an unwelcome sight to arriving Marines. Those responsible for preparing the camp had not expected the troops to show up so soon, and base construction had hardly begun. There were galleys but no cooking utensils, showers but no resupply of clean uniforms. Tents were still packaged and stacked, so the troops had to build much of their new home themselves. There were no blankets, so they shivered at night in the chill mountain air.

Red Mike found these inconveniences irritating, but he was much more concerned with the choice of the site itself. He called it "the best *Army* camp that I have yet seen in the Pacific," because there was no good place to conduct amphibious training. A quick reconnaissance of the island revealed only four small beaches; the majority of the coastline consisted of rocky volcanic flows reaching right into the sea. The few patches of sand were hemmed in by urban areas or cliffs and provided no access to further maneuver ashore. The camp itself was located many miles from the coast, and the main port of embarkation was on the far side of the island, connected to the base by only a single poor road. Hawaii may have been a tropical island, but it in no way duplicated the coral atolls of the Central Pacific.

Although imperfect, the site nevertheless was going to be home for the next several months. The division christened the base Camp Tarawa and named the streets after islands in the atoll and a few of the courageous buddies left behind there.

In the midst of the heavy demands of rebuilding the division, Edson was busy gathering afteraction reports from his staff and the subordinate commanders. Everyone was aware that this operation had been the first of its kind in the Pacific, a major assault against a heavily defended beach, and they immediately started drafting the lessons learned. Some of the remarks were unsolicited. A Navy officer who arrived on Betio the day after the battle wrote his own report. He recommended that the LVTs should have been taken to the beach in their mother tank landing ships (LSTs) to provide them additional protection, and that the assault should have been made against Green Beach to enfilade the Japanese defenses on Red Beach. The officer's comments overlooked the obvious facts that no LST could have made it to the beach on D day given the low tides and that Green Beach was more heavily mined and defended than Red Beach. His report did typify the raging debate over the Tarawa operation and the lack of knowledge of most of those who castigated the alleged failure.

The firestorm of controversy in the States began with the release of estimated casualty figures on 1 December. These made banner headlines in the newspapers, which compared the numbers unfavorably with Guadalcanal, Salerno, and other campaigns. Some commentators wrote it off as "ill-luck," but others characterized it as the result of poor planning, inept decision making, or cruel indifference to the lives of the troops. Only a handful, particularly those reporters who had participated in the landing, sought to justify it as necessary and unavoidable. One writer foresaw the public reaction and specifically addressed the issue in a story written on 24 November. "I certainly do not wish to minimize a scene of death and devastation, but it would be easy to overemphasize this aspect of the operation and thereby, perhaps, to weaken public confidence in the leadership of men like Maj. Gen. Julian Smith and Col. Merritt A. Edson and Col. Dave Shoup. . . . Every correspondent who knows these men and who knows the Tarawa story, believes they are among the finest military leaders we have."

Back home, HQMC decided to mount a campaign to protect the image of the Corps. The commandant needed a figure the public held in high esteem, someone who could explain Tarawa to them and justify the high cost. Smith and Shoup were unknowns prior to Betio. Red Mike, the hero of the Ridge, the fearless raider commander, the winner of numerous decorations, was someone who had already proven himself a top-notch combat leader. He was also intelligent, affable, well-spoken, and liked by the press. He was clearly the man for the job. On 24 December he flew to Pearl Harbor; three days later he went on to San Diego in Nimitz's personal plane. He arrived in the capital by commercial air on 30 December.

Although Red Mike's reputation required no boost, the Corps nevertheless gave him one when it promulgated his promotion to brigadier general on 21 December. He received the word in Hawaii and pinned the stars on his shoulders the next day. *Time* magazine found the event worthy of note and ran a brief article and his photo in their 27 December issue. It described him as "the Corps' ideal fighting man, full of military judgment, cold nerve and a complete devotion to his troops . . . the classic professional." In announcing his promotion, it noted, "For most leathernecks' money, it was about time."

His rapid rise did not please everyone. Edson had jumped ahead of more than a hundred senior colonels, to include some of his former commanders, such as Bob Blake. A fellow brigadier, perhaps only half in jest, believed that Red Mike might soon be writing fitness reports on him. Although rapid advancement based on merit was commonplace among the junior ranks in World War II, this was a rare event for senior officers, who had been steeped in decades of promotion by seniority. Moreover, the Corps was nearing its peak strength and there was little prospect of further expansion of the general officer ranks. Twenty-four men had made brigadier in 1942; Edson was only the fourth in 1943. Some colonels were undoubtedly jealous; some brigadiers were probably concerned that Red Mike might steal one of the coveted two-star slots in the future. For his part, Edson had been unhappy with the promotion lists since the beginning of the war, and he was certain he owed this advancement to Vandegrift, just days away from taking over as commandant. The former 1st Marine Division commander saw to Thomas's elevation as well just two weeks after Red Mike's promotion. His leap was even greater than Edson's and the two friends now had something else in common—the need to prove that they were worthy of the distinction.

Fresh from a bloody coral atoll in the Pacific, the new brigadier faced an entirely different type of battlefield in Washington. He jumped into the public fray on Monday, 4 January 1944. He began with a one-man press conference in the commandant's own office, an august location replete with walls covered by national marksmanship trophies, many of them won by Edson's teams. With those confidence boosters in the background, he spent the next two hours describing the Tarawa operation in detail, with frequent gestures to a map of Betio hung on an easel. He emphasized the two points that were the crux of criticism. First, he established that there had been no mistake about the tide; the planners had known that their information was sketchy at best, and they had decided to use the amphibious tractors precisely to deal with the possible lack of water over the reef. He further pointed out that the perception of heavy casualties due to the tide was simply wrong: More than 80 percent of the losses had been sustained ashore. The press questioned him at length on the matter and seemed satisfied with the answers.

Then he addressed the issue of the adequacy of naval gunfire. Edson was on shaky ground here. He had been the prime critic of the preparatory bombardment in the first place, and now the commandant had put him in the position of defending what had been done. He fudged the point in an artful manner, saying that the shelling and bombing were "as good support as anyone ever had," which was true enough, though he did not add that it was much less than he had desired. He did admit "off the record" that there had been considerable prebattle discussion about the probable effects of the bombardment. The planes and naval guns accomplished "about what we expected them to," inasmuch as they never had proven capable of completely destroying enemy fortifications. His amplifying statement ("By we, I mean Marines") did not make it into the press accounts, and he did not directly say that the Navy and even many Marines had expected a great deal more.

After his statements on firepower, Edson launched into a larger theme on the nature of the war in the Pacific. He pointed out that the entire Japanese strategy was built on the premise of inflicting casualties, not on achieving battlefield victory. "I think the American people should realize the psychology of the people we are fighting—to make the campaigns as costly as possible because they don't believe we can take it. They are willing to take large losses in the hope that we will be ready to quit before we can lick them." The enemy still held on to most of his conquests. It would take a complete defeat rather than a negotiated peace to ensure that the war did not break out again at some future date. Although he prefaced these remarks with the comment, "I am not sure whether this should be published or not," the latter observations—not the specifics of the Tarawa battle—grabbed headlines around the country the next day, though the stories did detail his justification of the operation. A Boston paper referred to him as "a grim-talking Marine."

The publicity campaign did not depend on this one battle. Edson met with combat correspondents that same afternoon, lunched with various luminaries of the press over the next several days, and made two radio talk shows. He repeated the same themes developed at the press conference. Even during a weekend visit to his mother in Vermont, he hammered home Tarawa. Nevertheless, the media continued to highlight his remarks on Japanese strategy and American will; one local newspaper carried his warning that it might take three or four more years to finally crush the enemy. The *Burlington Free Press* editorialized on the general's behalf. "He pays the American people the compliment of believing they do not have to be babied along in this war. He thinks the people should know the truth and face it, and he is doing his best to make it clear."

The Tarawa issue eventually faded away under the weight of fresh news of other battles in the war, but Edson had certainly done his part in ensuring that the reputation of the Corps survived what could have been a telling, if unjust, blow. Vandegrift was pleased with the brigadier's performance. Whenever anyone questioned him on the battle, he referred them back to Edson's press conference: "I think you could get everything right from that—from a man who was there and knew exactly what went on." The commandant had picked the best man for the job because Red Mike believed passionately that he and his division had done the right thing.

Despite Edson's efforts, the belief that "someone had blundered" never fully disappeared. The first semiofficial publication of the Marine Corps on the subject in 1944 was so full of errors that Edson felt compelled to draft a detailed rebuttal, most of which was incorporated into the final product. In his opinion the full campaign history in 1947 was even worse. "I think this thing stinks. Whoever wrote [the first chapter] has devoted about ten out of the twelve pages in apologizing for what took place at Tarawa." The misapprehensions would continue long after Edson died. The biography of Admiral Spruance is an excellent example. "All the amphibious planners apparently believed that an intense D-Day bombardment of several hours duration was going to be enough. Everyone was wrong." In reality, Edson and a few other Marines had predicted the outcome, but as is typical with prophets, no one had listened to them.

In one of his last appointments in Washington, the old match shooter got a chance to ride his favorite hobbyhorse. An editor of *The American Rifleman,* the NRA's magazine, interviewed him for an article on the role of marksmanship in the war. Red Mike discoursed at length on the value of accurate shooting, but a few of his supplementary points were most interesting. Despite his friendship with the manufacturer, he argued for a much more limited use of the carbine; he thought pistols should remain the mainstay for machine-gun and mortar crewmen and officers. "I don't think an officer needs a weapon, other than a strictly self-defense weapon. His job is to command. When he starts showing the boys how well he can shoot, his efficiency as a commander suffers." (Edson went a bit further in answering a question on the same subject at the Marine Corps Schools. He told the students that an officer should be armed with a swagger stick.)

Edson's two-week visit to the States seemed to go by quickly; he could not "recall ever having been as busy before in a comparable period of time." He joked that he would be glad "to get back to the field for a little rest and recreation." His anxiousness to return to the Pacific was part of his desire to keep his efforts focused on the war, but there was also the secondary motivation of spending as little time as possible with his wife. She took leave from her job to be with him, but he kept busy and made no effort to turn the trip into a vacation. In any case, she was a strong woman who could conceal her emotions; the officer who escorted her back from the airport when Edson left noted "she was dry eyed all of the way."

Red Mike must have found his first brush with a major public relations campaign invigorating, for he did not let the effort die when he returned to Hawaii. The press reaction to his comments on the war generated the idea of an article for *Reader's Digest* or the *Saturday Evening Post,* two of the most popular magazines of the day. He finally did finish a draft, but for unknown reasons he never published it. That may have been because Sherrod stole his thunder with an amazingly similar diatribe, titled "Afterthoughts," at the end of his March 1944 book *Tarawa.* In his manuscript, Edson not only repeated his comments on the Betio battle but also predicted that there would be "many other bloody Tarawas." His conclusion trumpeted an interesting theme that would, in time, serve as his clarion call on a different battlefield, though he could hardly have envisioned it at the time. "Perhaps I shouldn't be saying all this. I'm just a Marine, and a Marine's job is to fight and not mix in political or economic controversy. But sometimes a man has to get things off his chest. It's still a free country where everyone has a right to speak his mind. We're fighting to keep it that way."

Edson arrived back in Hawaii on 19 January 1944. A load of work awaited him. Julian Smith had fallen and broken a rib on New Year's Day and was laid up in the hospital. That did not derail previous plans for Edson's elevation to a billet commensurate with his new rank. Hermle detached the day of Red Mike's arrival and the fresh brigadier stepped up to be the ADC and the acting CG in Smith's absence. Julian Smith could not have been more pleased. In a mid-December letter to Vandegrift he had enthusiastically requested that Red Mike stay on. "Edson and I are a good team. He was a revelation to me. I knew he was a fine field commander but was not aware of his ability as a staff officer." Smith filled the vacancy at chief of staff with the capable Shoup, who had been doing the job anyway in Red Mike's absence. He had been spot promoted to colonel just two months earlier, so HQMC had planned to fill the billet with a more senior colonel, but Edson intervened with a personal letter to Thomas that allowed Shoup to hold onto the plum. Red Mike thought that Shoup (a future commandant) was "one of the outstanding and most capable officers of his grade."

The trio of men at the top of the division generally worked well together, but there was a certain amount of tension between them. Part of this was due to the precarious niche occupied by Edson and Shoup (and others who had received merit promotions). Under the system in force at the time, they continued to hold their lower permanent rank even as they filled slots at their higher temporary rank. In between those two positions on the lineal list were many officers senior to them in permanent rank but junior in terms of temporary status. Should any of those officers be promoted, they would automatically move ahead in seniority at the higher grade, even though they had been promoted to the new rank well after Edson or Shoup. The chief of staff's junior status (not only as a temporary colonel but also as a permanent lieutenant colonel) made it difficult to fill the regimental commander slots with officers who would not be senior to him, because the most senior colonel in a division traditionally rated the chief of staff billet.

Edson actually talked to Shoup about moving him back to a regiment, but Shoup was violently opposed to that idea. The chief of staff said he would rather have been killed on Tarawa than submit to what he saw as a demotion. Red Mike, perhaps at the behest of Smith, decided to write the letter to Thomas and let Shoup keep the billet. The ADC made a potentially big sacrifice to satisfy the chief of staff. During Edson's visit to HQMC, he and Thomas had discussed the likelihood that Julian Smith would transfer before the next operation. They decided that the possibility of Edson picking up a temporary second star and command of the division would be increased if a colonel worthy of temporary promotion to brigadier was available in the unit. Shoup was far too junior to fill that role, so if Smith moved on, HQMC would have to assign a brigadier to the division, and nearly all of them were senior to Edson. Red Mike was wistful but realistic about the dashed plans: "I may have guessed wrong on the whole setup anyway as there may never have been any intention of giving me the Division or two stars this summer."

The switch to ADC was a tough one for Edson, since the billet had no inherent responsibilities like that of CG or chief of staff. "In most places the ADC is an absolutely negligible personage as far as command and active direction of the Division and its policies are concerned." In his first staff meeting after the change, Red Mike found "it was something of an effort to keep quiet & let Dave do the talking as is the prerogative of the Chief of Staff." Edson conducted unit inspections and went out to the field to observe training, but he was not satisfied. "I am afraid I shall never succeed in keeping my fingers out of the pie—as it has always been customary for a good ADC to do, but will probably be interfering and upsetting somebody's apple-cart every once in awhile. . . . Anyway, everyone here expects that to happen."

Everyone, perhaps, except Smith, who was not too pleased when Edson gave a talk to the regimental and battalion commanders on training in early February. Red Mike suspected that the general's displeasure was over more than this particular incident. "I think, too, that Julian rather feels that I stole the show from him between August 1st and now, although he has never really said so. . . . I felt that someone had to carry the ball when I first joined the division. . . . At that time Julian was not too sure of himself in my opinion and if I had not joined as I did I seriously doubt if we would have been successful in November." Edson's claim to importance in the division later was seconded by Holland Smith. "I used to tell Julian Smith [to run his own division] but he never caught on. He let Edson run it."

Red Mike also was concerned that Smith was upset about press coverage focusing on Edson. Although there is no indication that Smith ever actually raised the point, growing public acclaim made the ADC feel uncomfortable. A prime example was the March 1944 issue of the NRA magazine, which carried the lengthy article on Edson's marksmanship views and featured his portrait on the cover. Semiofficial Marine publications were just as bad. *Leatherneck,* a magazine directed at enlisted members of the Corps, published an adulatory article in its March edition titled "Red Mike and His Do or Die Men," which recounted the story of the Raiders from formation through the Guadalcanal campaign. It summed up tales of his courage with a quote from one of his former Raiders: "I don't know what it would take to scare that man. . . . But it sure hasn't been built yet." Another article in the civilian press called him "the greatest amphibious commander." One of his friends wrote him that "you are quite a household word back here." Red Mike was fast becoming one of the well-known figures of the war; Julian Smith, by contrast, elicited yawns from the press.

Edson seized upon one photo in the *Marine Corps Gazette* as a means to rectify the matter. Under the caption "leaders of the assault," the periodical had listed the men shown in the picture: Edson, Shoup, and Carlson.

The ADC took advantage of his position as a director of the *Gazette* to write to the editor and call his attention to the fact that "in nearly every article published regarding Tarawa, General Julian C. Smith was either not mentioned at all, or never presented in his true light as the officer actually responsible for the excellent job done by his division." Edson urged the *Gazette* to publish a feature on Smith that would give the general his due credit.

Red Mike was not so willing to share the limelight with someone he disliked. In the same letter to the *Gazette,* the famed 1st Raider took umbrage at the characterization of his rival, Carlson, as a "leader of the assault." He thought it "very unfortunate that an official Marine Corps publication should have carried the impression conveyed by the public press, that he was in any way connected with the planning or direction of this operation." It was true that Carlson had been merely an observer, but he had also performed valuable services in the course of the battle, a fact Edson conveniently ignored.

If Red Mike was willing to allay any hard feelings over publicity, he was not about to become a shrinking violet in terms of the operation of the division, as he explained in a letter to Bibs. "I still intend to keep my finger on what is going on and to take an active part in this outfit, but I want to do it in such a way as not to appear to be doing so, that is difficult to do, although I certainly play ball with [Julian] and tell him everything I have in mind or do. Sometimes I think perhaps I have told him too much, but he is such a grand, honest, real person that I would not do otherwise."

Despite these squabbles over billets and fame, the first few weeks after Red Mike's return to Hawaii were a happy period for him. He and the principal division staff moved into a roomy ranch house, complete with electricity, hot water, beds, and a tennis court. He now rated an aide to take some of the mundane burdens off his shoulders. (He chose his first one, Lt. Carl W. Mesmer, for his combat leadership, demonstrated on Betio as an infantry officer.) The Parker Ranch even hosted a rodeo and barbecue for the division; Edson and Shoup (Smith was still recovering from his broken rib) opened the festivities on horseback, a pastime Red Mike had not enjoyed for many years. He also got the chance to delve into baseball again. The former first baseman threw out the opening pitch for the division world series between teams from the 2d and 10th Marines. Not content with a ceremonial toss from the sidelines, he went to the pitcher's mound in military uniform and, "field scarf flying," wound up for a fastball. If he had thoughts of reliving his youth after all this activity, reality soon set in; the doctors prescribed glasses to cure his growing nearsightedness. His weight, down a bit during Tarawa, also climbed back up to a hefty 154 pounds.

A cloud soon appeared on the horizon, however, as the Australian connection came back to haunt him yet again. The first hint had come at the end of January 1944 when he learned that a telegram he had drafted in San Francisco to Bibs had not been sent because it supposedly violated military security. He demanded his money back, the name of the censor who refused to pass it, and an explanation of the problem, none of which he ever received. The incident should have made him wary, but apparently it did not.

On 13 March Julian Smith received a letter from an Australian censor that accused Edson of multiple violations of the regulations and quoted from several letters written between 15 January and 6 February. "Although no single letter offers considerable information, these extracts taken as a whole enable an appreciation of the 2d Marine Division to be built up by inference." The facts themselves were generally innocuous, such as the names and billets of various officers in the outfit. A discussion of the number of mess halls being built and their capacity did reveal the relative size of the division, but that would not have come as a surprise to the Japanese at that point in the war. That the information was not too sensitive was borne out by the censor's actions; he had opened the letters, copied the contents, and then forwarded them to the addressee!

Smith's response to the censor indicated that Edson had no intent to evade the regulations, and that much of the information he had discussed was already available in the press and other public sources. This essentially brought the matter to an official close. Red Mike was grateful for that, since he had been concerned it might blemish his record, even though he was confident he had done nothing wrong. The accusation itself, of course, might have been a delight to those who were jealous of his rapid rise in rank and fame. The matter raised other problems, though, that did not go away with the CG's letter. First was Edson's embarrassment arising from the censor's verbal accusations, made to several senior 1st Marine Division officers, that he had divulged a "tremendous amount of secret information." He felt compelled to defend himself in lengthy letters to all those involved, particularly Rupertus and Brig. Gen. Lemuel Shepherd, the latter one of the few generals he admired. Edson was concerned enough about the spread of the accusation that he even asked the officers to destroy his explanations once they had read them.

The next difficulty was the contents of the letters themselves, for they contained his thoughts on Smith and others in the 2d Marine Division.

Edson was particularly incensed that "only those remarks which might be construed as derogatory were extracted while those of praise and commendation concerning the same or other officers were not objected to or quoted." Included in the extracts were references to Smith's handling of the division prior to Tarawa and his possible jealousy over Edson's fame. None of this could have endeared Red Mike to the CG, though the censor had included portions of his letter to the *Gazette* in praise of Smith, a copy of which had been enclosed in one of the letters to Australia. Smith apparently shrugged off the whole affair, because his last fitness report on Edson, written just two weeks later, recommended that he be given command of a division.

In addition to these professional concerns, the matter raised the visibility of Edson's relationship with the Australian woman; this caused some personal embarrassment, which Red Mike voiced to Shepherd. His 1st Marine Division counterpart told him he had been "indiscreet" but thought he had nothing to worry about. "Other than hearing that you had taken her around a bit which we were all doing, to dances and dinner parties, I heard nothing derogatory about either of you. I agree with you that companionship means a great deal to a man when he is away from home and I can see no harm in relaxation of that kind." Shepherd had tried to derail the whole thing in the first place by getting control of the letters and burning them, but he had been unsuccessful. The affair made Edson a more careful, but no less prolific, writer.

A bigger storm blew in shortly after this initial sprinkle on Edson's parade. The continued expansion and realignment of Marine forces in the Pacific brought about a major reorganization of higher headquarters at the end of March. I Marine Amphibious Corps, formerly part of MacArthur's Southwest Pacific command, had now joined the V Amphibious Corps in Nimitz's domain, which created the need for a new echelon of command in charge of both corps. Although it would take some time to sort out the details, this new headquarters was the genesis of the Fleet Marine Force Pacific. Holland Smith remained in charge of VAC, but IMAC was now subordinate to him. Julian Smith received orders to head a new supporting entity, the VAC Administrative Command, designed to relieve Holland Smith and VAC of some of the nontactical duties inherent in command of two corps. Contrary to Edson's hopes, but more in line with his expectations, he remained ADC; HQMC brought in newly promoted Maj. Gen. Thomas E. Watson to take charge of the 2d Marine Division.

Watson had just completed a successful stint as a brigadier in command of a hybrid unit of the 22d Marines and a two-battalion Army regiment that had seized Eniwetok Atoll in February. As a one star, he had been far senior to Edson, who even now had less than four months' time as a general. The new CG was the complete opposite of Julian Smith. Watson had a well-deserved reputation of being the hardest officer in the Corps to work under or with, as Red Mike knew only too well from their common tour at HQMC. Watson was definitely not the type to let his ADC run the division for him. More cautious after his bout with the censors, Edson left little record of their relationship during this period. He made only a brief allusion to it in a letter to his wife. "I have been fairly circumspect in my speech and actions; in fact I try to keep my mouth shut and have never done so little in my life." The distance between the two generals was noticed by even junior staff officers.

The dashed hopes of command and the uneasy truce with his boss put Red Mike in a funk. He went so far as to broach the idea to Thomas that he might consider a transfer to the Administrative Command, where Julian Smith was anxious to put him to work. Only his desire to remain in a combat division kept him from making a full-fledged request. Other things seemed to be eating at him, too. One of them might have been the additional burden of caring for his mother, who was now too frail to live on the farm by herself. He sold the property and took a large financial loss despite his years of effort to upgrade it.

His future seemed much less important to him, and his letters to his wife were morose. "Bobby is growing up, and doing it much better without me than he would if I were around." "There is nothing to worry about—for whatever happens is already in the book—and if [I die]—with a big IF—why that is alright with me too, and would probably be best for everyone." The gloom was so apparent that correspondence from others appeared designed to cheer him up. He began to keep a notebook containing choice words of that nature from friends and family, as well as similarly chosen poems and famous quotes. One short, unattributed piece dwelt on an alternate life he might have had: "Hadst thou been wedded to me, A great general thou wouldst not be, A lot of fun we would have had, But for success, t'would have been too bad. And then perhaps at close of day, Might not our idols have had feet of clay?"

His mother tried especially hard to boost his self-esteem with a cheery birthday message, which caused him to write back in a rare vein of nostalgia. "Somehow I cannot think of myself as 'a man whose heroic deeds are heard around the world,' but rather as still the small, tow-headed boy who would like nothing better than to be at the old home he still remembers . . . and to put my head in your lap to be cuddled and comforted as you used to do so often. . . . I have been scared half to death more than once, more often than anyone realizes, I hope." She responded with the story of a Vermont woman who had received a letter of condolence from him over her son's death. "I was never kissed before as she kissed my hand. It made me feel like perhaps my life had been worth living—in giving to the world a man like you." Red Mike noted their unusual openness. "It is not easy for me to say things, either—as you said about yourself. We are very much alike in that respect, I am afraid, and go around with our feelings all buttoned up which may, or may not be a good thing. Just don't worry about me, that is all, for I shall be all right."

Things that might have brightened his day just a few months earlier seemed to make little difference to him now. During May he received a gold star in lieu of his second Navy Cross, for Tulagi, and the Legion of Merit for Tarawa. At the end of that month Austin attended the commencement exercises at the University of Vermont and accepted an honorary degree on behalf of his father. The medals elicited almost no reaction in letters home. Of the diploma he only said to his mother: "I shall finally have a degree of sorts from all the expense that I caused you and Dad."

Although Edson was unhappy, and he had much less of a part to play in the daily business of the division after Smith's departure, he did not sulk in his quarters or waste his time. He asked Austin to send him books on diplomacy, politics, and Japanese history. And he devoted more effort to helping out the Marine Corps at a higher level. An observer sent out from HQMC in late May unwittingly noted in his report the ADC's changing emphasis: "General Edson has been most cooperative and has been quite generous in the amount of time he has given over to me for the discussion of points observed." Red Mike's impact on the direction of the Marine Corps in the latter stages of the war was little recognized at the time or since, but he played a major role that went far beyond his position as the ADC of a single combat division.

Edson's influence on the Corps rested on two things. First was his strong combination of intelligence and organizational skills. These capabilities allowed him to generate worthwhile ideas. Most of his thoughts would not have gone beyond that stage, however, were it not for the fortuitous location of Jerry Thomas. The director of the Plans and Policies Division at HQMC was a primary adviser to the commandant, and thus in a position to turn Red Mike's suggestions into reality.

A third officer who assisted for a while was Krulak, now a lieutenant colonel and head of the logistics section of Plans and Policies. He was equally respected for his combat prowess (he had commanded a parachute battalion in the raid on Choiseul) and his intelligence. He knew Edson from Shanghai and had established close ties with Thomas, too. Red Mike thought of him as "one of the brightest and most efficient youngsters that we have," and later noted "he is so far outstanding in comparison to most of his contemporaries that they do not like him."

The Thomas-Edson duo, aided by a handful of officers such as Krulak, wielded enormous influence on the organizational, logistical, and administrative direction of the Corps for the rest of the war. Melvin Johnson, the astute reserve officer trying to sell his weapon designs to the Marines, noted how things worked at HQMC in the spring of 1944. "As near as I can make out nearly everyone around there goes to Krulak to see if it is OK to leave the room. If it gets by Krulak it goes to the good Thomas, and then to the Commandant himself."

Thomas first informally drew on Edson's expertise during his brief trip to Washington after Tarawa. Several units had been experimenting with ideas for revamping the infantry squad, the twelve-man group that formed the backbone of Marine organization. For decades the Corps had operated with a unitary squad, meaning that every member worked under the direct supervision of the single leader, usually a sergeant. This created problems with span of control, since it was difficult for one man to monitor the activities of eleven others, especially in the chaos of combat. The theme of all the ideas currently being proposed was the subdivision of the squad into smaller groups whose leaders would report to the head of the squad. These subunits also could act independently of the squad when necessary.

In December 1943 the commandant had directed the formation of a three-man board headed by Sam Griffith to evaluate possible changes to the squad. The board completed its work in early January and recommended adoption of a thirteen-man squad of a leader and three four-man fire teams. Thomas forwarded the report to the commandant with an enthusiastic endorsement, but only after convening his own ad hoc group to analyze the proposal. He, Edson, Twining, Griffith, Krulak, and a few others discussed the matter and concluded that it was a worthwhile improvement. Word of the new squad went out to the divisions on 17 January 1944. The 2d Marine Division would be one of the first to begin the conversion.

Although his participation in the squad change was direct, Red Mike's later input would almost always be via the mail. He continued his old habit, formed in Nicaragua, of opening up lines of communication through personal correspondence and trying to influence policy through that channel. His friendship with Thomas made this a particularly effective method. His reacquisition of Sgt. Albert Tardiff, his highly capable stenographer from the 5th Marines, made this system work smoothly. The quick thinker and the efficient clerk turned out a steady stream of lengthy letters on innumerable subjects for the next two years.

The structure of the division would be one of the constant themes of Edson's letters. Most field units had barely received the commandant's 17 January announcement of the new T/O when Red Mike launched a counterproposal. Although the new squad was one of the most obvious changes made by HQMC, the basic thrust of the reorganization had been to reduce the size of the division to free up manpower for creation of the 6th Marine Division. The squad had grown larger, but many other elements of the division had been reduced or entirely eliminated. In a 30 January letter to Thomas, Edson forwarded an advance copy of the 2d Marine Division's comments on the new T/O and provided a well-argued case for the recommendations contained therein.

Edson thought that the authorized but unmanned division scout company and regimental scout-sniper platoons would draw off men from the other infantry units, thus making it impossible to actually maintain the thirteen-man squad at full strength, and defeating the purpose of that change. He also felt "very strongly, too, about the advisability of reducing the machine gun squad to five men." He cited his similar experience in trying to save manpower in the Raiders and the eventual problems caused in combat. He did not want the Corps to make the same "grave mistake." Red Mike recommended some areas where offsetting reductions in the infantry could be made, but he argued that other branches of the division, such as artillery and engineers, should share some of the burden. "Unless the Infantry Regiments and the Division Reconnaissance Company can perform their jobs successfully, the supporting elements of the Division can never be employed." He counseled Thomas to remember that "an efficient combat organization" was the prime goal, not the creation of additional units.

Despite the tenor of his first letter, Edson did not focus narrowly on his own infantry specialty. He had spoken to Thomas while in Washington about reorganizing the artillery regiment to provide increased firepower with more big guns, and reiterated in a letter that the division was ready to implement the change as soon as it might be authorized. He also wrote Krulak about the switch of the LVT units from the division to the corps. Although he agreed in principle, he argued that a company of the vehicles should remain organic to the division so that small numbers could be attached to each battalion to act as floating dumps in the amphibious assault and mobile dumps thereafter on land. This would vastly decrease the handling and loss of supplies between the ship and the using units. Krulak agreed, but he soon had to report that HQMC had not received the plan with open arms: "However, it is not dead yet—just resting for another attack."

Lieutenant Colonel William A. Kengla, an observer from Plans and Policies, arrived at Camp Tarawa in May and found Red Mike still pressing for improvements. One of the biggest was a change in the new fire team, which originally armed the assistant automatic rifleman with the small carbine so he could carry more ammunition for the team's Browning automatic rifle. Red Mike had beat the drums against the carbine in his *Rifleman* interview, and had not changed his mind. The observer discovered that in the 2d Marine Division the assistant BAR men carried the M1 rifle, which improved accuracy and allowed use of common ammunition.

Edson brought a host of other concerns to the attention of the observer, everything from his inability to outfit the division with boots instead of shoes to his opposition to further field commissions. He thought worthy men should be screened by Officer Candidate School (OCS) to ensure they had the qualities to perform at higher ranks and in staff billets. He complained that too many officers had become imbued with the cordon defense scheme of Guadalcanal and did not understand alternatives such as defense in depth. He argued that the division needed a tank dozer that could fit on the most available landing craft. He even demonstrated a modification to the entrenching tool that improved its utility. He appeared to convert Kengla into a believer, for the observer's report enthusiastically endorsed all of Edson's ideas. A few months later Kengla would tell Red Mike that he was "very agreeably surprised as to the amount of good our letters have done." He cited the removal of the carbine from the fire team, changes to the LVTs, the expansion of the machine-gun squad, and numerous other proposals now acted upon by HQMC.

Not all of these ideas originated with Edson, of course. Some were undoubtedly adopted from subordinates, such as recommended changes to the utility uniform, which Edson readily ascribed to Shoup. The important thing was that the ADC recognized that things could be improved and set about trying to make it happen. Furthermore, he knew how best to get the changes implemented. He noted in one letter that the same set of suggestions were also being passed up the chain of command through VAC, the route that his input would have followed if he had worked according to the system. But he knew that intermediate headquarters could pick and choose what they decided to forward to Washington, and he was concerned that many of his pleas would not complete their intended journey. When he thought an idea deserved serious consideration at HQMC, he immediately sent it to the place where it would receive that attention. It was not proper, but it worked.

Red Mike, as might be expected, took a definite interest in personnel and related training issues. He wrote Thomas about the serious shortcomings in the current replacement system. Among other things, he found that many men came out with "woefully inadequate" training, since they had spent much of their time in infantry or machine-gun schools performing duties as barbers or messmen instead of undergoing instruction. Some basic skills, such as digging fighting positions, were also being ignored in the rear, since units were expected to polish the men once they arrived overseas. However, many replacements joined just prior to or during an operation and were thus of little use. Thomas worked as best he could to correct these deficiencies.

Changes in division organization, equipment, and personnel policies were useful, but these were not the most important things to which Edson turned his mind in 1944. His ruminations on the larger role of the Corps in the war manifested themselves in two areas. First, he urged the staffers at HQMC to consider the future focus of the Corps. In the early campaigns in the Solomons the Marines had adapted to the exigencies of jungle warfare. Beginning with Tarawa, they had begun a shift to an entirely different type of fighting: the seizure of small, heavily defended atolls. These bunker-to-bunker campaigns were more like the trench warfare of World War I than anything else.

Red Mike believed there would be a third wave, a war for "large land masses" that would nearly duplicate the campaigns then underway in Europe. The final targets in the Pacific were not selected, but they would certainly be places such as the Philippines, Formosa, and the Japanese home islands. The Marines would spend more of their time fighting as a second land army than as an amphibious assault force. This would be a war of movement rather than trenches, which would necessitate important changes in the way the Corps operated. As an example, Edson cited the current T/O, which had done away with the weapons company and farmed the mortars and machine guns out to the rifle companies. This was fine for present circumstances, but eventually battalions would maneuver over larger, more open distances, and they would want to mass the fire of those guns. He recommended the creation of a new billet in the operations section, a battalion machine-gun officer, who would ensure adequate training for the separate platoons in each company and be available to take tactical control of them as a group as required. This type of warfare also would affect logistics. Long supply lines would require lots of trucks, a luxury the Corps currently could ignore when the beaches were so close to the front lines.

Edson's second area of interest was closely related to the first. As the targets got bigger in geographic size, the scale of Marine units involved would grow as well. It would take corps, and even armies, to do the job.

The Marine experience at that level of war was spotty. Vandegrift eventually had controlled more than a division at Guadalcanal, but the ad hoc nature of the whole operation and the limited offensive requirements had not forced the Marines to implement a higher echelon of command there. Holland Smith had taken VAC to the Gilberts, but that had been two one-division operations rather then a corps-sized attack. The problem that Edson foresaw was not Marine ability to control large tactical formations, but the capacity to supply such gargantuan appetites in combat. His concern was based on more than just the need for more trucks or service troops. In addition, he doubted his service's present knowledge and organizational skills in that arena.

Edson had first discussed the issue with Thomas during the visit to Washington. He reiterated his concern in a letter to Krulak in February 1944, in which he discussed the workings of the fledgling Supply Service created to support Marine units in the Pacific. "We feel strongly that the newly established Supply Service is now on trial and that the Marine Corps must prove itself from the logistic view-point in the next six months, or we will be seriously handicapped in our future employment in the Pacific Theater of Operations. The Army has accused us of being incapable of administering and handling a tactical corps or of supplying our combat divisions in the field. Unless we revise our previous concept of supply, I am inclined to agree with them. If we do not take some drastic action in this respect, our whole supply system will, I think, break down under the strain." He noted that the 2d Marine Division had taken only 30 percent of its supplies and equipment with it to Tarawa. "Something is radically wrong when seventy percent of the gear which a division has to handle, store, and maintain is not required for combat."

Red Mike easily identified the source of the problem and the beginnings of a solution. "The present system was developed when we were a very small organization. . . . I believe that we have passed far beyond that stage, and that we now have to develop a Supply Service comparable to the Army Service and Supply, which will relieve the tactical division of the responsibility of self supply. . . . Unless the whole question of supply is considered very carefully and properly handled, I think we will bog down before this war is over." Thomas was already thinking along the same lines, but he was having difficulty trying to reorganize both HQMC and the command setup in the Pacific. Krulak agreed wholeheartedly with Edson. He was already in the process of trying to lighten the load of the division; Edson's concerns caused him to recommend the addition of another truck company to the corps transport battalion then being created.

In subsequent weeks Edson began to flesh out his initial thoughts on the matter with details. He argued that the responsibility for carrying and distributing supplies in combat should be removed from the shoulders of the fighting units as much as possible. Battalions should have none at all, and divisions the barest minimum. "The proper place for most replenishment, in my opinion, belongs with the supply service once that service functions as it should." The ADC expressed equal concern about the development of Julian Smith's Administrative Command, which he saw as part and parcel of the requirement to support larger tactical formations. In a remark that would come back to haunt him, he noted the tendency to assign officers of marginal capability to the rear-echelon functions: "I do not think [Smith] has too much material to work with."

In May Edson again took up the subject with Thomas. "Although it is probably none of my business, the first thing on my list is further discussion of the Marine Administrative Command and Supply Service." He acknowledged that Thomas undoubtedly faced "obstacles and hurdles" in making changes, but he offered his observations anyway. He noted the incongruity of creating the Administrative Command to relieve the tactical commander of the burden, but then making it his subordinate unit, as was the case at present with Julian Smith reporting to Holland Smith. That made the tactical commander ultimately responsible. The personalities involved complicated matters; "Holland [Smith] and Bobby [Erskine] are loath to delegate authority, with the result that in my opinion the administrative command will never function as you visualize that it will."

It worked even worse in practice, for when VAC headquarters went off to battle, the senior officer in the VAC rear echelon, technically now Julian Smith's superior, was a Navy captain. "It is just not conducive to smooth operations when one officer has to combine in himself the tasks of a corps commander and an army commander in a combat zone and still retain responsibility over the administrative command in [the rear area]." On top of that the Supply Service was subordinate to the Administrative Command, which imposed another layer of bureaucracy between Holland Smith and yet another of his big responsibilities.

Edson thought the solution was comparatively simple: "It seems to me we have reached the point where we should parallel as nearly as possible the Army organization for a theater of operations." He saw Nimitz as the theater commander. Holland Smith should become the equivalent of an army commander, with corps commanders reporting to him. His authority would be limited strictly to combat operations, and his boss would be Nimitz. Julian Smith's Administrative Command would incorporate the functions of the Supply Service, be responsible for all rear-echelon functions, and report directly to Nimitz as well. Red Mike was sufficiently well versed on the subject to cite the relevant chapters of appropriate Army manuals. He disliked the Army intensely but he knew a good organizational setup when he saw one; at least it was more logical than the hodgepodge the Marine Corps was stumbling into in the Pacific.

Edson realized that he was getting far beyond the realm of an ADC. "As I have said in the beginning of this letter, none of this is really my business and I have been sticking my nose into something that I should probably keep it out of. . . . Whether such an organization can or cannot be effected, if you should agree with me, is something that I know nothing about. As I told Brute in an earlier letter, I do think we are on trial out here, particularly as regards supply and support of our combat organization. What I have written herein are simply my own ideas as to the best way to make the thing function."

The Edson-Thomas combination was not in a position to change Marine organization in the Pacific in 1944. The monster currently in place would continue to mutate in strange ways until the Corps realized that a major overhaul was desperately needed. Even then Red Mike's ideas would not determine the result, but his demonstrated interest and knowledge in the area almost ensured that he would get a shot at trying to make things work. At the moment, though, he and the division had more immediate concerns. They were just days away from mounting another operation against the Japanese empire.

Chapter 15

"If the Army and the Navy"

T
he 2d Marine Division's new assignment was the Marianas. The southern islands of this group—Saipan, Tinian, Rota, and Guam— were located roughly midway between the Gilberts and the Japanese homeland. The Marianas were another chapter in the continuing strategic debate between MacArthur and Nimitz over the relative importance of the Central and Southwest Pacific offensives. This time the Army Air Forces (AAF) unexpectedly threw its weight behind the Navy. The four main islands of the Marianas were big enough to hold several major air bases and were only fifteen hundred miles from Tokyo, which put Japanese cities and industry in range of the AAF's new B-29 bomber. The air generals were anxious to put their concepts of strategic bombing to work in the Pacific war, even if that meant siding with the Navy over their brethren in the Army ground forces. On 12 March the JCS issued its directive for the seizure of the Marianas beginning 15 June.

The organization of forces for the campaign was complicated. Holland Smith still headed VAC, but he bore the additional title of CG of Expeditionary Troops. Beneath him were the Northern Troops and Landing Force (NTLF), which would seize Saipan first and then Tinian, and the Southern Troops and Landing Force (STLF), which would take Guam. Smith also would command the Northern Force, while Maj. Gen. Roy S. Geiger took charge of the Southern Force. Given his dual role, Holland Smith created two staffs, one to serve him in each capacity. The NTLF consisted of the 2d and 4th Marine Divisions reinforced by the Army's 27th Infantry Division. The STLF, normally known as III Amphibious Corps (IIIAC), was composed of the 3d Marine Division, the 1st Provisional

Marine Brigade, and the Army's 77th Infantry Division. Substitution of the titles Expeditionary Troops, NTLF, and STLF for proper designations such as VAC and IIIAC highlighted the confused nature of the command structure at that point in the war.

Tarawa had been rough, but it had not been as draining as the endless jungle warfare of Guadalcanal. The division got back on its feet much quicker this time and launched into training almost as soon as the camp became habitable. The early focus was on physical conditioning, though it turned more toward tactical exercises as replacements poured in and brought units back up to strength. Edson played his usual role in this process, at least as long as Julian Smith remained in command. Typical of his efforts were those to obtain items needed for training. At the end of January he dunned VAC for a supply of demolition kits and more flamethrowers, since the division had only four weapons on hand. Always ready to ensure speedy action, he recommended that headquarters borrow them from the Army and ship them by air.

Hawaii provided an ideal training location in some respects. Much of the island consisted of geologically recent volcano flows, now endless fields of rock of absolutely no economic value. Thus the division had plenty of space available for live-fire training, and they used it to advantage to conduct large-scale exercises with artillery and aircraft and to hone the skills of infantry-engineer teams in assaulting fortifications. The downside of the Hawaiian terrain was the inability of the troops to dig fighting positions in most locations, a state of affairs that might have reinforced lazy habits, though commanders took steps to counteract this potential problem.

By March the division had already advanced to amphibious exercises with four transports, with the regiments taking turns spending ten days on board and practicing landing operations on the island of Maui. Edson found this a little premature, especially since there were no LVTs or LSTs, which "prevents the training from being as complete as we would like it to be." On the whole, though, he felt able to tell Thomas that the division was "rapidly rounding into shape for its next job." When Kengla came out from Plans and Policies in May to observe, he was greatly impressed by the progress of his former unit. "This is the finest outfit I've ever seen and the difference in it now and as it was when I left it last May is like getting hit in the face with a shovel." The division was ready for action, even more so than it had been for Tarawa. Obviously that was not all Red Mike's doing, but he had played a major role.

Edson exerted much less influence on the planning for the Marianas than he had for Tarawa. In part this was due to his new position as ADC rather than chief of staff. A larger factor was undoubtedly the greater scale of the operation—a multidivision assault in which Holland Smith's VAC headquarters would make the important decisions on the scheme of maneuver. Another reason, and probably the most important one, was his poor relationship with Watson. Under Julian Smith's tenure Red Mike had made his presence felt wherever it could help. Once Watson arrived, Edson found all but one of his suggestions "ignored or rejected."

That one point may have involved one of the most daring plans of the Pacific war. The island of Saipan, about eleven miles long and six miles across at its widest point, was dominated by a single terrain feature, Mount Tapotchau. Rising 1,554 feet from the center of the island, this mass afforded outstanding fields of observation in all directions. Anyone placed on the upper slopes of the mountain would be able to direct the fire of supporting arms on forces moving almost anywhere on the island. Holland Smith initially ordered 1/2 to prepare to seize the commanding height in an operation the night before the main landings. The plan clearly was the handiwork of someone intimately familiar with the raider concept. The battalion was to reorganize itself into units that would fit on six APDs. The troops would carry only light mortars and machine guns to facilitate foot mobility, and would get to the beach in rubber boats towed by landing craft. Once ashore they would use the cover of darkness to negotiate their way up Mount Tapotchau and take the summit. The comparison to Red Mike's old outfit was evident to those who soon nicknamed 1/2 "Kyle's Raiders" and the "Suicide Battalion."

Despite the obvious parallels with the Raiders, it was Erskine, not Edson, who instigated the idea. In fact, Red Mike probably played a substantial role in the move to scrub the operation. Although 1/2 was now attached to NTLF and no longer the concern of the 2d Marine Division, the division staff developed a study showing that the mission would likely fail with heavy losses. Red Mike's description of his efforts prior to Saipan gave a hint of his probable stand on the issue: "In the planning phase, only one suggestion of mine was accepted after I had repeated it several times, for the original was I believe impossible of accomplishment as it was set up." Whether his opposition carried any extra weight is unknown, but Holland Smith finally canceled the plan just days before the task force set sail.

The division began embarking at the port of Hilo in early May. Red Mike and the ADC staff went aboard the transport *Bolivar* (APA-34) on 13 May; Watson and his group boarded the *Monrovia* (APA-31). Based on the hard lessons of Tarawa, all assault echelons would go ashore in LVTs, so much of the outfit sailed in twenty-two slow, rolling LSTs. The initial stop on the itinerary was Maui, where the troops conducted a landing and a tactical problem ashore, then the ships moved on to Kahoolawe for a live-fire amphibious rehearsal. The task force then put into Pearl Harbor for replenishment.

Several accidents during this preinvasion period gave the superstitious cause to worry. During the rehearsals heavy seas swept overboard three landing craft deck-loaded on LSTs. As usual, many Marines were sleeping topside to avoid the crowded conditions below deck; nineteen were drowned and sixteen injured as a result. On 21 May, as men unloaded ammunition from an LST in Pearl Harbor, the vessel caught fire and exploded. Five other LSTs tied alongside were destroyed, too. The 2d Marine Division suffered a further 95 casualties in this disaster, and the 4th lost 112. Luckily, the LVTs and amphibious trucks (DUKWs) had disembarked and were not lost. In the next few days, the Navy replaced the ships and the divisions received new men, so the operation proceeded without delay.

The slower LSTs sailed on 25 May and the rest of the task force sortied from Pearl Harbor by the thirtieth. Now that they were finally headed to the objective, Red Mike found himself with even more time on his hands. He took the opportunity to get caught up on his correspondence and consider the future. In terms of the war, he found the news of the 6 June Normandy landings "marvelous," though he expected the fighting in Europe would "last through another winter." He was not so optimistic about the Pacific and continued to stick with his 1942 prediction that the war would not end until 1946 or maybe 1947. He feared that even a successful invasion of the Japanese homeland might not bring peace, that the enemy might continue a war of attrition from his self-supporting bastions in China and the East Indies. His concern about the American public finally seemed laid to rest, though: "By this time even the most ignorant of the Japanese high command should realize how sadly they misjudged us and our willingness and ability to fight."

Edson expected another hard battle in the Marianas. Robert Sherrod had joined the expedition and requested assignment to the *Bolivar* to be with his "friend from Tarawa." Red Mike called the reporter into his cabin one evening and provided the same cautionary prediction that he had prior to Betio. "This is not going to be easy. Maybe I'm wrong and I hope I am, but you know I've got a reputation as a pessimist." When Sherrod noted that the correspondents who had covered the easy Marshalls landings expected a repeat in the Marianas, the ADC replied, "The correspondents are not the only ones in that frame of mind." As if to bolster his point, two days later a message from VAdm. Marc Mitscher exuded overconfidence after a carrier strike on the targets: "Keep coming, Marines, they're going to run away." Colonel Jim Risely, the commander of the 6th Marines, echoed the feeling: "I've just got a hunch this is going to be the easiest one of all." Holland Smith agreed with Edson's point of view: "A week from today there will be a lot of dead Marines."

The final thing on Red Mike's mind was his own future, much of which revolved around his dislike for his commander. Sherrod was well aware of the chasm between the 2d Marine Division's two generals, since Julian Smith had informed him in Hawaii of Edson's unhappiness over Watson's appointment to the CG's slot. Risely told the reporter that he thought the ADC was trying to get a transfer to the 6th Marine Division, scheduled to form under Lem Shepherd after the Marianas. Many other officers in the outfit felt the same way; most considered their new commander "a cold, uninspiring leader." Sherrod sat in on one bull session and noted that the conversation was "mostly about Watson, whom all detest."

Despite the frustration of his earlier plans to get command of the 2d Marine Division, Red Mike still had some hope for "another promotion and a division of my own." He gave a glimpse of how he planned to achieve his goal when he counseled Melvin Johnson about the latter's own frustrations in selling weapons to the Corps. "I have learned the hard way it is necessary at times to burrow from within rather than to buck an impregnable combination. There is, I believe, an old saying: if you can't beat them, join them." Edson was doing his best to follow his own advice and get along with Watson.

Although he was somewhat downhearted at his relatively unimportant role in the upcoming assault, Red Mike made certain that he and his men would be prepared for it. A few days before the landing he brought his staff together in the wardroom for a briefing. The overcrowded space was suffocatingly hot; the general attended in his shorts, but he was all business. He stressed that they would have command of the division from the time they hit the beach until Watson's planned arrival later in the day, and that they would have to be prepared to take charge again if anything should happen to the primary staff. Moreover, all of them should be ready to take on the jobs of others in the group, "because we have to count on casualties among the staff as well as the infantry command." If any of them thought the life of a general and his assistants was one of comparative safety far behind the lines, they would soon see that the ADC meant every word he said.

He took similar precautions with the handful of enlisted men under his direct command. He had them assemble on deck in the gear they would carry into the assault and showed up in the same outfit to inspect them himself. He walked down the ranks and stopped to say a few words to each man. Red Mike tried to reach a wider audience with a prebattle communique published in the *Bolivar*'s newspaper. He noted that "our job will not be an easy one," but he also expressed confidence in the ultimate outcome. "You are physically fit, battle-wise, and your morale is high. You are without doubt the best combat division in the world today. You have won that reputation at Guadalcanal and Tarawa. You will add to it at Saipan. I am proud to be one of you."

While the Marine divisions made their way toward the objective, their Japanese counterparts were already fighting for their lives. Preparation fires had begun on June 11 with a fighter sweep by Mitscher's Task Force 58 (TF 58). The Navy destroyed an estimated 150 planes in the air and on the ground, and opened the way for an unhindered attack on other targets on succeeding days. Aircraft proceeded to soften up the island on 12 June, and the battleships, cruisers, and destroyers of Mitscher's force joined in on the thirteenth. The next day (D-1) the fire support ships of the amphibious group arrived on station and contributed their weight to the attack.

Although these three days of heavy bombardment provided impressive fireworks and far exceeded that thrown at the Japanese on Tarawa, the effect was not necessarily any greater. The ships of TF 58 had fired mainly at area targets and from great range, which meant that they had destroyed few of the defensive works that constituted the main threat to the landing force. The bombardment on the fourteenth benefited from the experienced, pinpoint, close-range fires of the old battleships of the amphibious support force, but it was again a case of too little, too late. The scale of fire support had grown, but so had the target: Saipan was seventy-two square miles, Tarawa less than one; the former was defended by nearly thirty thousand troops, the latter by just over four thousand men. The hundreds of tons of bombs and shells hurt the Japanese, but there were plenty of defenders left on the morning of the assault to give the invaders a rough reception. Holland Smith would later admit: "We did not soften up the enemy sufficiently before we landed."

The size of Saipan did allow more room for tactical options than had been the case at Tarawa. There were a number of possible landing sites, and enemy units that were spread out to defend each of them would not be able to provide immediate support to each other. The Marines eventually selected a wide swath of the southwest coast for the attack. The 2d Marine Division would land two regiments abreast over Red and Green beaches, while the 4th Marine Division came ashore nearby with two regiments on Blue and Yellow beaches. Each division had a regiment in reserve; these would make a demonstration near the northwestern beaches to draw enemy fire and troop movements away from the real point of attack. Reefs fringed the entire western side of the island, but this time there were sufficient amphibious tractors to carry all assault forces into the beach. H hour was 0830.

Edson and his group would board landing craft and wait for an opportune moment to go ashore, while Watson and the primary staff remained on their transport. This would allow the division commander to maintain effective communications with the assault elements until his ADC got a command post working on the beach. Red Mike asked Sherrod if he wanted to accompany him, and the reporter accepted.

The initial assault waves were in their LVTs and circling long before H hour. Edson and his party got into an LCVP (landing craft, vehicle and personnel) before 0800 and then transferred minutes later to a subchaser acting as a control vessel. The latter's job was to mark the line of departure for the amtracs and signal each wave when it should head for the beach. From this point just four thousand yards offshore the ADC had a good view of the action. Despite continuing heavy bombardment by naval guns and aircraft, the enemy put up a stiff defense from the very first. Once they crossed the reef the initial waves of LVTs came under a shower of fire from artillery, mortars, and machine guns. The Japanese had registered points of aim well in advance, and they exacted a heavy toll with a number of direct hits on the lightly armored amphibious vehicles. Some of the fire reached beyond the shallows, and occasional shells landed less than two hundred yards from the subchaser. As they followed the overall course of the battle by radio, Edson and Sherrod could see LVTs exploding. Even though casualties were significant, the assault was progressing satisfactorily. In the first twenty minutes seven hundred amtracs placed eight thousand Marines ashore.

The ADC staff busied itself with radio traffic to division headquarters, either describing what they could see or passing on transmissions received from units ashore. Although reports poured in of heavy fire sweeping the shallow beachhead, at noontime Edson requested permission from division to go ashore. The subchaser proceeded to the Green Beach control vessel, but the four LVTs it was to meet never showed up. Red Mike swore at the delay and quickly rounded up replacements from the multitude of craft shuttling to and fro. Japanese fire inside the reef had not slackened. As the general's party roared toward the beach, a shell struck an LVT just fifty yards away; Sherrod found the continual explosions "almost deafening." Typically, Edson ordered everyone in his craft to keep their heads down, while he himself remained erect, peering ahead at the beach. The

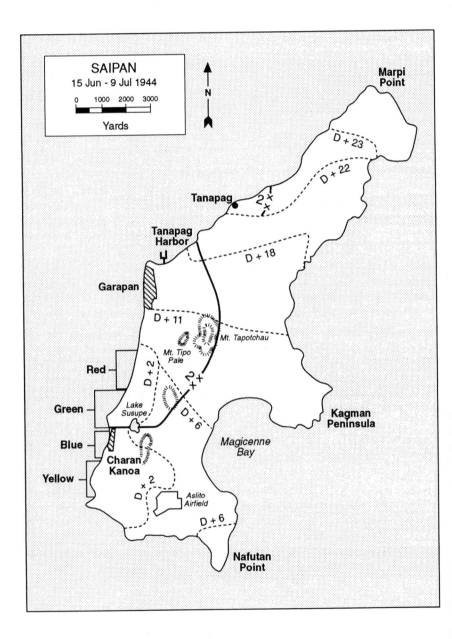

SAIPAN
15 Jun - 9 Jul 1944

0   1000 2000 3000

Yards

N

Marpi Point

D + 23

D + 22

Tanapag

2 x

Tanapag Harbor

D + 18

Garapan

D + 11

Mt. Tapotchau

Mt. Tipo Pale

Red

D + 2

2 x

Green

Lake Susupe

D + 6

Kagman Peninsula

Blue

Charan Kanoa

Magicenne Bay

Yellow

D x 2

Aslito Airfield

D + 6

Nafutan Point

fact that he was standing on a load of mortar ammunition seemed not to bother him at all. It was only at the urging of his aide that he finally doffed his cloth garrison cap and put on a helmet.

The general's party made it onto the beach about midafternoon. Before they could disperse and seek cover from the shelling, he had them unload the supplies and fill the LVT with wounded men from a nearby aid station. The group then moved just a few yards in from the waterline and set up a hasty command post in the limited shelter afforded at the base of a shallow rise. Shells continued to rain down on the beach and its immediate vicinity; Sherrod estimated them at one every three seconds. One explosion sent shrapnel tearing into the throat of a runner, who died just moments later. Machine-gun and rifle fire also whizzed overhead. At that time Marine lines were no more than five hundred yards inland. The inability to fight back against the incoming fire left many on the beach with a "most helpless feeling."

Once the ADC was certain that things were operating smoothly at the CP, he went in search of a more permanent home for the division nerve center. He grabbed Pfc. Robert Zang, a communicator, and the two men walked south along the beach. Near Green Beach 1, about the center of the division zone, he located the remains of a stand of trees between the beach and an unfinished airfield. He went into the middle, sat down, and had Zang put his radio into operation. With his new "command post" now operational, the rest of the ADC's party soon filtered south and set up a full CP nearby. Until that move was complete, Edson ran the show with a message pad and his single assistant. He scribbled out orders to the regiments or reports to Watson and passed them to Zang to send. The luck that accompanied Edson throughout his combat career was especially evident here. Hours later, after dozens of Marines had reinforced the general and his radio operator, a Japanese soldier popped up from a concealed hole just steps from where the ADC had been sitting. With better timing, the lone soldier might have ended Red Mike's string of good fortune.

Watson arrived on the beach at 1800, moved to the ADC's location, and took control of events. Not long after dark, though, artillery and mortar fire began to sweep the beachhead; numerous shells landed in and around the CP. Watson then decided to switch to a position farther inland and up the coast, to another grove of trees concealing a network of liberated Japanese trenches and shelters. Although night moves are habitually confusing and difficult, the ADC and his staff drew the worst assignment. They remained behind and braved the fires that returned intermittently throughout the night, then joined up with the main CP early the next day.

*   *   *

Those who had been confident of an easy victory now realized that they were mistaken. Casualties the first day were 238 killed and 1,022 wounded in the 2d Marine Division alone; the 4th was suffering just as much. Despite the similarity in cost, the nature of the problem was much different than it had been on Tarawa. There the Marines had absorbed heavy losses from Japanese small arms as individuals and teams assaulted the numerous fortified points on the small island. Here the enemy's defenses were not as well prepared, but he had lots of supporting arms, the space to hide the weapons, and the high ground from which to direct the fires. The type of casualties reflected the new style of fighting—many shrapnel wounds, fewer gunshot cases.

Manpower losses were not the main difficulty. The plan had called for the 2d Division to serve as a hinge as the 4th Division cut across the island and then wheeled to the left for a joint drive to the north. The southern portion of the island was simply too big and too tough a job for one division, though. As early as the morning of D+1 Edson answered a reporter's question with a more realistic appraisal than that contained in the operation plan. "Will we have to call in the Twenty-seventh Division? Sure we will, and we may need the Guam force, too, before this thing is over."

Edson was not far off the mark. Holland Smith and the Navy commanders decided later that same day to postpone for the time being the attack on Guam (scheduled for 18 June) and to commit immediately the 27th Division to the Saipan battle. (Within days Red Mike was writing Thomas about the deficiency he saw in the training of Marine planners. "I think we are suffering from years of kidding ourselves on the number of troops it takes to seize and hold a [beachhead]. . . . If we continue to teach that we can land a division against opposition, advance rapidly inland for five or six thousand yards, and then secure a beachhead line of ten thousand yards against an active and aggressive enemy, we are courting disaster. The place to correct this business, I think, is at the Schools.")

The 2d Division's door-hinge mission meant that it did not have to advance very rapidly in the first few days of fighting, especially since the 4th Division was moving much slower than planned. That did not mean there was a lack of action. On the contrary, the Japanese focused their attention on Watson's division during the first few days. On the night of D day the enemy launched a series of small counterattacks against elements of the 2d and 6th Marines holding the coastal road on the left flank of the beachhead. Although none of these disjointed efforts made much headway, they inflicted casualties and prevented the invaders from getting any rest. On the second night the Japanese injected a new element into the Pacific war, their first major armored counterattack. More than two dozen tanks spearheaded the assault, but bazooka teams and heavier weapons quickly destroyed the vast majority of them. Following that failure, the next night the defenders resorted again to small-scale infantry probes. Each day the division advanced a little bit, mainly to complete the juncture with the 4th Division and then keep pace with that organization's flank.

The 4th Division, now bolstered by the Army's 27th, began to make substantial progress in the south. On 18 June the Americans captured Aslito airfield. The next day they reached the shores of Magicienne Bay and cut the island in two. By 21 June the 4th Marine Division was oriented on a northwest-southeast line with the 2d Division and ready for the main push. The 27th Division had pocketed the remaining Japanese in the south into Nafutan Point.

The ADC was "impatient" with the slow progress of the attack, but he did not sit around the command post waiting for something to happen. During these first days ashore Edson "established a pattern . . . which he faithfully followed throughout the operation: get to that part of the division front where the action was most critical and offer advice, inspiration, or even active leadership as required."

Captain Carl Hoffman, commander of a company on the division's right flank, experienced Red Mike's brand of leadership early in the battle. He and his men were trying to crawl forward under intense enemy artillery and small-arms fire in order to make the linkup with the 4th Marine Division. As the captain lay on the ground he heard Edson calmly inquire, "How's it going, Hoffman?" The surprised officer looked up to see the general standing just behind him, oblivious to the shrapnel and bullets. Responding to the company commander's concern for his safety, Red Mike did put one knee down on the ground. In addition to exposing himself so openly, Edson wore his rank insignia, a shiny badge of importance bound to attract the notice of the enemy just dozens of yards away. Hoffman thought the general's actions extraordinary. "Edson was an individual who apparently had no fear at all. He was almost foolhardy. He really wasn't taking the normal precautions he should have." The ADC's calm words and demonstrated courage had the desired effect. Their confidence bolstered by the general's show of strength, the officers and men of the company pressed forward with renewed vigor.

This was typical of Edson, but there was added reason in this campaign for him to spend much more time at the front than an ADC normally would. One was a temporary failure of his program to get along with his immediate superior. The deterioration in relations between the two men reached a peak on D+5. They had initially shared quarters on shore, but Edson found the situation impossible after Watson "openly insulted" two Royal Navy observers who had come to visit him. This was the second incident of that sort, so Red Mike moved out and established a separate abode. The other reason was the CG's policy of giving his assistant next to no authority. Edson felt like "more or less of an extra number," so he focused on the only means by which he could make a positive impact on the outcome. He went to the front lines and attempted to inspire the men of the division by his personal example.

Red Mike may have been the most senior officer on the island to take such risks, but there were plenty of other Marine commanders who also believed in leading from the front. That trait, coupled with the pervasiveness of enemy indirect fire, resulted in high casualties among senior officers. Half of the division's original ten infantry battalion commanders had been wounded in the first two days, and the list grew longer as the battle progressed. As Edson had predicted on the *Bolivar*, division staff officers began to assume new duties. Lieutenant Colonel Rathvon McC. Tompkins, Red Mike's operations officer, took over 1/29, and the ADC assigned Maj. John Apergis to that battalion's operations slot. The major, one of the lieutenants Red Mike had shipped to Carlson in 1942, had been with the division motor transport battalion. Edson noted the unusually high level of attrition in lieutenant colonels when he wrote to Thomas about progress in the campaign. "Three months ago we were wondering how we would take care of rotation in that grade, but the problem seems to have settled itself in a way none of us anticipated or like."

On 22 June the two Marine divisions began their northward push, but it quickly became obvious that they would not be able to finish the job alone. The enemy's defenses in the broken, high ground around Tapotchau were particularly strong, and the continual drain of casualties made units less effective. In addition, the advance would soon uncover Kagman Peninsula and vastly widen the front to be held. As a consequence, Holland Smith decided to insert the 27th Division into the center of the line. The Army outfit occupied its assigned zone on 23 June, though one battalion remained at Nafutan Point to complete the mission of clearing that area. The 27th had done comparatively little hard fighting and had suffered few casualties, so it entered the fray as a rested outfit at nearly full strength. On the negative side, it faced an extremely difficult tactical situation. Enemy-controlled high ground on both flanks overlooked its zone; the left battalion had to advance along the base of a cliff honeycombed with hidden Japanese emplacements. The soldiers soon nicknamed the area Death Valley.

During the next two days of fighting the Marine divisions were able to make significant advances on their now smaller fronts. They might have gained even more ground, except that the 27th Division made little headway. As the center sagged, the interior flanks of the Marine outfits hung perilously in the air. On the afternoon of 24 June, Holland Smith relieved the commander of the 27th, Maj. Gen. Ralph Smith. Despite this change, the Army division's performance improved only marginally, but the Marine units on either flank adapted to the situation and still made gains. On 25 June the 4th Marine Division completed occupation of Kagman Peninsula; the 2d Marine Division, led by 1/29 and 2/8, seized the top of Tapotchau. Now the Americans were on the high ground staring down at the Japanese.

The 27th's travail was not over yet. On the night of 26 June, enemy forces counterattacked out of Nafutan Point, broke through the thin Army lines, and hit Aslito airfield, a Marine artillery unit, and the 25th Marines (NTLF reserve). Although the Japanese achieved initial surprise, the Americans reacted well and destroyed the more than five hundred attackers at comparatively low cost. Now that the point was nearly abandoned, the 2d Battalion, 105th Infantry, was finally able to clear it out. Meanwhile the rest of the Army division continued to make slow progress through Death Valley. It was not until 29 June that the 27th Division began to move forward at a significant rate. It did well again on the thirtieth, but this still left it more than a thousand yards shy of the front lines of the 4th Marine Division, which had been waiting in the same position since 27 June.

The 2d Marine Division was temporarily having its own troubles. Exhausted by the struggle for the dominating heights of Tapotchau and Mount Tipo Pale, it faced more strong enemy positions on its right flank. Edson noted that the combination of "steep cliffs, ravines, caves, and very thick brush" was "made to order for the type of defense the Nip is best at." He found their "reverse slope positions well located, since they effectively prevent close-in artillery support . . . except through high angle 105 howitzer fire." Red Mike's outfit moved forward slowly but steadily, though, and stayed ahead of the 27th Division until the latter's big leap of 30 June. The 2d Division's left flank remained almost motionless in the southern end of the town of Garapan, as the hinge continued to wait for the swinging door to catch up. Due to casualties, all three regiments of the 2d were in the front lines. The division reserve consisted of five provisional rifle companies: three of combat engineers and two made up of men released from the shore party.

Throughout this period Red Mike continued his daily journeys to the front. Tompkins's battalion had barely secured the crest of Tapotchau when the general appeared to inspect the position. Not content to look at the maps in a safe tunnel, he asked the battalion commander and operations officer to take him outside and show him their dispositions firsthand, even though enemy fire constantly swept the vital position. Despite the prohibition on wearing insignia, Edson was still displaying the same stars that had given Captain Hoffman so much concern. He also had disposed of his helmet and was back to sporting the garrison cap or wearing nothing at all on his head. Major Apergis, feeling a little bold due to his former association with Red Mike, asked the ADC if he would mind standing away from him, just in case the general attracted sniper fire. Edson grinned.

A few days later Red Mike was back with 1/29, now well north of Tapotchau. This time a mortar fragment caught Tompkins while the senior officers were in a forward observation post. Without hesitation the ADC told Apergis to take command. The general turned to the battalion executive officer, in whom he placed little faith: "You don't mind, do you, Mac?" Red Mike then suggested that the battalion skirt around the heavy fire coming from a strongly defended hill that had been holding them up. This indirect approach surprised Apergis, who thought of Edson as a by-the-book type who always made frontal assaults.

The daily visits to the front lines did more than boost the morale of the hard-pressed grunts; it also lifted the spirits of the ADC. During a lull on 29 June he wrote to Thomas and Julian Smith. He made it clear that his month-ago hint at a transfer was no longer valid. To Thomas he said: "You can forget about any assignment to the rear areas such as the administrative command. . . . I would never be satisfied with anything except this sort of business." Smith got a similar message. "Please forget any request of mine for duty with the administrative command. I would not have missed this show for anything, and I would hate to miss out on any in the future."

Edson's relationship with Watson was much improved, which may have contributed to his brightened outlook. Sherrod noticed this on 30 June after he and Edson came down from observing a battle on the slopes of Tapotchau. The correspondent had lunch with both generals in Watson's bunkered command post and later penned in his notebook that the two seemed "quite compatible now." Red Mike attributed the change in part to a confrontation over the incident with the British officers. "Since then we have gotten along quite amicably, and occasionally even my recommendations are solicited and often accepted, for I think he realizes by now I am interested only in results, and most certainly not in publicity or acclaim."

In the same visit with the generals, Sherrod pumped them for predictions on the course of the battle. Watson was noncommittal: "Ask me day after tomorrow." Edson was more forthcoming. "It's a tough battle, and it's drawn out—more like Guadalcanal than Tarawa. I wouldn't be surprised if it took three more days to get to the O-6 line, and seven more days after that to clean it up." His estimate proved nearly perfect in terms of the final outcome.

On the evening of 30 June the Japanese began an unexpected withdrawal all along the front. Over the next four days the American forces made large gains in the face of only spotty resistance. By 4 July the 2d Marine Division had seized the remainder of Garapan, as well as Tanapag Harbor and the western beaches reaching all the way to Flores Point. The 27th Division provided these Marines with a welcome holiday gift, since it pinched them out of the line by seizing its own portion of the coast beyond Flores Point. Following the big advances, the 27th and 4th Divisions reoriented their lines to split the remainder of the island between them. The 2d Division went into NTLF reserve, and it looked as though the worst was over.

The end was not to be so simple, however. The 27th Division had renewed troubles on 6 July with nightmarish terrain and strong enemy resistance beyond Tanapag village. The 4th Division was still surging along the east coast, so Smith redrew his offensive plan. The Army would continue to mop up the hornets' nest it had uncovered, while the 4th Division took over the entire front beyond that west coast enclave and completed securing the northern end of the island. These redispositions were not yet complete on the night of 6 July when the Japanese launched "the most devastating *banzai* attack of the entire war."

The assembled enemy force, probably more than 1,500 men, represented most of the remaining defenders. Many had only crude spears for weapons. Regrettably, the 27th Division had not properly tied in its lines or prepared for a night attack. The main assault surged forward about 0445. It quickly poured through a three-hundred-yard gap between the two battalions of the 105th Infantry holding the coastal plain, then overran both units and inflicted heavy casualties. The Japanese next came upon two Marine artillery battalions in the rear. The gunners put up a tough fight with small arms and the point-blank fire of their howitzers, but the attackers drove two batteries from their guns. The momentum of the attack subsided as enemy losses mounted, and it finally spent itself at the perimeter of the 105th Infantry command post. Although the Japanese force was nearly wiped out, friendly casualties were high. The two Army infantry battalions lost nearly 700 men, the Marine artillery more than 130.

The 27th Division regained most of the lost ground during daylight on 7 July, then easily handled a smaller banzai attack that night. Smith ordered the partially rested 2d Marine Division to pass through the 27th's lines on 8 July and complete the mop-up in the Army's assigned zone. The task was less difficult, though far from easy, now that few enemy remained in the rough country above the coastal plain. By the afternoon of 9 June, the 6th and 8th Marines reached the sea a second time and cleared the area. The 4th Division, with the 2d Marines attached, achieved the same feat at about the same time in its zone. Admiral Turner, overall commander of the amphibious operation, declared Saipan secured. Edson's prediction made on 30 June had proven exactly correct. The fighting was not over, though, and American troops continued to root Japanese from caves for months to come. The cost of the campaign was high. Total American casualties were well over 16,000; the 2d Division's share was 1,150 dead, 4,914 wounded, and 106 missing, figures that exceeded the losses at Tarawa.

Unlike previous operations, there was to be no extended period of recuperation for the 2d and 4th Marine Divisions in the aftermath of Saipan. On 7 July, while fighting still continued, Admiral Spruance, commander of the Fifth Fleet, set the date for the Tinian landing. Both divisions would attack the new target beginning 24 July. With Saipan finally secured on the ninth, the Marines had just two weeks to get themselves ready for another major amphibious assault. After twenty-five days of bitter combat, that would be no easy task. The average infantry battalion in the 2d Division had lost fully two-thirds of its strength to death, wounds, and illness. Although some of the men would recuperate in time for the next fight, every Marine was worn out.

The veterans could not rest, either; they mopped up the remaining enemy on Saipan, or they trained. The latter might seem superfluous after a battle, but the units needed to integrate replacements and perform essential tasks such as test-firing weapons for accuracy after weeks of hard use. Other factors conspired to make life miserable for the Marines on Saipan. The ADC himself spoke of the "obnoxious" flies that overran the island in the aftermath of the bloody fighting. A battlefield was simply not the place to recuperate for the next operation.

Edson supervised the training and continued with his self-appointed mission of improving fighting capability throughout the Marine Corps. He fired off several letters to Thomas and Krulak concerning the lessons of Saipan. Among his major points were those he had been putting forward for some time. He noted that the battalions would have to fight understrength on Tinian, as they had on Saipan, because it took too long for the manpower system to react to battle casualties. His idea was to take a substantial surplus of trained infantrymen into the battle, with the extras performing labor with the shore party until they were needed. "With such replacements immediately in hand the impetus of the attack can be maintained; otherwise it becomes progressively less over a protracted operation, which is the kind I believe we can anticipate in our future landings." He reiterated another important consideration arising out of the increasing scale of operations in the Pacific. "The need for additional transportation is going to increase with larger land masses, a thing I have already written about and which we must never lose sight of."

The ADC focused his greatest attention on the subject of assault engineers, the men who used flamethrowers and demolitions in support of infantry attacks on fortified positions. The T/O authorized a single platoon of these valuable men, but following Tarawa the 2d Marine Division had acted on its own initiative and reorganized its engineer units to form three companies of the assault variety. Now HQMC was promulgating a new T/O that would return all engineers to their traditional construction tasks. Headquarters intended to accomplish this by making demolition kits and a flamethrower available to each infantry squad for use as needed. The rationale behind the change was manpower savings, a vital necessity as the Corps struggled to find the men to flesh out new divisions.

In a letter to Thomas, Red Mike argued strongly against the proposed reorganization. He noted that the need for the assault engineer capability was increasing with each operation as the enemy burrowed ever deeper to avoid American supporting arms. In his opinion, the infantry could never satisfactorily perform this mission. They had too little time to train for it and no good method for carrying the additional weapons and munitions. Also, "the assignment of a flamethrower per squad destroys the very idea for which the present squad was developed," since one of its three elements would now take on a supporting role and thereby reduce the capacity for fire and movement by one-third. "I hate to appear insistent about this; but experience in Tulagi, Tarawa, and Saipan only serves to convince me that my ideas are right and that for once you are barking up the wrong tree."

During this brief lull between battles, Edson took some time to contemplate his own future. The intensity of combat had reinvigorated his spirits for a time, but now he was less optimistic. He was unhappy in his present role as an assistant with no authority and saw no appealing changes on the horizon. His letters home radiated dissatisfaction. "It seems to me that I have done very little in this particular campaign and as a result, I feel for the first time since the war started like a more or less useless appendage."

To add to his woes, his wife wrote that stories of the rift with Watson were circulating among senior Marines in Washington, and she was worried about his career. He tried to reassure Ethel on that point, at least.

I have very carefully avoided any references to T. W. in my letters to anyone. . . . There have been several regrettable incidents, not of my own making, during the past few months, which have occurred in the presence of other people, which I have taken without saying a word in front of anyone else or to anyone else. It is possible that some of them have been relayed in personal correspondence by officers who, as friends, considered they were doing me a favor, or by others, not as friends, who hoped to make things disagreeable for me. In either case, I can not be bothered or worried about it, nor need you be.

That was not the end of Edson's troubles. As Kengla wrapped up his observer mission and prepared to depart for the States, he questioned the general about a remark Red Mike had made during a meeting in Washington in January. To Edson's mortification, the young officer had taken it as an affront to his reputation. The general felt badly enough to write Thomas and all others present in an effort to correct the error: "It was one of those wisecracks which I often make only to those I like and consider my friends, believing that they already know what I think about them." In this downhearted mood Red Mike made his preparations for yet another battle in the long Pacific struggle.

Tinian was one of the most unusual objectives the Marines would face. It was located just four miles from the southern shore of Saipan and was almost as large (more than fifty square miles in area), but there the similarities ended. Tinian was generally flat. Its highest points (an unnamed hill in the south and Mount Lasso in the north) were less than six hundred feet above sea level. Neither was an imposing feature, and the surrounding areas tended to be plateaus rather than hills or jagged ridges. The only pieces of rough terrain were the cliffs that fell away from the plateaus to the sea at most points along the coast. Most of the island was covered with sugarcane or groves of trees, a far cry from the jungle or tangled undergrowth that the Marines had come to expect. A network of hard-packed coral roads and railroads ran in straight lines between the checkerboarded fields. It was an immense aircraft carrier awaiting development.

Terrain was not the only difference. The convenient location of the new objective allowed the American forces to undertake an unprecedented

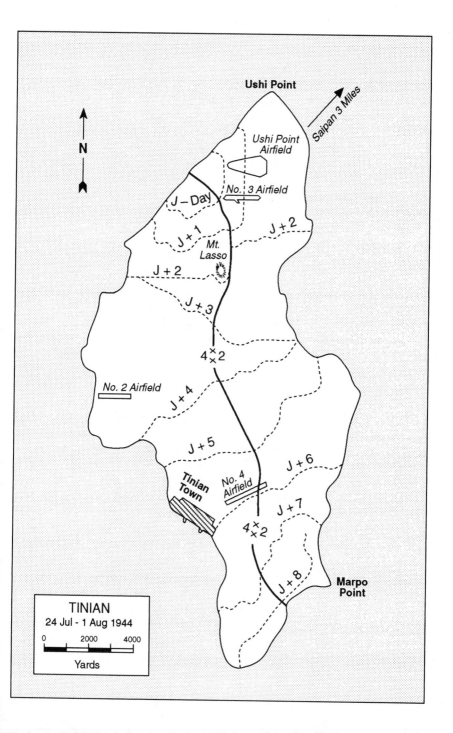

Ushi Point

Ushi Point
Airfield

Saipan 3 Miles

No. 3 Airfield

N

J – Day

J + 1

J + 2

Mt.
Lasso

J + 2

J + 3

4 × 2

No. 2 Airfield

J + 4

J + 5

Tinian
Town

No. 4
Airfield

J + 6

J + 7

4 × 2

J + 8

Marpo
Point

TINIAN
24 Jul - 1 Aug 1944

0   2000   4000

Yards

bombardment of the target. The Navy had started preparation fires against the island on the same day as those for Saipan—11 June—and turned their full fury in that direction after the fall of Saipan on 9 July. Warships and carrier planes were the traditional backbone of any prelanding bombardment, but here the attackers were also able to bring to bear land-based aircraft and artillery from Saipan. By the time of the landing there were thirteen battalions of Army and Marine artillery firing across the narrow straits, while aircraft shuttled the short distance from Aslito airfield to drop their ordnance and return for another load. Army Thunderbolts also tested napalm bombs, canisters filled with flammable substances that created large fireballs upon striking the ground. This weapon inflicted casualties and burned off the vegetation that had previously camouflaged enemy positions.

Despite these advantages, Tinian was no easy objective. The island's defenders consisted of nine thousand men, roughly split between four battalions of army infantry and a naval guard force manning most of the heavier weapons. The Japanese commander expected the American attack to come either on the southwest coast near Tinian Town or in the east along Asiga Bay. Both locations offered good beaches, so the defenders sited themselves and their guns to cover these likely avenues of approach.

Marine planners sought and found a means to surprise the enemy. The northwest coast of the island had two beaches, if one could dignify them with the name. White 1 was 60 yards wide; White 2 was about 160 yards wide, though less than half of it was free of boulders and rock ledges. The flanks of both beaches were hemmed in by low cliffs. Reconnaissance by Marine and Navy units indicated that the White beaches were usable and lightly defended; floating mines, barbed wire, and fortifications covered the other sites. On 12 July the admirals and generals decided to do the unexpected and land over the White beaches. The risk involved was considerable, since the narrow landing sites might slow the movement of troops ashore and create logistics problems. The 4th Marine Division would seize the beachhead while the 2d Marine Division made a feint against the Tinian Town area, then followed the 4th ashore. The two divisions would then advance side by side down the length of the island.

The landing proceeded smoothly on 24 July. Despite a fierce bombardment of the tiny beaches by warships, planes, rocket-firing gunboats, and armored amphibious tractors, a handful of Japanese troops were still alive and ready to fight at both sites. Mines on White 2 were a more serious obstacle, since they destroyed three LVTs before engineers swept the area. The 4th Marine Division bulled through this minor opposition and quickly fanned out to secure the beachhead. The 2d Division's demonstration in front of Tinian Town brought forth a fierce Japanese reception. Coastal guns scored twenty-eight hits on the battleship *Colorado* (BB-45) and the destroyer *Norman Scott* (DD-690), and mortars and artillery peppered tractors simulating a run to the beach. Before the day was out, all of the 4th Division's combat units were ashore, along with leading elements of the 2d Division (1/8 and both pack howitzer battalions). More than 15,000 Marines had landed at a cost of 15 killed and 225 wounded. Edson followed developments at sea and plotted the progress of frontline units.

The 4th Marine Division took extensive precautions against a night banzai attack. Units halted in late afternoon while there was sufficient daylight to dig fighting positions and tie in with adjacent units. Preloaded LVTs arrived at the front with extra ammunition and sufficient concertina wire to string around the entire beachhead. Tanks, 75mm half-tracks, and 37mm antitank guns bolstered every infantry battalion. The Japanese obliged and launched a major counterattack that night in an effort to drive the invaders into the sea. The result was predictable. The next morning the Marines counted five destroyed light tanks and more than twelve hundred dead in front of their lines. American casualties were less than a hundred.

At dawn the 2d Division began to pour ashore with the remainder of the 8th Marines leading the way. Watson ordered Red Mike to head for the beach at 1400; he debarked from his own ship shortly thereafter. A coast defense gun bracketed the four landing craft carrying the commanding general and his staff, although poor Japanese aim allowed them to reach the beach unharmed. Most of the division was on Tinian by the end of the day, and the 8th Marines, temporarily attached to the 4th Division, took over the left flank of the beachhead. Opposition was generally light on J+1, but the Marines advanced cautiously in doubling the size of their beachhead. That night the Japanese remained relatively quiet.

The next morning the 2d Division assumed responsibility for the left half of the beachhead and commenced a move to the northeast coast. The Japanese had largely withdrawn from the area, so the advance progressed rapidly. The 2d and 8th Marines completed seizure of the large Ushi Point airfield and reached the sea. The 8th Marines went into reserve, the 2d Marines reoriented its lines to the south, and the 6th Marines came into the line between the 2d Marines and the 4th Division. The men of the 2d Division then moved out again in the new direction. They nearly caught up with the 4th Division, which had been pushing steadily south all day and had seized Mount Lasso without a fight. The infantrymen had hardly cleared the airfield when artillery spotter planes landed and began to use it as a base of operations. The 2d Division's casualties for the day were two killed and fourteen wounded—that outfit's easiest day of fighting in a long time. The 2d Marines faced some probing activity by the enemy that night, but the Japanese seemed to disappear during the following two days. Both Marine divisions made large gains on 27 and 28 July; they were now in possession of more than half of the island.

Advances on 29 and 30 July were almost as great as the previous two days, but here the 2d Division ran into a bit more opposition. By the end of the seventh day ashore, however, the Marines had captured more than three-quarters of the island and had seen little enemy activity since the first night. It was obvious that the Japanese were conserving their strength for a final stand in the south. Just ahead of Marine lines was an escarpment, particularly steep in the 2d Division's zone, that led up to the plateau covering the remainder of the island. Three hills dominated the plateau, which fell off in steep cliffs to the sea. The Americans had made lavish use of firepower up to this point, but they vastly increased the scale of the bombardment prior to operations on 31 July. All supporting artillery kept up a continuous barrage from just after midnight. Two battleships, three cruisers, and more than a hundred planes joined in from 0600 until 0830.

The attack kicked off immediately thereafter and ran into the expected strong opposition. The two divisions seized all of the low ground in front of the escarpment, but they had great difficulty moving up to the high ground. By nightfall elements of the 8th Marines had a toehold at the top of the single hairpin road that climbed to the plateau in their zone. The Japanese launched counterattacks to close this breach, but failed. The next day the 2d and 4th Divisions completed seizure of the escarpment and overran the plateau. Large numbers of Japanese remained hidden in the cliffs along the coast, but with organized resistance at an end, the commander of the landing force declared the island secured the evening of 1 August. As on Saipan, mopping-up operations on Tinian would continue for weeks. The 2d Division's losses were the lowest for any of its campaigns: 104 killed and 654 wounded.

Within a few days the majority of the 2d Division began transferring back to Saipan, but the 8th Marines remained behind to scour the island for Japanese holdouts. The ADC and his staff also stayed on Tinian and assumed control of the effort. It was a welcome opportunity for the brigadier to be in charge again; he and his new command reported directly to NTLF headquarters. The mop-up campaign proved to be as difficult as the original battle. On successive nights after the island was declared secure, sizable

Japanese forces attacked 2d Division outfits. Marine casualties were light, but the enemy suffered more than a hundred dead in each case.

Edson put the comparatively small losses of Tinian in perspective when a correspondent asked him which Pacific battle had been the toughest. "They were all bad. There are no easy campaigns. At Guadalcanal it was the dirt and the strain, and having to lie there night after night in the lines and take it from the Japs. At Tarawa, for the first thirty hours the issue was in doubt. At Saipan it was the mortars and the artillery and the terrain." Red Mike then put his finger on the most important level of analysis for the individual: "The worst campaign is the one in which you get hit."

Throughout the Tinian operation, the ADC had continued his practice of roaming the front lines. Even after the battle, he was not content to settle into the mundane life of a garrison command post. When Vandegrift and Thomas toured the island in mid-August, they found him with one of the small units digging the Japanese out of their caves in the seaside cliffs. Watson recommended his assistant for the Legion of Merit medal for the Marianas campaign. A few understated phrases went to the heart of his role in the battles: "At great personal risk, he continually visited front line units of the division, advising and assisting in the operations against the enemy." Lieutenant Colonel Wallace Greene, then Watson's operations officer, said it more eloquently: "Edson was a brave and daring Marine officer—ice cool, calm, and collected during danger—a winner—and personification of the great fighting tradition of our Corps."

With the mop-up campaign well in hand, and no prospect on the horizon of a major battle, Red Mike again devoted time to considering his own future. The spark was a letter from Julian Smith that discussed potential billets for his former subordinate if the ADC still wanted to leave the 2d Division. Edson's reply made it clear that he knew what he wanted, but not how to get there. "I do not have to tell you that if there is any possibility in the near future I would prefer to accede to command of some division rather than to any other job in the Pacific Area. As I told you quite frankly when I came back from Washington, there seemed to be indications in some of the remarks made that such a thing might happen before the end of this year."

The picture was not quite so rosy now. Red Mike was still a very junior brigadier, and he expected the promotions of several colonels in the near future, all of whom would vault ahead of him in seniority under the rules then in effect. The other four division ADCs and three of the chiefs of staff were ahead of him on the lineal list, so that even if a command slot opened up, there would need to be additional transfers out of the division before he could take over. He assumed, correctly as it turned out, that when the 6th Division came off the drawing boards it would go to Lem Shepherd. Edson's only chance at the moment was Watson's elevation to assistant commandant, which would put him in position to lead the 2d Division, but even then he saw the odds as slim.

One small event on 4 August raised Red Mike's hopes a bit. After the official flag-raising on Tinian, Holland Smith remarked to the ADC: "I want to talk to you sometime about a job I have in mind for you in the reorganization which is to take place in this area." Edson knew that the senior Marine in the Pacific was "greatly displeased" with the leadership of the 3d Division then fighting on Guam, and he thought that Smith might be looking at him for the billet. He asked Julian Smith to see what he could find out from Holland Smith or Vandegrift.

The reorganization mentioned by Holland Smith was a pending change to the highest levels of the Marine command structure in the Pacific. The unwieldy system in effect in June 1944, with Holland Smith wearing two hats in the field and sharing rear-echelon authority with Julian Smith, was obviously unacceptable. The system had already been modified in the midst of the Marianas campaign. In mid-July Holland Smith had relinquished command of NTLF to Maj. Gen. Harry Schmidt, because the senior general could not effectively command the northern operation (Tinian) and provide the required oversight of the distant southern prong of the offensive (Guam). Now, acting solely as head of Expeditionary Troops, Smith had a proper role of supervising two subordinate commands.

Edson had already foreseen that this was only the beginning of the matter. In a letter to Thomas he had discussed the shifting of the pioneer battalion from the division to corps or army troops: "By 'army' I mean two or more Marine Corps corps under a unified command similar to a field army, and not the U.S. Army." At the moment Smith's force consisted of three Marine divisions, a Marine brigade, and two attached Army divisions. The likelihood was that he would have a force of five or six Marine divisions in the near future. That was much too big a force for the traditional corps structure, and Edson correctly identified that the next logical step was to create the first army-level command in the history of the Marine Corps.

Things began to clear up for both Edson and the Pacific command structure as August progressed. The visit of Vandegrift and Thomas to the combat theater allowed them to confer with Holland and Julian Smith regarding organization. The result was the creation of Fleet Marine Force Pacific (FMFPAC), which would have administrative authority over all Marine Corps forces in the theater. It would exercise its support functions through

Administrative Command FMFPAC and work with Marine aviation units through Aircraft FMFPAC (though the squadrons would continue under the operational control of the Navy air commander). In addition to maintaining administrative control of the six Marine divisions, FMFPAC would also serve as a field command as directed by Nimitz, the commander of the Pacific Ocean Areas. The III and V Amphibious Corps were now distinct, coequal tactical entities (soon to be composed of three Marine divisions each) that could operate independently or jointly under FMFPAC or an Army command. With the end of the Marianas campaign, Holland Smith's Expeditionary Troops headquarters ceased to exist and he took command of FMFPAC. Schmidt assumed the title of CG, VAC, and General Geiger remained in command of IIIAC. As Smith had intimated to Edson, one of his first actions was to fix the leadership problem in the 3d Division, but he did so by putting his longtime chief of staff, Erskine, in command. Before leaving the Marianas, Smith explained the new setup to Edson and asked him to fill Erskine's shoes and become chief of staff for FMFPAC.

The new job had great potential for Edson. At that level the chief of staff billet encompassed the duties of a second in command, and Smith rated a major general as his assistant. Red Mike had every reason to expect that elevation to the new job would bring a second star. There was also the likelihood that Smith would give Edson the same reward for performance that he had given to his last chief of staff, a coveted division command slot. Since Edson expected the war to go on for two years or more, there appeared to be ample time for him to achieve his goal. In the meantime, he would still be associated with a combat command whenever FMFPAC took to the field as an army-level headquarters.

Although this development was not exactly what Edson wanted, it appeared to be a step in the right direction. In a matter of days he would be out from under Watson and working for a man he liked and admired. And now there was a seemingly clear road to his ultimate goal of leading a division in battle. Even Watson was obliging in the latter respect; his fitness report on the ADC recommended him as "well-qualified to command a Marine division." Red Mike continued to build a substantial reputation beyond the Corps as well. In the late summer of 1944 he found himself the subject of a radio broadcast entitled "Thumbnail Sketches." "General Edson is a slight fellow physically, and always soft spoken. He is so polite to louder but lesser persons that one who does not know him might meet in a crowd one of the finest American soldiers and one of the great patriots of American history, and pass him quickly by unimpressed, to join some wittier group across the room. But his men swear by his swift, keen

Chapter 16

"You Will Find Us Always on the Job"

R ed Mike's transfer to FMFPAC headquarters did not go smoothly. During their August 1944 visit to the Marianas, Vandegrift and Thomas had left Edson with the impression that he would meet them in Pearl Harbor on their return trip to the States. Red Mike looked forward to the opportunity to discuss the reorganization with Holland Smith and the two top leaders from HQMC. The 2d Marine Division sent out orders terminating Edson's job as commander of the Tinian mop-up and recalling him to Saipan on 19 August. There he received orders directing him to detach only after the arrival of his relief, Brig. Gen. Leroy Hunt. Red Mike wrote Thomas that he was upset by the indefinite delay, since he would miss seeing Vandegrift and would lose the chance to influence the final decisions on the shape of FMFPAC. "As a result, I feel that I am going to have something dumped in my lap to execute which I know little about in the first place, and with which . . . I believe I am going to disagree."

Edson also sent a dispatch to FMFPAC headquarters requesting a modification to his transfer orders, so that he could detach immediately and take leave in Australia before reporting to his new duties. He explained to Thomas that he hoped the message might force headquarters to tell him when he would depart. But there was more to it than that.

I was not fooling when I mentioned last January that I wished to make a trip back to Australia, nor was I fooling when I mentioned it this time. . . . I consider it a personal affair of my own, and of no one else, whether I prefer to take leave which is due me in Australia, or the United States, or any place else within the limits of the time and space factor. While I am on the subject, there is another matter which I would like to straighten out. From occasional remarks made by both you and General Vandegrift, I am sure that both of you have a grossly mistaken idea of my relations with a certain party in Australia. It is true that I saw a great deal of her while in Melbourne, and although it may have appeared otherwise to you, actually that girl is as straight and honest and square as they come. If you have any other ideas, you are doing her an injustice.

Despite the protestations of innocence to a friend, Red Mike's interest in the Australian woman continued to be more affectionate than platonic. In addition to the daily letters, he frequently sent Bibs small gifts, some of them mundane wartime luxuries such as cigarettes, others more intimate items such as perfume and stockings. She expected him to return at the end of the war to marry her. He wanted to spend any available leave with her rather than his wife.

Things moved very quickly thereafter, though not quite the way Red Mike had hoped. Headquarters modified his orders on 24 August and he headed for Hawaii the next day. He formally assumed the duties of chief of staff on the twenty-sixth. However, he had little time to settle into the new job, because fresh orders sent him on an even longer flight back to the States for temporary duty at HQMC. This trip may have been in response to his 23 August request for the chance to discuss the Pacific setup. On 8 September Edson arrived at the airport in Washington, where Thomas met him and whisked him off to an immediate conference with Vandegrift. The remaining eight days of the visit were filled with meetings. Edson's only rest came in a thirty-six-hour layover in San Francisco on the return leg—time that he spent "doing practically nothing for the first time since the war began."

Red Mike had plenty of work awaiting him upon his arrival in Hawaii. The first priority was sorting out the bits and pieces of previous organizations and staffs so that they could be melded into the new FMFPAC headquarters. This was no mean feat, since the command element alone consisted of nearly 400 officers and more than 1,200 enlisted personnel. They in turn controlled operating and support forces totaling more than 170,000 officers and men. The second task was determining exactly what the headquarters was supposed to do. Although it was easy to list various responsibilities (a letter from Admiral Nimitz delineated eleven separate duties), one item presented a real problem: FMFPAC was to act as a task force command element in combat when directed.

This dichotomy between administrative authority and combat command had been the source of Edson's concern and the reason for his desire to see the commandant in August. Holland Smith envisioned the division of his headquarters into two wings: one a forward echelon that would fight battles, the other a rear echelon that would take care of all other responsibilities. Red Mike saw this as little more than a continuation of the structure in place during the Marianas campaign, and "it didn't work in the last show." He believed that once Smith became embroiled in planning and leading an operation, "somebody else [would have] to pick up the ball as CG, FMFPAC and try to carry it along." His solution was to adopt the Army's method of dividing a theater of operations into a communication zone and a combat zone, with separate commanders responsible respectively for fighting and for rear-echelon duties. The brigadier's concerns went far beyond immediate practicality: "For our own salvation, I believe that we must have an organization that not only fits in with the Navy set-up, but which also will fit into the Army system without necessitating a major reorganization if the time should ever come when we pass to Army control."

The issue was complicated by Holland Smith's own desire to remain a fighting leader and not an administrative one. The cantankerous senior general confided as much to Sherrod in September: "I told Nimitz he had to give me a combat command—if I make him mad again he'll probably send me back to the States." Nor was the decision entirely within the purview of HQMC, which had to tread lightly in Nimitz's Pacific domain. The end result was that FMFPAC would adapt to a changing situation without any senior leader ever declaring an official policy. Those who had to build an organization on these shifting sands were left to their own devices. Edson, for his part, accepted the challenge in his usual forthright manner: "I will do my damnedest to make the thing work, regardless of whether I agree with it fully or not."

Red Mike had the same eagerness as his boss to be at the front, and for a time it appeared as if both men might get their wish. One staff officer noted the "electric current of anticipation" that greeted the formation of FMFPAC and the possibility that a Marine would command a field army in battle. The prize was the April 1945 Okinawa landing, which would utilize the Marines' III Amphibious Corps and the Army's XXIV Corps. Nimitz would designate the commander. Edson realized that the decision would not be based solely on military considerations, but would result from "the usual political bickering." He lamented the fact that the senior Marine on Nimitz's staff was only a colonel, whereas the Army had three

generals emplaced around the admiral. He thought that the rank differ-
ential might foreclose the Corps from an important "entree to the topside
command," an issue he had raised more than a year earlier.

Nimitz made his decision in early October without even consulting Smith
on the matter. Although FMFPAC had come into being, in part, for just
such a contingency, command of the landing went to Lt. Gen. Simon Bolivar
Buckner and the Tenth Army headquarters. A large factor in the decision
may have been the Saipan incident, which still rankled the Army's leadership and no doubt increased the pressure they brought to bear on the
commander in chief Pacific (CINCPAC). They were not about to let the
man who had fired an Army general have authority over one of their corps.
Nimitz did assign Smith to command the February 1945 Iwo Jima landing, but Edson correctly saw that mission as "purely a corps commander's
job," since VAC would be the only tactical organization involved. That
left Smith with few practical duties, so he would not need the large operational staff that would have been necessary to command and coordinate an assault by two corps.

Although long-range plans contemplated more large-scale operations,
Red Mike read the decision as a final word on the future of his headquarters: "It looks as though we have lost out on the big picture for a
real job commensurate with the capabilities of [the] FMF." He was right.
In November 1944 Smith submitted a request for additional personnel to
man the fighting portion of his staff for campaigns subsequent to Okinawa.
Vandegrift came out to the Pacific in January 1945 to discuss the matter
with Nimitz, but they decided to leave things unchanged, which essentially restricted FMFPAC to an administrative role. For Edson, all this
meant that he was far removed from the action for the first time since
the war had begun. He lamented that fact to Sherrod as the war correspondent prepared to mount out for Iwo Jima. "The fortunes of war seemed
to have planted me behind a desk for the time being. It is going to be an
unusual experience to sit back here while the boys have a job to do out
where you are. I can tell you in all sincerity that I do not like it."

If Edson was in the unaccustomed position of pushing paper while others
fought, he was still contributing mightily to the war effort. He was not
boasting idly when he described his billet in October 1944 as "easily the
fourth, and maybe the third, most important post in the entire Marine Corps
and the success or failure of the Corps in the remainder of the war is largely
in my keeping." His importance stemmed only partly from the nature of
his position as second in command of Marine forces in the Pacific. He
had added authority because Smith gave him wide latitude of action, and

because FMFPAC's field commanders saw him as someone they could rely on to look out for the fighting forces.

His greatest source of influence continued to be his relationship with Thomas. The two brigadiers were not only close personal friends, but they often thought in similar ways. While Edson was pushing for the adoption of Army-style command-and-control arrangements in the Pacific, Thomas was trying to convince the commandant to reorganize HQMC along the same efficient lines as the Army's general staff. Both men were more than willing to steal good ideas from their institutional rival without regard for misplaced notions of service pride. They also shared a common focus on the importance of logistics, an area of warfare often slighted by other senior Marines, many of whom were ill-prepared professionally for handling the needs of units far larger than the Corps had ever fielded.

A factor that made the Thomas-Edson connection important was that Vandegrift trusted both officers; he had relied heavily on them in the tight pinches at Guadalcanal, he knew their capabilities, and he had placed them in key billets. This did not mean that the two friends had free rein to implement all their plans. Thomas's tour in Washington was marked by fierce bureaucratic infighting with officers such as Watson, now director of personnel, and Brig. Gen. W. P. T. Hill, the quartermaster general. Red Mike, in turn, had to deal with the network of senior generals heading the divisions, corps, and island garrisons. Despite these handicaps, the two friends worked closely together for the remainder of the war and used their positions to guide the Corps through the minefields that still lay ahead. Thomas did his best to shape headquarters policy to meet the needs that Edson identified in the field. Red Mike, in his turn, saw to it that Thomas's directives and ideas did not drift off course in the long passage from Washington to the far reaches of the Pacific.

As always, Edson carried on this shadow command channel through the medium of personal correspondence. Although Thomas did not think that was "proper," he had come to rely on Red Mike's policy-oriented letters. Now the director of Plans and Policies spelled out the heightened importance of the letters after Edson's elevation to FMFPAC:

> First, let's discuss the matter of letters between us and the use that I make of them. I need plenty of ammunition to shoot in problems that I work on here. The inertia can be terrific at times. The Commandant has as much confidence in you as I have and, therefore, anything that you write can be most effective if I am free to use it. However, I realize that sometimes you may write things that you would rather we keep between us. You must continue to pass on to

me the things which will be useful and they are many, as official letters carry very few real thoughts back from the field. I suggest that you separate material which you write—putting on separate sheets that which I alone am to see and on other sheets that which I may use broadly.

Thereafter the letters that flowed back and forth between "Jerry" and "Eddie" contained occasional reminders that the two friends needed to work as a team. One pair of letters that crossed in the mail in mid-October demonstrated this symbiotic attitude. Edson told Thomas: "What I am really trying to say is, there must not be any misconceptions or disagreements so far as you and I are concerned." Thomas wrote: "The ideas that I now advance I put forth with humbleness and sincerity as they are of such great importance that we must be together in handling them."

Thomas laid out the challenge that they faced. "There is no getting away from the fact that this present Marine Corps organization was to a degree haphazard in that it has grown from day to day and the growth has not been in accordance with any well-developed plan. Consequently, you and I are trying to tie things together with the few strings that are available to us. . . . You must share with me the responsibility for the most effective use of the men at our disposal." For the rest of the war the greatest concerns of the two staff officers would revolve around personnel and logistics, issues that were often intertwined.

Edson had hardly returned from the States when he opened up the dialogue with a long letter on the island commands, the units left behind to garrison conquered territory. As these proliferated with the growing success of American operations, FMFPAC found itself devoting more and more of its precious pool of manpower to the task. At the same time, each of these units required logistic support, which stretched resources to the breaking point. As it was, only one in nine FMFPAC Marines worked in the Supply Service. Edson considered that ratio inadequate to the task. Given its personnel ceiling, the theater headquarters could devote more men to the island commands or logistics only by disbanding combat units, or by using the replacement pools, which would leave the divisions shortchanged in any future fighting. Red Mike thought that one possible solution might be to turn over more garrisons to the Army, though some Marines opposed this as a loss of prestige. Edson argued: "It seems to me that it is not a question of how many island commands we set up during the present war so much as how effectively and how capably we administer those we do have assigned to us."

The ability of the Corps to operate and support large formations was important, because it was becoming an issue in the Army's attempt to stifle the growth and employment of the Marine Corps, not only in the present war, but afterward as well. The Army justifiably saw each legislated increase in the size of the Corps as a drain on the limited pool of quality manpower available for its own expansion. Although the debate would be settled in the halls of Congress, the performance of Marines in the Pacific theater was a key weapon in the struggle. The Army argued that senior Marines had neither the experience nor the professional background to control corps and armies. Edson and others had to prove that they could, though Red Mike thought that current efforts did not bode well for the outcome. "Although I would not admit this to the Army, within the family I am frankly of the opinion that we are already overextended so far as logistic support is concerned."

The island commands were not the only source of the manpower crunch. The establishment of two corps and a theater command had created major new requirements that the operating forces were only now beginning to recognize. Artillery units needed more personnel so they could effectively coordinate their activities. Future assaults on territory with large civilian populations necessitated the creation of military police battalions to handle the people. If FMFPAC actually assumed a field command, the signal battalion would have to be enlarged by a factor of nine. Headquarters was also shipping five hundred amphibious trucks (DUKWs) to the Pacific to improve motor transport, but it had not authorized the creation of any new units to man and maintain the vehicles. As it was, the two amphibious corps had not yet fleshed out the units created on paper to man the trucks already available. Red Mike noted that these specific requirements came to more than seven thousand men, though he estimated that the final total of additional men needed for a fully functioning FMFPAC would reach fifty thousand.

In the past, the preferred solution of HQMC in such situations had been to recommend the formation of provisional units. These outfits would not be authorized by T/O, and local commands had to staff them by raiding manpower from existing units. Edson gave Thomas his candid opinion regarding that option: "It is akin to the ostrich who hides his head in the sand and fools nobody, including you at Headquarters Marine Corps." On the other hand, the chief of staff had no ready solution. He did not want to resort to augmentation from the Army or the disestablishment of one of the combat divisions, and he soon learned from Thomas that it would be impossible to push through Congress further increases in the size of the Corps. Edson hoped that the reduction of island commands would free up some personnel, but that would not be enough.

As a consequence of the cap on the strength of the Corps, personnel problems continued throughout the remainder of the war. Edson and Thomas often went to extremes in generating ways to overcome the handicap. At one point Thomas contemplated closing the engineer training establishment in the States to provide manpower to fill out engineer units in the Pacific, though that would mean no fresh, trained replacements within that specialty for the future. He did shut down the seacoast and antiaircraft schools after Edson successfully negotiated with the CINCPAC staff to disband many of those battalions. As always, Red Mike kept one eye on service politics when making such decisions. When Tenth Army asked for various Marine support and service units for the upcoming Okinawa landing, Red Mike told Thomas of his unsympathetic and calculating reply: "My answer was that if they would give us the overall command of the job we could do it with what was available."

In October 1944 Edson turned greater attention to logistics requirements, and began to champion a reorganization of FMFPAC's Service of Supply, which would be redesignated as Service Command. He thought the change in name was needed to reemphasize its broad missions. Up to that point the logisticians had devoted too much attention to supply to the detriment of other important duties such as maintenance. Red Mike proposed that the antiquated staff system be reshaped along general staff lines (that is, G-1, G-2, G-3, G-4). In addition, he sought to reorganize the aggregations of specialists in the large base and field depots into separate platoons of repairmen, communicators, ordnance experts, and so forth. With this building-block approach, headquarters could configure each depot to the particular needs of the unit to be supported instead of following a common, but possibly wasteful, table of organization. As the war advanced farther across the Pacific, rear area logistic organizations could also move forward piece by piece as required, with the eventual goal of abandoning backwater depot locations.

Vandegrift took the recommendation seriously enough to schedule Thomas for a trip to Hawaii. Thomas arrived on Oahu on 9 January 1945 for "head to head discussion" with his "old compeer." Many of the primary FMFPAC staff officers, as well as Holland Smith, were unavailable, since they were boarding ships to rehearse for the Iwo Jima landing, so Red Mike carried the load for the Pacific headquarters. With much of the spadework accomplished in letters, the director of Plans and Policies found the three days of conferences on manpower, reorganization, and the Supply Service especially fruitful. "As usual Edson and I were not long in solving our problems."

Smith's pending departure for Iwo Jima put Edson in the mood to march toward the sound of the guns. He thought he had his chance to do so when Brig. Gen. Arthur Worton, ADC of one of the assault divisions, severely injured his leg in a landing accident. Since no other brigadiers were available as a replacement, Red Mike volunteered to take the position on a temporary duty basis, but he "did not get to first base" with Smith. The CG took time just before his departure to pin the Silver Star medal on Red Mike for Saipan and Tinian, but the award did not improve the chief of staff's mood. Edson expected that the operation would be another tough one. As acting head of FMFPAC he estimated that the entire on-hand pool of 11,500 replacements would be used up before the fight was over.

As former subordinates transferred back to the States, Edson's correspondence network at HQMC expanded. Shoup, now the logistics officer in Plans and Policies, asked the chief of staff to send comments direct rather than through slower official channels. Lieutenant Colonel Tompkins, also now in Washington, made a similar plea to his old boss. "I know that you have definite ideas on equipment, and if you would care to jot some of them down, we will get to work on them and see what can be done at this end." These informal connections often resulted in significant changes. During the Iwo Jima operation, former Raider Joe Chambers commanded his own battalion and was impressed by the utility of rocket launchers. Upon his return to Hawaii he passed his opinion on to Edson. When Chambers reported to HQMC shortly thereafter, he discovered that Red Mike had not only succeeded in derailing a planned cutback in rocket units, but had gotten them increased instead.

Red Mike made similar use of personal correspondence to keep tabs on the far-flung empire of FMFPAC. Generally he made direct contact with commanders who knew him well, such as Maj. Gen. Pedro del Valle, Graves Erskine, and Cliff Cates, CGs respectively of the 1st, 3d, and 4th Divisions. Sometimes he used officers at a lower level. When Col. John McQueen left his billet as operations officer of FMFPAC to become chief of staff of the 6th Marine Division, Edson asked him to make monthly reports. Oftentimes these letters made it possible for Edson to make a difference in relatively simple but important ways. During the 1st Marine Division's preparations for Okinawa, del Valle asked for shipping so he could rotate his units from their inadequate base at Pavuvu over to a bigger island for live-fire and maneuver training. When IIIAC rejected the request, he passed it on to Edson, who saw that he got what he needed.

The nonofficial nature of the letters was an important feature, because it allowed the writers to say things that they would be reluctant to put on the record. On occasion the system backfired. At the behest of General Shepherd, commander of the 6th Marine Division, Edson tried to obtain orders home for colonels who did not perform up to standard. Vandegrift fired back a tough reply: "I thought I had made it definitely clear to the Fleet Marine Force Pacific and to each division commander that I did not approve, nor would I tolerate, the relief of officers . . . on personal letters or personal reports not backed up by official action. . . . All it requires is the moral courage to go on record as stating that this or that officer, in the opinion of the division commander or higher command, is not competently exercising command over his unit and in the opinion of the division commander is not competent or efficient to hold the job he now has." Red Mike took the rebuff in stride and passed it on to Shepherd: "I think that the action indicated in General Vandegrift's letter is absolutely correct." Apparently not all commanders got the word even then. A few months later Cates tried to get Edson to switch a lieutenant colonel. "Have you done anything about [his] transfer? I do not want to smear his record but there must be a change. Another case of bad judgment since I wrote you." Red Mike turned him down.

Finding quality colonels was a Corps-wide problem by that point in the war and no doubt served as the catalyst for Vandegrift's tough stand on the issue (though he himself had been guilty of similar behavior on Guadalcanal). Officers in that rank were a tightly knit group that had served many years together in the small, interwar Corps, and those of their peers who had made general were reluctant to deal harshly with old friends. As a result that deadwood clogged up the promotion system now that the Corps was no longer growing and automatically creating fresh billets at the higher ranks. Pedro del Valle noted the problem after relieving two of his subordinates. "The situation would seem to call for a search for suitable young, active, capable regimental commanders." Thomas echoed that frustration. "We have from forty to fifty colonels, not one of whom anyone would take. If we could get rid of that group and promote an equal number of youngsters, the overall number of colonels now authorized would be entirely adequate." Edson was caught in the middle, since he bore responsibility for assigning colonels to particular units, and there seemed to be too few unimportant slots in which to hide the marginal performers.

The shortage of good colonels was even more disturbing to Red Mike due to the priority he placed on joint staff billets with Navy and Army commands. Whereas Thomas believed that quality junior officers would fit the bill, Edson argued that rank was an important factor in whether or not the other services would even listen to the Marine point of view. He cited as a recent example the requirement for a more senior officer at Nimitz's Joint Intelligence Center, because Navy captains disregarded the lieutenant colonel posted there. Another factor was the tendency of some Marines to gravitate to the "enemy" after too much time with another service. Edson noted that one Marine "sounded like a naval officer to me," after opposing the effort to have Navy construction battalions build camps for divisions returning from campaigns. "I think his viewpoint would be considerably different if he had spent a few months in the field with combat units and seen what they go through not only in combat but when they have to start building their own camps when they should be rehabilitating and training."

As the Army's efforts in the Pacific expanded, Edson devoted more attention to working with that service. That became especially important when Nimitz made it clear that FMFPAC would never command in the field, which meant that Marine forces would henceforth fight under the Army in the large-scale offensives to come. Since IIIAC made up half of the Tenth Army fighting on Okinawa, a number of Marine officers served on the staff of that Army command element, the senior one being Brig. Gen. Oliver P. Smith. While the battle raged on Okinawa, Red Mike was looking ahead to the pending invasion of Japan and trying to plant Marines on the Army staffs that would head that offensive. The Sixth Army was to land on Kyushu in November 1945 in Operation Olympic, while MacArthur's own General Headquarters (GHQ) would command an assault by two reinforced armies on Honshu in Operation Coronet in March 1946. The dozens of Army divisions involved would swamp the six Marine divisions, so Edson wanted a voice in the planning counsels from the earliest possible moment to protect the interests of the Corps. His campaign targeted not only GHQ and Sixth Army, but the U.S. Army Service of Supply (USASOS) as well, "since logistics play such an important part in the whole setup."

The campaign was not an easy one. Although USASOS was enthusiastic about obtaining the services of the additional two dozen officers offered by FMFPAC, the other headquarters were interested in maintaining their current setup of having only one or two liaison officers to answer questions. Edson wanted Marines filling actual billets on the staff, to include a general at each command element who would act as a deputy chief of staff and senior Marine adviser. At the close of the Okinawa campaign, the Tenth Army even tried to return the Marines on its staff, though it was scheduled to employ an amphibious corps in Coronet. General O. P. Smith unwittingly seconded the Army view that only token Marine liaison officers would be required in the future.

The Navy provided little assistance in the matter. Nimitz's headquarters enforced the protocol that only its representatives could talk to GHQ. Vice Admiral Forrest P. Sherman, the CINCPAC plans officer, promised that he would pass Edson's memo on the subject to Nimitz, that he would take up the issue with GHQ in an upcoming trip to Manila, and that he would call in Red Mike to participate in talks with the Army at that time. The FMFPAC chief of staff made the trip to the Philippines with Sherman in May, but the admiral's call never came. When Red Mike confronted him afterward, Sherman replied that "they had been so busy settling the affairs and relationship of the Army and Navy that they did not get down to the small fry." After great effort Red Mike finally won his fight, and Marine staff officers went to all Army headquarters.

The concern over relations with the Army, and the questionable support of the Navy in the matter, were symptomatic of a greater problem that forward-looking Marines such as Edson, Thomas, and Vandegrift saw on the postwar horizon. The Army was pushing the concept that all the services should be unified, a prospect that frightened Marines, since they would disappear altogether in such an organization. Their air groups undoubtedly would merge with the air component of a single service, and their ground forces with the ground component.

The threat was great enough that it impacted on decisions regarding operational capability. Marines in the field requested the conversion of at least one battalion of corps artillery from 155mm guns to eight-inch howitzers, because they needed the high-trajectory and explosive power of the latter weapons to deal with Japanese fortifications. Red Mike wanted to make the change but had to inform proponents that Vandegrift and Thomas found it unacceptable. "It is in the category of army artillery and the Commandant thinks it inadvisable for us to go to anything more than normal corps artillery. Their feeling is that if we parallel the Army in all respects of organization and equipment, we will be in a very precarious position at the end of the war since the Army will have an added argument for either our disbandment or our absorption within the Army itself. The basis, of course, would be that there is no excuse for the American public to sustain two armies, one of them being called the Marine Corps but actually organized and trained to perform the same functions as the Army does."

The Navy was also uncooperative on matters closer to home. After the capture of Guam, Admiral Nimitz planned to move his CINCPAC headquarters to that island, since the rapid progress of American forces was stretching the lines of communication between the front and Hawaii. In divvying up the island for various units, FMFPAC selected fifty acres for itself, but Nimitz decided to limit FMFPAC representation on the island to twenty officers and fifty enlisted. That posed a quandary for the Marines. If Smith and his primary staff officers went to Guam, they would be divorced from the vast majority of the FMFPAC headquarters personnel that implemented their decisions. If they did not go, they would lose face-to-face contact with their counterparts in CINCPAC. Smith ended up sending a small forward echelon under Col. Capers James to the island with Nimitz, but it was little more than a liaison unit. As Edson anticipated, problems soon began to crop up as CINCPAC made decisions on Marine matters without consulting FMFPAC.

The Navy's rationale for the limitations was not wholly without merit, since Guam could not accommodate all the personnel of various subordinate commands located in Hawaii, and Nimitz himself initially took only a forward echelon of his own headquarters. However, that scheme soon broke down as CINCPAC found that it could not operate effectively with the tip of the iceberg isolated from the mass that normally kept it afloat. As Nimitz transferred more and more of his staff out to Guam, Edson waged an unrelenting but unsuccessful campaign to get FMFPAC included.

Perhaps in part due to the geographic split between CINCPAC and FMFPAC, Edson jealously guarded the prerogatives of the latter in the early months of 1945. Whenever he felt that the Navy had encroached on his territory or slighted the Corps, he lodged a protest. On one occasion CINCPAC formed its own board to investigate 2d Marine Division complaints about training facilities, even though it was FMFPAC's responsibility to prepare its units for combat. Red Mike admitted it was "a minor matter, but it did not set very well back here." Sometimes the issues were weightier, as when CINCPAC tried to take charge of the disposition of replacement drafts and defense battalions supposedly under the operational control of Smith's headquarters. Edson thought this implied "a complete lack of confidence at CINCPAC in the ability of Headquarters, FMF to perform its ordinary functions." He then testily noted: "If this is to be your policy, Headquarters, FMF is in effect no more than a First Sergeant's office, and it might just as well be disbanded."

The relationship between the two headquarters may have reached a low point following the Okinawa campaign as a result of an Army-Marine dispute over the conduct of that operation. At the height of the battle, several senior Marines (to include Vandegrift and Thomas, who were touring the Pacific at the time) tried to convince General Buckner to use Marine forces to land on the coast behind the strong enemy lines that were chewing up Tenth Army's frontal ground attack. Buckner, with the support of Sherman and Nimitz, declined to change tactics. A civilian correspondent later denigrated the Army for the resulting heavy losses, an argument picked up and expanded by David Lawrence, an influential columnist in the States. Nimitz was incensed by the charges, which threatened to reopen the wounds of the Smith versus Smith controversy on Saipan. Edson felt compelled to tell CINCPAC that neither Smith nor anyone else at FMFPAC knew Lawrence. These various disputes between the Army, Navy, and Marine Corps in the Pacific, seemingly quite innocuous in many cases, foreshadowed the bigger interservice battles to come after World War II. Red Mike would reprise his role on a much bigger scale then, and would even get to know Mr. Lawrence.

Events in the latter part of the war proved that some of Edson's earlier ideas were exactly right, though the Marine Corps had not always listened to him. During the initial phases of the Okinawa campaign, IIIAC advanced rapidly up the northern half of the island against light Japanese opposition. Krulak, now the operations officer for the 6th Marine Division, wrote that logistics suffered in part due to "the pitiful amount of transport we have." More than a year earlier, as ADC of the 2d Division, Edson had tried to convince HQMC to increase the number of trucks available to Marine units before they began to attack bigger targets. Now he found himself returning to the same issue as he tried to prepare all of FMFPAC for the invasion of the Japanese home islands. "If [our] employment involves rather deep penetration in large land masses, there are certain things we have to think about right now." One of them was more motor transport, which he saw as the greatest current deficiency. Not only did it affect logistics, but the trucks would be needed to motorize infantry units for the "rapid mechanized movement" that would be possible.

Official Marine Corps policy was heading in the opposite direction; an April 1945 HQMC directive ordered the disbandment of FMFPAC's provisional DUKW companies. Edson argued that they should be expanded instead, since the operating and maintenance skills were similar to the ones required for trucks, so the units could be readily converted once the battle moved inland and DUKWs lost their utility. Edson thought he could produce sufficient personnel for the DUKW companies by disbanding unnecessary amphibious tractor and antiaircraft battalions. By June, Red Mike had "the ball rolling" for the creation of the 13th Motor Transport Battalion, the first of four that he thought would be needed to match Marine capability with that of the Army.

In 1945 he was also still venting his concern over the loss of marksmanship skills, first voiced when he was the inspector of Target Practice in 1940. An Army captain working with NBPRP asked for Red Mike's input on the state of military shooting skills and received a lengthy reply describing the reasons for Marine success in the interwar period and for the decline since then. "The result, in my opinion, has been disastrous and is reflected in every engagement. Our new men no longer have confidence in their weapon or in their ability to hit a target with it." As if to confirm Edson's analysis, Erskine wrote the chief of staff about poor marksmanship skills in his division and the inability of junior officers and NCOs to rectify the problem due to their own lack of training.

Edson's primary concern continued to be logistics. Although that certainly came within the ordinary scope of his job as chief of staff, he gave it much greater attention than he might have, particularly since another brigadier on the FMFPAC staff already had complete cognizance over the issue. Some of his efforts were directed toward reorganizations that would improve logistics support. More often Red Mike simply evinced a high-level interest in the functioning of logistics units. As Smith prepared to return from Iwo Jima, Edson asked him to stop off in the Marianas and make some inspections, with particular attention to the field depots located there, which he thought were in poor condition. "If this is so, sooner or later some enterprising Island Commander or Army or Navy officer will submit a report which will be deleterious to us, in an effort to show that we cannot handle our logistic support properly." He told Erskine to expect a thorough inspection of the 3d Division following the operation, for the sole purpose of collecting accurate data on battle losses of equipment. Surprisingly, the Marine Corps was still making prebattle requisitions for replacement gear based on estimates developed prior to Tarawa.

Red Mike had no trouble putting his finger on the root of logistics shortcomings in FMFPAC. "The Supply Service . . . has not yet functioned as it should. We are going to try to do something about that. We can make a going concern of it, however, only if we get them good officers to work with." Part of his definition of quality in this case was someone with combat experience in a line outfit, a leader who could thus understand the challenges of battle. He did not want permanent quartermaster officers to dominate the logistics function. Although they might be experts in filling out requisitions, they often had little knowledge of the "turmoil of war," as Thomas put it in describing General Hill, the chief quartermaster.

Edson and Thomas both lacked confidence in Maj. Gen. Cecil Long. That officer had been head of the Supply Service since Vandegrift created it in 1943. The director of Plans and Policies quoted one wag on the situation: "The Supply Service is like a bunch of people working in the bottom of a bucket who have not yet found a way to look over the top." He thought they needed a new leader to "correct that situation." Thomas was having his own fight with Hill and the quartermaster department, and that gave him an additional reason to want a line officer in the Pacific's top logistics post. His initial candidate was Worton, the brigadier recovering from a leg injury. Although Vandegrift had expressed an interest in keeping Long in the job, there was the potential for a change in spring 1945 as the commandant contemplated a wholesale shakeup of general officers. A factor in the timing of the moves may have been that all six divisions were wrapping up operations and would not be engaged again for several months.

When Vandegrift and Thomas came out to the Pacific for a tour in April, Thomas indicated that Edson might head one of the Marine staff delegations to the Army headquarters scheduled for the invasion of Japan. Red Mike had no great qualms about the shift, though he still hoped to get command of a division, a move that many others anticipated would occur. At some point the thinking at HQMC took a decidedly different turn, perhaps in part due to Thomas's continuing frustration over logistics. Thomas did not feel that he himself possessed the requisite knowledge of the actual state of affairs in the Pacific, and his ongoing fight with Hill crippled his ability to press for change in that area. It occurred to him that Edson not only had the interest and skill to do the job, but would be an absolutely trustworthy ally in the key billet.

On Sunday, 10 June 1945, a message arrived at FMFPAC with orders for Edson to take charge of the renamed Service Command before 1 July. He could not have been more surprised if Japanese planes had appeared at sunrise to stage another attack on Pearl Harbor. The news spread quickly around the Pacific and elicited positive reactions from those who had not been pleased with the level of logistics support. Pedro del Valle's response was typical. "All of us are looking forward with high hopes to a more beneficial system of supply than that now in effect. . . . Incidentally, I wish that you would see fit to come here and make your own investigation of supply agencies here. *Their relation to us and their services to us as a Division have been, in my opinion, highly unsatisfactory.*" (Emphasis in original.)

For his part, Red Mike was ambivalent about the switch. He knew that it was an important and challenging assignment, and his hopes were raised again that a second star would accompany the transfer. He was, after all, replacing another major general, and would be commanding more troops than a division reinforced for combat. Moreover, promotion would be a well-deserved reward for the performance that had elevated him to the vital slot. For a time he and many others thought that the new rank was guaranteed. Some even assumed that the promotion had already occurred; congratulations poured into his office.

o On the other hand, the chance of commanding a division in combat receded. It was unlikely that HQMC would transfer him in the foreseeable future, certainly not before Olympic or Coronet. Once all six divisions were engaged in battle, the probability of a change in leadership was even more remote. Sherrod wrote Edson expressing his mystification at the new assignment. "The Marine Corps command philosophy is still outside my scope of understanding. In Washington about six weeks ago I had a long talk with General Vandegrift about it. He was most enthusiastic about three of the younger generals in the Corps—of whom you were one—and I could see your getting a division command, Shepherd getting the III Corps, and some of the more elderly generals moving into less active posts. It doesn't seem to have happened that way." For Red Mike, it was clear that he had lost the last opportunity to achieve his greatest dream of the moment: "From where I sit, it is doubtful if the war will last long enough for me to ever get to a division and I feel that I will see the end of it still sitting behind a desk back here."

He was definitely disappointed at the unexpected turn of events. "I little expected three years ago that I would probably finish the war pushing bullets up to the boys instead of yelling for more." Occasional reminders of his status as a major public hero may not have helped. Nearly a year after his last battle he still received adulatory letters. One from an Oakland lawyer to HQMC highlighted how things had changed from the difficult but glorious days of Guadalcanal and Tarawa. "In the early part of the War, we heard a great deal about Col. Edson who was doing some mighty fine work in the Pacific war area. I see nothing about him now. Is he still alive or did he pay the supreme sacrifice!" Later on Red Mike would note the irony of the reward for doing too good a job: "That's one of the penalties we pay for striving to become 'educated' Marines; we get the 'staff' tag." In June 1945 his receipt of the staff tag dashed his hopes for the remainder of the war. In many respects, it was almost the same for him as if he had paid the supreme sacrifice.

If Red Mike was unhappy with his new assignment, he at least could take satisfaction in a job well done in his old billet. Many officers made certain that Edson knew how much they appreciated his efforts. Red Mike's most recent deputy chief of staff wrote: "It looks as though you are stepping into another job where you will have to put the pieces together and get the machine running as you have done with the FMF." Thirty years later, Brig. Gen. Russell Jordahl, who had served as G-1 at FMFPAC, recalled the four men for whom he had worked during his tenure. "The greatest of those chiefs of staff was Edson. Edson was a tremendous individual: he was not only a fighting man, but he understood how to operate."

Red Mike went right to work on the task of fixing Service Command. He told Thomas on 19 June that he intended to carry through the reorganization along general staff lines as soon as possible, and he put his personal staff to work outlining the scheme. The director of Plans and Policies had agreed to that in principle during the January 1945 conference in Hawaii, but the commandant then had deferred to Long's ideas, which HQMC was in the process of formally approving as a new T/O. Bound by that decision, Thomas recommended that Edson give the current setup a test before changing it. Red Mike was in a hurry because he felt considerable pressure to succeed quickly. Part of this was due to the high expectations of those requiring better support. Another factor was the looming invasion of Japan, which would leave little room for sloppy logistics.

The Service Command faced several immediate problems. The most obvious one was its perceived inability to perform its most important mission—supplying combat units in action. Complaints from supported units were widespread, but the 7th Field Depot came in for the greatest criticism. Edson gave the accusations considerable weight, because they came from people he respected, such as Shepherd, del Valle, and Lt. Col. Dave McDougal. The 7th Field Depot's failure was especially frightening because it had been responsible for logistics during the invasion of Okinawa, one of the largest objectives to date and a harbinger of the invasion of the home islands. If the Marine Corps could not support its divisions on Okinawa, it would face grave difficulties on even larger land masses, unless things improved significantly.

Two items highlighted the challenge. Until that point in the war, the Marine Corps had geared its supply system to support each division in two operations per year, each of thirty days' duration. Since the coming invasions would last far longer, those calculations were now inadequate. The second fact was much more worrisome. Despite having operated on the above planning basis for more than a year, the Service Command could not tell what quantity of supplies it actually had on hand in the theater, and therefore could not determine whether it was meeting its goal. Edson's first step was to ask commanders for detailed information about their supply problems so that he could start corrective action. Before making an inspection tour to check things for himself, however, he decided to spend the month of July gaining an appreciation for Service Command's headquarters and rear echelons, the starting point for the logistics operation stretching out into the far reaches of the Pacific.

Another major problem was spotty leadership, which undoubtedly contributed to the weak overall performance of Service Command. There were several reasons why officers as a group in this particular branch of the Marine Corps seemed not to measure up to their counterparts in the rest of the FMF. One aspect was the lack of senior commanders who had experience in running a large logistics operation. Another factor was the traditional favorable bias in the military toward combat jobs, which meant that service units got more than their fair share of cast-offs and failures. That attitude also had a negative impact on morale; service troops sometimes did not have the same sense of mission or accomplishment as their brethren in the fighting units. There were many fine leaders in Service Command, but not in the same proportion as in other Marine outfits. This, of course, was one of the reasons that Vandegrift had assigned Red Mike to the job.

Edson made some small but important changes to turn things around. He took an interest in the fitness reports of all officers, even lieutenants, and insisted that commanders rank them in a way that would allow him to sort out the bad from the good. He started official action to improve the promotion possibilities for the neglected Service Command and successfully gained support for it from Lt. Gen. Roy Geiger, the new head of FMFPAC. Then Edson launched a program to enhance publicity and recognition for his troops to boost their sagging morale. With Thomas's help, he also won approval to bring in more line officers to replace quartermasters in key leadership billets. But Service Command did not even know which of its officers were quartermaster specialists.

Red Mike had another leadership problem at the very top. His chief of staff and second in command was Brig. Gen. Evans O. Ames, an officer who had been far senior to Edson until Tarawa vaulted Red Mike ahead. Edson retained that seniority now only because he had a temporary promotion that ranked in status ahead of Ames's spot promotion. To complicate matters, the chief of staff was a competent officer who had managed to keep the Supply Service from sinking during its darkest days. Red Mike believed that "Ames has felt and still feels keenly that he should have succeeded Long rather than I." In addition to the frictions of seniority and potential jealousy, Edson did not care for his subordinate's leadership style, which he found ill-suited to the requirements of a chief of staff position. He lobbied Thomas for a replacement, but he did not get his wish right away.

A third problem looming on the horizon involved joint operations with the Army. Although Marine Corps units had landed under Army command before (in the Southwest Pacific and at Okinawa), the two services had yet to establish an efficient method of dividing supply responsibilities. The difficulty arose from the many items distinctive to the Marines, which required separate requisitions and processing. Obviously this needed to be solved before all six Marine divisions began large-scale operations under MacArthur. The Navy and Army supposedly reached an agreement on the issue in a June 1945 conference, but Edson found that the statement of principle lacked too many specifics to be of much use.

Finally, there was the problem of organization. Despite Thomas's plea to let things lie for a while, Edson was hardly on board when he became convinced that his initial concerns were fully justified. Red Mike found his new headquarters riddled with confusion and duplication. Thomas's yellow caution flag on change conflicted with his desire to have Edson prove the desirability of the Service Command concept: "I am particularly anxious that everything sound be developed between now and the end of the war; as I have insisted that the post-war FMF contain a Service Command I'll need everything possible to defend our stand that officers and men must be alloted to that task." Edson agreed with that goal and offered a pledge of continued team effort, but his bias for action caused him to step on the accelerator instead of the brake. He brought Jesse Cook on board and assigned him the task of developing an entirely new T/O, which he promised to submit for HQMC's approval. However, he intended to implement it immediately without waiting for that bureaucratic engine to creep into gear.

On 6 August 1945, the atomic bomb leveled Hiroshima, and at the same time blew away many of Edson's most pressing problems. He would still have to support occupation forces in Japan, but they would be smaller than those scheduled for the invasion and would not require the same volume of supplies as in combat. The new situation brought with it new difficulties, though, as the old plans collapsed and were replaced by a confused future. No one seemed to know just which units would go where, and when, or how long they would stay. Demobilization also required fresh thinking about reversing the flow of men and material from the Pacific back to the States. Red Mike saw that his organization would have an even bigger role now, "the cleaning up of evacuated areas and the disposition of the vast amount of material which has accumulated." His force would have to increase in size as the rest of the FMF shrunk, since departing units would leave behind large stocks of equipment and supplies that would need to be cared for until shipped home or discarded.

The atomic bomb was a surprise to Edson. Barely a week before it burst onto the scene, he was certain that the war would last for at least another year, and that the talk of a negotiated peace in the American newspapers would only buttress the will of the Japanese to continue the fight. In fact, he hoped that they would not negotiate an end to the conflict, because that might result in a muddled peace like that of World War I. "Although we have certainly destroyed their fleet and are in a fair way to destroy their industry, none of the major ground forces have yet been defeated. If the Kwangtung Army comes out of this without being defeated and the Japanese homeland itself is not invaded, I feel that we will be heading for trouble in another forty years or so. Considering the future rather than the present I think we should beat them thoroughly while we know that we can do it. A couple of generations from now it may be different." The power of the atom supplied a finality that Red Mike had not foreseen.

The quick and unexpected end to the war equally upset Edson's calculations about his personal life. The first casualty was his hoped-for second star. With the Marine Corps about to plummet in size, no one would get promoted anytime soon, and there was even a strong possibility of demotions, as had occurred after the last major war. His final reward for his recent effort in the war was a single sentence of congratulations from the commandant.

Red Mike had another concern. Throughout the war he had maintained that he did not want to go back to the States until the conflict was over. Just days after Hiroshima and Nagasaki, he redefined that goal to Thomas. "This is just a short and hurried note to reiterate a desire which I have expressed numerous times to stay out here until the job is finished. Having just assumed command of this outfit and, in fact, just beginning to get my feet on the ground, I hope that the Commandant will see fit to leave me here to carry the thing through." Edson estimated that it would take Service Command two years to complete the mission of cleaning up the theater. He had already been on duty in the Pacific for more than three years, which made him, quite possibly, the senior Marine with the longest continuous service in the war zone.

There was more to this, of course, than a simple sense of duty. Red Mike was enjoying his life in the tropics and had no desire to give it up. The perquisites of a senior officer overseas were certainly tempting. As chief of staff for FMFPAC he had shared a large house with Smith in the

Navy compound at Makalapa, with a panoramic view of Pearl Harbor. When he took over Service Command he moved to his own house just down the road. He had an aide, a driver, a cook, and two stewards to look after his needs, and a Beechcraft plane at his disposal, which he flew himself in trips to bases throughout the Hawaiian Islands. As a hero and a senior leader, he enjoyed the same sort of entree into important civilian circles that he had received in Australia. Although he worked long hours, seldom an evening went by that he was not involved in some social activity. With the large number of officers either stationed in Hawaii or passing through, he never had a problem bringing together a few old friends from the Raiders or the 1st or 2d Divisions.

Edson was undoubtedly enjoying his freedom from Ethel, too. He continued his long-distance affair with Bibs, but he developed a series of relationships in Hawaii as well. He met one woman when he served as best man at Hank Adams's wedding in July 1945, and she dominated his social schedule for the next two months. Then he was with a reporter for the Hearst newspaper chain. The rumor mill churned out gossip about his activities, but he was careful to avoid any overtly scandalous behavior. When the reporter accompanied him on one inspection tour, an enterprising Navy billeting officer asked the aide if the general and the woman were to share quarters. Red Mike provided a rather curt negative reply. On the other hand, his social habits were not those of a happily married man, and Ethel suffered from his lack of attention. Over the course of the final year of the war, she received just four letters from him, though she was quick to excuse his inaction due to his press of work. One general noted that Ethel was unhappy when he saw her on Christmas Day 1944, and with good reason. Red Mike was somewhat repentant when he finally sent her season's greetings in February. He did send her flowers in March, but he spent three times as much on a bouquet for Bibs at the same time.

On 6 August, undoubtedly with the implications of Hiroshima reverberating in his mind, he wrote Ethel his longest letter of the war. After some introductory small talk, he repeated his intention to remain in the Pacific "until the war is over—and longer." He then launched into a blunt assessment of their marriage and his own life:

> You should not love me the way you do, for I am not, nor have I ever been, worth it, not even a small part of it. I wish that you did not, for it makes me feel even more of a cad than I naturally am, and that is bad enough. I have never been a good husband to you, nor a good father to the two wonderful sons which you produced. Whatever they are and whatever they may become, for they will both

grow into better men than I have ever been, will be because of you and your influence, not mine. You and they, too, would be infinitely better off without me, even though you have never admitted it altho I am sure you have often felt that way, too.

I came out here over three years ago with the expectation that I would not return. It would be better so, for you and Bobby and Austin. If the Nips could have shot straight enough on Tulagi or Guadalcanal, Saipan or Tinian, that expectation would have been fulfilled long ago. They had plenty of opportunity in all four places, and a little at Tarawa, but missed each time. With every change of jobs out here I have moved progressively farther from the front lines, and now it looks as though I would finish the war sitting safely back here behind a desk. That is not of my own choosing, and I hate it and almost loathe my job, in spite of the fact that I know it is one of the most important they could have given me.

I had hoped that in these months I have been away you would have gone out more than you have—for in fact you have gone no place and done nothing but work—and that in the going you would have found someone far worthier than I. That would be so easy to do—someone who could make you far happier than I ever have. You have been loving a dream ideal, and not the lousy man who is your husband. Again, my dear, you would be so infinitely better off without me—if only you would realize it.

You told me a long while ago that I had no heart—no morals— that I was selfish—inhuman—all of which is undoubtedly true—as you knew then and have known for years. Knowing me as you do, I cannot see why you should ever want to see me again. I certainly have done nothing to make your life happy for the past 15 years. The fault is not, nor has it ever been, yours, for you are a marvelous and a wonderful woman, only far, far too good for anyone like me. . . .

I have never been able to talk with you—truly. Now I cannot even write to you—for in the writing I can only add hurt to all the pain and hurt that I have given you for so long. Am I worth it? I do not think so. If I had been killed out here in these past 3 years, you would long ago have recovered from it. And yet, in many ways, I have been dead for years, which I think you realize, too.

There are any number of reasons why you could and should have divorced me years ago—and it would have been far better for you and the boys had you done so. Why you have not done so, I do not know, for you have taken a beating from me that no one should stand for. That, I know, is up to you, for God knows that you have been a better wife than I would ever find again, or I have ever deserved. I have not even accumulated a decent living for you—but whatever there is belongs entirely to you anyway.

This is a rotten letter—especially at this time. I have written it mentally a thousand times because I was and am too much of a coward to say what I should have said a long, long while ago. If you could only give up loving me—if you could only forget about me—you would be so much happier. . . . Do not worry about me—ever. Take care of yourself—and I hope that someday you will find the happiness which I have never—never given to you. Goodnight, my dear.

This was a unique outpouring of feelings for Red Mike. The news of Hiroshima probably played a part in it, since that crushed his dreams of promotion and command of a division in battle. The imminent end of the war also forced him to face the reality of eventual return to the States and Ethel, a prospect he had assiduously avoided for some time. But why did he write this at all, and why now, when he claimed that he had been "too much of a coward" to say it before? One reason might have been to goad her into divorcing him, which would then free him to lead the carefree life of a bachelor or to marry someone else. And his only recourse if he wanted a divorce was to have her initiate the action.

His discussion of death may provide another potential motivation behind the letter, for he seems to have been consumed by a sense of guilt. He had hinted at that in the past, not only over his unfaithfulness to his wife, but also over his failure to rescue Lillian from an unhappy marriage. References to his own worthlessness cropped up from time to time in his diaries and in letters to his mother, sister, and wife. Although he seldom attended church services anymore, the moral beliefs of his Congregationalist faith were deeply imbued in his psyche, which undoubtedly increased his anguish.

It may be that he thought death an appropriate punishment for his misdeeds, whatever they might have been, or that it would at least be a release for his tortured conscience. If he went off to war in hopes of dying, why did he not choose the simpler alternative of suicide? There is evidence that he considered that a valid option. In January 1944 Cal Lloyd, one of Red Mike's closest friends, walked into the woods above Quantico's football stadium and shot himself through the heart with a .45-caliber pistol. Hod Berry wrote Edson that the family believed that Cal had killed himself only because he had lost his mind as the result of injuries sustained in an auto accident. Red Mike thought otherwise: "I believe that he was true to his own ideals even to the last, for I am firmly convinced that what he did was influenced solely by the idea that he might become a burden to his family, the last thing that he had any intention of ever permitting." Edson saw nothing dishonorable in a decision to end one's life when there was no longer any reason to continue it.

There is no indication that he ever thought about killing himself over his troubled marriage, perhaps because his life was good in other respects. But he seemed willing to submit his destiny to the final judgment of the hands of fate, a sentiment he repeated on many occasions. He would take extreme risks. If he died, he and his family would be better off. If he lived, he would soldier on and do his best, just like Rustum, the ancient Persian warrior. In that respect, the letter was revealing about his willingness to seek out grave danger, to a point unusual even for brave Marine officers. That did not detract from his unmatched record of courage during the war. It may have been easy to decide to risk death; it took nerves of steel actually to put one's life on the line time after time.

A few days after Ethel received her husband's letter, she wrote to Lelia in a vein that suggested she had received his bombshell. "I wish I were young and beautiful maybe it would be more fun for him to come home but my youth is gone and I feel very uninteresting. A woman I know just my age has just divorced her second husband, a commander in the Navy, and married an Admiral. But somehow I never could bring myself to such casual changes."

In November Ethel ran into Vandegrift and asked him when her husband would return. The commandant apologized to her, said she had received "the worst deal of all Marine wives in the war," and promised to get Edson home for a visit at Christmas. She described the encounter to Lelia and asked rhetorically: "The next difficulty is 'Will Merritt *want* to come home at Christmas?'"

Ethel generally put up a brave front to the world, but her own mother knew she was unhappy. After reading one "discouraged little letter" she tried to console her daughter.

And altho others have hurt you badly—yet you have kept on so bravely and wisely, that some day you are going to be the happy woman you deserve to be. Dear heart, isn't it something for you, when your boys, in looking backward, can most honestly say—"I never knew my mother to do anything to hurt anyone"—and certainly Austin who has seen and known so much, and kept all these things to himself—

things which have hurt him far more than we will ever know—can look back with more pride in his mother's life than anyone else's—can say, "My mother never failed us—never!"

In her own way, Ethel Edson was courageous, too. Ultimately, Red Mike's letter accomplished nothing. Ethel did not seek a divorce, and he continued in his old ways.

He at least had cause to take great pride in the achievements of Austin during this period. In January the young man had graduated seventeenth in his class of 252 in officer candidate training and received his commission as a Marine lieutenant. Regrettably, his poor eyesight made him ineligible for the regular commission that any other reserve officer would have received for that performance. Red Mike made discreet inquiries to Thomas and others about a waiver of the physical standards, but he did not press the point too far. "I would not think for a moment of asking you or anyone else to give him a boost if he can not stand on his own two feet so far as professional qualifications are concerned."

Edson took time out to provide some useful advice for his son on a subject in which he had considerable personal experience. "You will find our people extremely negligent in the matter of cover. All too often both our officers and enlisted men expose themselves needlessly which accounts for many of our casualties. I do not mean by this that a man should dig himself a hole and never get out of it. There are plenty of times when exposure is absolutely necessary. . . . On the other hand it is not a sign of bravery but just damn foolishness when a man needlessly stands up for someone to take a pot shot at him." Austin ended up having no need for the advice, at least not yet, because he did not arrive in the Pacific until just after the war ended.

With both his personal and professional life in disarray, Red Mike had plenty to keep him busy in the fall of 1945. His plans to make a circuit of the Pacific in August to inspect his command were upset by the changes wrought by the bomb, but in October he finally had things sufficiently under control to make the trip. As he laid plans for a month-long journey, problems with the demobilization process added a new twist. Everywhere the troops were clamoring to come home now that the war was over. Things got out of hand in some Army units, but Marine leaders kept a tight rein and there was no lapse in discipline. That did not stop Marines from writing to their families, congressmen, and even the president, and complaints about living conditions and other problems threatened the Corps with a public relations crisis. The commandant charged General Geiger with investigating these matters and making a full report. Since

Edson was about to inspect his service units anyway, it made sense to give the mission to him.

Geiger provided Edson with his personal command plane, an R4D specially outfitted with executive seating. Red Mike took with him only his new aide (2d Lt. J. Angus MacDonald), a single staff officer, his female reporter friend (who had official credentials and orders for the trip), and an enlisted photographer. The small party toured all major Marine installations in the Central Pacific, the Philippines, Japan, and China. At each location Edson spoke with commanders and inspected the quarters and mess halls of the men. At his own subordinate commands he went a step further and spoke to the assembled troops. He also took the opportunity to inspect some of the battlefields he had not experienced firsthand in the war. He toured the Shuri Castle defensive line on Okinawa, and stopped at Iwo Jima, Peleliu, and Eniwetok. In Japan he spent a few hours at Nagasaki and saw for himself the destructive power of nuclear weapons. The general visited with his son, stationed with the 6th Marine Division in Tsingtao, and the two took a four-day side trip to Shanghai.

Red Mike met up with numerous old comrades along the way, and at least one party lasted until dawn. But Red Mike demonstrated his own philosophy that a leader could drink hard at night only if he was ready to go to work the next day as if nothing had happened. He had his own cagey method for maintaining a reputation as a man who could hold his liquor. "Every time someone else has three drinks, you have two. The next morning all the other guy will remember is, 'Christ, can that guy drink.'"

Edson's trip highlighted the odd situation that the American military faced in late 1945. For a large proportion of the junior officers and men, those who had been drafted or who had joined for the sole purpose of winning the war, the end of combat meant that it was time to go home and resume civilian pursuits. For those who had called the service "home" before the war, it was a different story. They could take institutional pride in a tremendous victory over major opponents on opposite sides of the globe, but that same success posed a personal threat. Those who had risen rapidly on the crest of the war wave now faced the possibility of an equally dizzying fall as demobilization progressed at a frantic pace. Headquarters was wielding an ax throughout the officer corps. Many reserve officers had to leave the service, and most regulars were reverting to their permanent rank. Since Congress had not yet reached a final decision on the ultimate size of the armed forces, no one knew where the process would end.

After twenty-five stops in forty-four days, the R4D landed at Ewa airfield,

Oahu, on the morning of 11 December. Edson had barely settled into his routine three days later when a telephone call upset all his carefully laid plans for Service Command and his own life. The FMFPAC chief of staff rang up Red Mike a few minutes before morning colors on 14 December and told him that a dispatch had just arrived from HQMC with transfer orders. Edson was to depart immediately for Washington, where he would report to the office of the chief of Naval Operations (CNO) as a relief for Brig. Gen. Omar T. Pfeiffer. There was emphasis on the speed of execution—pack up and move by air as soon as possible.

The orders came as an unpleasant surprise for Edson. "So far as I am concerned, congratulations are not in order. I would much prefer to have stayed at Pearl Harbor until I had completed the reorganization of Service Command in line with my ideas." He would have to give up the perquisites of a commanding general, the social life of an important official in a distant outpost, and the comfortable weather of a tropical paradise. Worse still, he would be stationed at home for the first time in nearly four years. He did not relish the return to domesticity.

But orders were orders. Within a few hours he had turned over his duties to his chief of staff and was back at his quarters to arrange his personal affairs. The next forty-eight hours were a whirlwind of packing and quick good-byes to Marines and civilian friends. As if in preparation for the lonely job ahead, there was no parade, no formal change of command, not even a farewell party at the officers' club. The last visitors were his aide and the reporter. Lieutenant MacDonald found it difficult to express his feelings over Edson's departure, so he tinged his regrets with humor; he said he was sorry to see the general go, particularly because he would miss the jeep assigned to him as the aide. Edson considered that statement for a moment, smiled, and replied in a similar vein: "Mac, if we had more time and I had been a better teacher, you might have made a good aide." Shortly after, the hero of the Ridge quietly boarded a plane in Oahu and left the Pacific behind.

Chapter 17

"For Right and Freedom"

The American armed forces focused their attention on foreign foes during World War II, but another conflict was percolating on the back burner. When Japan surrendered, the other crisis boiled over and erupted into open warfare. This time the armed services of the United States were fighting each other. Interservice rivalry had been a feature of the American military landscape for decades, but the roots of the current row lay in the just-completed war. The unprecedented buildup of military power had stretched resources to the breaking point and left the services competing bitterly for shares of limited production capacity and manpower. Added to that were numerous disputes over strategy and command, particularly the contentious debate between MacArthur and Nimitz in the Pacific.

The Army had a plan to solve the problem. In November 1942 its chief of staff, Gen. George C. Marshall, asked the Joint Chiefs of Staff to consider the merger of the War Department (the Army and Army Air Forces) with the Navy Department. Under this setup, a single civilian secretary of defense and a single military chief of staff would ensure unity of command and efficient utilization of national resources. Although many naval officers initially favored the idea of unification, Navy opposition to the Army's version of it began to develop as the end of the war approached.

The issue of defense reorganization disturbed the sea services because it arose from wartime rivalries that promised to intensify during the ensuing peace. With the advent of atomic weapons and long-range bombers, the Army Air Forces now claimed that they played the primary role in national defense. In a time of increasing fiscal austerity for the services, a shift in strategy seemed to presage a defeat for the Navy in the battle for shares of a shrinking military budget, particularly if generals dominated the single department, as seemed likely.

Secretary of the Navy James Forrestal commissioned a study of the subject in June 1945, and chose investment banker, government executive, and longtime friend Ferdinand Eberstadt to conduct it. The report, completed in September, found the Army unification idea unworkable and instead proposed the creation of various coordinating bodies that would improve cooperation between the War and Navy departments. With its independence maintained under the Eberstadt Plan, the Navy would have some hope of protecting itself in the struggles over strategy and money.

In October 1945 the Senate Military Affairs Committee began hearings on two bills, each calling for creation of a single military department. Both pieces of legislation were comparatively short, which meant that the details of reorganization would be left up to the Executive Branch. The second piece of legislation, Senate Bill 1482, was most worrisome to the Navy Department; it specifically authorized President Harry Truman "to consolidate, eliminate, or redistribute the functions of offices, bureaus, agencies, branches, and organizations." Thus the Navy and Marine Corps would be at the whim of Truman, a former Army officer and an avowed partisan of the War Department plan. Since the Army saw the Marines and naval aviation as prime examples of duplication, both might well face extinction. Those concerns would be amply justified in the months ahead.

Red Mike had first become aware of the importance of the merger issue during his visit to Washington in September 1944, when Thomas showed him interservice memoranda on the subject. In September 1945 Thomas had flown out to Hawaii to confer with Edson and Geiger; undoubtedly the conversations encompassed postwar plans for the Corps and the shadow of unification that hung over them. Not long thereafter, Edson drew an assignment to make a Navy Day speech to the Hilo Chamber of Commerce. His preliminary remarks at the Hilo luncheon hinted at the threat that he and other Marines perceived; he referred to "our Corps—which has always been, and, I hope, always will be an integral part of the United States Navy." The speech, entitled "A Strong Navy Is the Guarantee of a Strong Peace," began by highlighting the strategic value of a capable navy and the role of the sea services in the victory over Germany and Japan. But then Red Mike moved quickly into the heart of his talk: "I mention this primarily because of the current discussion regarding a unified department of defense."

Edson agreed that there might be some budgetary advantages to merger, in terms of common procurement and transportation, and he supported continuation of the JCS and the system of unified commands employed in the war. However, he saw a need to maintain independent services that could develop the specialized equipment and expertise required to meet the vastly different needs of combat on the ground and at sea. As an example, Edson opposed the creation of a separate air force encompassing naval and land aviation, since it "would result in decreased efficiency and support to both the Army and the Navy on the field of battle." In his closing remarks, he argued that, despite the advent of atomic weapons, naval power would remain the nation's first line of defense and the primary means of preventing future war. And an important element of that naval force would be "a strong and adequate Marine Corps—the ground forces of the Navy."

The general spent most of the next day discussing the merger with Krulak, who had stopped briefly in Hawaii while on his way to a new assignment at Quantico. He was going to work for Twining, now head of the Marine Corps Board. This newly created body had the mission of studying unification and other postwar policy concerns. Edson's hasty departure from Service Command was likewise connected to the unification battle. He hinted as much to his aide, saying that he was going home "to protect the Marine Corps." Thomas, the leader of the antimerger campaign up to this point, was preoccupied with his overwhelming duties as director of Plans and Policies. He needed someone who could devote nearly full attention to the unification debate. As the senior Marine representative on the CNO's staff, a less demanding billet, Edson would have the time. He would also be in position to coordinate efforts with the Navy. He possessed the seniority, intellect, and presence to represent the Corps in the public arena, and his wartime reputation could be expected to carry considerable weight with Congress and the voters. Finally, Thomas knew that Edson had strong feelings on the issue and, perhaps more importantly, the courage to fight for those convictions.

As usual, Edson immediately jumped into his new duties. A few hours after his plane arrived in Oakland on 17 December he held a press conference. The Associated Press story later led off with his reputation as a "famed Marine Raider commander and hero of many a bloody Pacific battle." The media obviously had not focused yet on the merger issue, for the opening paragraphs concerned Edson's thoughts on the drawdown in the Pacific and the occupation of China. The story finally turned to his views on unification, a prospect he considered "most unwise" and "not in accordance with national policy." His rationale followed that laid out in the Hilo speech.

● Despite his orders, Edson was in no hurry to get to Washington; he requested and was given a modification that authorized him to complete the trip by rail. When he finally arrived in the capital at 0830 on Sunday, 23 December, he reported immediately to HQMC and spent two hours in conference with Thomas. Then he finally went home after an absence of more than a year. The reunion was not a happy one. Ethel put the best face on things; she told the family that his vanity had been hurt because of the loss of the command perquisites and high society he had become accustomed to in Hawaii. She tried hard to please him, and even quit her job the day before he arrived, but nothing seemed to work. At the same time, she was still quite proud of him. In her eyes, his sudden orders occurred "when Admiral Nimitz decided Merritt was the only officer in the Marine Corps that he wanted on his staff and he wanted him badly and immediately."

For the moment, personal concerns outweighed Edson's dedication to the Corps: "This is supposed to be an important job, and I suppose I should feel flattered that they gave it to me, but I did not want to come back to Washington for duty. . . ." He dutifully attended to his family. He phoned his mother, sister, son, and mother-in-law, and even helped entertain Ethel's former coworkers on Christmas Day, but he also found time for calls to his reporter in Hawaii.

If his home life was not satisfactory, he at least had work to keep him busy. The day after Christmas he went into HQMC again, this time for meetings with Vandegrift, Thomas, and Shoup. The merger issue had been a hot topic during Edson's transfer. On 19 December, President Truman addressed Congress and strongly advocated a single department of defense. In his opinion: "Further studies of the general problem would serve no useful purpose. There is enough evidence now at hand to demonstrate beyond question the need for a unified department." He concluded ominously that "however strong the opposition that has been expressed by some of our outstanding senior officers and civilians, I can assure the Congress that once unification has been determined upon as the policy of this nation, there is no officer or civilian in any Service who will not contribute his utmost to make the unification a success."

The move to enforce support began the same day in a Navy-wide directive (AlNav) from Secretary Forrestal: "In view of the President's message to Congress urging the passage of legislation for a department of national defense, officers of the Navy and Marine Corps are expected to refrain from opposition thereto in their public utterances." An exception was made for testimony to Congress, and officers were encouraged to stress the important role of the Navy in national security. The press quickly jumped on the Navy's attempt to stifle dissent (an eventuality that Forrestal may have foreseen and desired), and reporters questioned Truman about it the very next day. A subsequent attachment to the AlNav incorporated the president's 20 December reply: "I want everybody to express his honest opinion on the subject . . . nobody has been muzzled. It will be necessary now, though, for all people who are in the services to make a statement that they are expressing their personal views and not the views of the administration." This exchange would not be the end of the issue.

On 2 January 1946 Edson reported to Main Navy and began the turnover of duties with Pfeiffer. The title of the position was officer in charge, Marine Corps Strategic Plans Sub-Section (known by its office code, Op30M). The senior Marine was one of twenty-three officers reporting to the assistant chief of Naval Operations for Strategic Plans (Op30), RAdm. Mathias Gardner. It was a considerable change from the setup in Hawaii, where he had commanded nearly twenty thousand Marines. Edson's new organization consisted of himself, his military secretary (a lieutenant), and an enlisted clerk-typist. All three shared the same cramped office, with the general's corner partly enclosed by a portable screen.

Edson looked through the files and asked about the job, then he and Pfeiffer made their formal call on Nimitz, now the CNO. In the course of conversation about the occupation of Japan and the future of the Corps, the admiral revealed the substance of a recent meeting with Eisenhower, the new chief of staff of the Army. The two service heads were conducting negotiations to settle differences on unification in the wake of the president's address to Congress. Eisenhower's initial memo on the subject included a recommendation that the Marines be limited to no more than forty thousand men, possess no supporting arms, and focus solely on duties involving shore party and the operation of landing craft. This would reduce the Corps to a naval auxiliary incapable of ground combat. Nimitz asked Edson for Marine input for a reply to the Army.

The general promptly went to HQMC, where he passed the disquieting information to Vandegrift and Thomas. They in turn contacted Twining and his crew, and the Quantico officers spent that night drafting a suitable passage for inclusion in Nimitz's proposed response. The memo stressed the need for an organization dedicated to the development of amphibious doctrine and available for employment with the fleet on short notice. It was signed by Vandegrift and forwarded to the CNO the next day. Edson spent all of Saturday, 5 January, in meetings drafting Nimitz's reply to Eisenhower. In the morning he and Pfeiffer (still formally Op30M) met with senior admirals. In the afternoon Vandegrift and Thomas joined the sessions.

Pfeiffer detached on 16 January and Edson assumed complete responsibility for the job. For the moment, he was occupied with normal work, such as observing congressional budget hearings on the Navy Department's annual appropriations and trying to fulfill the secretary of state's request for a standby force to meet a possible emergency in the Western Hemisphere. The latter seemed difficult enough; the only Marine combat units readily available on the East Coast consisted of an infantry battalion and a couple of artillery batteries used as demonstration troops at the Marine Corps Schools in Quantico. Red Mike held no romantic notions based on his own experience in the Banana Wars. He recommended against relying on ships detachments since "the calibre of opposition encountered on landing will be vastly different than pertained in the 1917–1933 period and should be met by well-trained, coordinated units." The only ways to make a force available were to maintain reservists on duty beyond the scheduled demobilization date, withdraw forces early from China and Japan, or increase the proposed peacetime strength of the Corps.

The occupation forces presented another aspect of the hurried drawdown of U.S. military power. The Corps had 226,000 men on active duty but had to reach its planned size of 100,000 by the end of the year. The commandant's request for disbandment of some Marine units in China and Japan met with opposition from the Army commanders and diplomats in charge there, which meant that the Corps was falling behind its schedule for manpower reductions. Edson pressed the CNO to support USMC efforts to effect the reductions in occupation forces. Although the Op30M memos on these subjects were unrelated to the unification fight, they highlighted the strained resources of all services and the resulting scramble for control over postwar reorganization.

As part of the CNO's planning staff, Edson was well placed to participate in the concurrent debate over strategy. Many officers of the Army Air Forces were arguing that nuclear weapons rendered the Navy and Marines obsolete, since bombers striking at an enemy's homeland would quickly win a war; in any case, massed fleets of combatants or amphibious ships would make inviting targets for an opponent's atomic arms. Edson and the naval services publicly disagreed with that view. In one speech the general pointed out that military forces always developed technological or tactical counters to every new wonder weapon, and the same would hold true in this instance. Bombers could be shot down, while more exotic means of delivery were only on the drawing boards and not yet a practical threat. Moreover, the spread of atomic bombs would eventually deter their use, in the same way that poison gas arsenals had remained in storage throughout World War II.

Edson did not stick his head in the sand and ignore the emerging challenges to the old order. New developments, such as nuclear weapons and missiles, commanded his attention. When he heard reports that shelters had proven effective against the atomic blasts in Japan, he recommended that the Bikini Atoll nuclear tests scheduled for the summer of 1946 incorporate ground fortifications containing live animals. He arranged orders to observe the firing of a V-2 missile at White Sands, New Mexico—an experience he found impressive and "thrilling." He took a strong interest in the commandant's Special Board and its work on amphibious tactics. Some of the finest minds in the Corps were looking at the fledgling helicopter as a response to the atomic threat. This new device would allow the dispersion of both ships at sea and the landing force ashore.

Edson occasionally got to demonstrate his grasp of strategy and tactics by doing what was allegedly his primary job, developing contingency plans for war. As time passed, that effort focused increasingly on the potential threat from the Soviet Union. When one preliminary draft plan came to his office, Edson found it rather poor from the Marine standpoint. In a rehash of the early days of World War II, it called for immediate occupation upon the outbreak of war of Iceland and the Azores by USMC units. The general found this to be a waste of assets until such time as these areas were related directly to operations of the fleet; otherwise the Army should provide mere garrison forces. Nor should the Marines be inserted into Egypt, North Africa, or Palestine, which were clearly land masses more appropriate to Army operations. Instead, he touted a landing on Crete as a means to bottle up the Soviet Black Sea fleet, deny an advance base to the enemy, and protect the Navy's eastern flank in the Mediterranean.

A subsequent draft incorporated the Crete option but placed it well down the list of priorities. Edson pressed to rank it higher. He also criticized the scale of the force envisioned for the operation; Army and Navy reserves would be required and it would take nine months to get the force ready. He thought it would be much better to use a small Marine unit to take the island immediately upon the outbreak of war before the Soviets could get there. That would be in accordance with the traditional role of the Corps as a force in readiness supporting a fleet campaign.

Strategic debates did more than simply determine future war plans. In a period of limited availability of resources, the outcome would affect access to funds and, perhaps, even institutional survival. This point was driven home to the sea services in a battle of memorandums reminiscent of the Eisenhower-Nimitz exchange that had welcomed Edson to the CNO's staff. The previous Army chief of staff, Marshall, had initiated this series of related papers in August 1945 when he recommended that the JCS develop postwar strength requirements for each service. He wanted these numbers to reflect personnel savings to be achieved by the elimination of duplication in the services. Specifically, he saw land-based naval aviation and the Marine Corps as falling into this category. In his view, the single department would achieve economy and resolve the muddle resulting from overlapping roles and missions. The CNO disagreed; he believed the JCS should base its figures on the present organization of two military departments. Ultimately the JCS ordered a subordinate committee to study the roles and missions of the services. These documents, known collectively as the JCS 1478 papers because of their filing designators, would have an impact on the outcome of the unification controversy.

On 20 February the JCS received the report on the "Missions of the Land, Sea and Air Services." The fifteen-page document, known as JCS 1478/8, was classified top secret, which meant that it could not be used in public debate. A special distribution limited access to just nineteen senior Navy and Army officers. The Marine Corps received no copy and might have remained unaware of the contents, except for Edson's presence on the CNO staff. When he got wind of the document, he promptly informed Thomas, who sent Twining and Krulak to meet with Edson.

The joint committee that crafted the report could not agree on all things. The Army Air Forces sought control over land-based naval aviation, and the Army argued that the Marine Corps should be limited to "small lightly-armed forces" no larger than a regiment. This obvious attempt by the War Department to diminish the Corps did not send the Marines involved with the antiunification effort to general quarters. Rather, it was the Navy's view of things that raised great concern. If implemented, the document would limit the Marines in the future to "minor operations," while the Army would gain responsibility for the development of amphibious tactics and techniques. If the Corps was reduced to small units that performed the same missions as their Army counterparts, it would be only a matter of time before it would be absorbed by its larger rival as an unnecessary duplication.

Subsequent memos in the same series made the Army position absolutely clear. General Carl Spaatz, head of the AAF, repeated the "duplication of forces" theme. "During the war the Navy developed and employed the Marine Corps as a major force in land and air warfare. This is patently an incursion by one service into the normal roles of the other two services." Eisenhower went slightly farther and characterized the disputes as "land-based versus naval aviation or Army Ground Forces versus Marines." The exchange degenerated into a dispute over which services had won the recent war. The Army argued that it had been prepared for amphibious operations at the outset of the war, that it had conducted in the Pacific more successful assaults than the Corps, and that such work did not require dedicated forces. The Marine rebuttal, a thirty-five-page compilation of facts, many taken from the Army's own reports, argued that it was the doctrine and strategy of the sea services that had triumphed in the Pacific. The drawn-out debate widened interservice differences. Nimitz recommended that the entire series of papers be filed without further action, and on 7 June 1946 the Joint Chiefs agreed to shelve the issue for the time being.

Many naval leaders had been complacent about reorganization in the past, but nearly all now agreed with Edson that "the Army has finally laid their cards on the table." Nimitz saw the roles and missions controversy as an attempt to "eliminate the Marine Corps as an effective combat element" and to "abolish an essential component of Naval Aviation." Vandegrift was equally concerned about the future existence of his service. These fears were justified. Clark Clifford, an important Truman adviser, later stated that the president "always felt that there was no need for a separate Marine Corps."

The issue was not solely one of institutional prerogatives. Edson soon came to believe that the outcome of the unification debate would have a far-reaching impact on the future of the country. Reorganizing the Marine Corps or land-based naval air out of existence certainly would weaken American military power. More important, however, was the Army's quest for a single secretary and general staff. Under the current system, the War and Navy departments fought a public battle before Congress over budget shares and defense strategy, just as they were presently doing. Critics of the Army plan argued that in a unified military the single chain of command would enforce conformity on all subordinates. Representatives of the military thus would speak with one prearranged voice, and Congress would have no free discussion of service opinion to inform its deliberations. Edson and others found ready evidence that the War Department was already sanitizing its own house to get rid of wayward views on unification. And one of the Army's own arguments for the merger bill seemed to prove the point that a single service would give Congress short shrift. One officer later testified to a congressional committee to the effect that it "should not question too closely the legislation proposed by the military," because the men in uniform were the experts.

Coupled with this was the War Department's desire to gain greater influence in the management of the national economy, for the worthy goal of improved industrial mobilization. Red Mike thought the armed forces had tried to gain too much control over economic production during the war, and that the War Department now hoped to perpetuate that policy and even expand it. He equated the unified services, the general staff, and enhanced industrial control with the system from which he believed the War Department had copied the ideas—the German military. Once started down this road, Edson felt that it would lead inevitably to militarism and dictatorship as service leaders wielded more and more power to enhance military readiness. In his mind, the obvious compromise between preparedness and democracy was the Navy's Eberstadt Plan, which would achieve the desired efficiencies through coordination while leaving the two-department system intact and assuring "Congressional and democratic control."

Other officers in the Navy and Marine Corps used similar arguments, frequently for purely parochial and expedient reasons, but Edson was one of the few who truly believed that the threat was real. In a long letter to his mother he pointed out the growing practice of appointing retired, and even active, officers to government positions, Marshall's ascent to secretary of state being a prime example:

> I am very much worried about the latest moves for unification—not so much for its effects on the Marine Corps . . . but primarily because of its eventual effects upon the policies and security of this nation of ours. It will impose upon this country a strong military clique which will surely change our foreign policy from one of defense to aggression—and will dominate our domestic policies as well. . . . It will mean the adoption of the same system which ruined Germany and Japan and is now in force in Russia.

As the debate wore on, fewer military men resorted to this argument. The conviction that civilian control of the military should remain undiluted would guide Edson's actions for the remainder of his years.

Red Mike's views probably were shaped by the populism of his Granger roots and the progressivism of his Republican politics. He thought that any monopoly was bad, and used that economic comparison to deride a single military. He also harked back to the philosophy of the "founders of our nation" and agreed with James Madison's argument for the separation of powers between three branches of the government: "Ambition must be made to counteract ambition." He thought that the division of the armed forces served the same purpose.

Edson's fears were genuinely held but probably overblown. Men such as Marshall and Eisenhower were not about to subvert the government. (MacArthur would later step beyond the bounds of propriety in challenging Truman, but the president would leave little doubt who held the whip hand in that case.) The Marine general did have some good points. At that time the War and Navy departments constituted by far the largest activities of the national government. To concentrate that power even further in a single agency was more of an apparent threat then than would be the case today. Edson's prediction that the initially small staffs of the secretary of defense and Joint Chiefs would burgeon into large bureaucracies proved correct. And he was right that the Department of Defense would attempt to impose conformity on the services despite sincere differences on policy, though it has never been completely successful. The failure to do so might be traced, in part, to the success of Edson and others in preventing the total merger that the War Department desired. Without the diversity of independent services, recent history might have turned out much different if various weapons systems and doctrines had been discarded because they did not fit the dominant plan.

As the primary point of contact between the Marine Corps and the Navy, Edson played a vital part in the roles and missions debate. After each salvo from the War Department, the Navy looked to Edson for Marine input to any response. The actual writing chores frequently fell to Twining's think tank in Quantico, but once a position paper left the hands of those staff officers, they had little impact on the outcome. It was generally Edson and Thomas who counseled the commandant firsthand. Sometimes all three generals then attended the flurry of meetings that gave birth to the CNO's memos, but more frequently it was Edson who lobbied Nimitz's staff in person or in writing. He was not always successful in getting the Marine point of view adopted. In fact, although the Navy invited the participation of the Corps in these efforts, it did not keep its junior partner fully informed of developments. When Edson tried to provide his thoughts on one draft document to Gardner and Admiral Sherman (now the deputy CNO for operations), he was surprised to find that it already had been completed, signed, and sent forward.

Edson felt that the battle should not be decided in an exchange of secret documents, and he began to push for a coordinated campaign to develop public and congressional support for the Navy Department's position. In a personal memo, he pressed Sherman to create such a mechanism. "It is my opinion that we are engaged in a campaign which is as important to the continuing welfare of the Navy and Marine Corps as was the campaign of Okinawa toward winning the last war. If this opinion is correct, then, it is necessary that we have as definite a plan of action as was necessary at Okinawa. I believe that this plan should cover the line of attack, that is, what contacts will be authorized and made with Senators and Congressmen and with influential citizens throughout the country; what speeches will be made, by whom and when and where; what the approach will be to the American press."

The Navy had already made a move in this direction. Forrestal had created the Secretary's Committee of Research on Reorganization (SCOROR) in the fall of 1945. Headed by RAdm. Thomas H. Robbins, Jr., this group was supposed to wage the Navy's public relations battle against unification. Edson thought Robbins was afraid to take strong action and that his committee's scope was too limited. Red Mike wanted an entity that could deal with all facets of the campaign, not just public relations. As it turned out, SCOROR's efforts would be hampered by a more fundamental problem— vacillation at the very top rungs of the Navy Department.

The Marine Corps was certainly not hesitant to fight on its own behalf in the interservice squabbles. One idea floated at the time involved the United Nations, which was then considering creation of a standing military force for use in enforcing the peace. Thomas and Edson saw this as a ready-made mission for the Corps and launched an effort to have the American share of this postwar plum assigned to the Marines. They believed that USMC participation in this potentially important role would guarantee the existence of the Corps.

The Army took exception to this idea. In a subsequent debate over allocation of forces to the United Nations, Eisenhower argued that Marine participation as a ground component hinged on the definition of roles and missions "currently under review" in JCS 1478/8. Apparently, if the Army had its way, the Corps would not even be capable of playing a peacekeeping role. Edson pointed out to the CNO that "unless JCS series 1478/8 on the one hand definitely establishes the development of amphibious doctrine and the conduct of amphibious operations as a responsibility of the Navy, and JCS 1567/28 on the other definitely specifies that the Fleet Marine Force will constitute a part of the 'ground' elements of our commitment to the Security Forces of the United Nations, the Fleet Marine Force will be destroyed and the Marine Corps relegated to impotency with its sole mission that of furnishing ships detachments and Navy Yard guards."

In Edson's opinion, the battle needed to be decided as soon as possible. "The Marine Corps stands especially high in the opinion and good will of the American public at this time as evidenced by editorial comment and the public statements of members of Congress. It is believed that this favorable position should be exploited to the fullest to the benefit of the Naval Establishment in the matter under discussion." Edson saw the importance of the public and Congress from the first, and these two areas would be where he would contribute most to the unification battle.

His initial postwar foray into the legislative arena was not related to the merger, but it provided Edson with valuable experience for the upcoming fight. The Navy Department was then in the process of trying to pass a bill that would set strength levels for the naval services. In preparation for the committee hearings, Navy leaders left nothing to chance and demonstrated levels of skill and thoroughness that seemed to bode well for any legislative battle with the Army. The CNO's office tasked Edson with preparing arguments in support of the Corps's portion of the bill, which he incorporated in a detailed memo based on input from HQMC. He and the other naval witnesses (Edson would be the only Marine to testify) then repeatedly rehearsed their presentations. This included two practice briefs in front of Nimitz and Forrestal. Edson's testimony on 14 February 1946 met with a positive reception from the House Naval Affairs Committee, a group already favorably disposed toward the legislation. Among the rationales advanced for a Corps of 100,000 enlisted men was the ready adaptability of the FMF to the United Nations mission.

Shortly after his congressional testimony, Edson began to carry the antiunification message to the American people. His first speech was prompted by a letter from a former Marine in upstate New York, who complained that the area was being bombarded by promerger propaganda from the local Army Air Forces base and requested that Adm. William F. Halsey speak at a fund-raiser for the city war memorial. Edson took on the assignment and picked up a similar speaking engagement at Rhode Island State College. He gave the talk, entitled "The Enormous Challenge," on 20 and 22 February 1946.

Since both occasions concerned war memorials, he had to deftly steer the subject from honoring the heroic dead to the partisan issue of unification. He did so, in a manner reminiscent of the Athenian Pericles, by arguing that those who gave their lives in service to the country had passed on a challenge to the living to maintain the peace, and that an important element in doing so was maintaining an effective organization of the military forces so they could be strong enough to prevent war. He argued that it was not simply a technical issue for the services, but one that had to be decided by the people through their representatives in Congress. As such, he was talking to them as a fellow citizen rather than as a military man, and his ideas were his own, not those of the Navy Department or the administration (phraseology that worked neatly in the obligatory disclaimer).

His arguments touched on several themes, including the manpower inefficiency of the Army in the past war, the preference of Army ground troops for Navy and Marine Corps close air support, and the importance of naval forces in bringing strategic bombers into position to conduct their campaigns. He further noted that unified military systems traditionally lost wars, and that the "effect of monopoly is to retard progress."

The speeches made headlines in local newspapers, and Edson reinforced his point at the grass roots level in both towns by getting out to various clubs, such as the Rotary and the VFW. He was not particularly happy with his initial effort on 20 February, since he had felt "very tired," but the 22 February talk before two thousand people seemed to go much better. In all likelihood he had not written the speech himself; probably it came from the busy pens of Twining's group. But that was in keeping with Edson's style in delegating work to a staff. Moreover, his reputation assured that the speech would receive attention. And he was no mere front man, reciting by rote the words of others. Upon his return from New York, he noted: "This is entirely too long—I briefed it verbally at both places—but still not good. Covers too much. Better magazine article than speech." Nor was he content to let others do all the research. During this period he expanded his library with volumes such as Fuller's *Armament and History,* Mahan's *Influence of Seapower Upon History,* and Huie's *Case Against the Admirals* (a promerger, pro-AAF diatribe against the Navy).

Edson and others continued to carry the issue to the public. The well-known war hero made good copy wherever he went, and he traveled and spoke frequently during the spring of 1946. He participated in major events in Ohio, New York, Missouri, Michigan, Vermont, Illinois, and Massachusetts. And always he asked his local contacts for additional forums, such as radio talk shows and dinner meetings, where he could "express my views on the merger."

President Truman was making that task more difficult. In an 11 April press conference he castigated those officers who spoke out against unification and undercut the support he felt he should receive from the Navy and War departments. He hinted darkly that he would have to "alter the situation" if his subordinates did not "get into line." Later that same day he told Forrestal and others that discussion of the unification issue by the military should be limited to congressional testimony. In another press conference the following week he attacked the Navy for its antimerger "lobbying" effort. Although Truman and Forrestal did not repeat the mistake of issuing written policy, it seemed clear to all officers that opposition to the president would henceforth have to be more circumspect.

The outspoken leader of the Marine campaign seemed unfazed. One newspaper stated that Edson was unable to comment on the merger bill itself due to a presidential "gag rule," but his quotes made clear exactly what he really thought. He insisted that amphibious operations were a naval responsibility and required a specialized, separate force. If there were no Marines, the country would have to reinvent them before the next war.

Edson organized others who were completely unfettered to assist in the publicity effort. He contacted people around the country, such as Marine reservist and Louisiana businessman Walter McIlhenny, and asked them to do their "bit to help the Corps" by making speeches whenever possible. His letters laid out the major points of the issue and promised that supporting material would arrive via Lt. Col. Hunter Hurst (the Marine representative to SCOROR). In a revealing slip of the pen, Edson referred to McIlhenny's own problems and then wrote, "If you need any help from *another Ex-Marine,* give me the word and I will be there." (Emphasis added.)

The Marine general tried to open yet another front in the publicity war. In early April he had the Marine public information officer in New York circulate the draft of one of his unused speeches to various national magazines, "as an illustration of General Edson's thinking on the merger question." The raider hero offered to write an article or submit to an interview on the subject. The initial effort failed. *Liberty* was the only magazine interested, but its editors noted the president's recent, strongly expressed sentiments and commented: "Truman seems to have had the last word." The fearless Marine might be prepared to sacrifice his career, but no national magazine seemed willing to help him cross the president.

Edson soon passed on to the public information officer the latest official policy promulgated by Forrestal. "The Secretary . . . expressed the opinion that the public is fed up with this question and that, therefore, an aggressive campaign is not desirable from the Navy's standpoint. Of course, the Secretary is much closer to public opinion than I am. My feeling, however, is that the attitude of the public is not so much that of being fed up with the question as it is of ignorance. . . . It is not a Navy versus Army question but one which concerns the nation as a whole."

Edson's earlier proposal to launch a coordinated offensive was now dead. What he probably did not know at the time was that Forrestal was already searching for a means to develop a compromise position. The secretary ordered SCOROR to prepare possible concessions, and suggested to Truman that Eberstadt serve as a mediator between the services. In a 13 May conference with the secretaries of war and the Navy, the president approved Forrestal's scheme and gave his two civilian chiefs until the end of the month to complete the effort.

The president's interest in a compromise may have arisen in part from the successful opposition of the sea services to the administration merger proposal then wending its way through Congress. Introduced in early April 1946 as Senate Bill 2044, it largely followed the Army's plan for unification and contained the same language that would allow the president to transfer agencies and functions within the single department of defense. The Senate Naval Affairs Committee held hearings on the bill and encouraged a parade of witnesses to criticize it. Among these were Forrestal, Eberstadt, Nimitz, and Vandegrift.

The commandant, under pressure from Thomas and Edson, reluctantly used strong remarks prepared by Twining and Krulak. His testimony on 6 May revealed the existence of the 1478 papers and the threat to the Corps contained therein. He then closed with an emotional appeal. "The Marine Corps thus believes it has earned this right—to have its future decided by the legislative body which created it—nothing more. . . . The bended knee is not a tradition of our Corps. If the Marine as a fighting man has not made a case for himself after 170 years, he must go. But I think you will agree with me that he has earned the right to depart with dignity and honor, not by subjugation to the status of uselessness and servility planned for him by the War Department."

The Senate Military Affairs Committee blessed the bill with a thirteen to two vote on 13 May, but unfavorable press rising from the Naval Committee hearings made it clear that it would not pass the Congress in its present form. Forrestal, whose testimony had been as damning as any to the Army viewpoint, contemplated compromise, not surrender. The Marines, however, were unsure whether they fell into the realm of the protected or the expendable.

In the public struggle, Red Mike was by far the most active of all Marine generals. His efforts increasingly focused on the Marine Corps League, though he still touched wider audiences through speeches, radio, and newspapers. The thrust of his league presentation was always what present and past Marines could do to help ensure the survival of the Corps. At the Michigan state convention of the league, he pumped up the faithful and called them to action. "We are Marines first and last, and we belong to the most select, the most elite corps of fighting men which the world has ever produced. We feel the pride of having been a member of the Corps and of having shared in its achievements. I know that you are as loyal to the Corps and as interested in its future as I am." In Kansas City he stressed the ultimate goal: "I foresee a constant threat to our organization unless some legislation can be enacted which properly protects our functions as one of the combatant branches of our armed forces." He made use of other ties as well. In Vermont he spoke to the UVM class of 1919 reunion, and in Chicago to the national convention of Alpha Tau Omega.

In accordance with the president's earlier directive, the War and Navy departments submitted the results of their negotiations to the commander in chief on 31 May 1946. They were only slightly closer to a compromise. The Navy still insisted on coordination rather than unification; the Army continued to pursue its goal of stripping land-based naval aviation and amphibious warfare from its sister services. The two secretaries and their uniformed chiefs then made a joint presentation to Truman on 4 June. On the fifteenth, the president issued his determination on the points at issue: the Navy lost on land-based air and the single department, but the Marine Corps would maintain its ascendancy in amphibious operations. At the end of the month S.2044 was duly revised to incorporate the new administration position; however, it contained none of the language in the president's 15 June letter supporting the claim of the Corps to the amphibious mission. The Senate Naval Affairs Committee held new hearings; Forrestal and other naval leaders registered their displeasure with the bill, and the situation reverted to its earlier impasse. There would not be enough votes in Congress to pass S.2044. Merger was a dead issue in the current session, but it was sure to crop up again after the November elections.

In addition to the public battle over legislation, the CNO's senior Marine waged a constant guerrilla campaign against Army encroachment onto Marine turf. Edson had considerable experience in that game after his tour at FMFPAC. He noted that the Navy's Amphibious Warfare Planning Subsection had an Army colonel assigned, but no Marine, and asked that one be requested from HQMC. He noticed that the Navy's billet on the Joint Logistics Plans Committee was unfilled, and offered a Marine colonel for the job. Regarding a proposed Army-Navy Secretariat, he pressed for USMC representation on it.

When the new Army-Navy Staff College (ANSCOL) contemplated developing a Joint Operations Manual that wandered into the realm of amphibious doctrine, Edson wrote a strident memo to the vice CNO denouncing it as an infringement on Navy-Marine Corps's prerogatives. He continued the fight with ANSCOL's successor, the Armed Forces Staff College. He argued to Admiral Gardner and the commandant that the new institution appeared to be "an entering wedge" that might destroy the Marine

Corps Schools by taking over their amphibious warfare curriculum. In a similar fashion, he decried the Navy's offer to the Army to participate in an upcoming operation to develop and test cold weather amphibious techniques. Given the ongoing debate over roles and missions, he was "amazed" that the Navy would "weaken our position so far as leadership in the amphibious field is concerned." The development of doctrine and technology should stay in the naval family, as it had in the 1930s.

The wily general continued to employ the same unorthodox channels to get things done that he had used throughout his career. In the case of the cold weather amphibious operations, he not only raised the issue with Gardner and Sherman, he also went outside the chain of command and wrote to the senior Marines in the Pacific and Atlantic Fleets. They were to use their influence at that level to ensure that Navy commanders kept the Army at arm's length in the future. In another personal letter to a colonel at the Amphibious Training Command, he provided direction on how to prevent the Army from achieving parity with the Marines in the number of instructors assigned to the staff. Later, a Drew Pearson newspaper column produced a tentative list of U.S. units for the UN command; it did not include Marines. Edson then pressed Gardner to ask Nimitz to take up the issue with the JCS. When his boss refused to pass along those concerns, the general sent the memo to a colonel serving on the UN staff and asked him to give it to Admiral Turner, the senior American military representative. Edson was not one to let a few bureaucratic hurdles slow him down.

On occasion some of the Marine officers involved in the campaign seemed paranoid (though the top secret 1478 papers gave them good reason). Newspaper articles on the 1944 Smith versus Smith controversy began to appear in late March, for no apparent reason. Certain Marines suspected that this phenomenon must be connected to the unification fight, that the Army somehow intended to use it to discredit the Corps. Edson promptly wrote to Brig. Gen. Ray Robinson, a CINCPAC staff officer, and asked for a copy of the official investigation into the incident, so that it could be "briefed and digested by Krulak and Twining." When the document arrived a few days later without its proper enclosures, Edson immediately asked for them, since they were more sympathetic to the Marine point of view than the official report. Robinson quickly complied, with the contents going to the CNO's office under a secret classification. The Marines were learning from their Army counterparts.

Often Edson and the Corps seemed to be as much at odds with the Navy as with the Army. He fought to get the headquarters of the FMF's Atlantic branch colocated with its Navy counterpart. Strangely, the Navy initially disapproved, on the grounds that there was no room on the flagship or at its Norfolk base and, in any case, coordination would be better effected if the two headquarters were not "cheek by jowl." In another instance, Edson tried to obtain an amphibious command ship (AGC) for a lengthy exercise to be conducted by the 1st Special Marine Brigade, which was being offered instead a tiny space on board a cruiser. The former chief of staff at Tarawa, no doubt recalling Julian Smith's problems there, argued that "full advantage should be taken of the lessons learned and special craft developed during the war." Three AGCs were available, but the Navy told the brigade to make do with the cruiser anyway.

Although OP30M was theoretically just the Marine representative to the Navy's strategic planning staff, Edson set about building an empire out of his tiny office. His activities ranged far beyond his narrow charter and covered every issue of interest to the Corps. Shortly after his arrival at Main Navy, he instituted a weekly meeting of all Marine officers attached to the CNO's staff. He opened it with a review of events significant to the Corps, asked each officer in turn about his recent activities, and then issued marching orders for the coming week. In this manner he ensured that they were all working toward the same end, to safeguard the interests of the Corps within the Department of the Navy. Where previously there had been individual officers operating independently in various Navy sections, he established a team effort under a parallel Marine chain of command. Since he was now coordinating "all Marine Corps matters which came under the cognizance of the Chief of Naval Operations," he asked the deputy CNO to create a new billet for a lieutenant colonel in OP30M. Headquarters promptly assigned Red Mike's choice for the position, Lt. Col. William T. Fairbourn.

Edson also had to replace his inherited military secretary. He picked Lt. Victor A. Kleber, Jr., who had served as a reconnaissance platoon commander on Iwo Jima. To the young officer, it soon seemed that he had to work as hard in peacetime in Washington as he had in the field in war. The staff of OP30M typically stayed late every evening and came in on Saturdays as well. Kleber did not mind, for he received a tremendous education from his mentor: "Every day included lessons in leadership by example."

One of the things that impressed Kleber most was the general's ability to remain calm and dignified in the most trying situations. He felt that Edson must have had tremendous emotional strength in order to retain his self-control and patience when others invariably lost theirs. The lessons could be hard ones sometimes. Kleber once volunteered to come into the office on a day off to assist his boss. His alarm clock failed to go off and he arrived very late. Red Mike's brief, low-voiced admonition—"Vic, when a Marine officer gives his word that he will be some place, he is always there"—cut much deeper than the loud tirade he would have received from other commanders.

The lieutenant discovered, as everyone else had, that it took a while to win the general's trust and friendship. But once that point was passed, Edson's quiet, courteous demeanor gave way to warmth and humor. At the end of a long day at Main Navy, the two officers often would repair to a nearby Chinese restaurant and unwind. The senior man regaled his junior colleague with stories, demonstrated his skill with chopsticks, taught him that the proper drink for a Marine officer was scotch and water, and passed along the wisdom gained in thirty years of military service.

Although Edson was heavily committed to the unification struggle, he tried to maintain his professional expertise. He requested and received orders to observe an amphibious exercise in Puerto Rico. In the middle of May he flew to San Juan, boarded the USS *Huntington* (CL-107), and participated in a landing at Roosevelt Roads. Apparently he was not satisfied with what he saw in the Caribbean, for he soon tried to reinvigorate a flagging proposal to procure land on Culebra and Vieques islands for live-fire amphibious training. No current base was suitable for such activity, which was absolutely necessary to maintain the precious skill levels gained through hard experience in war.

If Red Mike was unsure of his celebrity status now that the war was receding into the past, he had it confirmed by events in mid-August 1946. The General Electric Company sponsored a commemoration of the first anniversary of V-J Day, a television broadcast built around ten of the premier naval heroes of the Pacific war. Edson was ordered to New York, where he starred in the show along with Admiral Nimitz. From there he traveled on to Chester, Vermont, for his first visit to his hometown in years. He was the guest of honor and principal speaker at a veterans' homecoming celebration, which drew an amazing twenty-five hundred attendees from the surrounding area.

The Chester speech stood apart from Edson's other public presentations and their focus on unification. He honored the war dead, as he had at numerous similar ceremonies, and argued the necessity of maintaining a strong defense to prevent such sacrifice in the future. Then he closed with an unusual appeal. "There is a growing tendency to elect our representatives on the basis of local considerations alone, completely disregarding the viewpoints of the candidates for office on national and international issues. As a leader among nations, we must learn to act as such."

The unique and public mention of politics hinted at Edson's growing fascination with elected office. He picked up books on local history, subscribed to Vermont newspapers, and began to keep a scrapbook of articles concerning state politics. He expressed his tentative feelings on the matter to Ethel: "I still have a bee buzzing around which may or may not bite me." He went a bit further and made "casual remarks" to Paul Ballou about "senatorial possibilities a few years hence." The well-connected Vermont banker initiated a quiet campaign to make Edson's qualifications known among leading politicians in the state. The general made his own connections, too. He sent a congratulatory letter to Ernest Gibson, a progressive Republican who swept into the governorship in September on an antimachine platform. The new state leader responded and expounded on the potential for a wave of new blood in Vermont government. He added: "Sometime when I am in Washington, I shall give you a ring because I would like to talk over a couple matters with you."

One of the main reasons for Edson's look at politics was an ongoing assessment of his future in the peacetime Corps. He had survived the spring 1946 "plucking board" created by Congress to winnow the senior ranks of the naval services in the face of demobilization of 80 percent of the enlisted force. Vandegrift had pressed for the law in order to retire involuntarily some older officers rather than revert many of the younger, better colonels and generals to lower rank. That panel, composed of Lt. Gen. Holland Smith, Harry Schmidt, and Roy Geiger, did not entirely follow its precept to favor "youthfulness and wartime performance"; a few officers with mediocre records made it through the process. Edson and Thomas held onto their rank but were the two most junior brigadiers to do so.

Edson was not so confident about the promotion board to major general coming up in late fall. He rated his chances for selection as poor: "It looks to me as though the wind is blowing in the old channels of seniority and I doubt if they will promote me over the heads of some eight or ten of the old guard." (All but two of the fifteen brigadiers ahead of him on the list had reached that rank after he had.) If he did not make it this time, it would probably be several years, given that openings in a smaller, stable force would come only through retirements. Beyond that things looked even bleaker. "So far as I can see, my chances of getting more than two stars are so nebulous that they can be counted as nil. I would like to get them, but on the other hand I do not believe that I want to hang on for the next twelve years, filling innocuous jobs or stifling the wheels of progress as Julian did, for example, if I can find any other lucrative or interesting thing to do on the retired list."

• Another factor in his thoughts may have been the seemingly endless press of work in the Corps. The long hours at Main Navy left him constantly exhausted; on his rare days off, he often slept away the entire morning. (He would not discover until months later that a medical problem accounted for his unaccustomed fatigue.) A new law on military leave also may have caused him to evaluate the hold that the Marines had on his time. In order to comply with the legislation, Edson requested a summary of his leave history and discovered that he had lost 343 days of vacation over the course of his career—days he rated but had been unable to use. He had not taken any leave since 1941 and had four months of it on the books. He rarely had time to see his youngest son, still living with Ethel's mother in Maine while he completed grade school. The general's thoughts must have turned in that direction when he received a plaintive letter from Bobby during the summer; the youngster wanted to move to Washington in the fall to be with his parents instead of going off to boarding school.

Edson had other reasons to be restive. Several months at home had done nothing to improve his personal life. If anything, it made the situation worse, for he had to be more circumspect in pursuing his relationships with other women. His correspondence with Bibs had tapered off and slowly died after her marriage in the fall of 1945, but he remained close to the reporter. She returned to the States in January 1946 and Edson got together with her on those few occasions when she could come to Washington. They had lunch or dinner, and even took a drive through a park one afternoon. But those rare moments were not enough. Generally he felt tired, unmotivated, depressed; he hated the trap that Washington had become. "I dislike it as much as ever, with the result that my job is not being done as well as it should be, and I feel that I am not doing myself, or anyone else, or anything else, much good." He was ready to consider an alternative to the straitjacket of peacetime staff work and domestic unhappiness.

In late August Edson requested his first vacation in five years. He asked for thirty days to go home to Vermont, visit with his mother-in-law in Maine, make a trip to Canada with his sons, and bring his mother and sister to Washington. He was scarcely halfway through his schedule in late September when an urgent letter from the commandant sent him scrambling to San Francisco on unification business. After the interruption he picked up where he had left off.

It was a thoroughly enjoyable time. He went on a successful deer hunting expedition, basked in the unusually warm fall weather, and attended a large family gathering reminiscent of the old Edson reunions. He mixed in a little business too; Paul Ballou introduced him to various editors and leading citizens, and the two men dropped in on Governor Gibson. But it was mainly a badly needed chance to relax and recharge his energy before returning to Washington and the unification fray, which was just beginning to heat up again.

His fellow Vermonters found him as congenial as ever, in spite of the heavy burdens, and humble, in spite of his fame. The Chester High School seniors dedicated their yearbook to the Pacific hero, but after they recounted his exploits, the students remarked: "Yet on his return to Chester . . . one of his major interests was to tramp again these stairs and poke his head into this classroom and that, where once he learned about the future." Paul Ballou's wife also felt Red Mike's attitude worthy of note. "May I pass on to you what seemed a wonderful compliment? After your visit to Chester, one of the women there said to me, 'He is the same old Merritt. All his successes have not changed or spoiled him at all.'"

Chapter 18

"And to Keep Our Honor Clean"

T he victory of the naval services over the 1946 Senate unification bill was short-lived. Truman called his service secretaries together on 10 September and assigned them to negotiate another compromise, so that legislation could be introduced in the new Congress in January 1947. The burden of developing an acceptable bill fell largely to two men, Maj. Gen. Lauris Norstad of the Army Air Forces and Vice Admiral Sherman. The latter choice did not please Red Mike, who no doubt recalled the admiral's failure to assist him in getting representation on Army staffs in 1945. Edson considered him "a two faced rat," an ambitious man bent on becoming CNO by any means possible. The Corps could not expect the admiral to look out for its interest.

After a late summer lull, the publicity battle revved up again in the fall of 1946. Army partisans introduced a promerger resolution at the American Legion convention in San Francisco in September, which prompted Edson's recall from leave and an emergency trip out west. After much lobbying with the Standing Committee of the legion, the general thought he had things under control, but the rank and file ignored the executive body's recommendation and voted for the measure on the floor. Edson then fell back to a second line of defense; since the Standing Committee was favorable to the Navy-Marine point of view, he would try to persuade them to take no overt action to implement the resolution or speak out on behalf of merger.

In evaluating the legion affair, Edson fingered the real threat to a successful antiunification campaign. "There are many men of influence in the American Legion who will back the Navy's and Marine Corps's battle provided, of course, the Navy Department can determine upon a definite policy within its own household." As the primary liaison between the two naval services, the general knew better than anyone else that his earlier recommendation to develop a common plan of attack had generated no result. Increasingly the Navy acted unilaterally without even keeping the Corps informed. In one instance Edson could tell Thomas only "of a conference which rumor states will be held between a representative of the Navy Department and a representative of the Air Forces on this matter."

The Marine Corps had internal divisions of its own. The antimerger effort was geographically split between Quantico, HQMC, and Main Navy. The officers involved were not always able to maintain close liaison. Moreover, even when they had a common policy, the views of these men did not always coincide with those of their seniors and contemporaries. Many officers hesitated to get involved, either because they feared for their careers or they saw it as a dirty political battle beneath the dignity of the military profession.

The commandant, in particular, was reluctant to sail into the prevailing wind blowing from the White House and the Pentagon. Nor did he always see the issues as important as his subordinates portrayed them. At one point the Army raised difficulties about the FMF headquarters in the Pacific and Atlantic, since it saw them as corps-level organizations violating the Navy's agreement to limit Marine units to division strength. Edson wanted to fight the issue as a matter of principle, but Vandegrift "tacitly acceded" to Army demands and limited the two commands to administrative functions. As one Marine later phrased it, after the bended-knee speech the commandant had been "taken to the woodshed by President Truman" and "was never again in the forefront of the battle."

After pressing especially hard on one issue, the raider hero feared he had alienated his closest friend, Thomas. But the commandant's right-hand man reassured Edson. "I am not easily offended and don't fool yourself—you and I are sticking together and there will *be no misunderstanding*. It must be that way as you and I are trying to make an awful lot out of a little and I believe we are getting away with it. As far as matters both official and personal are concerned I rate you as tops for this outfit of ours. I mean it that way too."

The Navy's lack of direction was reflected in its failure to generate a coherent publicity campaign. In October 1946, long after Edson and his cohorts had geared up the Marine Corps League, Admiral Robbins was still pleading with the assistant secretary of the Navy to goad the Navy League into action. Red Mike was particularly angry after he participated in the Navy Day celebration in Detroit, which he criticized in a report to

Forrestal's director of public relations. He found that "press coverage was poor," the only advance notice was in the "social columns," and the downtown ceremony "attracted only curious passers-by such as happens at a Salvation Army street meeting."

In December 1946 the general took an opportunity to get away from the Washington scene and participate in a more enjoyable pastime. In the aftermath of the war some western European nations decided to revive the moribund International Shooting Union (ISU). The NRA asked Edson to be the American delegate to an ISU organizational meeting in Sweden. Edson flew there for the conference. It was a pleasant trip until it came time to return home. Bad weather and mechanical problems turned the transatlantic journey into a three-day marathon spent in planes, trains, and airport lounges. That brought on a severe cold, and aggravated a condition that had been bothering him for some time.

During the previous summer Edson had experienced a sudden onset of back pain that radiated down his left leg. For three or four days he could hardly walk. A similar bout occurred in November and never fully went away, though a numbness or tingling in his left foot sometimes replaced the pain. Prolonged sitting seemed to make it worse, so he developed the habit of slouching low in his chair and propping up his feet on his desk or the wall. His staff found this behavior unusual for someone normally so fastidious, but he never hinted of his trouble. After the trip to Europe it was bad enough that he went to the dispensary. The doctor found him not qualified for duty and recommended hospitalization. He put that off for the moment, but pain and fatigue became his constant companions.

As if the physical problems were not enough, Edson's worst fears about promotion were realized. He had not expected to be among "the chosen few," but he received a telegram in Sweden confirming that seniority had returned as the guiding principle. The four officers selected were the three ground officers at the very top of the list and the most senior aviator (just one number below Edson). That would not have bothered him, except for his belief that the ground officers did not deserve it based upon their war records. Leo D. Hermle already had been passed over twice for two stars. Alfred H. Noble had been passed over once during the war, and Red Mike thought he had not performed well as chief of staff for III Amphibious Corps. Franklin A. Hart had been promoted to brigadier nearly a year after Edson. (In terms of time as a general, Red Mike was third in seniority and thus should have had the promotion, except for the odd quirk that placed latecomers to brigadier ahead of him because they were senior in their permanent rank of colonel.)

It was obvious to Red Mike that "from now on it is going to be seniority and good-fellowship which count, and combat records will be secondary." That would affect his plans. "I do not know yet what I shall do, but I have no intention of doing the work of some officer I consider inferior to me for the next five or six years just on the hopes of eventually being promoted. It is not worth it, even though I could well use the difference in retired pay between that of a brigadier and a major general."

Red Mike might have been down emotionally and physically, but he was not about to declare himself out of the merger fight. The election in November of a Republican-dominated Congress had buoyed Marine hopes, since they expected that body to naturally oppose the Democratic administration's plans. But events in late December gave Edson reason to be concerned. He was "considerably distressed" that the reorganized Senate committee system had diluted the influence of the Navy and Marine Corps. The new Armed Services Committee (SASC) tentatively included four members of the old Military Affairs body and no representation from its former Naval Affairs counterpart. Edson telephoned an influential constituent of Senator Chan Gurney of South Dakota, the SASC chairman, and stated that Senator E. V. Robertson was willing to forego the chair of the Commerce Committee if he could get the same spot on SASC's Naval Subcommittee. Red Mike asked if the man would pass that information on to Gurney and urge him to appoint Robertson. The Wyoming senator ended up in SASC, where he would prove to be a stalwart on behalf of the Corps.

The negotiations between Norstad and Sherman continued throughout the fall and into the winter. As they progressed, Edson funneled copies of some of their work to the commandant and Thomas. These documents included proposed legislative language and a draft of the joint letter that the War and Navy secretaries were preparing for the president. Since Red Mike stressed repeatedly that these papers were only for the eyes of the two generals, he probably had obtained them in a surreptitious manner. The secretaries forwarded their final compromise to the president, who announced the new plan on 16 January 1947. Vandegrift and Thomas must have closely held Edson's inside information, for the news came as a "complete surprise" to other Marines involved in the fight.

Truman sent a letter to Congress the next day, spelling out his legislative plans. The new bill would incorporate most of the 1946 compromise, but he promised that roles and missions would be set forth in an executive order. Since the latter could be changed by the stroke of a president's pen, it provided no real protection to the Corps. Edson fumed over the proposal:

Although this looks like a compromise by the Army, it is actually a sell-out by the Navy horse-traders, and the thing is so worded and the ground work so laid that the Army will achieve its full objectives in only a matter of a few years. This will include elimination of the Marine Corps as a combatant force; the absorption of naval air; and the creation of a great, super, General Staff. The last in particular, in my opinion, will eventually prove disastrous for this country. The whole thing stinks of politics, undercover deals, and a complete sell-out by the Navy; and it was so unnecessary if the Navy could before now have reached a definite policy on this merger question within its own house. . . . The failure to achieve this end rests with no one except Nimitz and Sherman.

Obviously the general was not so upset with the politics and undercover deals as he was with the outcome, for he had been using the same tactics himself for quite some time. The day after the president's announcement, Edson, Thomas, Twining, and others met to plan their strategy for the coming campaign. Their goals were simple: Prevent the creation of a unified staff, have the roles and missions of the services spelled out in law, and get the commandant on the Joint Chiefs of Staff. To achieve these aims, they would educate the public on the dangers of a general staff, seek allies among other organizations (such as the National Guard), and lobby Congress.

Secretary Forrestal acted promptly to forestall any activities that might undermine the new compromise. In an 18 January message he extolled the virtues of the unification plan and stated his belief that it provided sufficient protection for the Marine Corps and naval aviation. "The plan therefore is deserving of the loyal and wholehearted support of all within the naval service." Accompanying extracts from Navy regulations made his meaning plain. The rules prohibited any officer, active or retired, from communicating with Congress on pending legislation, or even responding to congressional requests for information, except as authorized by the Navy Department. The Navy had finally promulgated a single, clear position on unification, but it was not to the liking of the Corps.

This latest effort to muzzle military opposition made the news in late January. When the VFW's National Security Committee met to consider its stand on the merger, Army witnesses made strong statements in favor of it, but Navy officers refused to say much at all. The VFW commander, Louis E. Starr, wrote the president about this and received a public response. The *Washington Post* headlined the story "Truman's Gag on Navy Views of Service Unity Seen Relaxed," but the actual words of the president's statement were less reassuring. He said he had not prohibited officials from talking to bodies such as the VFW, but he did object to "newspaper articles and other propaganda by unauthorized members of either the Army or the Navy. Any member of the naval organization *who has authority to speak for the Navy* certainly has the right to appear before your committee and state *the Navy's position* on this or any other subject." (Emphasis added.) Given Forrestal's earlier actions, this effectively meant no one could speak against unification.

Edson was not in position to do much publicly at the moment. He finally entered the naval hospital at Bethesda on 9 January, and the doctors made a preliminary diagnosis of a ruptured intervertebral disc. Over the next few days X-rays and tests seemed to confirm the nature of the problem, and Red Mike insisted upon surgery when the choice was put to him. The doctors had to postpone the operation, though, until they could cure the case of hookworm they had discovered. Now the general realized why his energy seemed so depleted. He traced both problems to the summer of 1944 and the Marianas operation. He had fallen and landed on his back on a rock, and later he had experienced some difficulty walking. He guessed that he had picked up the hookworm during the same campaign.

While Edson awaited surgery scheduled for 28 January, he was free to come and go. Although he spent a few nights at home and went into the office occasionally, he generally entertained visitors and conducted work in his hospital room. Kleber brought out the news and paperwork from Main Navy, and the general dictated memos and letters to a clerk. Among the visitors was Hunter Hurst; he delivered a copy of the merger bill then being drafted by Sherman and Norstad. It contained few of the already minimal redeeming features of the president's message to Congress and seemed a complete capitulation to the Army point of view.

After a conference at his home, Edson assigned two officers to develop a thorough brief on the entire unification question, a document the general could use to persuade key figures in Congress and the media. Krulak would draft a memorandum outlining the main points of the debate, and Hurst would compile supporting documents in a series of appendices. Then Edson began the lobbying campaign he and Thomas had envisioned during a mid-January strategy session. The two brigadiers attended the annual dinner of the Alfalfa Club, a select group of capital insiders, and sat at a table with several congressmen, including the chairman of the House Armed Services Committee. A few days later Edson went to the Capitol and called on Senators Aiken and Flanders, both of Vermont. He promised to provide them with a detailed memorandum of his views on unification. He also visited Gen. Milton Reckord, head of the NRA, legislative liaison for the National Guard Association, and an acquaintance from the prewar matches. Edson gave the general a Twining paper outlining the dangers of unification for the Guard. The Marines saw these weekend warriors as excellent allies, since they were "politically potent in every state," and there was a reservoir of ill feeling among the many Guard generals who had lost their commands to regular officers during the war.

The doctors wielded their knives on 28 January. It was a relatively short operation, only thirty-five minutes, and Edson (under spinal anesthesia) was awake throughout the entire procedure. Pain and fever ensued for the next few days, but the doctors had Red Mike up and walking a few trial steps just seven days after the surgery, even though he could not yet stand or sit up straight. Daily physical therapy followed, and he took his first walk outdoors two weeks later. A little over a month after the operation, he went home on an outpatient basis.

Red Mike was not idle in spite of the handicaps, and Ethel found it amusing that he was labeled unfit for duty. "He has been carrying on his job with his secretaries coming to the hospital almost as well as if he were at the office. Also having conferences in his room! I expect our house will become a small Marine Corps Headquarters when he gets back."

In the days immediately following Edson's surgery, he, Hurst, and Krulak conferred several times over the initial drafts of their antiunification brief. Krulak completed his memo before the appendices were ready, so Edson wasted no time and fired off that part of the document to Senator Aiken. The general's cover letter focused on what he saw as "the most dangerous potentiality of the proposed plan for unification of the armed services—the growth of a National General Staff," which would "destroy our type of government from within." He argued that it also made no sense to abandon a system that had won two world wars for the one used by the losers in those same conflicts.

Aiken visited Red Mike in the hospital several days later, and the two Vermonters conferred by phone in succeeding days. It appeared that this relationship might bear some fruit when the president sent the Sherman-Norstad merger bill to Congress in late February. Senator Aiken, chairman of the Committee on Expenditures in the Executive Departments, waged a floor fight to get the proposed legislation into his domain, but a Senate voice vote gave it to the Armed Services Committee instead.

The day after this unsuccessful effort, the commandant convened a meeting of Marine generals in the Washington area and announced his official policy on the latest merger bill. The Corps would not oppose the legislation, but it would make an effort to have the bill amended to "adequately protect the status and traditional functions of the Corps." One other thing became clear; the Marines would go it alone in this fight and no longer look to the Navy for guidance or assistance. When Sherman forwarded a copy of the bill to Vandegrift for his input, the commandant stated simply: "There is nothing to be added to the views which I have already expressed in my numerous memoranda and statements on the subject."

Thomas and Edson moved quickly to ensure that the Marine Corps would mount its own fully coordinated campaign. After a lengthy meeting on 7 March they decided to establish a formal mechanism to guide the effort. Red Mike spent the next few days getting the group organized. The commandant gave it official sanction in a 14 March order that named the raider hero senior member of the ponderously titled Board to Conduct Research and Prepare Material in Connection With Pending Legislation. The group included Thomas, Twining, Krulak, Hurst, and seven other officers.

The board operated out of a conference room at HQMC, though the group had only one formal session. Edson announced that he intended to organize the operation "on a businesslike basis," and he assigned each officer to lobby specific congressmen. Twining "shuddered in horror" at what he thought was a "ham handed approach." He and Krulak returned to Quantico, where they continued to work largely on their own. Since no one was assigned full time to the board, Red Mike never did produce the type of smooth-running staff that had become his trademark, though that made little difference in the end.

Given those limitations on the board, the conference room became a command post; officers showed up as necessary to receive new orders, make progress reports, turn in drafts of documents, and discuss plans. Major Jonas Platt and his staff of three clerks handled the flood of letters and memos, but the real work generally occurred elsewhere. Individuals and small teams generated ideas; met in private with legislators, reporters, and prominent citizens; and tried to broadcast their views to the public. Given the stance of Truman and Forrestal, all this had to be done as quietly as possible. The Quantico officers adopted a name befitting their awkward status; they became "The Chowder Society," which evoked "a mythical institution appearing in a popular comic strip." Edson always thought of his group in more descriptive terms; in his view they were "termites," small insects invisibly burrowing away in the heart of a huge structure. For the next few months the officers of the Edson Board and the Chowder Society would carry the ball for their fellow Marines and for the nation.

*　　*　　*

The Senate Armed Services Committee opened hearings on the administration's merger bill (S.758) on 18 March 1947. A parade of senior defense officials and military leaders unanimously supported the legislation. Forrestal, Nimitz, and Sherman each insisted that the proposed law provided adequate protection for all service branches and would enhance national security. With favorable testimony from both military departments, Edson grew pessimistic about the outcome in the Senate. In private he criticized the Navy for adopting the political course of compromise and inadvertently delivering a complete victory to the Army: "They have lost their shirts, as any amateur would when playing against experts." At the same time, he recognized his own inexperience in the field and his vulnerability. "But who am I to talk like that? For I am dabbling in the political pond, too, trying my best to defeat the thing—and if I get burned at it, I will have no one else to blame. But feeling as I do that the adoption of the proposed unification will be such a national calamity, I can not do otherwise."

The notion of an ill-fated battle against the odds began to permeate Edson's thinking. He likened the situation to "having a bull by the tail. . . . I am in this thing so far now that I can not let go." His concern seemed to go beyond a sense of duty, though, and he exhibited a rare level of emotion. He confessed to friends that he thought of little else and had begun to lose sleep worrying about the outcome. A friendly letter to Edwin Bond, a United Service Organizations (USO) official, turned into ten pages of single-spaced, typed arguments against the merger. "I did not intend to write a book when I started this letter. But . . . if I have made you see only a fraction of the potential dangers which lurk in the shadows and haunt me day and night . . . then I will consider my time has been well spent." Edson wrote his mother that "it has become something of an obsession with me."

If he felt pessimistic about the outcome, he nevertheless redoubled his efforts to prevent passage of the bill. On 15 April he flew to New York in an attempt to generate media opposition to the merger. He spent the morning talking to a senior editor in the Hearst newspaper chain, which had not yet taken a strong stand on the issue. In the afternoon Edson kept an appointment with Hanson Baldwin, the influential military analyst for the *New York Times*. The writer agreed that the military was encroaching into the civilian sector, but he was unconvinced that the merger and the joint staff presented a threat to democracy. Although the general found the second meeting much less satisfactory than the first, it did open up a channel of communication that Baldwin made use of later.

Things looked bleaker upon his return to Washington. Twining and Krulak had drafted yet another hard-hitting speech for the commandant's upcoming SASC testimony, but Vandegrift decided to substitute a milder statement that addressed only the narrow issue of Marine Corps roles and missions. Edson guessed "some unknown skullduggery had been at work on the CMC." Others later learned that the commandant's counsel and liaison with Congress, Col. John W. ("Buddy") Knighton, had been one of the primary instigators. It probably did not take much persuasion, since the revised speech was in line with Vandegrift's policy announced on 4 March. Edson sought to lessen the damage by talking to Joe Chambers, the former Raider and fellow Medal of Honor winner, now legislative assistant to SASC. The two men discussed questions that friendly committee members could ask to elicit the desired information from the commandant.

Vandegrift's testimony on 22 and 24 April accomplished little. He offered amendments to the bill that would incorporate Marine Corps roles and missions, but under intense questioning the commandant seemed unable to articulate a strong defense of his position. On 24 April, when Edson tried to convince him to read a Hurst-drafted statement of clarification, Vandegrift turned him down. In his memoirs, the commandant would state that his testimony had carried the day, but at the time the termites were downcast, for in their eyes Vandegrift had failed to achieve even his narrow goal of protecting the Corps.

Retired Admiral Halsey and Marine Reserve Maj. Gen. Melvin Maas followed with denunciations of the bill, but their efforts appeared to carry little weight in the absence of significant opposition within the active duty ranks. Maas, a former congressman from Minnesota, elicited one interesting observation from Senator Styles Bridges: "I would like to have a few [more] witnesses like him . . . to break the monotony of having so many from the departments who are just following a very stilted course here and who are under orders."

Edson was doing his best to oblige the senator. Upon his return to Washington several days earlier, he had continued his frenzied lobbying efforts. On 16 April he saw Senators Aiken, Flanders, and Robertson and deposited copies of the Hurst-Krulak brief with each. When Edson spoke to Robertson, he repeated his earlier offer to appear as a witness in the SASC hearings. The Wyoming senator was still reluctant to accept, since he did not want to be responsible for the consequences (presumably the negative impact on Red Mike's career).

Edson spent the rest of the day trying to reach yet more people. He visited General Reckord to reiterate the need for National Guard input.

He spoke to General Worton, his replacement on the CNO's staff, and asked him to pass a copy of the brief on to his friend and fellow Bostonian, Representative John W. McCormack. Edson and Lt. Col. Robert D. Heinl, Jr., another board member, then met with the senior assistant to Mark Sullivan, a syndicated newspaper columnist. The staffer seemed impressed by their arguments and accepted a copy of the brief; later Sullivan advocated some of the Marine positions in his columns. Edson next spoke to General Shepherd, the assistant commandant. He left yet another copy of the brief with him and convinced his friend to incorporate many of the arguments into a scheduled speech before the Marine Corps League. Red Mike, still on convalescent leave, wrapped up the day by meeting with Hurst, then finally headed home at midnight.

The next day Edson flew to Burlington. Although his trip included a visit home, his main activities were speeches to the Vermont VFW gathering in honor of the national commander, and to the UVM Alpha Tau Omega alumni banquet. The topic, of course, was unification. The Vermont papers carried a surprise for the general on 19 April. Under headlines touting a new state law, he read: "With the Department of Public Safety a legal reality, Statehouse rumors indicated that Brigadier General Merritt Edson of the U.S. Marine Corps has been offered the post of head of the new state police." Although the details were news to Edson, the idea of a state job offer was not entirely unexpected. Back in January Aiken had told him that the governor had a position in mind for him. Red Mike later wrote and asked Paul Ballou for additional information, but he had since given it little thought.

During Edson's stay in the hospital, his future had been the subject of considerable interest from other quarters as well. The NRA had offered him the directorship of the skeet organization, a position the general considered "worth thinking about." The day after Red Mike's operation, Thomas had stopped in for a visit and informed Edson that, when his recovery was complete, he would report to HQMC to fill Thomas's shoes as director of Plans and Policies. Edson asked Austin for his opinion. The former lieutenant, now working for an American bank in the Philippines, found the NRA job the most appealing because the Corps was no longer worth the mental anguish, and politics depended "too much on public caprice."

On his return to Washington Red Mike found the expected letter from the governor. Gibson did not offer the state police job, but only wondered when Edson might retire and come back to the state, "because I foresee where you can be of great service to us." In his response, the general wrote that he was slated for an important post at HQMC, though retirement was an option and he was willing to consider alternatives. Edson found the governor's letter "peculiar," but he hoped his reply did "not close the door to any offer he wants to make and yet tells him that I am not around begging for a job." Although he called Vermont to get a copy of the state police law, and asked HQMC to calculate the exact date when he would reach thirty years, Red Mike was still a long way from deciding to leave the Corps.

Edson's antiunification activities were in the process of making the decision for him. On 23 April he left a copy of his brief with the commandant; the next morning he received a phone call from Vandegrift requesting his immediate presence at headquarters. Edson had a fair idea what the meeting would entail, so he drafted a letter of resignation. It got right to the point. Since he was a likely witness before both the Senate and the House of Representatives, he requested retirement "in order to feel free to express my personal views on this proposed legislation without embarrassment to or as a representative of the Marine Corps."

At headquarters, the commandant wanted to discuss the brief. He noted that the document bore signs of having been prepared by the Marine Corps and might be construed as representing an official position. To avoid that eventuality, he asked Edson to sign any copies he provided to others. Red Mike agreed and then handed his letter to the commandant. Vandegrift was astonished; he rejected the offer, and said he had no intention of preventing anyone from expressing personal views on the matter. Afterward, Edson felt that the confrontation had been useful. The commandant now knew how strongly he felt about the merger and how far he was prepared to go to fight it.

A few days later, Senator Robertson told Edson about a conversation with Forrestal. The secretary had remarked that a small group of Marine officers was working against the merger bill in spite of express orders forbidding unauthorized contact with Congress. Apparently Forrestal had a similar discussion with Vandegrift. The next day Thomas told Edson that the commandant had talked to someone at Main Navy and he now wanted "to warn the termites to watch their step or they might find themselves in trouble."

Edson kept up his contacts with politicians and the press. At a conference of most of the termites on 23 April, Edson gave them guidance and put them to work drafting a completely new bill that would incorporate protection for the Corps and many of the coordinating features of the Eberstadt Plan. The next day (after the commandant's final SASC testimony and his rejection of Edson's resignation), Robertson and Edson met to plan further action. The general provided information on how to subpoena the 1478 papers, suggested some amendments to the senator, and offered to supply an entirely new bill. Robertson especially liked the latter idea. Over the next three days Edson and his board worked feverishly to complete the draft legislation and produce a statement for the commandant's use before the House committee. At the same time, Edson used Twining and Krulak as a sounding board to prepare his own testimony.

In the middle of this hectic schedule, the general took time out to celebrate his fiftieth birthday. At breakfast Ethel gave him his present, a Remington portable typewriter, which both surprised him and struck his fancy. In addition, he received a set of tickets to hear Oscar Levant in concert that evening. He took his wife and Bobby, and for the first time in quite awhile he seemed positive about his family life: "It was quite enjoyable and a very pleasant day in every way."

The reporter no longer seemed to factor in his thoughts, but he was coming to rely more and more on a younger female Marine officer he had met at headquarters. This relationship seems to have been a simple friendship, since he and Ethel often joined the Marine and her boyfriend in social activities. However, the officer was a strong influence in his life at a rare time when he needed a shoulder to lean on. Whenever he felt down, he talked to her or took her for a brief drive in the country, which invariably raised his spirits. "She is a grand person—a sincere and sympathetic friend to windward—whose understanding and friendship cannot be expressed in words, nor would they be understood by hardly anyone else, including ERE."

As the end of April 1947 approached, Edson waded deeper into the political morass. He delivered the completed draft bill to Robertson. The senator recommended minor changes and then asked the general to find someone to sponsor a companion measure in the House. Red Mike passed his brief and the draft bill to Representative Clarence Brown. Robertson then asked Edson to provide detailed comments on a Sherman-Norstad letter regarding the supposed economies of merger. The general put board member Lt. Col. Samuel R. Shaw to work on that project and the senator eventually used it in the committee hearings.

Subsequently, Robertson and Edson discussed means to involve civilian groups in the antimerger effort. They hoped to persuade politically powerful bodies such as the National Chamber of Commerce and the Association of Manufacturers to oppose the expanded government control of industry inherent in the present bill. Edson and Hurst met with Senator Joseph McCarthy on 30 April and gave him a copy of the brief. He promised to appear at the remainder of the hearings and make unification his first order of business. The termites were more than lobbyists now. They were assuming the role of legislative staffers for those in Congress fighting the merger.

After an unbroken string of favorable government witnesses, Chairman Gurney began to press for an end to the SASC hearings. Robertson, now looking desperately for a means to derail the political express train, insisted that one more witness be called. When questioned by Army supporters on the committee, the Wyoming senator refused to provide a name. On 2 May he told Edson that he was scheduled to testify on the seventh. A House committee had already asked the general to appear at a later date, so the stage was set. Red Mike would have ample opportunity to make his case before Congress and the nation.

Edson's intervention in the legislative process came at just the right time, for the commandant was waivering even more. He may have been influenced by Knighton's gloomy assessments, because he directed that officer to develop a new amendment to replace those previously submitted to SASC. The proposed paragraph would water down the strong protection provided by the initial listing of roles and missions. When Knighton passed the commandant's decision to Edson for action, Red Mike decried it as the same backsliding that he had observed earlier from the Navy. In his view, the Corps had to hold its ground and depend on strong support in the House to force the other side to compromise. Thomas agreed with Edson, but they could only comply with Vandegrift's wishes.

The morning papers of Monday, 5 May, broke the story that an unidentified Marine would be among the last witnesses before SASC. The articles quoted Senator Robertson's description of the secret individual as "a good American" and "no little lieutenant." When Thomas and Edson went in to see the commandant later that day, Vandegrift asked if they knew the Marine's identity. He grinned when he heard the answer and commiserated over what he considered to be Edson's misfortune. Red Mike's name leaked out the next day; he received a call from Admiral Robbins, who demanded a copy of any prepared statement so that it could receive appropriate approval. Edson dodged that requirement by saying simply that his remarks would be extemporaneous.

The commandant continued to draw himself further back from the brink of opposition. Edson asked that Lt. Col. DeWolf Schatzel, a board member, be allowed to sit behind him at the SASC hearings and provide assistance. Vandegrift refused, because it might put a seal of official approval on what was supposed to be Edson's personal views. The commandant testified before the House committee the evening of 6 May and made essentially the same pitch that he had made to SASC for writing the roles and missions of the Marine Corps into law. Here the reception was much more sympathetic. In fact, several congressmen prodded the commandant to reveal the Army's designs on the Corps as stated in the 1478 papers. But he refused to be drawn into criticism of the other services or their leaders. The result was a halfhearted plea to protect the Corps from a threat that Vandegrift would not describe. The termites again were disappointed at the lost opportunity to hammer home the dangers of the bill to the Marines and to the nation.

The commandant did face a tough situation. He had to make his concerns known, but he did not want to go so far as to antagonize Forrestal and Truman into relieving him, which would prevent him from exerting any influence at all. On the other hand, a strong statement by the leading Marine, coupled with his relief, might have created sufficient controversy to doom the administration bill. The courtly Virginian shrank from that type of confrontation, so his role in the battle became a marginal one. Edson, ever the fighter, had no sympathy for Vandegrift's predicament.

Edson's disgust came to a head between Vandegrift's testimony on 6 May and his own scheduled presentation to SASC the next morning. During the commandant's testimony before the House, a committee member had asked Vandegrift to respond to a proposed compromise solution on roles and missions. Shepherd and Knighton advised him to wait until after Edson's testimony so that the reaction of Forrestal and Truman could be determined. In Red Mike's parlance, their stance was "if his neck is chopped off we will fall in line; if it isn't, we will take a firmer stand." Edson grew angry at his situation: told to defeat a bill without visible support from the superior who had given the order; in fact, with the commandant sometimes working at cross purposes.

The raider hero felt more alone now than he had on the Ridge or along the Coco. "I am getting a bit tired of doing the dirty work—something which [Vandegrift] has shoved off on me ever since the war began five years ago. If this present bill is modified as it should be, and as I believe both the CMC and the Navy would like to have it—it will be because I stuck my neck out when no one else would do so."

In that defiant mood, Edson reported to the Capitol on 7 May. He began his testimony with a brief statement highlighting the dangers of giving the military too much influence in the development of policy for defense, foreign affairs, and the economy. Senator Robertson, the first questioner, began by noting that the general "has this matter very clearly and firmly in mind, and has made a great study of it." Edson's advice over the past few weeks obviously had impressed him. Robertson and McCarthy then presented the general with a series of questions that allowed him to bring out specific shortcomings in the merger bill.

Senators Gurney and Tydings frequently interrupted, with mostly antagonistic questions, but Edson succeeded in making all the points that Vandegrift had ignored. When the general started in on the defects of the proposed Joint Staff, the chairman cut him off and explained that the language would be rewritten to include Marines on that body. Red Mike fired back that he had more on his agenda than just a parochial concern for the Corps, that he wanted no such staff at all, since it was a danger to the nation. After one exchange, Tydings admitted that he favored the military domination made possible by the bill. "When the atomic bomb is pretty well scattered in other nations, your one hope of survival will be the strong authority at the top. It will have to regulate, whether we like it or whether we do not like it, the civilian as well as the military population. Do not use that against me in the next election."

In the afternoon session, Edson touched upon the issue of budgetary savings; he brought out a 1932 quote from General MacArthur that opposed the added expense generated from additional layers of bureaucracy, a statement made about a similar unification proposal of that era. At the end of his testimony, it seemed obvious that Edson had changed few minds within the committee. But he had registered a telling critique and made the point that there was not universal support for the bill among officers. Nor was his concern that of someone merely looking out for his service, which would have softened the impact. For the first time there was a public record of opposition within the military.

The immediate effect on public opinion was muted. The *Washington Post* did not even mention Edson's testimony the next day, nor did the Associated Press news service. Perhaps the one-star general was not sufficiently newsworthy. Red Mike felt that it was "censorship at the source" by those elements of the media in favor of merger. Many major newspapers continued to carry favorable commentary on the administration bill. The *New York Times* found a "near unanimity of sentiment behind it"; the *Washington News* thought that the American people had "long ago made their decision . . . for a unified command." The *Washington Post,* using data suspiciously like that contained in the Army's 1478 papers, argued that the Corps had no lock on the amphibious mission.

A *Washington Times* editorial cartoon of 9 May at least noted that there was opposition. Captioned "Is this shotgun marriage going to last?" it depicted the service secretaries as husband and wife, Congress as the preacher, and Truman as the gun-toting father. When the minister noted the couple's promise to live happily ever after, the president replied: "That's what I told them to say." Oddly enough, Vandegrift (the most mild Marine critic) was cast as a baby shaking his fist at the secretary of war.

Edson was not the only person to testify before SASC against the merger bill, but he was the only active-duty officer to do so, and his was the strongest criticism. Retired Admirals King and Halsey both argued against the proposed legislation, but they made little impression. King thought only that the process should go slower, that minor changes should precede radical ones to allow a testing period. Halsey prefaced his remarks by saying that he had made only a brief study of the bill, then largely limited his concerns to the future of the Marines and naval aviation. He spoke for only a short period and generated few questions from the committee. Eberstadt focused on many of the same faults outlined by Edson, such as the "disturbingly general and indefinite" powers of the proposed defense secretary. But he demonstrated little of the passion that Edson brought to the issue.

The day after his testimony, Edson wrote a supplemental statement, which Robertson inserted in the record the next day. Then he wrote a speech for the Wyoming legislator to use when he introduced the Marine-written bill into the Senate. Schatzel worked on a draft too, but Robertson eventually picked Edson's version and delivered the speech and the bill to the Senate on 14 May. Edson and various members of the board lobbied additional senators and media leaders. The general sent copies of his brief to Bob Payne, involved with West Coast newspapers, to Eddie Jones of *Time,* and to the Washington head of the United Press. He talked at length with the UP representative soon thereafter and seemed to make some headway.

Edson met or talked to Robertson almost every day during this period. The SASC hearings were now over, but the committee met regularly in closed session to discuss revisions to the administration bill and the new Robertson/termite bill. Most of the meetings were so secret that not even staffers such as Joe Chambers were allowed to attend, but the senator kept Edson informed of events. The picture grew increasingly bleak. Finally, on 24 May Robertson informed Edson that nearly every vote was now going against them. The senator's alternate bill was dead, and the committee was throwing out even those amendments to the administration bill that earlier had appeared promising.

The commandant himself put the nail in the coffin on 27 May. When the committee asked his opinion of an amendment that provided cosmetic guarantees for the Corps, he gave his approval. At the completion of an important, losing vote on 29 May, a thoroughly discouraged Robertson gathered up his papers, walked out of the conference room, and gave up the fight. When SASC voted twelve to zero for the merger bill on 4 June, the strongest Marine supporter did not even bother to show up. The committee's proposed law was almost exactly the same one that had been introduced by the administration.

*   *   *

The termites had lost the battle in the Senate, but they had not yet lost the war, for the struggle continued in the House. Through a combination of luck and foresight, the odds were better in the lower chamber. When Truman introduced the merger legislation in the House, the House leadership steered it away from the Armed Services Committee, which contained old Navy friends such as Representative Carl Vinson. Instead, the bill went to the Committee on Expenditures in the Executive Departments, where the administration expected that a subcommittee headed by James Wadsworth, an "ardent supporter of unification," would handle it. However, Lt. Col. James D. Hittle, who worked with Twining and Krulak in the Quantico branch of the Edson Board, came to the rescue. Hittle's father was an influential Michigan lawyer, longtime state representative, and friend' of the committee chairman, Representative Clare Hoffman. With that entree, Hittle met with Hoffman, discussed the dangers of the bill, and convinced the Michigan congressman to take a personal interest in it. Hoffman soon announced that the issue would be addressed by the entire committee.

The House hearings opened on 2 April, though they did not get seriously underway until late in the month. Initial witnesses followed the administration line, but each met with tough questioning from the numerous Marine partisans in the committee. They were well supplied with ammunition for the effort, since Hittle was now working nearly full time with Hoffman. Despite open invitations to rebellion made by various committee members, Navy witnesses continued to support the bill. Nimitz stated that it was too difficult to incorporate roles and missions into law, so an executive order was the appropriate solution. He also maintained that he never felt the Army had been out to destroy the Corps, though he soon had to backtrack when Hoffman asked if he had signed a 1478 paper saying exactly the opposite. Sherman maintained that the 1478 papers were not an accurate picture of current Army feeling.

The Senate fight held Edson's attention for much of this period, so he relied on Hittle to carry the ball in the House and keep him informed. When the Senate appeared to be a lost cause, Edson increasingly redirected his efforts to the House. The general delivered copies of his brief and discussed the issue with several members of the committee. On 20 May he met with six former Marine representatives, including committee member Henry Latham of New York. He also arranged with Krulak to use family influence in Colorado to get access to Representative J. Edgar Chenoweth, another committee member.

If the commandant's support for the fight had been tepid in April, it grew downright cold in May. The break between the two Guadalcanal veterans began with a 29 April meeting of Vandegrift and Eisenhower. The latter agreed to support the commandant's efforts to get Marine roles and missions into the merger bill (a promise he soon reneged upon). A few days later Edson was approached by an assistant of Drew Pearson, a leading newspaper columnist. The writer had wind of the meeting and hinted that he wished to publicize it. Edson tried to straighten out misimpressions and asked that it be kept quiet, but the story appeared a few days later. An angry Vandegrift threatened to court-martial the leaker. When Edson got that news he went to see the commandant, admitted his part, and explained the circumstances. He thought Vandegrift was mollified at the end of the conversation, but was unsure if his boss had revealed his true feelings. The bond of trust between the two seemed increasingly fragile, if not already broken.

In a conference immediately after that meeting, Thomas and Edson decided to close down the official activities of the board due to the rising heat. The next day, 10 May, Red Mike cleaned out his desk in the conference room and the staff removed all the files. Although the commandant's order formally dissolving the board was dated 6 May, he must have signed it later and backdated it to just prior to Edson's testimony in the Senate, so that Vandegrift could disavow any connection with that activity.

Another incident followed quickly. The evening papers of 13 May carried an interview with Edson and his criticism of the administration bill. Nimitz called Vandegrift the next morning and reminded him of the orders preventing unauthorized public comments. Edson found himself on the commandant's carpet shortly thereafter. Red Mike explained that he had not expected his private discussion with a reporter, arising from a chance meeting in the corridor just after his 7 May testimony, to end up in print. Vandegrift accepted the explanation and smiled as he told Edson to consider himself reprimanded. However, there was obviously high-level interest in the matter; the commandant had to pass the substance of the meeting on to the White House via Forrestal. The cordial censure left Edson confused about his old division commander. "Maybe he admires my guts—or my stupidity—more than I thought he did."

That the commandant took the administration ban on public opposition seriously was evidenced by an article in a New Orleans newspaper. After an interview with Vandegrift, the reporter commented, "It would be easier to eat steak through a straw than to pry words loose from him on the merger of the armed forces and what it would mean to the Corps. . . . About the proposed merger, he minced no pretty talk: 'Never talk about it—only to the congressional committee.'" But the commandant never told Edson what he thought of the brigadier's Senate testimony or his lobbying efforts, though he privately expressed the feeling to a retired general that attempts to change the opinion of congressmen were not "the thing to do." Consequently, Red Mike continued to feel that he had been put out on a limb by his commander. He told Hanson Baldwin about the commandant's smiling reprimand and observed that "I do not know exactly where I stand other than knowing full well that I am trying to walk a tight wire without losing my balance along the way."

If reaction from the commandant was ambivalent, Edson knew that it was certainly negative at higher levels. The interest of the secretary and the president in his activities was not something that could be ignored easily. "The top brass have every reason to dislike the things I have said, and I have every reason to believe that they will pull no punches (and most of them below the belt) to get even with me eventually." That he was the only active-duty officer to testify against the bill made matters that much worse.

The future seemed to hold only two possibilities. If the administration bill passed, Edson wanted no part in implementing it. "I do not have to remain in an organization to which I am so fundamentally opposed; I do not have to carry out orders to support it, and I have no intention of doing either." On the other hand, if the general and his termites succeeded in stopping the bill or amending it to their liking, things would not appear appreciably better. Melvin Johnson thought that Truman would accept Edson's opposition as a simple difference of opinion and that the general's status as a combat hero would protect him. Edson disagreed; he felt that any hope for promotion or useful employment would be destroyed. (The general was right; Truman later expressed considerable unhappiness regarding even Vandegrift's weak opposition.) Shepherd also counseled Red Mike not to resign, though he made the mistake of saying that the Corps could not afford to lose one of its two best leaders (the other being Thomas). That only caused Edson to think bitterly of "the action of the last selection board."

Edson had good reason to ponder the future; outside opportunities were still available but would not necessarily remain so. Governor Gibson formally offered him the job of Vermont commissioner of public safety in a meeting in Washington on 19 May. Less than a week later, the NRA reminded him that their position was still open for him. Red Mike weighed the possibilities in a manner befitting a top-notch staff officer; he drafted a complete study of the issue. First he compared incomes from each of the alternatives. Then he contemplated what his career would look like till he reached the mandatory retirement age of sixty in 1957. Since he was only eleventh on the brigadier list and many of those ahead of him would remain in place until they had to retire, he foresaw at least four years and maybe six before he would be eligible for promotion based on seniority.

As a brigadier, he would spend the next three years at Plans and Policies, then probably move back to being an assistant division commander. By the time he was promoted and eligible for an independent field command, he feared that force reductions might leave no Marine divisions to lead. There was some hope for eventual elevation to the commandancy, but that was "nebulous" given the politics involved in the selection process. For the present, Major Generals Cates and Shepherd seemed to have the inside track. And this assumed that Truman, Forrestal, and other unification supporters would not be in a position years hence to block his promotion. He thought that his chances would be better under a Republican administration (though he could hardly foresee that it would be headed by his nemesis, Eisenhower). He made one other serious miscalculation: "The picture would be different if there should be another war, but I consider those chances practically nil within my remaining twelve years."

Edson sought counsel from Thomas, who agreed that his prospects in the Corps were "not too promising" and recommended the Vermont position as a good alternative. Two things drew Edson toward his home state. Although the NRA job offered more money, his first instinct was to remain in public service. At the time that Gibson offered the public safety position to Edson, the two men discussed the possibility of using it as a springboard into politics. The governor thought that the two Vermont senators were strongly entrenched and reasonably effective, but he believed that the state's lone representative was "ripe to be plucked at any time." When Edson broached the same subject with Aiken, he received an enthusiastic response. In his retirement study, he noted his Medal of Honor and wartime reputation, and felt that successful creation of the state police would further enhance his credentials in his home state. "Where it would lead politically would be, I believe, largely in my own hands."

Overlaying all these rational considerations was a thick coating of emotion. Physically, the general still was not completely recovered. A medical board found him fit for full duty at the end of May, though he still suffered from stiffness and fatigue. The cured hookworm notwithstanding, he frequently felt that he had never been more tired in his life. He attributed this to the unrelenting schedule he had pursued during the past four months of convalescent leave. That would not have bothered him, except that his efforts seemed to meet with censure rather than approbation. He resented his treatment at the hands of Vandegrift and blamed the entire mess on the commandant's lack of support. "It would have been fairly easy, I believe, to have defeated this thing . . . if the CMC and the Marine Corps had been officially behind it. It was almost impossible for me, as an individual, to bring the necessary prestige and influence to bear in spite of all my efforts." Edson felt he had been "doing a lot of dirty work for the top people. . . . It is a pretty lonesome feeling; and I am getting tired and weary of it—mentally, physically, and in every other way."

His past seemed unimportant to promotion boards and political leaders, the present was a thankless staff job, and his military future seemed to offer more of the same. There was a window of opportunity to "try something else for a change," a new career where he might be able to influence events on an even larger stage. In his mind, "the wisest thing for me to do is to turn in my suit and retire." There was only one problem—he loved the Corps far too much to leave it so easily. In early June Shepherd came "fishing for information" about Edson's plans, but Red Mike found it easy to be evasive: "After all . . . I do not yet know my own mind."

The decision was not long in coming. On 3 June Edson learned that the House committee had placed his name on its list of witnesses. Since the commandant was even less receptive now to merger opposition, the general felt compelled to resubmit his letter of resignation prior to any testimony. But this time it would not be an offer. Three things seemed uppermost in his mind. First, resignation would prove that his testimony was not connected to service rivalry or careerism. Second, the fight seemed doomed to failure, and remaining in the service under the new law would give it his "tacit approval." Finally, this might be his only chance to do something important in retirement. If he went now, he would make his own destiny. If he remained, he might pass up an opportunity and end his days in the Corps as just another time server waiting for age limits or a personnel board to force him out.

On 7 June Edson visited Vandegrift at HQMC and tendered a new letter of resignation. This time he removed the preamble concerning congressional testimony and stated simply: "I hereby submit my request for retirement." There followed a few lines summarizing his career in subdued and sparing prose, with little hint of his spectacular accomplishments during thirty years of service. The commandant took it this time, though Edson had given him no choice. The soon-to-be-retired Marine then telegraphed his acceptance of the Vermont job to Governor Gibson.

Vandegrift may have hoped that Edson would relent, for he did not forward the retirement request to the Navy Department until 16 June. Events at that point must have convinced the commandant that his strong-willed subordinate had burned the bridges behind him. The assistant secretary approved the request immediately and orders were issued the next day; the general would go home on leave on 23 June and formally retire on 1 August. In the meantime, Red Mike had to finish one last battle.

Although Edson had reduced his speaking schedule during his convalescence, he had not gotten altogether out of the public eye. In early May he had been the guest speaker at a gathering of UVM alumni in New York City. The association wanted Edson to talk about the Pacific war, but the hero replied that he was not very good at reminiscing about his own exploits. Instead, he spoke about unification. One of the attendees was university president John Millis, which may have brought about an invitation for the general to speak at the alumni luncheon during the June commencement at UVM. Edson accepted, since it fit in with his plans to meet with Gibson.

The general's 14 June speech before a thousand alumni assailed the proposed merger bill and focused on its origins in the Army. "When we have reached the point where the military are directing instead of supporting this Country's policy, we are far along the road to losing what this Country has stood for." He spoke of his pride in the armed forces but warned against allowing any increased influence of uniformed men in civilian life. Then he made the first public announcement that he was resigning, citing the prospective merger as the chief reason. At the end he received a vigorous ovation from the large, friendly crowd.

Although the general repeated many of the same points he had made to the Senate committee, his remarks created a much greater stir this time. They made newspapers around the country and met with a favorable reception in at least some quarters. The *Chicago Tribune* described the "famed leader of Marine raiders on Guadalcanal" as a man of "courage and honesty." The *Burlington Daily News* called it an "explosive speech" and editorialized: "Thank God that there are men like Edson still in Washington." A radio station opined that he had "deliberately strayed off the military reservation to deliver a well documented attack."

Edson's continuing efforts to sway media figures may have accounted for the coverage, or his news value may have been heightened by a recent spate of articles on military opposition to merger, stories that spoke of unnamed officers working behind the scenes. Often the comments were negative; the *Minneapolis Star* had referred to "a potent combination of well meaning but hidebound brasshats and stubborn, prestige-hungry military reactionaries." Now, finally, there was a face and a reputation to represent the anonymous group. That it was a well-known war hero ready to sacrifice his career to prevent an increase in the power of the military must have destroyed the stereotype and generated unusual interest.

The same stories of mysterious opposition had been creating problems for the administration. During his testimony before the House committee, several representatives grilled Forrestal about naval opinion on the merger. He replied that nearly everyone in the Navy Department was in favor of the bill. Pressed further, the secretary assured the committee that anyone was free to speak his mind in congressional testimony without fear of retaliation. He would have reason to regret those assertions.

Edson returned to Washington the day after the Burlington speech, visited with Clare Hoffman on 16 June, and then testified before the House committee on the seventeenth. As an avowed opponent of merger, he received a warm reception. Representative Latham introduced him and noted he was "in no sense of the word an armchair general." Edson's testimony, "the most comprehensive critique of the issue yet articulated," never varied from the theme of maintaining civilian control of the military. He noted that the bill itself had been drafted by military men and that the powers of the proposed secretary, joint staff, and Central Intelligence Agency (CIA) needed to be "carefully delineated and circumscribed." At the end of those remarks, Representative George Bender declared that Edson had "tossed an atom bomb into the works." Chenoweth thought the general "should be commended for appearing before this committee and expressing his frank criticism of this measure." In response to a question regarding concrete suggestions to fix the bill, Edson promised to forward amendments and a completely new draft law. The congressmen did not agree with everything Edson said, but they at least now had an expert to support their own opposition stance.

They soon heard many more. Six days after the general's testimony, Forrestal responded to the earlier criticism that he was preventing naval officers from speaking their minds. In a message to the naval services he stated that "I have recently become aware that a feeling of restraint may exist among certain Naval personnel" regarding discussion of the merger bill. Therefore, he decided to temporarily waive previous limitations on congressional testimony. The result was a flood of witnesses against the administration position. Vice Admiral Gerald F. Bogan probably spoke for his colleagues when he explained his previous silence. "We were given to understand that this legislation was favored by the high command and it was hoped that we would all support it. Being unable to support it, we had nothing else to do but keep our mouths shut." Edson, of course, had demonstrated that everyone had an option, if they only had the courage to pursue it. Later, he would evaluate his willingness to speak out as his greatest contribution to the struggle. He believed that his example had been the primary factor in the subsequent public opposition by other officers: "The fact remains that not a single one of them would have done so had I not led the way."

The day after his testimony, the general wrote a letter to Hoffman to clarify some points, and the congressman inserted it in the record. Red Mike also forwarded his legislative proposals to the committee, sent additional copies to Senator Aiken, and conferred several times with key congressmen. He had done all he could for the moment. It was time to move on to the future. He spent most of the next few days in Washington visiting with J. Edgar Hoover and learning about police work from Federal Bureau of Investigation (FBI) experts. On 26 June the movers came and packed the house, and he got in his car and drove north late in the afternoon. As in Hawaii eighteen months before, there was no ceremony to honor his departure, no brass band or marching men as befitted a Medal of Honor winner. He simply doffed his uniform and faded out of the military.

Even Marines closely connected to the merger battle were astonished at Edson's resignation. Lieutenant Kleber had just reported to Plans and Policies so that he could continue as the general's military secretary, only to find that Edson would not be going there now. The news gave Krulak "a solid shock." Melvin Johnson, aware that the general had been contemplating such a course, registered his disappointment at the final decision: "I can only say that it was a very sad day when you were ordered to duty in the Navy Department and in turn thrown into contact with that legislation."

Although Edson's interest in politics was an even closer secret, many assumed that it would be a logical course for the retired general. Jesse Cook wished him luck and said: "I hope to address you as the Governor in the not too distant future." Johnson recommended that Edson run for Congress because he had what it took to get elected and to do a "tremendous" job once there. Bob Blake registered his concern about merger with a similar suggestion: "What you may be able to do about it I don't know but I do know that you are set up to get into the Senate from Vermont where you can, at least, try with the backing of a constituency by whom the concepts of republican (with a small 'r') government are understood and appreciated."

The Corps did not recognize Red Mike's departure, but some of his friends did so informally. Krulak told him it was a major loss for the service, "since the number of senior officers who are willing to stand firm on their convictions is certainly numbered, and in all the time I've known you, you have taken no other position." Johnson noted Edson's reputation for "combat heroism and administrative brilliance," and called him "one of two or three of the most outstanding and most prominent Marine officers in the service." Blake discussed the irony of the general's quiet retirement from a service that owed him so much. "You have had official recognition of the manner you fought for it in battle, but only your friends know how you fought for its survival. We will always remember that battle and admire you for having the guts to lead it, and whether we survive or not we admire your courage." A *Burlington Daily News* editorial best summed up the situation. "It may be true that General Edson might have been wiser had he waited until he is out of uniform on July 1 before making his speech. But Red Mike doesn't play ball that way either. He speaks his mind; he tells the truth without fear of consequences. God bless him for this forthrightness. It will stand him in good stead here in Vermont, where the truth still keeps men free."

Chapter 19

"In the Snow of Far Off Northern Lands"

R ed Mike's first few days in Vermont were busy ones. He attended numerous meetings with his new subordinates and the governor. The weekend of 4 July he drove Ethel and Bobby up to Maine to stay with Mollie until he could find a house in Montpelier, the Vermont state capital and their future home. There also was an "impressive and historic ceremony" on 1 July to inaugurate the Department of Public Safety. The governor swore in Edson on the steps of the gold-domed, stone-columned Capitol building. The new commissioner then led the seventy men and women of his infant force through their oath of office. In his brief speech, Red Mike praised Vermont, for "nowhere else are the principles of constitutional government more firmly entrenched." And he said that he expected loyalty to the department from each of its members. "That does not mean that I want you to be 'yes' men, for no man can be truly loyal to his superior unless he expresses his honest opinion when asked for it."

Those words had real meaning to a man still intimately engaged in the struggle against the unification of the armed forces. On 14 July he received a delayed telegram from Congressman Hoffman asking him to be in Washington on the fifteenth. Red Mike immediately drove south, but arrived in the nation's capital too late to participate in anything more than one late-night meeting with Hoffman and Schatzel. The next day, 16 July, Hoffman's committee sent to the House a bill that incorporated many of the suggestions made by Edson and other Marine officers. Unsatisfied with the diluted committee report accompanying the bill, Hoffman added his own minority report echoing the themes advanced in Red Mike's June testimony. Although the congressman supported the much-improved bill, he still thought that "the possibilities of a dictatorship by the military are in this legislation."

The House passed Hoffman's bill with a single amendment, engineered by Schatzel and Heinl, that required a civilian director for the Central Intelligence Agency. The Senate had already approved its competing version that hewed more closely to the original submitted by Truman. A conference committee representing both houses of Congress worked out a compromise that generally followed the House version. Most important from the Marine Corps perspective, it included language spelling out the roles and missions of that service. The Senate and the House passed the conference bill and Truman signed the National Security Act of 1947 into law on 25 July.

Few of those involved in the battle over unification were pleased with the outcome. Supporters of the War Department position had achieved much less than their original goal. Edson thought the law had given them far too much. On the day of its passage he addressed the Vermont state convention of the American Legion. "History has amply demonstrated that military might and authoritarian government go hand in hand," he told the audience. In his opinion the bill contained some good features but also the seeds of "potential danger." "Those things must be recognized by all, and they must be closely watched." His call for vigilance was prescient. The Army's General Marshall saw the legislation as only a temporary compromise. "Let us take the half loaf. It is my belief that experience will ultimately give us the whole loaf."

Although the battle had come down to a draw, Edson had "no personal regrets" at his part in it. His only concern was the light in which history would cast his retirement. Vandegrift seemed to justify his fears when he awarded official letters of commendation to the other members of the Edson Board, but not to its namesake. Instead, he sent Red Mike a brief personal note as a "very meager expression" of his thanks. His final fitness report on the brigadier rated him as outstanding overall, but marked Edson down in the categories of cooperation, military bearing, and physical fitness. That last rating must have been especially galling to the Marine who had given up his convalescent leave to help the Corps, because part of its official definition was "endurance under hardship, adversity, or discouragement." Red Mike also noticed that the military newspapers, which normally printed career reviews of retiring officers, had ignored his departure from the service. He thought that headquarters considered his retirement to be "something reprehensible."

In response, Edson sent a long letter to Vandegrift explaining his part in the unification battle. He insisted that the document go into his official record. Red Mike also sent his own letters of commendation to the Marines and politicians who had fought the battle with him. In later years historians and commentators would find it difficult to sort out who was most responsible for the legislative success of the Corps in 1947, but the efforts of all involved were so intertwined and interdependent that everyone could claim a vital role. The thinking of Krulak and Twining; the dogged lobbying of Hittle, Heinl, and Schatzel; the legislative skill of Hoffman and other Marine friends; and the moral courage of Edson were all indispensable to the final outcome.

The nature of his departure from the Corps left Red Mike unhappy, a feeling he expressed after receiving his promotion to major general (a purely honorary elevation required by law due to his gallantry in action). Governor Gibson surprised him by performing the ceremony in front of an assembly of the state's senior civil servants. Edson noted that it was "more than I could have expected had I received the promotion while on active duty." The hero of so many tough fights could have taken his isolated retirement to heart and left future battles to others, but he did not direct his bitterness toward the institution that had been his home for thirty years. Instead, he asked his former assistants on the Edson Board to keep him apprised of the implementation of the National Security Act, and he heavily involved himself in the affairs of the Marine Corps League. His service to the Corps was not complete yet, as one of his friends correctly predicted. "It is so much a part of you that you cannot, wilfully or otherwise, cast it aside or sever its blood stream."

Vermont had first considered the idea of a state police force in the mid-1930s, but conservative legislators had vetoed the proposal. In December 1946 a coed disappeared from Bennington College. The unsuccessful investigations of city police and county sheriffs provided political fuel for a proposal by the newly elected governor to establish a statewide agency unhampered by jurisdictional boundaries. Governor Gibson got the law he wanted in April 1947. It consolidated a number of small, specialized enforcement bodies, doubled their numbers with new recruits, and gave them broad powers to enforce state statutes related to crime and safety.

Gibson was about the same age as Edson, and the two had been acquainted since their youth (through Paul Ballou, a relative of the governor). Gibson had given up his seat in the U.S. Senate in 1941 to go on active duty in the Army; he had served in combat in the Solomons. A progressive Republican, he had won election to the governorship in November 1946 on a platform to reform state government. Ballou described him as a man who "does not hesitate to say what he thinks." It was not surprising then that he turned to a decorated officer with a similar outlook to head one of the major initiatives of his young administration. Edson's goal of unseating one of Vermont's conservative Republicans in Congress was probably an added bonus for the governor.

While Edson kept one eye on Washington in the summer and fall of 1947, his hands were full in Montpelier. He found it no easy task to create an entirely new organization. His service background served him well in some respects. He established policy by issuing general orders in military format, created efficiency rating forms that looked suspiciously like Marine Corps fitness reports, and even promulgated a method for using panels to signal airplanes in emergencies. He also headed the board that designed uniforms, which were a cross between those worn by American Marines and their Royal Marine counterparts.

In other areas he demonstrated an astute awareness of local politics, probably a result of his willingness to accept advice from subordinates more familiar with the terrain. His very first order kept his troopers out of matters traditionally handled by local law enforcement agencies, unless those bodies specifically requested help. That policy wisely defused potential turf battles with the politically powerful sheriffs. A tougher problem was deciding where to locate district offices, since many localities wanted one. Requests came from a number of influential citizens, to include Paul Ballou on behalf of Chester. Edson also undertook an extensive public relations program. He spoke at club meetings and other functions around the state and he initiated a weekly radio broadcast. This helped him sell the state police force and raise public awareness on issues involving crime and safety. It made him a more familiar face with the voters, too.

Red Mike's hopes of raising a garden and living inexpensively in his home state did not pan out. Finding a house took some time and cost much more than he had expected; the only thing cheap in postwar Vermont was labor. In September he finally settled on a large, turreted, multigabled place at 67 East State Street, just a few blocks from downtown Montpelier. The second floor was a separate apartment that he could rent to cover part of the mortgage. A brand-new Pontiac did come with the commissioner's position, and that helped the finances a bit.

Edson was invigorated by the return to his native state, and he shook off the sense of foreboding that characterized his last months in uniform. Ethel remained in Maine till their new house became available in November; his letters to her were affectionate and humorous for the first time in more than a decade. And he signed off all of them with "love to you." He attended services, "believe it or not," at the Congregational church while visiting Chester, and also rejoined the Grange chapter in his old hometown.

Red Mike finally seemed content to spend the rest of his life with Ethel, although his rekindled affection for her did not wholly crowd out his relationship with the woman Marine officer. That friendship had blossomed into love. In many respects this affair was similar to his earlier ones, carried on at long distance primarily through letters and telephone calls. There was one difference: This time he gave no thought to leaving Ethel and he apparently made that clear to the other woman, who referred to their relationship at one point as a "dead end street." Nevertheless, it would continue on in that manner for the next few years.

A number of problems confronted Edson in his first year as commissioner. The state's inability to provide a suitable office site created many difficulties. After considerable searching he and the governor settled on Redstone, a large brick mansion set in the middle of eight wooded acres on a ridge above the state capitol. They leased the premises for $1,000 per year but had to spend $35,000 to renovate the building, which had been unused for three decades. Another state account picked up most of the cost, which otherwise would have crippled the department's $390,000 annual budget. Various delays kept Red Mike from occupying his new headquarters until February 1948, so for seven months he and his office staff had to operate from widely scattered locations around the city.

Installation of a statewide radio network proved even more difficult. It took months to pick a contractor and even longer to get approval for frequencies from the Federal Communications Commission. The work of erecting antennas and transmitter buildings on the state's highest peaks took until spring 1948. The final cost of the radio system exceeded the $60,000 contract price by $40,000. Edson also discovered that he had too few men to meet all the duties levied upon his force. His uniformed troopers worked an average of ninety hours per week, so he had to ask for a 50 percent increase in manpower.

The cost of the state police force had been a significant point of debate in the legislature at the time of the law's passage. The department's budget overruns thus became a "political football" in the 1948 election campaign. Lieutenant Governor Lee Emerson, a candidate for governor in the Republican primary, pressed hard on the point to demonstrate his fiscal conservatism. Simple expenditures such as the cost of two flagpoles in front of Redstone became big news. Although Gibson eventually defeated his archrival, the debate over spending created some doubt in the public mind about Red Mike's stewardship of the state police. The campaign also generated animosity between Edson and Emerson.

At first Vermonters welcomed the retired general's no-nonsense attitude toward his duty. He made headlines when he used his personal car to chase down and capture a youthful speeder who flashed by him on the highway. Later his unbending attitude created some discontent. A local chapter of the American Legion invited him to their hall, which housed several slot machines. Although these gambling devices were outlawed by the state, many fraternal organizations used them as fund-raisers anyway. Edson felt compelled to have his troopers sweep the lodges of veterans' groups two days later. They seized machines at several locations, but mysteriously found none at the legion hall, which was crowded with state convention delegates.

The legionnaires were outraged that he had abused their hospitality, but he correctly observed that it was they who should have apologized to him for putting him in an awkward position in the first place. This time the editorial writers were not all supportive. One newspaper called it a "slap-happy raid." Edson publicized his opinion that groups that did not agree with the law should seek to change it rather than flout it. Some agreed, but the politically potent private clubs were not mollified.

There were some legitimate complaints about state police failures, mainly due to the lack of manpower. On one occasion an officer failed to respond in a timely fashion to a call from a man who had been beaten and robbed on a Friday morning. A neighbor telephoned the Montpelier headquarters to complain. Red Mike personally returned her call twenty minutes later and immediately dispatched his deputy to investigate. When reporters questioned the governor about the incident on Monday, he made a public demand for an inquiry. The next day the newspapers noted that there was a complete report of the matter on Edson's desk on Saturday that had been available if the governor had requested it. The governor was no doubt embarrassed at having moved too publicly and hastily to shift the spotlight to the commissioner, and Edson probably regretted not having informed his superior before the press got hold of the story. This did not create a rift between the governor and the commissioner, but it was another public setback for both of them.

Despite the criticism leveled from several quarters, Red Mike kept up his program to win over the state. In addition to public appearances and radio broadcasts, he offered to meet with people "to answer in person such criticism and such questions as they may care to raise." At the end of one newspaper interview he extended an invitation for anyone to visit any of his installations at any time: "We're open twenty-four hours a day." At the same time, he was wary of the power of the press after his years of experience in the Corps. His school for new troopers included a course on how to deal with reporters.

The demands of the job kept Red Mike extremely busy during this first year. When he was not off visiting a distant part of the state, he was in his office till late at night. He remarked to Ethel that "I do not know where I ever got the idea that I would have more leisure here than in Washington." His mother, in frail health for some time, grew increasingly worse in late 1947, so he made frequent round-trips to Burlington to spend evenings with her. She died just a few days after the new year began. The long hours and the mental strain made him tired and caused some pain in his stomach and back. He thought his ulcers and his spinal disc problem might both be recurring. Toward the end of January 1948 he went to Washington and checked into the Navy hospital at Bethesda. Tests and X-rays revealed neither an ulcer nor any other reason for the stomach troubles. The doctors diagnosed his back problem as muscle spasms; a few sessions of therapy relieved that. Red Mike returned to Vermont feeling better, but not perfect. The doctors had done nothing about his stomach, and the commissioner's job still had "its ups and downs," though he optimistically believed that "one of these days it is bound to get up and stay there."

Red Mike may have been retired, but he was still earning the free medical care he had received at Bethesda. Schatzel, Hittle, Heinl, and Kleber had kept in close touch with him in the fall of 1947 regarding the interservice jockeying for position after the passage of the National Security Act. They were concerned about the implementation of that law, since Truman and the generals of the Army and Air Force were doing their best to ignore those features they had opposed. Vandegrift was in no mood for further battles in Congress, so the former termites turned to "a distinguished gentleman from Vermont" to lobby for them.

Edson's opposition to defense unification received a boost in December 1947. Hanson W. Baldwin, the respected military analyst of the *New York Times,* published an article in *Harper's* magazine titled "The Military Moves In." He noted with alarm the increasing "militarization of our government and the American state of mind." Too many military people were assuming positions of authority in the civilian realm, and the 1947 legislation had "potentially dangerous provisions." He was not ready to go as far as Edson, though he did quote him and mention his retirement in protest. The article contained numerous points obviously culled from the material Red Mike had fed him earlier in the year. A national broadcast picked up on the theme the next day and prominently mentioned Edson. Other commentators gave the topic wider play in following days. Heinl suggested that it would be a good time for Red Mike to arrange a national interview "as the man who started all this."

Early 1948 brought a change in leadership for the Corps. Vandegrift's four-year tenure was complete. As Edson had suspected, the two leading candidates were Cates, the commanding general at Quantico, and Shepherd, still the assistant commandant. Neither of them had played any significant role in the unification battles. Truman interviewed both and selected Cates because he was older and senior. The president promised Shepherd that he would be the next commandant. Cates asked Shepherd to stay on in his position, but Shepherd elected to take the now-empty slot at Quantico. Edson wrote his old friend, asking him to reconsider because he thought Cates and his designated assistant, O. P. Smith, were ill-prepared to ward off further encroachments from the other services. Shepherd demurred; he thought Cates was "prepared to resist to the last the Army's attempts to circumvent the National Security Act."

The new commandant's powers to fight for the Corps were quite limited. Legislation reorganizing the Navy Department appeared to weaken his status as the head of an independent service. Then the Navy Department issued yet another "gag order" restricting public statements. Finally, the Marine Corps had no representative at the conference in Key West, which the secretary of defense called to settle the roles and missions question. The results of that March 1948 meeting were a setback for the Corps.

As the president and Congress squeezed the defense budget ever tighter, all the services fought harder for scarce dollars. The Marines suffered the most, because they had no voice at the highest levels. The Army and Air Force, and even some in the Navy, thought amphibious assaults were a thing of the past, and they planned to cut down the Corps to just six battalion landing teams. Edson worked behind the scenes through the press and Vermont's senators to get out the Marine point of view, but he also continued his philosophical opposition to military encroachment into civilian affairs. He publicly spoke out against Truman's proposal for Universal Military Training. Red Mike thought the answer to readiness was stronger reserve and active forces, not a misguided program that put generals in charge of the civilian population.

As 1948 progressed Edson found additional forums for propounding his views. Herbert Hoover's Commission on Reorganization of the Executive Departments spawned a subcommittee on national defense chaired by Eberstadt. Red Mike managed to get himself called as a witness before that group, and then incessantly lobbied individual members while they worked on their report. One of them admitted that "none of our committee—certainly none of the advisors or consultants—has shown more interest in this tremendously important business than yourself." Edson's conversations with leaders of the Veterans of Foreign Wars resulted in his appointment to their National Security Committee, which developed that influential organization's stand on defense issues. For a time he hoped that after the election, Governor Thomas E. Dewey, the Republican nominee for president, might make him his military chief of staff, an advisory role held by Adm. William D. Leahy under Roosevelt and Truman. That goal dissolved when Truman snatched an unexpected victory at the polls in November.

The issue of defense unification received renewed interest in early 1949 when Senator Tydings introduced a bill that would amend the 1947 Act to bring it more closely into line with the original intent of the Army and Air Force, thus fulfilling Edson's predictions. This new legislation would create a chairman of the Joint Chiefs of Staff, enlarge that body's supporting staff, strengthen the office of the secretary of defense, and downgrade the status of the Departments of the Army, Navy, and Air Force. The president also had replaced Secretary of Defense Forrestal with Louis Johnson, a man who would faithfully execute Truman's wishes without any independent analysis of the policy.

Throughout the unification battles of 1946 and 1947 the press largely had backed the War Department's proposals, but the media's attitude changed slowly as time passed. Baldwin was one of the first commentators to shift closer to Edson's position, but others soon followed. Tregaskis, always a Marine supporter, got the *Saturday Evening Post* to print an article in February 1949 revealing the inside story of Marine opposition to the original legislation and using that as a springboard to attack the Tydings bill. "The Marine Corps Fights for Its Life" gave prominent play to Edson's previous efforts, though Red Mike felt that it put too little emphasis on his larger political objections to unification. He did not want "to be publicly branded as nothing more than a rabid Marine Corps partisan." Columnist David Lawrence wrote stronger pieces pushing the more Edsonian theme of the threatening shift to a German general staff system. Red Mike had provided much of the material used by both writers, and he fed more to Dave Merwin, an Illinois newspaper editor. Merwin made regular mailings of editorials on the subject to congressmen and fifteen hundred other newspapermen around the country. Edson was still lobbying individual legislators, but he had determined that "the approach must be through the press and the public in order to have any effect whatsoever on the members of Congress."

Tregaskis's article had painted General Cates as a worthy successor of Edson, ready to defeat any renewed assaults on the existence of the Corps. That was not entirely accurate, at least not at first. In 1948 the new commandant refused to publish an article, prepared for him by Heinl,

Schatzel, and others, that sought to counteract the Air Force's campaign to prove that strategic air power would be the primary determinant of victory in future wars. Cates forbid Schatzel to print his own piece comparing the need for competition in the armed forces to the free enterprise system. The commandant also called some of the old termites to his office about suspected leaks to the press concerning interservice disputes.

Any hint of discord met with disapproval. *Leatherneck,* a semiofficial Marine publication, had to delete an article on Red Mike's career just as the June 1948 issue went to press. Edson would authorize publication only if it told the true reason behind his retirement, but headquarters remained adamant that the magazine had to ignore that subject. The commandant even considered killing the Tregaskis article when the reporter asked headquarters to clear it. As Edson had suspected, Cates was not ready for the rough and tumble political scrapping required to protect the Corps or defeat further unification moves.

When the Tydings bill appeared in early 1949, Edson made an offer of assistance to both Cates and VAdm. Arthur W. Radford, the vice chief of Naval Operations. Neither man took him up on it right away, though both said they would have their assistants keep in touch with him. Cates said he found the situation in Washington "puzzling," and he was not yet sure what course of action the Corps would pursue. The Navy and Marine Corps became much more worried when Secretary Johnson used his authority over the budget to make fresh inroads into their strength. He canceled the Navy's premier project, construction of the supercarrier *United States,* and was ready to sign an order transferring Marine aviation to the Air Force (until certain congressmen stepped in to dissuade him from that drastic action). Even then Cates seemed slow to act. One of the former termites could not understand why the commandant was sending Lieutenant Colonel Hittle, the "ablest lobbyist and public relations officer in the Marine Corps," to the Naval ROTC unit in Utah just when headquarters most needed his services.

In early summer 1949 Cates finally turned to Edson for help. Red Mike had already done considerable lobbying and public speaking on his own; now the commandant provided his own plane to fly Edson to the West Coast for a series of appearances. The retired general met privately with people such as the editor of the *San Francisco Chronicle*; made speeches to groups as diverse as the Sierra Club, the Commonwealth Club, the Los Angeles Press Club, and the Marine Corps Newsmen Association; and held several press conferences. His remarks that the Tydings bill replicated the general staff system used by Hitler and other dictatorships received wide broadcast in the media. The *Chronicle* summed up its article with one of his most compelling quotes. "People in Congress tell me they only get one official armed services point of view now. Before, they used to find things out by asking each branch in turn." The Tydings bill threatened to decrease open interservice debate even further.

Edson's importance in the publicity offensive stemmed in large measure from the reticence of active-duty officers to risk their careers by openly defying the administration. In April 1949 the president had issued Consolidation Directive No. 1, which contained yet another order designed to stifle military dissent. It applied not only to those on active duty, but also to reservists, retirees, and civilian defense employees. It required prior review, "for security, policy, and propriety," of any public utterance on defense matters. The CNO, Adm. Louis E. Denfield, noted its effect when the press first asked for his reaction to the cancellation of the *United States*. "How can I comment? Look at the directive."

In Edson's mind, the sweeping nature of the directive was proof that the public had cause for alarm. In one speech he explained that coupling that policy with passage of Universal Military Training would eventually give the defense establishment the right to censor the speech of the entire adult male population. Marines certainly were wary of this latest gag rule. Red Mike received several requests from active-duty officers about submitting their manuscript articles for publication under his name. He found one by Heinl promising, and circulated it to a number of officers for comment. Thomas, no stranger to a political brawl, counseled caution. "I believe you know that I have been an advocate of working on our enemies with a baseball bat—still am—your article does that. . . . *You must, however, be certain of your position before you consider publication.* Though this article is good it is not worth giving those gnats a real chance to knock you off."

The danger was real. Legislation revamping the military legal system was then working its way through Congress. The resulting Uniform Code of Military Justice would give the president the power to recall a retired officer to active duty for court-martial for any violation of orders. Although Edson had no career to risk, there was the possibility of losing his retired pay. For a time that gave him pause, but he soon reached the same conclusion he had in 1947, a decision he communicated to Thomas just prior to the California trip. "When I get through there plus what I have already said and what has already appeared in the newspapers I see no reason why I should back away from going whole hog with the magazine article." His stand was not quite as courageous this time; he suspected that any move to silence a retired officer of his stature would create such a political backlash that the administration would not risk it. Still, he was again the lone wolf carrying the position of the Marine Corps to the public.

After redrafting the Heinl piece to his own satisfaction, Edson submitted it to the *Saturday Evening Post* in late April. Editors there disliked the strident tone. Red Mike massaged the draft again, but the *Post* demurred, in part because they thought that the passage of the Tydings bill was now a foregone conclusion. He next tried *Collier's,* another weekly national magazine. His chances were better here because the editor was Louis Ruppel, a Marine reserve captain. That almost backfired when Ruppel thought about redirecting the article to address the Corps's fight for survival instead of Edson's wider concerns. Red Mike reacted with vigor to that proposal. "If you read the piece carefully, you will notice that the Marine Corps is not even mentioned. . . . I will not agree to the publication of any piece under my signature which attempts solely to set forth the Marine Corps viewpoint."

Ruppel confined himself to minor changes, and the article appeared in *Collier's* in mid-August 1949. Titled "Power-Hungry Men in Uniform," it reiterated Edson's well-developed arguments about the dangers of further centralization of military power. By the time the article hit the newsstands, the administration had withdrawn its restrictive policy on public statements. But Truman had also won congressional assent to most of the Tydings bill through arm-twisting tactics that brought his party into line. Attempts by Marine partisans in Congress to get a seat on the JCS for the commandant and to fix Marine strength at 6 percent of the total armed forces both went down to defeat, despite strong testimony in their favor by Cates. Red Mike acknowledged that his latest contribution had come too late to make a difference, that his opponents "could simply shrug it off as a petty annoyance," since they had achieved their aims.

The article was not welcome at headquarters, at least not by the commandant and his closest advisers. It did not focus on their narrower interest in securing the future of the Corps, and it contained tough words against senior Army and Air Force leaders. Cates was already upset with Edson after the 1st Marine Division reunion in New York in early August. Red Mike had been grand marshal of the parade and one of the featured speakers at the banquet. His speech criticizing Marine efforts to defeat unification embarrassed several luminaries at the head table, since they were the ones obviously responsible for the shortcomings. Their reaction was sufficiently visible that Edson cut off his talk before he was halfway through. Afterward he sent apologies to Vandegrift and Senator Paul H. Douglas (a former Marine), though he told Shepherd that his comments were justified. "If we are going to deliberately close our eyes to what is going on and refuse to discuss the situation even within the family group, then I think that the Corps is indeed in a bad way." Many other Marines were inclined to agree with Edson, as one noted in a letter describing Cates's reaction to the reunion: "I find myself wondering if he were displeased by that speech so much as by the relative volume of cheers."

The Marine Corps had lost the 1949 legislative battle, and Edson expected more to come as the Army and Air Force continued to push toward their goal of a completely unified military. Red Mike still believed that the most effective way to influence Congress was to enlist public support. And the best method for achieving that was a media campaign that would shift public opinion. The reaction to his own first step into national journalism was generally positive. *Collier's* received little mail on the subject, but many people wrote directly to Edson. Those who congratulated him ranged from retired Admiral King to *Life* editor Richard W. Johnston to ordinary citizens.

Tregaskis's earlier piece had also generated interest in the cause. One businessman's response to Edson on that article was typical. "As long as America has men like you on the alert we are secure. I'm awfully proud and grateful to you Sir." Even Senator Wayne Morse, a unification partisan, had been moved to write Edson to ask for details on his views. Tregaskis had convinced the legislator that Red Mike was the best man in the country to discuss the subject and "certainly one of the most brilliant Marines I know." With that praise ringing in his ears, Edson determined that he should carry his own standard in the journalistic arena instead of merely feeding information to others. He hoped to become a regular contributor to a national newspaper or magazine.

Edson had been well aware for some time of his literary potential. His efforts in the *Gazette* had demonstrated some skill, and he had a reservoir of fame from his wartime exploits. Just days after his retirement, a leading New York publishing house had approached him about writing a book on the Pacific war. Edson expressed an interest in the project but replied that he was too busy at the moment. Several Marines with media contacts had suggested possibilities for articles, too, and Red Mike authorized them to do some "missionary work" with various publications. Nothing came of those early attempts, but now he was ready to devote time to the effort. Sherrod and Lieutenant Colonel Heinl encouraged him to undertake a book about his life.

His interest was heightened by the $1,000 fee from *Collier's*, the equivalent of two months of his commissioner's salary. Holland Smith's recently released *Coral and Brass* was a ready example of the possibilities. It briefly made the *New York Times* best seller list and netted $20,000 just for serial rights in the *Saturday Evening Post*. The book also rekindled a national debate about Tarawa and renewed public interest in one of Red Mike's greatest battles. In late August Edson took a few days out of his busy schedule to attend a writing workshop given by literary greats Robert Frost, Catherine Drinker Bowen, Samuel Eliot Morrison, and Fletcher Pratt.

An unexpected event arose to disrupt his plans. The stomach pains he had been experiencing for some time continued to grow worse, so he checked into Bethesda Hospital in mid-September 1949. After a thorough battery of tests, the doctors finally discovered the cause, a diaphragmatic hernia. He had a large hole in the left side of his diaphragm and his stomach protruded up through it into his chest cavity, particularly when he was lying down. It had escaped previous X-rays because he had always been standing up; this time he had been horizontal. That explained why the pain seemed worse at night and why his habit of sometimes sleeping sitting up in a chair had helped relieve it. The doctors guessed that there had never been an ulcer, that the hernia had been the source of his problem for some years.

The surgical procedure entailed some serious risks, so Edson put his financial affairs in order just in case. He was not much better off than before, with a savings account of just $800 and debts on the house equaling its potential sale price. He switched the beneficiary of his insurance policy from Mary to Ethel so that she would face no immediate hardship given their lack of ready cash. A long letter to Austin spelled out all the details. Another one to Ethel, signed "lots and lots of love," made light of the operation, but he was not quite so optimistic with Mary. "I'm sure that everything will be all right—and if it isn't—so what!! No one can live forever."

The surgery went well, but his recovery proved long and difficult. There was a great deal of pain that lasted well beyond the expectation of the doctors. A month later they traced that to a pinched nerve where they had broken his ribs to gain access to the chest cavity. The aftereffects of this operation were "several times worse" than his back surgery. He had "no pep or ambition" for some time and did not leave Bethesda until just before Thanksgiving.

In the midst of Edson's stay in the hospital, another of his longstanding interests came to the fore. Vermont's Senator Aiken mentioned at a press conference that he expected the commissioner of public safety to run against him in the 1950 primaries. Edson had no such intention, and he announced that fact while still in Washington. It was an unlikely rumor because Aiken and Governor Gibson were close political allies, and the senator was far and away the most popular figure in the state. However, Red Mike was giving serious thought to the only other national race to be decided in his home state in 1950, Vermont's lone seat in the House of Representatives.

He had begun discussions on the issue with Senator Flanders and Stephen Kelley, a Montpelier public relations consultant, as early as June 1949, though he was far from making a decision.

Vermont's current representative was Charles A. Plumley, a seventy-five-year-old lawyer who had first entered politics three years before Edson was born. He had been in Congress since 1934, but there were indications that he might retire, or that a more progressive Republican might be able to defeat him. Just before Christmas 1949 a national radio broadcast announced that a group of Vermonters were trying to persuade Edson to run against Plumley. It just so happened that the commissioner had a press conference already scheduled for the next day concerning minor state police business. To the inevitable questions encountered there, Edson answered that the report was "news to me." Very likely the event was orchestrated as a trial balloon to test public reaction to the notion, an interpretation supported by his reiterated intention not to run against Aiken. He made no such promise regarding Plumley's seat.

In the spring of 1950 Edson canvased editors of the state's leading newspapers to determine the amount of support he might receive. They gave him a generally warm welcome; most estimated that he could probably beat Plumley, though it might be a tough race. Despite Red Mike's status as a hero, he had spent too little time in the state to develop a strong following. One public opinion survey ranked him only forty-fourth among Vermont's most influential leaders, well behind several potential opponents, to include Plumley. More disconcerting was the news that Robert W. Mitchell, editor of the important *Rutland Herald,* would not support him in the race. He told Edson that he was "no politician" and had "no business being in Congress anyway."

In mid-May Plumley announced his retirement from politics. Within days several people indicated that they would run for his seat. Edson refused to make any commitment to the press, but they mentioned his name prominently as a likely candidate. Some editorial reaction was positive, but not all. Several things tended to discourage Red Mike. The number of candidates and the lack of strong, broad-based support reduced the odds to less than fifty-fifty in his estimation. That conflicted with his oft-stated policy that "I never willingly entered any scrap that I did not expect to win." (He considered the unification battles an exception because they were "moral" ones.) More important was the cost, estimated at up to $20,000. Since the statute creating his position specifically forbad his participation in an election, he would have to give up his job and that income for several months, and then look for a new position if he lost. Given his financial status, he thought that an unwise risk. He was even more concerned about fund-raising after Paul Ballou rejected his request to serve as campaign treasurer. Finally, his political patron and strongest ally, Gibson, had accepted a nomination to the federal judiciary at the end of 1949 and was not available to assist him. With all those negative considerations in mind, he reluctantly announced his decision not to run in early June.

Edson did not give up his desire for elected office, he merely postponed it. He continued his intensive schedule of public appearances and kept a close watch on political developments. Editor Mitchell may have been right when he said that Red Mike was "no politician," but the retired general had all the makings of an excellent choice for Congress. He had strong convictions and was not afraid to make them known even when they were unpopular. In March 1950, while he was still a potential candidate, he vigorously attacked Senator Joseph McCarthy's anticommunism campaign as "rule by smearing" and repeatedly objected to legislation seeking to outlaw communism (what eventually became the McCarran Act). He lumped those efforts and the drive for defense unification together as threats to democracy. "It is in such times that our freedom is most imperiled, for unscrupulous men will play upon our fears to gather unwarranted power unto themselves." He noted that the Emancipation Proclamation was a century old, but "there are many who will say that emancipation of the negro has not yet been reached." He also supported the United Nations. In 1950, few of those positions were very popular, particularly in the Republican party. His stand against McCarthy was especially revealing, because the senator was one of the strongest legislative supporters of the Corps.

The passage of the Tydings bill had not been the only setback for the sea services in 1949. In addition to canceling the *United States,* Secretary of Defense Johnson (a former Army officer, assistant secretary of war, and director of the company building the Air Force's B-36 bomber) halved the Navy's force of carriers from eight to four in the fiscal year 1950 budget. He also increased funds for the B-36, the centerpiece of the Air Force's plan to deter or win the next war with nuclear bombs. That clear defeat in the budget battles sent shock waves through the Navy. The secretary of the Navy resigned in protest. Denfield, the CNO who had been reticent earlier due to Consolidation Directive No. 1, finally spoke out against the cutbacks during congressional hearings. Johnson fired him. This short outburst from the Navy, dubbed the "Revolt of the Admirals," came too late to affect the passage of the Tydings bill. It did elevate Admiral Sherman to the CNO slot, a switch that brought no joy to Marines worried about their own future. Edson's reaction to Sherman was "No comment fit to print!"

Red Mike continued his fight against unification in 1950 with more speeches and work on the National Security Committee of the VFW. And the Marine Corps continued to struggle for its life under the increasingly centralized Department of Defense. Marine supporters in Congress again introduced legislation to make the commandant a member of the JCS, but it made no headway. Sherman argued against the proposal and compared the Corps to another subset of the Navy such as submarines or aviation. Only events beyond the control of Edson and the Corps brought the issue to a successful but temporary close. On 25 June 1950 the North Korean army invaded South Korea and embroiled the United States in an unexpected war. Courageous battlefield fighting by Marines in the next few months, and politically inept criticism of the Corps by Truman, led Congress to pass a bill giving the commandant a voice in the deliberations of the JCS and permanently fixing the strength of the Corps at no less than three divisions and three air wings.

For Red Mike it was a very limited victory, since it did nothing to reverse the flow of power to the Department of Defense (DOD) and the JCS. In fact, the war emergency led to changes that he considered "dangerous precedents." In September 1950 Truman nominated Marshall to head the DOD. Although the 1947 National Security Act contained a provision preventing any former military officer from serving as secretary of defense for ten years after leaving active duty, Congress voted to waive that restriction and approve Marshall's appointment. Edson was especially worried about the retired Army general because he had been a major proponent of the original unification scheme. In Esdon's opinion Congress had put the fox in charge of the henhouse.

The Korean War may have saved the Corps, but it was a source of some consternation for Edson. He had retired in 1947 on the assumption that there would be no major conflict before he reached mandatory retirement age in 1957. Now he had to stand on the platform and watch a train depart with the Marine reserve unit he had helped create in Montpelier. As the war expanded and dragged on, he wished that he were "in the hills of Korea instead of the hills of Vermont." This was not the first time he had regretted his decision to retire. In March 1948, with the Berlin crisis just getting underway and a war scare sweeping the nation, he had looked into the possibility of a recall to active service. He told one of his former Raiders then that if he thought he had passed up the chance to command a division in combat, he would "kick himself all over the place." In the fall and winter of 1950, with the 1st Marine Division covering itself in glory at Inchon and the Chosin Reservoir, that chance appeared to be at hand.

It did not help that *Time* magazine featured a story recounting the division's history. Edson's picture accompanied the text, which mentioned only two heroes of Guadalcanal, Edson and Vandegrift. In January 1951 Red Mike talked to Cates about returning to active duty. The commandant suggested there might be a spot for him and told him to file a formal request. Edson sent one in, but he sensed that "a field command is almost beyond the pale of possibility." Cates's reply confirmed his expectations. The commandant had no intention of recalling any retired officers to active duty at present; if he did, Edson would return as a brigadier and would serve at headquarters.

Even if Red Mike had remained on active duty in 1947, he might still have missed out on his dream of commanding a division in combat. In January 1950 a promotion board had met to pick two brigadiers for major general. Since postwar selections had been almost entirely by seniority, Edson initially would have been considered for promotion at this time, as was the case with Thomas (just one number below him on the lineal list). Much to the surprise of Thomas, Edson, and most other Marines, the board passed over Thomas. The head of the committee was Watson, no friend of Thomas or Edson. In all probability the selection board would have passed over Red Mike too. Thomas seriously considered resigning over the "injustice and insult." As he later told Edson: "They do not pay off on a scale of values in D.C. today that you or I understand."

The Korean War halted the assault of the budget cutters on the Corps, which had dropped to just seventy-five thousand officers and men by the summer of 1950. With renewed expansion in the fall, the commandant gained authority for supplemental promotions to major general. A new board met in October 1950 and selected four men, among them Jerry Thomas. He pinned on the rank in January 1951, and Cates picked him to be the next commander of the 1st Marine Division. Assuming Red Mike would have been promoted at the same time, he would have found himself in competition with his friend for the only Marine division in combat. Thomas took charge in May and remained in Korea until January 1952, when he returned to the States to become assistant commandant to Lem Shepherd, the new commandant.

▼ As it was, the Edson family's major contribution to the war came from the next generation. The Corps activated Austin in February 1951; he ended up as a company commander in the 5th Marines under Col. Lew Walt. His battalion commander was Lt. Col. Jonas Platt. In June 1951 Bobby (now called Bob) graduated from high school and joined the Naval ROTC unit at Tufts as a Marine option. Red Mike's service during the Korean War centered on maintaining the strong ties of allegiance built up among a generation of men who had fought in World War II, many of whom had gone back to civilian life. He played a prominent role in the Marine Corps League and the division associations. Although these organizations were primarily fraternal, they provided a vital source of political support for the Corps.

The group that was closest to his heart, however, was a much smaller one. In February 1950 Walt invited former 1st Raider officers to Quantico to celebrate the eighth anniversary of the creation of the battalion. In the midst of a party that lasted nearly till dawn, the fourteen men present decided to form an association of those who had served in the 1st Raiders. Griffith later suggested that they broaden it to include all the Raider battalions, but Walt opposed that idea. He thought that there had been no special tie between the battalions; in fact, as Walt put it: "There was an opposite type of feeling between the First and Second Raider Battalions, at least throughout the first months of their existence." In a move that made it unique among Marine groups, the members voted unanimously to name it "Edson's Raiders Association." Even those men who served after Red Mike's departure from the battalion approved of the title. It was a tribute to their "devotion and admiration for General Edson."

● The gulf between the first two raider battalions was part good-natured rivalry between competing units, but there also was an element of genuine dislike. Much of that may have percolated down from the respective commanders. Edson never forgot the shabby treatment that Company A received on the West Coast in early 1942. Nor did he appreciate the 2d Battalion's ongoing claim that it was the original raider unit. Carlson's obituary in the 1 June 1947 *Washington Post* repeated that fallacy. Red Mike took the time to get the facts from headquarters so he could straighten out the misconception. (His unit was redesignated the 1st Separate Battalion on 7 January 1942 and 1st Raider Battalion on 16 February 1942. The respective dates for Carlson's outfit were 12 and 19 February 1942.) Edson carried the grudge even after Carlson's death; he refused to chair a memorial service to his rival. "I have never been nor am I now an ardent admirer of General Carlson's. Although I respected his bravery as an individual, I have never agreed with the doctrines and policies which he espoused."

Edson had concerns closer to home in early 1951. Emerson, the toughest political critic of the state police, won the governorship in November 1950. His inaugural address dwelt at length on a proposal to merge Edson's organization with the Department of Motor Vehicles. Although the governor billed it as a cost-saving measure, Red Mike was certain that his true goals were to cement ties with the powerful sheriffs, who stood to gain from the change, and to reorganize Edson's position out of existence so he could bring in his own man to fill the new billet. By law Emerson could not otherwise cut short the retired general's six-year term except for misconduct. Red Mike canceled all his out-of-state activities in February 1951 to concentrate on winning this latest "merger fight."

With years of experience working the halls of Congress, Edson was well prepared for this legislative struggle, though it proved to be a tough one. The bill narrowly passed its first vote in the Vermont House. Walt and Schatzel noted after a visit that they had never seen Edson "so downhearted and pessimistic." Further efforts by opponents overcame the initial appeal of the cost-cutting measure, however, and the bill went down to a decisive and final 142 to 89 defeat at its second reading in mid-April. Red Mike's dislike for Emerson showed through when he gloated in private over "beat[ing] the little s.o.b.'s ears back to where they belonged."

The political crisis in spring 1951 forced Edson to reassess his future in Vermont. He had won the battle, but in defeating the "major plank in the governor's legislative program" he had widened the rift between himself and the man he would have to work with for at least the next year and a half. In addition, Emerson had been successful in preventing the needed increase in the department's budget, which only added to the difficulty of the commissioner's job.

That was not the main problem. Red Mike had come north in 1947 with the goal of becoming a U.S. senator. He had expected that the position as commissioner would help him build "prestige and a friendly and receptive atmosphere" among Vermont's voters. Instead, he had been embroiled in controversy for most of his four years in office. Those difficulties would not prevent him from winning an election, but he had not attained his objective of being an overwhelming favorite. In between the initial victory of Emerson's police merger bill and its final defeat, Edson lost whatever taste he once had for the political arena. "As I have watched politics of the worst kind being played here in the State during the past nine months and more, I realize more and more how little stomach I have for it—and I am glad I made the decision which I did last spring. My skin is not thick enough; nor do I have the ability to play the game below the belt as it is being played here now."

Edson's options for staying in Vermont were not promising. Once he gave up his political dreams, all he had left was his position as commissioner. That promised continuing fights with the governor, with no assurance that whoever sat in the executive office two years hence would reappoint Edson to the job. General Cates had also just informed him that there was no prospect of a return to active duty. There was only one other line of work that Red Mike knew anything about, and chance stepped in to provide a ready solution to his dilemma. In early May 1951 Edson's close friend C. B. Lister died after a long illness. That left vacant Lister's position as the National Rifle Association's executive director, the top full-time position in that organization. With Red Mike's background as a competitive shooter, his standing as a national hero, and his ties to Congress and the military, he was a natural for the job. On 8 May the NRA offered him the position at a salary more than twice what he was making in Vermont. Edson took it.

He kept the decision a closely held secret until 15 June, when he informed the governor and made a public announcement. The move came as a surprise to everyone, and there was much speculation in the press over his motives. He explained simply that it was "a better job," but many assumed that the police merger battle had something to do with it. Everyone was sorry to see him go. His troopers appreciated his fair-minded, common-sense approach and his efforts to improve their working conditions and pay. One paper remarked on his ability to adapt to the procedures of civilian life after so many years in the military. Even Emerson, in accepting his resignation, commended him for "a splendid job." Robert Mitchell, the editor who had played a substantial part in dissuading Edson from politics, had fulsome praise for him, too. "Vermont has lost an outstanding man as head of the state police . . . a man who has an illustrious place in the history of our state and nation."

Chapter 20

"From Dawn to Setting Sun"

E dson's association with the NRA reached back three decades. He had joined the group in 1921 during his first season of competitive shooting. That was the same year that C. B. Lister came to work on the association's staff at its Washington headquarters. At that time the NRA was still a small organization of 450 clubs and 3,500 members. Edson and Lister became close friends over the years as each man rose to prominence in the sport: Red Mike as a shooter, then a team coach, captain, and match official; Lister as an administrator who eventually became the executive director of the NRA. World War II introduced the NRA to a wider segment of the population. The services were so overwhelmed with the influx of manpower that the NRA played a valuable role in providing initial marksmanship training. As a consequence, the association grew dramatically after the war as demobilizing veterans joined its ranks.

Edson's shooting background, national prominence, and seat on the board of directors of the NRA made him one of the leading figures in the shooting world in 1946. His authority in the area was so great that following his retirement in 1947 the Corps asked him to continue as its representative to the NBPRP because there was no senior active-duty officer with comparable qualifications. In 1948 the members of the NRA elected Edson vice president. As Red Mike involved himself more closely in the affairs of running the group, he discovered that all was not well. Its organization and bylaws had changed little since the 1920s and were now ill-suited to a rapidly expanding association. General Reckord served as the executive vice president, a part-time position on the NRA staff but one with greater authority than the senior full-time billet, Lister's executive director slot. Reckord had been an important leader in the NRA since 1926, but his range of duties began to exceed his capacity to do them all well. He also opposed some of the changes that Lister and others saw as necessary to modernize the group.

By tradition, the association elected the previous year's vice president to the presidency, a progression that provided continuity at the top and some training for the incoming president. Although the latter position did not involve its holder in the daily operations of the NRA, it was a seat of some real power. In 1949 Reckord proposed that Edson volunteer to remain the vice president for the next two years so he could serve out an honorary period as president to close his long association with the NRA. Lister asked Edson to refuse the request so they could ease Reckord out the door: "So, my friend, there is the baby right on your doorstep." Red Mike took the diplomatic course of not running an active campaign for the presidency, but also announcing that he would refuse to serve another term as vice president. At the 1949 convention in Denver the members elected Edson to the presidency as he recovered from his surgery in Bethesda. The man who had been so thrilled in his youth when he could hit a deer or the bull's-eye of a target was now head of the largest shooting organization in the nation.

He was soon assisting Lister and the rest of the staff in getting the NRA onto a fresh course. He established a board to draft new bylaws, reorganized the system of committees that recommended policy in various areas, and moved to "rejuvenate" the leadership of those bodies. He abolished Reckord's old position of executive vice president in order to clean up the lines of authority. Taking advantage of considerable member interest in hunting, Red Mike directed the association to develop more programs in that area. He also pressed hard to restore the preeminence of the national rifle matches and to convince the services to push the maximum marksmanship distance from six hundred yards back out to a thousand.

Competitive shooting was not yet back on its feet in 1950 when the Korean War interrupted things. The NRA even canceled its 1950 convention, scheduled for October in San Francisco, though Edson did bring together the board of directors. They adopted the new bylaws and discussed plans to reactivate the NRA's successful Civilian Basic Small Arms Course, the program that had helped the services and the NRA during World War II. When Red Mike took over as the executive director in the summer of 1951, the NRA was a flourishing organization of 230,000 members, but there was still a lot of room for growth.

The new job seemed much like Edson's state police position in some respects. Although he did not have to create a new organization, the NRA was undergoing a major transformation, and there were a number of loose ends to deal with in the aftermath of Lister's long illness. Red Mike also found himself on the road again, except this time he was traversing the nation, not a state. He was not running for office, but his efforts to build up the association and to affect legislation required many of the same skills he had practiced as a budding politician in Vermont. As he explained to one reporter, this was "no armchair desk task."

Edson quickly outlined his goals for the association—themes he would stick with throughout his tenure as executive director. One was the continued emphasis of the NRA on gun legislation. He stressed, however, the need to differentiate between good laws and bad ones. There should be no general prohibition or limitation on the ownership of weapons, but he wanted the NRA to vigorously support laws that provided stiff mandatory sentences for crimes committed with guns and barred convicted felons from possessing weapons. He also wanted strong programs to teach users proper safety techniques. Another goal was increased marksmanship training for both civilian enthusiasts and service members. Edson believed that the rifleman was the backbone of national defense and needed to be thoroughly trained in the use of his weapon to be effective. Civilian shooting programs contributed to that aim by providing preservice familiarity with weapons. Finally, Red Mike emphasized the need to expand membership and use the group's strength to pursue loftier goals. "If we will only lift our sights a little above the competitive target range . . . this Association can and will become one of the most important, one of the most influential organizations of patriotic citizens in the United States."

From his headquarters at 1600 Rhode Island Avenue in Washington, Edson pursued his effort to push the NRA to a higher plane of activity. He asked every staff member to explain his duties, and he set about realigning the organization to make it more efficient. He wrote the editorial that led off each issue of the association's magazine, *The American Rifleman*. His topics closely followed his goal of broadening the usefulness of the organization. He addressed issues such as getting out the vote for elections and the course of U.S. defense policy.

Not all of Red Mike's activities were related to the NRA. A side trip to Mexico City was at the behest of the CIA, which now employed him as a consultant. He also kept busy in his new capacity as president of the 1st Marine Division Association. He could say truthfully that he had "never been busier anytime or anyplace." He sometimes found the pace overwhelming, and his sister Mary counseled him to slow down.

In addition to the never-ending work, he had to worry about money, despite the big raise in pay. He had been unable to sell the house in Montpelier and had to rent it out, which meant that the Edsons had to settle for leased quarters in Washington. Given the cost of living in the nation's capital, they ended up with a much smaller but more expensive house. When Bob mentioned that he was considering going on to law school, he received a letter containing the ancient refrain of parents: "that money does NOT just grow on trees, and that your father is NOT rolling in wealth." Edson did at least enjoy some perquisites with the NRA. He described his new office glowingly, noting "the thick rug on the floor, and the air-conditioner and whatnot that would make the good Vermonters shake their heads in criticism."

That last comment seemed to contain a sigh of relief at finally being out from under the microscope of state politics. He soon made it clear that his former ambitions to achieve high elective office had disappeared altogether. In August 1952 Judge Gibson called from Vermont with a plea to enter the Republican primary for governor, since he thought Edson could handily defeat Emerson's weak candidacy. The chance to strike back at his old nemesis did not move Red Mike, though he did send a strongly worded letter to the state's newspapers supporting the relatively unknown man that Gibson finally persuaded to run. Emerson won the race by a narrow margin and Gibson lamented Edson's absence from the field: "You could have been our next Governor." Despite the hard work and the cost of living in Washington, Red Mike was comparatively happy with his new lot in life. "It is much better in every respect than trying to be a Chief of Police or a second-class politician."

Edson still had plenty of interest in political battles involving unification and the protection of the Corps. He kept in close contact with Thomas, Krulak, Heinl, and others in 1952 as they fought for the bill to put the commandant on the Joint Chiefs of Staff. He made occasional visits to Congress and received requests for advice from senators and representatives. And he continued to hold his seat on the VFW National Security Committee. In the winter of 1952–53 he served as the Marine Corps representative on the Sarnoff Commission, a board created by Senator Lyndon B. Johnson's Preparedness Subcommittee. Its mandate was to recommend changes on the use of manpower in the military, since the armed forces were under heavy criticism for wasting the time of many draftees.

The Sarnoff Commission died in February 1953 without having accomplished anything, due primarily to the election of Eisenhower as president. The former Army chief of staff launched a new unification battle with his Reorganization Plan No. 6. This proposal to strengthen the secretary of defense and the chairman of the JCS was a logical continuation of the drive to centralize control over military power. Red Mike did more lobbying and testified before a House committee. He emphasized that this was just "another girder added to the structure" that would result in eventual creation of the general staff that Congress had rejected in 1947. There were no witnesses from any of the services, but Commandant Shepherd sent a statement that opposed the legislation. Based on this input the House Committee on Government Operations voted against the bill, but the president eventually got his way in Congress.

Shepherd's ascendancy to the commandant's office in 1952 was an important turn of events for Edson. Whereas Vandegrift had acted as if Red Mike's retirement were "reprehensible," and Cates had kept him at arm's length, Shepherd wholeheartedly embraced Edson. The two men were not close friends—they had never served together—but there was considerable mutual respect. Edson made the commandant an honorary life member of the NRA. Shepherd invited Red Mike to be the reviewing officer at the sunset parade at the Marine Barracks in Washington. He also arranged for Edson to inspect the 1st Marine Division in Korea in spring 1953 so he could visit with Austin, on the front lines there in Red Mike's old 1st Battalion, 5th Marines. Edson received red carpet treatment throughout the theater, to include an audience with Syngman Rhee, the president of South Korea.

Red Mike became a regular speaker at Basic School graduation exercises in Quantico, particularly after Col. Lew Walt took charge of the program. Edson invariably spoke on his favorite topic, the rifleman. He told the young lieutenants that nuclear weapons had enhanced rather than diminished the importance of the individual, since greater dispersion on the battlefield and the vulnerability of rear areas meant that every man had to be prepared to operate effectively on his own. The executive director of the NRA was a welcome speaker at Army graduation exercises, too.

In August 1952 Shepherd asked Edson to assume the presidency of the Marine Corps War Memorial Foundation (MCWMF), a nonprofit corporation created to raise money and oversee the construction of the commemorative statue of the flag-raising on Iwo Jima. Felix de Weldon, a noted sculptor, had conceived the idea as soon as he saw the famous photo in February 1945. Congress had passed a joint resolution authorizing the monument in 1947. The MCWMF, originally an offshoot of the Marine Corps League, had begun operations in 1949. The amateurish fund-raising schemes of a handful of retired and reserve officers had turned into a debacle by 1951, when it was discovered that a reserve major, Harry R. Dash, had embezzled a large portion of the money. Red Mike's job was to straighten out the mess and push the embarrassingly bungled project to completion.

It was only after Edson took charge that he and the commandant realized just how bad things were. After a detailed study, Red Mike created a list of actions needed to clear up past problems. Chief among them was negotiating a contract with de Weldon, who had been working on the project for some time with no fixed agreement as to the amount he would receive for his services. Red Mike's formal "Estimate of the Situation" determined that the committee needed to raise an additional half million dollars, three times the amount previously thought sufficient. The study also highlighted the ineffectiveness of past fund-raising efforts. An expensive appeal by mail to the eighteen thousand members of the Marine Corps Reserve Officers Association, for instance, had brought in less than $600. The only significant source of income came from the recruit depots, which had no difficulty raising "contributions."

In 1953 and again in 1954 the commandant made appeals through his commanders for donations from active-duty Marines. The first drive netted $250,000; the second nearly brought the foundation to its final monetary goal. In the meantime, Edson and the foundation secured a seven-acre site for the memorial on a sought-after tract of land adjacent to Arlington National Cemetery. On the February 1954 anniversary of the landing on Iwo Jima, Shepherd and Edson jointly wielded a shovel to break ground for construction. In his brief address Red Mike described the future statue as an "immortal scene" that "symbolized the determination, the pride, and the patriotism of the American people." The commandant reached back to paraphrase the ancient Greeks at Thermopylae in describing the symbolism of the monument honoring all Marines who had fought for their country: "Go tell all Americans ye who are passers by that somewhere, faithful to their trust, we lie."

The occasion, with Edson making a rare appearance in his dress blue uniform and the Marine Corps band blaring Sousa marches in the background, should have been a triumph for the retired general. Instead, he was decidedly unhappy. The process of constructing the memorial and raising funds was proceeding well, but he was frustrated over a continuing series of disputes with the foundation's board of directors, many of them the same men who had run things so poorly prior to his arrival on the scene. They disagreed over a number of issues, but the primary problem seemed to be the board's proclivity for spending money.

The relationship between the president and the board reached a low point when it held an unscheduled meeting while Edson was out of town and approved an additional payment of $5,000 beyond a price already agreed upon in a contract. At least two members of the board also had conflicts of interest involving business ties to the project. Red Mike was disgusted with such arrangements. He himself was scrupulous in his dealings; he even refused to accept the gift of a scale model of the statue from de Weldon. Nor was he the only one to object to the situation. Ruth Cheney Streeter, former head of the Women Marines during World War II, had resigned from the board for similar reasons before Edson assumed the presidency.

In June 1954 Red Mike made a final attempt to put the board on a sound legal footing and to alter its membership. His efforts failed. After discussions with Shepherd, Thomas, and Streeter, he resigned from the foundation. He was "delighted, indeed, to be out of it." Edson attended the international shooting matches in Venezuela and was "happy" to miss the dedication of the memorial on 10 November 1954. Instead, he participated in a small Marine Corps birthday celebration with the Marine guards at the embassy in Caracas. His difficulties with the project did not dim his view of it. He believed that the dedication was "a truly momentous event in the history of the Corps," and he congratulated de Weldon for the impressive result. "I could not visualize until I saw it finally erected the grandeur of your work." The commandant was equally pleased with Edson's energy and resourcefulness in managing the project, but the strongest praise for Red Mike came from another congratulatory letter: "It will not only be a memorial to our Corps, but to you as well in the years ahead."

In May 1955 the secretary of defense appointed Edson to another board, the Defense Advisory Commission on Prisoners of War (POWs). This group had its roots in the Korean War, where the Communists used some American captives as political propaganda tools. A few POWs had given in to enemy pressure and confessed to things such as the supposed U.S. use of germ warfare. After the return of the prisoners, the Marine Corps conducted a court of inquiry on Col. Frank H. Schwable, a pilot who had signed a confession. The court recommended no action because the Communists had tortured Schwable, but it did note the lack of clear policy governing the conduct of POWs. In passing the results of the inquiry to the secretary of defense, Shepherd suggested the need for "well defined" guidance. The situation was further exacerbated because the Army took a hard line against its collaborators, whereas the Air Force absolved all its men of any blame for their actions. The result was a board to recommend a joint policy for the future.

The committee deliberated from late May through the end of July. They investigated a number of options, including a recommendation that prisoners be authorized to say or sign anything. According to that line of reasoning, the United States would announce beforehand that any communications from its captured men would be considered false and thus no harm would result to the nation or to the prisoners. Edson hewed to the tough line favored by Shepherd and the Army, which encouraged a POW to hold out against pressure and refuse to divulge any information but name, rank, and serial number. The majority of the committee ended up agreeing. The result of their deliberations was the Code of Conduct for POWs, a set of brief principles ingrained into American fighting men from that time forward.

● The POW committee placed an unusually heavy burden on Edson. Since it brought him onto active duty, that was his daily job for two months. As a consequence, he had to fit in his full-time responsibilities with the NRA whenever he could. He had a full plate of other activities, too. There were occasional meetings in his new position as a director of the National Savings & Trust Company, work with a national committee of the Boy Scouts of America, speeches to the Basic School classes, and attendance at the annual 1st Marine Division reunion. He was living proof of the maxim that one of his friends had sent him: "The man who has time for all he wants to do, surely cannot want to do very much."

Edson's sister, Mary, took him to task again for his overburdened schedule when he announced his appointment to the POW panel. "I don't know whether to congratulate you on being on the advisory committee or not, for the reason you just do too much, just are wearing yourself out." In physical terms Red Mike was actually on the rebound in the early summer of 1955. After retiring from the Corps and taking command of a desk, his weight had gone up to the high 160s and remained there. In March he instituted a strict diet and tried to keep his daily food intake to 1,700 calories; some days he ate as little as one-third of that amount. By the beginning of June he was down to 153 pounds. He had also begun taking special vitamins recommended by an Army doctor.

The summer of 1955 also marked the first time in many years that all of the Edson family was together for any length of time. Austin was still on active duty and stationed at Quantico on the staff of the Basic School. Bob had graduated from Tufts in June and won the Marine Corps Association award for being the top Marine option in that Naval ROTC unit. He was now undergoing training at the Basic School. With both sons close to home, the family went out together on a regular basis for dinner or entertainment, events Red Mike made time for despite his hectic schedule. In early August he spent a day down at Quantico speaking to another Basic School class and witnessing the donation of a perpetual trophy for marksmanship from the lieutenants of one company to the school. They had been so impressed by the general's remarks on a previous occasion that they created the award and named it in his honor. The general, Austin, and Bob had their picture taken in front of the replica of the Iwo Jima memorial located at the main gate to the Quantico base. It was the only photograph of all three in uniform, since this was the first time all of them had been on active duty together.

Edson's only apparent concern was the ever-present problem of money. He had finally sold the Montpelier house in 1954, but for only $13,000. That was much less than he had paid for it, and barely half what he had hoped to get. His retired pay also had gone down in 1954 when he elected to reduce it by one-quarter to provide survivor's benefits for Ethel. That program entitled her to continue to receive a portion of his retirement benefits should he die first. He was so "strapped" for money in January 1955 that he borrowed $2,500 from Mary. (He needed it to buy stock in the trust company in order to meet the legal requirements for a director's seat.) He had some investments, mainly still in life insurance policies, but he and Ethel had little in the way of savings. The sale of the house removed their only major debt, however, and his salary and military retirement pay covered their monthly expenses.

On Saturday, 13 August 1955, Merritt and Ethel attended a late-afternoon wedding. He slept through the ceremony and when they returned home he laid down to rest, after which he expected to go to the office. With the POW commission just completed and a long trip to Camp Perry for the National Matches just ahead, there was much to do. He got up briefly at 2300 and told Ethel that he was going to sleep a little more, but he still intended to go in to work that night. She was a bit worried about him, though it was common for him to take naps whenever he had some free time. It made up for the sleep he lost during his typically long days. Bob was up from Quantico for a weekend visit. He returned from a date at 0200 and parked the family car in the driveway. Shortly after 0800 on Sunday morning, Ethel found her husband in the car in the garage. The key was in the ignition and turned to the "on" position, but the motor was no longer running. He was dead.

The newspapers reported General Edson's death as a "mystery." The coroner ruled that it was due to carbon monoxide poisoning, but would make no pronouncement beyond that. Surprisingly, no one decided to conduct an autopsy. The general's will specified a preference for cremation and the family quickly carried out his wishes. A few days later, the deputy coroner announced that he had ruled Edson's death a suicide. Since there had been no autopsy, he based his decision on the amount of carbon monoxide in the general's blood and the circumstances surrounding his death.

The coroner's announcement came as a shock to Red Mike's family and friends. Ethel refused to believe he could do such a thing: "No problem was too great for Merritt." Lew Walt said that it "was completely out of the question for a man of Edson's character and temperament." Several people who had been close to the general sought to prove the coroner wrong. They discussed the facts with doctors and developed various explanations, all involving some form of heart failure. There were significant problems with each of these scenarios. Red Mike's annual physical examinations at Bethesda, to include one done just two weeks before his death, revealed no evidence of a heart problem. All the doctors who had answered queries from Edson's family and friends had based their diagnoses on second-hand information. They had never examined Red Mike and did not have access to his medical records.

The circumstantial evidence points strongly toward suicide. After pulling the car into the garage, Edson had either left the car running while he closed the garage doors, or started it up again after getting back into the car. Both suggest an intentional act. The position of the body also was such that it was clear he had lain down on the car seat, not slumped over. It seems most unlikely that he felt strong enough to open the garage doors, put the car away, close the garage doors, get back in the car, and lay down, but felt too poorly to notice that the engine was still running.

Since the physical facts are not conclusive, Edson's state of mind takes on great importance. There is evidence to support Ethel's contention that "all facts of his manner of living show how he was looking toward the future." His appointment calendar was full for weeks to come. On the other hand, several friends later recalled incidents that seemed relevant in light of the circumstances of his death. One officer who saw him that summer noticed that "the fire seemed to be gone from his eyes." Thomas was "shocked" when Edson confessed to him one day that he was tired, an unusual public admission for a man who always seemed to exhibit boundless energy. A former Raider recalled an odd discussion with Red Mike over lunch at the Army-Navy Club. Edson asked him which medal he thought was the most beautiful, and then revealed that his choice was the Purple Heart: "I always wanted to have it but it never happened."

In spite of the belief of many that the general was "too big a man" to kill himself, he had for many years expressed the feeling that his own life was worth little. During World War II he actually had looked forward to the prospect of dying in battle. To all outward appearances he had no fear of any challenge, but he also was fond of saying that he would never fight a battle he did not expect to win. And he apparently subscribed to the notion that suicide was an acceptable alternative in the right circumstances; he had found no shame in Cal Lloyd's decision to kill himself.

The last few years of his life had been productive, but each success had bred disappointment, too. His skill as a staff officer had taken him away from combat, but not brought him the promotion he deserved. His effort to prevent unification cost him a career that might have ended with the commandancy instead of an early retirement. He brought the state police to life and prevented encroachment on their powers, but in the process lost his hopes of political office and even his livelihood in his home state. He continued to fight for the Corps in retirement, but that institution left him at home when it went off to Korea and greater glory. Even his valuable role in bringing the Iwo Jima Memorial to life ended on a bitter note. There will never be conclusive proof as to the cause of Edson's death, but it may be that in the summer of 1955 Red Mike decided that life was a battle with no more victories in sight.

Edson's funeral took place on Tuesday, 16 August. Although the Marine Corps had sent the hero of the Ridge into retirement without fanfare, this time Red Mike received full military honors. After a service in the base chapel at Fort Myer, the funeral cortege wound its way to nearby Arlington National Cemetery. Colonel Walt led the escort, a battalion of Marines in dress blues. A riderless horse, with empty boots facing backward in the stirrups, accompanied the caisson carrying the general's remains. The Marine Corps band provided the funeral music. After the casket was in the ground, General Shepherd, the commandant of the Marine Corps, handed Ethel the folded American flag that had draped the coffin. A bugler played taps and a detachment of riflemen fired a final volley in honor of the man who had heard so many shots in battle and in competition. Red Mike was gone, though one of the eulogies hinted that he would not be forgotten.

> There is no death! The stars go down
> To rise upon some other shore;
> And bright in heaven's jeweled crown
> They shine for evermore.

Epilogue

dson's contemporaries greeted the news of his tragic death with shock and disbelief because they knew him only as a courageous and invincible leader, one who never shrank from any confrontation. At the end of World War II Red Mike had been one of the greatest heroes in the Corps. Few Marine officers could point to a list of engagements as impressive. No other senior leader had an equal reputation for bravery under fire in the front lines. He was less well known for his superior staff work, though his contributions to the Corps in that area were every bit as important. His combination of courage and competence made him an excellent choice for commandant, a position he might have held in the 1950s if the unification crisis had not intervened.

In the first few years after his death, Red Mike maintained a place of importance in the hearts of fellow Marines. The shooting community honored him with a minute of silence and the playing of taps on the firing lines of the 1955 National Matches. Within a few months, Thomas dedicated a new building at Quantico as Edson Hall. In 1958 the Navy named one of its destroyers (DD-946) after the Marine hero. The firing range at Camp Pendleton, a Vermont reserve center, a Marine Corps League detachment, and a number of other entities eventually bore Edson's name.

Despite these physical commemorations of Red Mike, modern Americans are only vaguely familiar with the man and his deeds. Several dictionaries of military biography take note of Carlson and Puller, but not Edson. The Coco Patrols have been reduced to a footnote in the Banana Wars, which have themselves been washed away by the tidal wave of a

414

bigger war of counterinsurgency, Vietnam. The Corps has recently resurrected the *Small Wars Manual* as a teaching tool, but the reprints bear no indication of Edson's role in creating that doctrine. Most of his battles in the southern Solomons are largely forgotten. Tulagi is regarded as a sideshow to Guadalcanal, while Tasimboko and the Matanikau engagements pale beside the bigger and bloodier struggles later in the war. Edson's name barely appears in the accounts of Tarawa, Saipan, and Tinian—since he was not a commander—and Shoup has long worn the mantle as the sole architect of the Betio assault plan. Only Red Mike's heroics on the Ridge generate some recognition, but he too often appears as a one-dimensional figure, the stereotypical leader who instills courage by screaming at his men about "guts."

One might easily write off Edson's loss of status as a function of the passage of time, but that is not a complete explanation. After all, Puller's legend has grown stronger over the years, though he was probably no more than co-equal with Red Mike at the end of World War II. The reasons are not hard to discern. While Edson suffered one disappointment after another following that war, Puller went on to greater fame at Inchon and the Chosin Reservoir. Finally, the nature of Red Mike's death undoubtedly diminished the general's stature in the eyes of those who considered suicide a disreputable act.

History has not treated Edson kindly, but the loss has fallen most heavily on his successors. Modern Marines could make good use of many facets of Red Mike's legacy. Today's Special Operations Capable battalions have much to learn from the Raiders. The Coco Patrols are vital to understanding the strategy and tactics contained in the *Small Wars Manual*. And the unification battles of the late 1940s may yet replay themselves before the current restructuring of the armed forces is complete. Red Mike was also one of those rare individuals who combined administrative ability with leadership. He knew how to plan an attack as well as command one. More importantly, he understood logistics better than most military men, who too often like to think of themselves as battlefield commanders first, and staff officers only when necessary. Edson's career reminds us that a leader must be skilled in both areas to be truly great.

While Red Mike's example of bravery on the battlefield is valuable, he also demonstrated the rarer commodity of moral courage. He was not a man to shrink from telling his superiors what he really thought, even when they had no desire to hear those ideas. He was quite willing to sacrifice his own future if that served a higher purpose. He noted in his later years that many men go through life thinking they are strong, when in reality they have only played it safe. Edson always challenged the boundaries of his profession instead of accepting the status quo.

Red Mike had weaknesses, but they were primarily in his personal life. Those feet of clay both tarnish and enhance his reputation. Most everyone fails somewhere in life; few rise above their problems to do great deeds. Edson placed himself in that select group because he recognized a simple truth: "If it is a fear you would dispel, the seat of that fear is in your heart and not in the hand of the feared." Merritt Edson knew how to overcome most of the fears that crept into his heart. He deserves to be one of the greatest legends in the history of the Corps.

Essay on Sources

The richest sources of information on Merritt Edson are his personal papers, an unusually complete collection of more than twenty thousand documents held by the Manuscript Division of the Library of Congress. I also used some recently uncovered material that the Edson family has since added to the collection. Those documents will probably not be cataloged for some time, although the main body of material is readily available. A valuable supplement to the papers are Edson's twelve thousand photographs maintained by the Photographic Division of the Library of Congress. The photographs have not yet been cataloged.

The Marine Corps Historical Center (MCHC) in Washington, D.C., possesses a wide range of information on the Corps and on individual Marines. The National Archives (NA) in Washington holds all official Marine Corps records through 1940. The Washington National Records Center (WNRC) in Suitland, Maryland, holds official Marine Corps records after 1940, to include the campaign records of World War II. The *Marine Corps Gazette* (*MCG*) is also an important source. Finally, I have supplemented the available primary and secondary sources with a large number of interviews, particularly with members of the 1st Raider Battalion. I conducted these either in person or by telephone or mail. I have used that information sparingly and only when corroborated at least in part by documentary evidence.

Most personal details in this biography are drawn from family letters and diaries contained in Boxes 1, 2, and 3 of the Edson papers (EP). Many basic facts of Red Mike's military career are contained in his enlisted Service Record Book, Officer Qualification Record, Officer Selection Jacket, and Medical Record. The first three are held by the National Personnel Records Center in St. Louis. His medical records are maintained by the Veterans Administration. These heavily used sources will not be cited hereafter.

PROLOGUE

The quote on Edson's eyes comes from "The Best Soldier I Ever Knew" by Richard Tregaskis, *Saga* (Feb 1960), p 18. Although the article was published in a men's magazine not noted for high scholarly standards, the piece is a reliable summary of Edson's career. The "shriveled up" quote comes from the Lee N. Minier papers (MCHC).

CHAPTER 1

Primary sources are Boxes 7, 35, 42, 55, 57, 59, and uncataloged material (EP); the Paul Ballou papers, held by the Ballou family; the UVM newspaper (the *Vermont Cynic*), yearbook (the *Aerial*), and catalogs of that era (all in the UVM Archives); the *Burlington Daily Free Press*; the personnel records of the 1st Vermont Infantry (State Veterans Affairs Bureau, Montpelier); and the official records of the regiment (Vermont Militia Museum, Camp Johnson). Secondary sources are *Put the Vermonters Ahead: A History of the Vermont National Guard* by Peter Haraty (Burlington: Queen City Printers, 1978); *Edson Family History and Genealogy* by Carroll A. Edson (Ann Arbor: Edward Brothers); *In Many A Strife* by Allan R. Millett (Annapolis: Naval Institute Press, 1993); "As It Was Before" by J. C. Jenkins, *MCG* (Mar 1941); and "Red Mike Edson" by Edward Dieckmann, *MCG* (Aug 1962). The last source is not very reliable, but correspondence between Dieckmann and Paul Ballou provides insight into which information to accept or reject.

CHAPTER 2

Primary sources are Boxes 4, 7, and 15 (EP); "History of Company E, 11th Regiment," Jacob Stein papers; "The Schleswig-Holstein Expedition," James H. Draucker papers; the Thaddeus Sandifer papers (all MCHC); a postcard booklet of Quantico entitled "Devil Dogs in the Making," and a unit newspaper called *The Schleswig Patrol* (both MCHC). Secondary sources are *Semper Fidelis* by Allan R. Millett (New York: Free Press, 1982); *Maverick Marine* by Hans Schmidt (Lexington: University Press of Kentucky, 1987); *The Reminiscences of a Marine* by Maj. Gen. John A. Lejeune (Philadelphia: Dorrance & Co., 1930); "History of the 11th Regiment U.S. Marines," *MCG* (Jun 1942); "A History of the Education of Marine Officers," *MCG* (May 1936); and "American Islands in France," *Collier's Weekly* (21 Sep 1918). "Moving Like Prairie Fire" by David Brown, *Washington Post* (15 Mar 1992), details the history of the flu epidemic. A valuable source is "That So-and-so Grin," a draft article on Edson in the possession of its author, Col. Houston Stiff. Stiff interviewed Edson for it in 1947, and the original bears the general's comments in the margins.

CHAPTER 3

Primary sources are Boxes 15–17, 31, 35, 42, 45, 49, and 55 (EP); Austin Edson's "Memoirs" describing his life; the Adjutant & Inspector files, RG #127 (NA); and the oral history of Lt. Gen. Louis H. Woods (MCHC). Secondary sources on shooting are *The History of Marine Corps Competitive Marksmanship* by Maj. R. E. Barde (Washington: HQMC, 1961); "America's Distinguished Marksmen" by Sue Ann Sandusky, *American Rifleman* (May 1991); "The Training of a National Match Team" by Maj. W. D. Smith, *MCG* (Dec 1919); and "The March of Events," *MCG* (1921). Sources on aviation are *History of Marine Corps Aviation in World War II* by Robert Sherrod (Washington: Combat Forces Press, 1952); *United States Naval Aviation 1910–1980* (Washington: Dept. of the Navy, 1981); *Marine Corps Aviation: The Early Years 1912–1940* by Lt. Col. Edward Johnson (Washington: HQMC, 1977); and *Unaccustomed to Fear: A Biography of the Late General Roy S. Geiger* by Roger Willock (Quantico: Marine Corps Association, 1983). Other sources are Lejeune's *Reminiscences*; Schmidt's *Maverick Marine*; Millett's *Strife*; *Marine Officer Procurement: A Brief History* by Bernard C. Nalty (Washington: HQMC, 1958); "The Mail Guard," *MCG* (Dec 1926); "Marine Corps Order #8," *MCG* (Jun 1921); "Education in the Marine Corps" by Col. R. H. Dunlap, *MCG* (Dec 1925); and "Professional Notes," *MCG* (Sep 1927). Box 17 is especially interesting because it includes Edson's flight logbooks.

CHAPTER 4

An important primary source for this chapter is Edson's own account of this period, "The Coco Patrol," *MCG* (Aug, Nov 1936 and Feb 1937). His extensive records saved from the patrol, and a short diary, are now in his uncataloged papers (EP). Other primary sources are Boxes 18–23 and 28 (EP); the Harold Utley papers (MCHC), which contain most of the original message traffic of the Eastern Area; the Nicaragua files (MCHC Reference); the 2d Brigade files, RG #127 (NA); and the Ballou papers. I also interviewed CWO3 Raymon Clark, probably the last surviving member of the patrol. His vivid recollections correlated extremely well with the written sources and provided invaluable additional insights. Secondary sources on sea duty are "With the Special Service Squadron" by Capt. John W. Thomason, *MCG* (Jun 1927); and "The State Department's Navy: A History of the Special Service Squadron" by Richard Millett, *The American Neptune* (Apr 1975).

CHAPTER 5

This chapter makes use of most of the same sources as Chapter 4. Additional primary sources are Boxes 9 and 15 (EP); and Stiff's "Grin." Secondary sources are *A History of the United States Marine Corps* by Lt. Col. Clyde H. Metcalf (New York: Putnam, 1939); "The Saga of the Coco" by Maj. Edwin McClellan, *MCG* (Nov 1930); "Professional Notes," *MCG* (Dec 1928); "The Coco Patrol" by Maj. Houston Stiff, *MCG* (Feb 1957); and the oral history of Gen. Edwin A. Pollock (MCHC). "U.S. Marines, Miskitos, and the Hunt for Sandino" by David C. Brooks, *Journal of Latin American Studies* (May 1989), provides an important perspective on the campaign.

CHAPTER 6

Primary sources are Boxes 4, 15–17, 20–22, 28, 53, 55, 59, and uncataloged material (EP). Of special note is the copy of *Small Wars Operations* in Box 21, perhaps the only copy left in existence. Other primary sources are the Utley and Ridgway papers (MCHC); the oral histories of Brig. Gen. Edward C. Dyer, Samuel B. Griffith II, Frank Schwable, and Robert H. Williams (MCHC); the Adjutant & Inspector Files, RG #127 (NA); the Clark interview; and Austin Edson's "Memoirs." Secondary sources are Millett's *Semper Fidelis* and *Strife*; Barde's *Marksmanship*; *Progress and Purpose: A Developmental History of the USMC* by Lt. Col. Kenneth Clifford (Washington: HQMC, 1973); "The Education of a Marine Officer" by Brig. Gen. Dion Williams, *MCG* (Aug 1933); "Tactics and Techniques of Small Wars" by Lt. Col. Harold Utley, *MCG* (May 1931, Aug 1933, Nov 1933, and Feb 1935); "Final Report of the M.G.C." by Maj. Gen. John Russell, *MCG* (Nov 1936); "The Training of a National Match Team" by Maj. W. D. Smith, *MCG* (Dec 1919); "The Training of a National Match Team" by Maj. Merritt Edson, *MCG* (Feb 1937); and professional notes in the *MCG* (Aug 1933, May 1935, Aug 1935, Jul 1936, and Aug 1936).

CHAPTER 7

Primary sources for the Shanghai period are in Boxes 4, 5, 8, 16, 29, 35, and 45 (EP); the 4th Marines' *Walla Walla* newspaper (MCHC); the oral histories of Lt. Gen. Robert E. Hogaboom, Victor H. Krulak, and Herman Nickerson, Jr. (MCHC); an interview with Lieutenant General Krulak; and Austin Edson's "Memoirs." Secondary sources are *Hold High the Torch* by Kenneth W. Condit and Edwin T. Turnbladh (Washington: HQMC, 1960); *The 4th Marines and Soochow Creek* by F. C. Brown (Bennington, VT: Int'l Graphics, 1980); *The Old Corps* by Brig. Gen. Robert H. Williams (Annapolis: Naval Institute, 1982); Millett's *Semper Fidelis*; "Shanghai Emergency" by Maj. Richard B. Rothwell, *MCG* (Nov 1972); "North China, 1937" by Capt. S. B. Griffith, *MCG* (Nov 1938); and "Military Lessons from the Chinese-Japanese War" by Capt. C. Rodney Smith, *MCG* (Mar 1940).

Primary sources for the HQMC period are Boxes 4, 8, 13, 15, 21, 22, and 33 (EP). Of particular interest are partial diaries for 1940–41 in Box 3 and the uncataloged correspondence with Ashurst. Other primary sources are the Lt. Gen. Julian Smith papers (MCHC); the biographical files of Maj. Gen. Thomas Watson, Maj. Gen. William Rupertus, Brig. Gen. Vernon Guymon, and Lt. Col. Ernest Linsert (MCHC); and the hearings of the Senate Committee on Military Affairs, 29 May 1940 (NA). Secondary sources are *Once a Marine* by A. A. Vandegrift with Robert Asprey (New York: Norton, 1964); Barde's *Marksmanship*; Millett's *Semper Fidelis* and *Strife*; *Schouler Divorce Manual* by Oscar Leroy Warren (Albany, NY: Banks & Co. 1944); "Headquarters Marine Corps and Arlington Annex," *MCG* (Dec 1991); *American Rifleman* (Mar 1943); "The Marine Corps Rifle and Pistol Teams and the National Matches, 1939" by Maj. Merritt Edson, *MCG* (Sep 1939); "Command of Native Troops" by Lt. Col. Harold Oppenheimer, *MCG* (Oct 1951); "Marine Corps Rifle Tests" *MCG* (Jun 1941); and "The Marine Corps Rifle Team, 1940" by 1st Sgt. Robert Thompson, Jr., *MCG* (Nov 1940).

CHAPTER 8

Primary sources are Boxes 4, 7, 8, 15, 23, and 35 (EP); Amphibious Force Atlantic Fleet files, Boxes 1–3, Series 63A-2535 (WNRC); 1/5 unit file (MCHC); the oral histories of Krulak, Brig. Gen. Samuel B. Griffith II, Col. Justice M. Chambers, Gen. Graves B. Erskine, and Gen. Gerald C. Thomas (MCHC); correspondence with Gen. Merrill B. Twining in the possession of Dr. Allan R. Millett; and interviews with Brig. Gen. John Antonelli, Col. John Apergis, James Blessing, James Childs, Capt. Frank Guidone, John Ingalls, Col. Ira Irwin, James Mallamas, Anthony Massar, GySgt. Edward Roche, Dr. Robert Skinner, Col. John Sweeney, and James Thomas, all members of the 1st Raider Battalion. Secondary sources are *A Brief History of the 5th Marines* by Maj. James M. Yingling (Washington: HQMC, 1963); and *U.S. Marine Corps Special Units of World War II* by Charles L. Updegraph, Jr. (Washington: HQMC, 1972). Edson's 1941 diary in Box 3 (EP) and the AFAF files are valuable sources for this period.

CHAPTER 9

This chapter uses many of the same sources as Chapter 8. Additional primary sources are Boxes 5, 9, 16, 24, 47, and 55 (EP); the Lee Minier and Gen. Thomas Holcomb papers (MCHC); 1st Raider Battalion muster rolls (MCHC); the Marine raider files (WNRC); the Nickerson oral history (MCHC); the Henry Poppell diary (possession of Edson's Raiders Association); and interviews with Herb Coffin, Col. John Erskine, Marlin Groft, Lt. Gen. Foster LaHue, Maj. Gene Martin, Thomas Mullahey, Lt. Col. Robert Neuffer, Thomas Pierce, Thomas Powers, Irv Reynolds, CWO Forrest Tyree, Jack Tracy, and James Vittitoe. Secondary sources are *The U.S. Marines and Amphibious War* by Jeter Isely and Philip Crowl (Princeton: Princeton University Press, 1951); *Commandos and Rangers of World War II* by James Ladd (New York: St. Martin's Press, 1978); *Semper Fi, Mac* by Henry Berry (New York: Arbor House, 1982); Vandegrift's *Once a Marine*, p 100; "The Worst Slap in the Face" by Lt. Col. R. E. Mattingly, *MCG* (Mar 1983); "Combat As I Saw It" by T. D. Smith, *The Dope Sheet* (Jul 1990); "Guerrilla Warfare in China" by Samuel Griffith, *MCG* (Jun 1941); and "A TBX Team On the Tasimboko Raid" by Fred Serral, *The Dope Sheet. The Dope Sheet,* the newsletter of Edson's Raiders Association, contains many useful details of raider history.

CHAPTER 10

This chapter uses many of the same sources on the Raiders. Other primary sources are Boxes 5, 13, 15, 24, 35, 46, 54, and 55 (EP); the oral histories of Maj. Gen. Chester R. Allen, Brig. Gen. Robert C. Kilmartin,

Jr., and Gen. Merrill B. Twining (MCHC); interviews with Col. Houston Stiff and John Ingalls; the Claffy papers (MCHC); Stiff's "Grin"; and the Guadalcanal campaign records (WNRC). Secondary sources are *Guadalcanal* by Richard Frank (New York: Random House, 1990); *The Amphibians Came to Conquer* by George Dyer (Washington: HQMC, 1991); *The Guadalcanal Campaign* by Maj. John Zimmerman (Washington: HQMC, 1949); *The Battle for Guadalcanal* by Brig. Gen. Samuel Griffith II (Annapolis: Nautical & Aviation Publishing, 1979), p 36; *Fighting on Guadalcanal* (Washington: War Dept., 1943); *Guadalcanal Diary* by Richard Tregaskis (New York: Random House, 1943), pp 79–84; Millett's *Strife*; Tregaskis's "The Best Soldier I Ever Knew"; "Red Mike and His Do or Die Men" by George Doying, *Leatherneck* (Mar 1944); "Raiders on Tulagi" by Pete Pettus, *The Dope Sheet* (Jul 1959); and "The Night by the Ditch" by Gene Martin, *The Dope Sheet* (1956).

CHAPTER 11

Additional primary sources on this period of the 1st Raiders are Boxes 6, 8, 9, 15, 16, 24, 26, and 58 (EP); interviews with Col. J. A. Daskalskis, Col. Clarence Schwenke, Martin Clemens, and Roche. Secondary sources are *Guadalcanal Remembered* by Herbert Merrilat (New York: Dodd, Mead & Co., 1982); *The Island* by Herbert Merrilat (Washington: Zenger, 1979); *The Quiet Warrior* by Thomas B. Buell (Annapolis: Naval Institute Press, 1987), p 126; Frank's *Guadalcanal*, pp 222, 232; Griffith's *Battle for Guadalcanal*, pp 109–110, 116, 119; Tregaskis's *Diary*, pp 228, 232; Tregaskis's "The Best Soldier I Ever Knew," p 84; and "Do or Die Men" by Herbert Edson. The latter unpublished account is especially useful, since it is based on Herbert Edson's interviews of his father after the war.

CHAPTER 12

Primary sources for this chapter, in addition to those cited above, are interviews with Brig. Gen. Gordon Gayle and Charles Morris; the oral histories of Col. Victor Croizat and Lt. Gen. John McLaughlin (MCHC); and correspondence between General Twining and Dr. Millett. Secondary sources are *Marine!* by Burke Davis (Boston: Little, Brown & Co., 1962), p 146; *Into the Valley* by John Hersey (New York: Alfred A. Knopf, 1943), p 91; *The U.S. Marine Corps in World War II,* ed. by S. E. Smith (Random

House: New York, 1969); Millett's *Strife*, p 201; and "Second Battle of the Matanikau" by Pete Pettus, *The Dope Sheet* (1958). There is no general agreement on the names of the battles along the Matanikau. Although some authors refer to the late-September battle as "First Matanikau," there was an earlier battalion-sized operation that probably rates that title. Edson called the late-September battle "Second Matanikau," and I have adopted that usage.

CHAPTER 13

Primary sources are Boxes 4, 5, 6, 9, 16, 22, 35, 54, 55, and 58 (EP); the oral histories of Lt. Gen. Leo D. Hermle, Lt. Gen. Julian C. Smith, Thomas, Twining, and McLaughlin (MCHC); the Tarawa campaign files, Box 13, Series 65A-4556 (WNRC); and my interviews with Gayle, Morris, and Apergis. Secondary sources are *Follow Me* by Richard Johnston (New York: Random House, 1948); *History of U.S. Marine Corps Operations in World War II: Central Pacific Drive* by Henry I. Shaw, Bernard C. Nalty, and Edwin T. Turnbladh (Washington: HQMC, 1966); *Coral and Brass* by Gen. Holland M. Smith (New York: Scribners, 1949); *Line of Departure* by Martin Russ (Garden City, NY: Doubleday, 1975); *Tarawa* by Robert Sherrod (Fredericksburg, TX: Nimitz Foundation, 1973), pp 24–25, 122; *The Battle for Tarawa* by Capt. James R. Stockman (Washington: HQMC, 1947); Buell's *Quiet Warrior*, p 192; "Tarawa" by Maj. Gen. Julian Smith, *USNI Proceedings* (Nov 1953); "The Stick Wavers" by Clay Barrow, *Naval History* (Summer 1990), p 32; *MCG* (May–Jun 1943); and *Life* (25 Oct 1943).

CHAPTER 14

Primary sources are Boxes 4, 5, 6, 8, 9, 13, 22, 32, 35, and 36 (EP); Gen. A. A. Vandegrift and Gen. David M. Shoup papers (MCHC); Thomas's oral history (MCHC); *Lineal List of Marine Corps Officers* (Washington: HQMC, 1943 and 1944); Robert Sherrod's wartime notebooks; and interviews with Brig. Gen. James D. Hittle and Apergis. Secondary sources are *Betio Beachhead* by Earl Wilson (New York: Putnam's Sons, 1945); Buell's *Quiet Warrior*, p 227; Sherrod's *Tarawa*; "U.S. Rifleman M-1944," *American Rifleman* (Mar 1944); *Time* (27 Dec 1943); "Developing the Fire Team" by 1st Lt. Lewis Myers, *MCG* (Feb 1946); and Doying's "Red Mike and His Do or Die Men." The Edson-Thomas correspondence in

Boxes 5 and 6 (EP) provides an unprecedented inside view of high-level matters in the Marine Corps during this period.

CHAPTER 15

Primary sources are Boxes 4–6, 8, 9, 13, 16, 36, and 55 (EP); Sherrod's notebooks; the oral histories of Thomas and Maj. Gen. Carl Hoffman (MCHC); Boxes 67, 77, and 78 of Series 65A-4556 (WNRC); and interviews with Apergis, Hoffman, Gen. Wallace M. Greene, Jr., and Robert Zang. Secondary sources are *Saipan: The Beginning of the End* by Maj. Carl Hoffman (Washington: HQMC, 1950), pp 65, 221; *A Fighting General* by Norman Cooper (Quantico: Marine Corps Association, 1987); *On to Westward* by Robert Sherrod (New York: Duell, Sloan & Pierce, 1945), pp 38–43, 56, 63; *Coral and Brass* by Gen. Holland M. Smith (New York: Scribners, 1949); *The Seizure of Tinian* by Maj. Carl Hoffman (Washington: HQMC, 1951); Johnston's *Follow Me*; and "Beachhead in the Marianas" by Robert Sherrod, *Time* (3 Jul 1944).

CHAPTER 16

Primary sources are Boxes 4–6, 8, 13, 45, 46, 54, and 55 (EP); the oral histories of Thomas, Chambers, Maj. Gen. William Battell, and Brig. Gen. Russell Jordahl (MCHC); the Lt. Gen. John C. McQueen papers (MCHC); Thomas's manuscript autobiography (MCHC); the Sherrod notebooks; "Marine Corps Logistics in World War II: A Personal View" by Brig. Gen. Edwin Simmons, USMC(Ret); and interviews with Margeret Carnegie, Col. J. Angus MacDonald, and Stiff. Secondary sources are *American Caesar* by William Manchester (Boston: Little, Brown & Co., 1978); Vandegrift's *Once a Marine*; Millett's *Strife* and *Semper Fidelis*; Stiff's "Grin"; and "Historical Outline of the Development of Fleet Marine Force Pacific: 1941–1950" (MCHC).

CHAPTER 17

Primary sources are Boxes 5–12, 15, 22, 36, 55, 58, and uncataloged material (EP); the oral histories of Hogaboom, Thomas, Twining, and Maj. Gen. Omar T. Pfeiffer (MCHC); Joint Chiefs of Staff Papers series 1478 and 1520; *Federalist #51* by James Madison; the Ballou papers; and interviews with Col. Gordon Keiser, Col. Victor A. Kleber, Krulak, and MacDonald. Secondary sources are *First to Fight* by Lt. Gen. Victor Krulak (Annapolis: Naval Institute Press, 1984); *The U.S. Marine Corps and Defense Unification: 1944–47* by Col. Gordon W. Keiser (Washington: National Defense University Press, 1982), p 52; *Eberstadt and Forrestal* by Jeffrey M. Dorwart (College Station: Texas A&M Press, 1991); *Counsel to the President* by Clark Clifford (New York: Random House, 1991), p 149; *The Politics of Military Unification* by Demetrios Caraley (New York: Columbia University Press, 1966); and "The Marine Corps Fights For Its Life" by Richard Tregaskis, *Saturday Evening Post* (5 Feb 1949).

CHAPTER 18

Primary sources are Boxes 7–9, 11–15, 17, 28, 36, 45, 46, 55, 56, and uncataloged material (EP); the Thomas papers (MCHC); the oral histories of Maj. Gen. Jonas Platt, Thomas, Twining, and Krulak (MCHC); the hearings of the Senate Armed Services Committee and the House Committee on Expenditures in the Executive Departments; and interviews with Kleber and Hittle. Secondary sources are Buell's *Quiet Warrior*; Krulak's *First to Fight*, pp 28, 40, 49; Vandegrift's *Once a Marine*, p 326; Keiser's *Defense Unification*; and Tregaskis's "The Marine Corps Fights For Its Life." Probably the most valuable source is Edson's diary for 1947 (Box 56), which provides a daily account of his activities and thoughts during this crucial period.

CHAPTER 19

Primary sources are Boxes 4, 8, 9, 11–13, 15, 17, 23, 24, 26, 28, 32, 34, 36, 37, 39, 46, 49, 52, 56, and uncataloged material (EP); the oral history of Thomas (MCHC); the papers of Governors Ernest Gibson and Lee Emerson (Vermont State Archives); the Department of Public Safety file (Vermont State Archives); the 1st Raider Battalion file (MCHC); the Ballou papers; and interviews with Stiff and Glenn Davis. Secondary sources are *General of the Army* by Ed Cray (New York: Norton, 1990), p 683; *For the Common Defense* by Allan R. Millett and Peter Maslowski (New York: Free Press, 1984); *Sea Power*, ed. by E. B. Potter (Annapolis: Naval Institute Press, 1981); Krulak's *First to Fight*; Cooper's *Fighting General*; "Power-Hungry Men in Uniform" by Merritt Edson, *Collier's* (27 Aug 1949); "The

Military Moves In" by Hanson Baldwin, *Harper's* (Dec 1947); Tregaskis's "The Marine Corps Fights For Its Life"; and *Time* (14 Aug 1950), p. 19.

CHAPTER 20

Primary sources are Boxes 8, 9, 11–13, 15, 22, 23, 25–29, 37–39, 41–43, 45, 46, 48, 49, 54, 56, 58, and uncataloged material (EP); Thomas's oral history; the Ballou papers; "Notes Re Enquiry by Col. Lew Walt Into the Demise of Maj. Gen. Merritt A. Edson" by Col. G. T. Armitage (possession of Maj. Gen. Hoffman); and interviews with Herbert R. Edson, Kleber, MacDonald, Stiff, and Sweeney. Secondary sources are *Americans and Their Guns* by James Trefethen (Harrisburg, PA: Stackpole, 1967); Krulak's *First to Fight*; *The Dope Sheet* (Sep 1955); and Tregaskis's "The Best Soldier I Ever Knew."

EPILOGUE

The dictionaries of military biography are *Who Was Who In American History: The Military, Dictionary of American Military Biography,* and *Webster's American Military Biographies.* Edson used the quote on fear as the opening to an article titled "Vermont's Heritage" that he published in 1948. It comes from *The Prophet* by Kahlil Gibran.

Index